PROCEEDINGS OF

THE
ARISTOTELIAN
SOCIETY

New Series—Vol. XCVII

CONTAINING THE
PAPERS READ BEFORE
THE SOCIETY DURING
THE ONE HUNDRED AND
EIGHTEENTH SESSION 1996/7

Published by
The Aristotelian Society

First published 1997 by
The Aristotelian Society

© The Aristotelian Society 1997

ISBN 0 907111 36 X

ISSN 0066-7374

THE ARISTOTELIAN SOCIETY PUBLICATIONS

PROCEEDINGS: as a journal, three times a year, and as a bound volume annually in June.

SUPPLEMENTARY VOLUME: annually in June. This records the papers read at the annual Joint Session of the Aristotelian Society and the Mind Association.

BOOK SERIES: (in co-operation with Blackwell Publishers). The Society has editorial responsibility for these books, which are published by Blackwells. They are available at less than half price to members of the Society. Currently available:

Barry Taylor:	*Modes of Occurrence: Verbs, Adverbs and Events* (1985)
Kit Fine	*Reasoning with Arbitrary Objects* (1985)
Christopher Peacocke	*Thoughts: An Essay on Content* (1985)
David E. Cooper	*Metaphor* (1986)
Jonathan Westphal	*Colour: Some Philosophical Problems from Wittgenstein* (1987)
Anthony Savile	*Aesthetic Reconstructions: Lessing, Kant and Schiller* (1987)
Graeme Forbes	*The Languages of Possibility* (1989)
E. J. Lowe	*Kinds of Being* (1989)
Ian McFetridge	*Logical Necessity and Other Essays* (1990)
Tim Maudlin	*Quantum Non-Locality and Relativity: Metaphysical Intimations of Modern Physics* (1994)
John Martin Fischer	*The Metaphysics of Free Will* (1994)
John Bacon	*Universals and Property Instances: The Alphabet of Being* (1995
S. Lovibond & S. Williams (eds)	*Essays for David Wiggins: Identity, Truth and Value* (1996)

ORDERS for past *Proceedings* and *Supplementary Volumes* and all institutional enquiries should be addressed to the Distributors.

OTHER ENQUIRIES should be addressed to the Editor.

Printed in England by
The Longdunn Press Ltd.
Barton Manor
St. Philips
Bristol BS2 0RL

Distributed by
Blackwell Publishers
Journals Subscriptions Department
Marston Book Services
PO Box 87
Oxford OX2 0DT

Edited by
Jonathan Wolff
Department of Philosophy
University College London
Gower Street
London WC1E 6BT

Please check in most recent volume for current addresses

CONTENTS

DISCUSSION

Habermas's Moral Cognitivism

GRADUATE PAPER FROM THE 1996 JOINT SESSION

Self-Respect and the Stepford Wives

TRUTH: THE IDENTITY THEORY

by Jennifer Hornsby

I want to promote what I shall call (unoriginally, and for the sake of its having a name[1]) 'the identity theory of truth'. I suggest that other accounts put forward as theories of truth are genuine rivals to it, but are unacceptable.

A certain conception of *thinkables* belongs with the identity theory's conception of *truth*. I introduce these conceptions in Part I, by reference to John McDowell's *Mind and World*; and I show why they have a place in an identity theory, which I introduce by reference to Frege. In Part II, I elaborate on the conception of thinkables, with a view to demonstrating that the identity theory's conception of truth is defensible. Part III is concerned with the theory's relation to some recent work on the concept of truth: I hope to show that the identity theorist not only has a defensible conception of truth, but also, in the present state of play, has appropriate ambitions.

I

I. 1 McDowell introduced the notion of a think*able* in order to fend off a particular objection to the following claim (1994, p. 27).

> [T]here is no ontological gap between the sort of thing one can… think, and the sort of thing that can be the case. When one thinks truly, what one thinks *is* what is the case…. [T]here is no gap between thought, as such, and the world.

Someone who objects to this supposes that, by denying any gap between thought and the world, one commits oneself to a sort of idealism. But such an objector confuses people's thinkings of things with the contents of their thoughts. If one says that there is no ontological gap between thoughts and what is the case, meaning

---

1. For 'the identity theory' in recent and contemporary philosophy, see Candlish 1995.

*Meeting of the Aristotelian Society, held in the Senior Common Room, Birkbeck College, London, on Monday, 14th October, 1996 at 8.15 p.m.

by 'thoughts' cognitive activity on the part of beings such as ourselves, then one is indeed committed to a sort of idealism: one has to allow that nothing would be the case unless there were cognitive activity—that there could not be a mindless world. But someone who means by 'thoughts' the contents of such activity, and who denies a gap between thoughts and what is the case, suggests only that what someone thinks can be the case.

> [T]o say that there is no gap between thought, as such, and the world, is just to dress up a truism in high-flown language. All the point comes to is that one can think, for instance, *that spring has begun*, and that the very same thing, that spring has begun, can be the case. That is truistic, and it cannot embody something metaphysically contentious....

In order to avoid the ambiguity in 'thought' which would be exploited if a metaphysically contentious idealism were reached, McDowell suggests using the word 'thinkables' for what may be thought. My policy here will be to use the word 'thinkable' generally, in place of any of the more familiar 'content', 'proposition' or 'Thought'. Further reasons for this choice of word will show up in due course.

McDowell's demonstration that his position avoids a simple idealism may strike some people as an inadequate defence. I think that it can help to defend it to locate it by reference to debates about truth. One may view the quotations from McDowell as encouraging an identity theory of truth.[2] This says that true thinkables are the same as facts. True thinkables then make up the world of which McDowell speaks when he dresses up a truism. The world is 'everything that is the case', or 'a constellation of facts', as McDowell puts it, following Wittgenstein.

I. 2   The identity theory is encapsulated in the simple statement that true thinkables are the same as facts. But it may be wondered how that statement could amount to a *theory* of truth: 'If someone asks what truth is, and receives an answer which helps itself to the idea of a fact, then hasn't she been taken round a very small circle?' Yes. But the simple statement on its own is not supposed to tell us anything illuminating. A conception of truth can be drawn out from an elaboration of what the simple statement can remind us of. And,

---

2. I do not say that McDowell himself would see a point in viewing them thus.

as we shall see, the conception can be set apart from the conceptions of other accounts that go by the name of theories of truth.

The identity theory is not vacuous. It cannot be vacuous because it takes a stand on what the bearers of truth are, calling them thinkables. This is not an uncontentious stand. For there are philosophers who have told us that the notion of proposition (and thus of thinkable) is so dubious that we should take the truth-bearers to be sentences.[3] The identity theory proceeds without such doubts, taking it for granted that we can make adequate sense of what is meant when someone says, for instance, 'She told me something that isn't true'.[4] And the identity theory not only asks us to understand such 'something's in appreciating where truth is applicable, but it also asks us to understand such 'something's in saying what truth's applicability consists in. Certainly there is no illumination at the point at which the word 'fact' is resorted to in order to say what this applicability consists in. But the identity theory makes definite commitments nonetheless.[5]

3. The doubts are induced by Quine's attack on propositions, which I touch on below (at §II.2, and see nn. 6 & 10).
  I think that someone who had never encountered logic or semantics might have encountered predications of truth to thinkables without encountering predications of truth to sentences; and the question *what truth is* surely concerns a concept which might feature in a language about which logicians and semanticists had never had anything to say. At a minimum, then, a philosopher who takes *truth* primarily as a property of sentences must say something about what appear to be its predication to thinkables. Although I accord priority to thinkables' truth here, I acknowledge that, when returning answers to particular philosophical questions, the application of 'true' to sentences is indispensable: see below, Part II. I acknowledge also that what appear to be predications of truth to thinkables may be treated as no such thing, as in the prosentential theory (see nn. 6 & 16). *Pro hac vice* I talk as if the surface appearances were sustainable.

4. In saying that the identity theorist proceeds without doubts, I do not deny that hard work has to be done to give accounts of what appears to be talk about propositions/thinkables. An identity theory of truth evidently places constraints on such accounts. See e.g. Rumfitt 1993's account of the construction of propositions: Rumfitt's constructionalism goes hand in hand with a paratactic treatment of the logical form of sentences containing 'that'-clauses; but his kind of constructionalism might be entertained outside the context of such treatment.

5. Candlish says, of what he calls a 'modest' identity theory, that it is 'completely uninteresting—trivial… precisely because it has no independent conception of a fact to give content to the identity claim' (1995, p. 107). Candlish here assesses the theory as if it had the ambitions of a definition. But what I call 'the identity theory' has no such ambitions (and indeed it acknowledges truth's indefinability: see below). The interest of the theory derives from what it can be seen, from what it says, to be opposed to philosophically. Candlish allows that an *im*modest ('robust') identity theory might be interesting: its interest could derive from its 'independent conception of facts', independent, that is, of the conception of thinkables, or truth-bearers. For my own part, I cannot see a point in thinking that such a theory deserves the name of *identity* theory. (Here I disagree with Julian Dodd 1995, from whom Candlish takes the robust/modest distinction. There is much about which Dodd and I agree, however: see our 1992.)

I. 3   Whether or not its title to be a theory can be made out, it may be unclear why the word 'identity' belongs in it. What could be the point in saying that true thinkables *are the same as* facts, rather than—more simply and apparently to the same effect—that true thinkables *are* facts?[6]

A familiar argument in Frege (1918) may help to show the point. It is an argument against the correspondence theory of truth. Frege introduces it with the words 'It might be supposed... that truth consists in the correspondence of a picture with what it depicts'. 'This is contradicted, however', he says, and then argues by *reductio* (pp. 18–19):

> A correspondence... can only be perfect if the corresponding things coincide and so just are not different things at all... [I]f the first did correspond perfectly with the second, they would coincide. But this is not at all what people intend when they define truth as the correspondence of an idea with something real. For in this case it is essential precisely that the reality shall be distinct from the idea.

6. The introduction of 'identity' might seem to have the consequence of upping the ontological stakes (so that thinkables are to be treated as OBJECTS). That is not so. When we have understood, for example, 'She does it in one way, and he does it in another way', we have also made sense of 'They don't do it the *same* way'—but not at the expense of treating either things that are done or ways of doing them as OBJECTS. I think that hostility to propositions derives partly from Quine's assumption that all quantification is objectual or (in Quine's own sense) substitutional. This assumption has seemed to have the consequence that unless we give a Quinean substitutional account of these 'something's, we shall be forced to treat propositions as OBJECTS, in a sense of the term caught up with a particular understanding of singular reference. But Quine's assumption is not compulsory: see e.g. Davies 1981, Ch. VI, §3. Some of the interest of the prosentential theory of truth, defended in Grover 1992 and Brandom 1994, derives from the directness of its challenge to Quine's assumption.

The identity theory is not formulated in order to take a stand on the logical form of predications of truth. If taken to reveal logical form, it would take an erroneous stand—the one which is contradicted by Frege's remark that '"true" is not a relative term'. Comparison with Russell's Theory of Descriptions may be helpful here. In the analysis of 'the' provided by Russell, the word 'the' is not treated as the simple quantifier which, presumably, so far as logical form is concerned, it is. One point of giving the analysis which Russell's theory states is to show what is involved in seeing 'the' as a quantifier, and to show which quantifier it is. Something analogous goes on when 'identity' is introduced into an account of truth. Just as Russell's Theory can present the negative semantical claim that 'the' does not combine with predicates to form names, so the identity theory of truth can present its own negative metaphysical claims—claims such as emerge from seeing how the identity theory arises out of rejection of a correspondence theory.

One point of a formulation including 'same' might be to draw attention to the principles of distinctness of facts presupposed to the theory: those principles cannot allow a coarser grain to facts than to thinkables. (This means that it is not a target of the so-called slingshot argument; see Neale 1995.) A naive account of facts, attractive to those who seek facts in line with a correspondence conception, might incorporate the principle: Where $a = b$, 'Fb' does not express a different fact from 'Fa'. Such a principle, obviously, is at odds with the identity theorist's conception of facts. (In Neale's terms: 'the fact that ( ) = the fact that ( )' is –PSST.)

But then there can be no complete correspondence, no complete truth. So nothing at all would be true; for what is only half true is untrue.

Putting this only slightly differently, we hear Frege saying: if truth were explicated in terms of any relation, it would have to be identity, since anything less than a candidate for truth's coincidence with a putatively corresponding thing would lead to the intolerable conclusion that there is no truth. Someone who takes herself to think that true thinkables correspond to the facts has it right, then, only if she actually means that any true thinkable is the same as some fact—which is what the identity theorist says.

Frege's argument has a sequel. This starts by showing how Frege thinks his opponent will respond. The opponent asks (p. 19):

> But can't it be laid down that truth exists where there is correspondence in a certain respect?

Here it is conceded that truth cannot be unspecified correspondence, so to speak. The problem with taking truth to be unspecified correspondence is that there can be correspondence in this respect, or that respect, or that other respect, so that there can be less or more correspondence according as there is correspondence in fewer or more respects; but there can't *in any analogous way* be more or less truth.[7] The opponent supposes that he can get out of this difficulty by picking on one respect of correspondence. To this Frege has a response.

> But in which [respect]? What would we then have to do to decide whether something were true? We should have to inquire whether an idea and a reality, perhaps, corresponded in a laid-down respect. And then we should have to confront a question of the same kind, and the game would begin again. So the attempt to explain truth as correspondence collapses.

---

7. Frege pointed out that 'with every property of a thing is joined a property of a [thinkable], namely that of truth' (p. 20). For illustration, suppose that Fred is tall. Putting it in Frege's way, a property of Fred (being tall) is joined to a property of a thinkable: if Fred is indeed tall, then a true thinkable is put forward when Fred is said to be tall. But if this is correct, then it can seem that we should allow that *truth* can have any of the features which the property of *being tall* can have, so that if *being tall* admits of degrees (if *x* can be to some extent tall), then *truth* admits of degrees (it can be to some extent true that *x* is tall). But now it seems that Frege appreciates a characteristic of 'true' which ensures that, when treated as a predicate, it will seem to admit of degrees, if any does. This makes me think that when Frege invokes the claim that what is half-true is untrue, he is relying on the thought that any *relation* introduced to account for truth cannot be a relation which admits of degrees. And that is why I say that there cannot *in any analogous way* be more or less truth.

The idea now is that if there was something distinct from a thinkable such that establishing that some relation obtained between it and the thinkable was a way of getting to know whether the thinkable was true, then someone could be in the position of knowing what is known when the thinkable is known, yet of still not knowing whether it was true. But of course one could never be in that position: to discover whether p is already to discover whether it is true that p.

This reveals a general difficulty about defining truth—the difficulty which shows up 'when we confront the same question again'.

> In a definition certain characteristics would have to be stated. And in application to any particular case the question would always arise whether it were true that the characteristics were present.

'Consequently', Frege concludes, 'it is probable that the word 'true' is unique and indefinable' (p. 19).

When one follows Frege's argument through to this general conclusion, about the definability of truth, explicit opposition to the correspondence theory is lost: the correspondence theorist's definition fails to meet a constraint on any adequate definition; but it turns out not to be alone in that failure. Frege accordingly might be thought to have argued against an especially naive correspondence theory in the first instance, and then turned to opposing the whole idea of truth's definability. But there can be a point in thinking of Frege's initial argument as meant to show that a correspondence theory in particular—and *any* correspondence theory—is untenable. This is an argument which is sound only if the identity theory escapes its *reductio*. Its conclusion may be dressed up in high-flown language: there cannot be an ontological gap between thought ('an idea') and the world ('something real').

I. 4   The identity theory, at any rate, is distinguishable from any correspondence theory. And the identity theory is worth considering to the extent to which correspondence theories are worth avoiding. I think that correspondence theories *need* to be avoided. I mean by this not merely that they are incorrect, but that people are apt to believe them.

It is common for philosophers to speak as if a correspondence theory of truth had no metaphysical import whatever. We are sometimes told that the idea of correspondence is recorded in a series of platitudes that any theorist of truth has to respect. Simon

Blackburn has spoken of the phrase 'corresponds to the facts' as sometimes a piece of Pentagonese—a paraphrase of 'is true' deployed with the purpose of saying something important sounding (1984, p. 255). But of course this is not all that has ever been read into the phrase. Someone who says 're-rendered it operational' for 'got it going again', may be criticized for needless portentousness, but not on other grounds; but when 'corresponds to the facts' gets in, the phrase's wordiness should not be the only source of doubt. Certainly there are glosses on 'is true' that are platitudinous: 'is a fact' is one such—the one that the identity theory singles out for attention. Perhaps it is also a platitude that true sentences say how things are. And this again is unobjectionable, so long as the 'things' in question are ordinary objects of reference: the true sentence 'that book is red', for example, says something about how things are by saying how one of the things (sc. that book) is (sc. red).[8]

From the point of view introduced by the identity theory, it will be distinctive of correspondence theorists to seek items located outside the realm of thinkables, and outside the realm of ordinary objects of reference, but related, some of them, to whole thinkables. The idea is widespread, and it takes various guises. In the Russell of *An Inquiry into Meaning and Truth* (1940), the basic correspondents are percepts. Percepts can be 'surveyed but not defined'; utterances appropriately associated with them get their particular meanings from them; and propositions, the truth bearers, can be constructed out of percepts. In the Quine of *Philosophy of Logic*, the correspondents are cosmic distributions of particles. 'Two sentences agree in objective information, and so express the same proposition, when every cosmic distribution of particles over space–time that would make either sentence true would make the other true as well' (1970, p. 4). These very different candidates for things that make sentences true—percepts and particle distributions—reflect the very different obsessions of Russell and

8. This platitude points up the independence of thinking from what there is. Whether you want to know the book's colour, or to know something of what I think about the book, you have to think of something that is not sustained in existence by your thinking. But the thing to which you are then related (that book) is obviously not something which corresponds to a thinkable.

Davidson used to say that a relation like Tarskian *satisfaction* could provide the language–world links sought by a correspondence theorist of truth. But Davidson now regards this as a mistake (1990, p. 302). It must indeed be a mistake if opposition to correspondence theories can be combined with thought about mind-independent objects.

Quine, epistemological and cosmic. But what is common to their accounts, despite this vast difference, is a willingness to reconstruct thinkables from posited entities of a different sort, entities which make things true. Percepts and particle distributions, then, are supposed to be items which we can specify independently of an account of thinkables, items which may confer truth upon a thinkable. When they are introduced, however, we cannot hold onto the truism that inspires the identity theory. The fact (as it is) that autumn has begun, if it were to be a cosmic distribution of particles, would not be the same as what I think when I think (truly) that autumn has begun.

It is evident now that the words 'corresponds with' do not have to be in play for an ontological gap between thought and the world to open up. This is something that we see in formulations used over the years by Michael Dummett and Crispin Wright in stating the semantic anti-realist's case. Their formulations often appear to invoke a conception of a truth-maker which will suit a correspondence theorist but which an identity theorist cannot allow.[9] Dummett asked 'If it were impossible to know the truth of some true statement, how could there be anything which *made* that statement true?'. Wright spoke of 'a truth-conferrer for a sentence': in the case where the truth of the sentence cannot be known, he said that this is something that 'the world fails to deliver up'. And he spoke of 'the states of affairs' that are in question when a sentence is undecidable as things that 'could not be encountered'. These ways of speaking give rise to an image of something with which a thinkable might have connected up, but a something which we are expected to think of the world as taking sole responsibility for. This is the image that an identity theory may help to rid us of. For when the conditions for the truth of a sentence are supplied by

9. See Dummett 1976, at p. 61 in the version reprinted in Dummett 1993.
   A different sort of illustration may be got from Frank Jackson, Graham Oppy and Michael Smith 1994. They argue for the compatibility of versions of non-cognitivism (in ethics, say) with minimalism about truth. They follow Michael Devitt in characterizing minimalism as holding that 'terms for truth and falsity are linguistic devices for talking about reality by appending the truth predicate'. Their claim then is that it might not be that any old sentence is such as to talk about reality: non-cognitivists, they say, 'precisely deny that (e.g.) ethical sentences talk about reality'. But someone who is opposed to correspondence theories in all their versions will not allow this 'talking about reality'. Suppose that Devitt had characterized minimalism by saying that truth and falsity are terms for going on talking while adding a word or two. Would Jackson et al. then have said 'Non-cognitivists precisely deny that (e.g.) ethical sentences are used in talking'?
   This example may serve to show how easily ideas of correspondence get in through the back door.

an identity theorist, nothing is brought in besides the thinkable that is expressed by the sentence itself. By introducing 'sources of truth', 'truth conferrers' and 'states of affairs', Dummett and Wright drive a wedge between what is demanded by a thinkable and what is demanded by a thinkable that is true. The identity theorist leaves no room for any wedge.

Of course these remarks about Dummett and Wright do not get to grips with the position which was their concern. But they can illustrate a point—that philosophers' formulations are apt to create an outlook which is forsworn when an identity theory displaces a correspondence theory. I hope that they also suggest how the identity theory may displace forms of anti-realism more subtle than the crass idealism which results from equating thinkables with thinkings of them.

II

II. 1   It would be laborious to attempt to show that the identity theory is incompatible with all things irrealist. In order to show that it embodies nothing metaphysically contentious, I shall attempt only to reveal its actual compatibility with a perfectly common-sense realism.

McDowell's rebuttal of any simple idealism emphasizes the independence of thinkables from thinkings. One way to grasp this independence is to see that there are (so to speak) more thinkables than there are thinkings. I suspect that those who find the theory problematic are apt to suppose that it could be part of commonsense that there are (so to speak) more facts than there are true thinkables. If this is right about where the opposition lies, then further reflections on the identity theory, if they are to serve as a defence, must expand on the notion of a thinkable. By the identity theorist's lights, our grasp of the notion of a fact cannot exceed our grasp of the notion of a true thinkable. But someone who wishes to express doubts on that score might be helped by having it made apparent how generous the notion of a thinkable nonetheless is.

II. 2   There can seem to be an immediate obstacle, however, to *any* account of thinkables—of the contents, the meaningful things that bear truth. Quine's attack on the Myth of the Museum is directed against the assumption that there could be things external to thought and meaning, lodged like exhibits in the mind, whose relations to other things could constitute the foundations of meaning (1960). The identity theorist agrees with Quine about the incoherence of the hope that intersubjective sameness of meaning might be explained in terms of relations with things external to thought and meaning.

From the identity theorist's point of view the correspondents of correspondence theories of truth play the same role as the exhibits in the museum of the mind: they are items located beyond the bounds of human play with concepts, in terms of which one is supposed to explain meaning. As Quine puts it, speaking himself of particle distributions, the item assigned to one sentence as a condition of its truth is the same as the item assigned to another sentence as a condition of *its* truth if and only if the two sentences have the same meaning. But such items as cosmic distributions of particles are in the same boat as items in the mind's museum according to the identity theory: neither can be used in the reconstruction of thinkables from something else.

If one countenances the cosmic items, but is led by the problems of the items in the mind's museum to think that ordinary talk of meaning is unsupported, then one may invoke a double standard. Quine tells us that a second class standard is appropriate so long as we are tolerant of such everyday psychological talk as involves any notion of a thinkable (1960, §45). But he said that we can, and in science we must, employ a first class standard; it is then that objective information, corresponding to (say) cosmic distributions of particles, can do duty for thinkables, Quine thinks. The upshot of this is hard to make coherent. For the view of everyday reports of people's psychological states which is required by Quine's lower standard for them is not a view that can be sustained by someone who takes herself (for instance) to seek the truth in some area. A person's being an enquirer of any sort requires that she be interpretable as aiming at gleaning the facts, and we have no conception of what that is excepting as we can think of her as more generally intelligible—as apt to perceive things, and to think them, and to draw conclusions. We cannot then be in a position to make statements about Quine's first-class reality but of refusing (according to the same standard) to make any statements which say, for instance, what people are doing when they are investigating that reality. The identity theory helps to make this difficulty with the Quinean picture vivid. The first-class standard was meant to be the standard of genuine facts; the second-class standard was to be invoked when the language of thinkables was used. But if any fact is the same as some true thinkable, then we cannot endorse facts and despise thinkables.

II. 3   It can seem as though the identity theorist had nowhere to turn for an account of thinkables. At least there is nowhere to turn for an account besides an investigation of other predications to them—predications other than 'is true'. This brings me to further reasons (which I said I would come to) for using the term 'thinkable'.

'Thinkable' is a word for a sort of things to which a person can be related in various modes. I say that the Labour Party will win the next election. I have just said something (that Labour will win) which many now believe, which a good few hope, which John Major fears. The example then shows that thinkables can be beliefs, hopes and fears. They are called beliefs when thought of in connection with one psychological attitude towards them; they are called hopes or fears when thought of in connection with other attitudes. They are thought of as propositions when thought of as propounded.[10] A modal term, like 'thinkable', may serve to remind one of the variety of relations here: it is not only thought which relates to think*ables*, because a thinkable can be believed and hoped, for instance. (And just as we must not confuse a thinkable with a thinking, so we must not confuse a thinkable with someone's believing one, or with someone's hoping one.)

Besides '—— is true', then, there are predicates of thinkables, such as '—— is believed by Tony', '—— is hoped by members of the crowd'. Yet other predicates of thinkables show people as related to them by their speech acts: a statement, for instance, is what we call a thinkable when we think of it in connection with someone's making a statement. 'Thinkable' gives a word for what is truth-evaluable which is indifferent between the case where the evaluable thing is presented as the object of a state of a thinker's mind and the case where it is presented as having been put into

---

10. It seems worth remembering that propounding is a propositional attitude, and that Quinean hostility to propositions is hostility equally to beliefs (say). Because the opposition to certain abstract conceptions of thinkables has typically been directed against things called propositions, we find philosophers whose attitude towards beliefs and statements is one of acceptance, but towards propositions is one of rejection. (See e.g. David 1994, p. 12.) Of course it might be stipulated that the term 'proposition' is to mean what is meant by those who use the term illicitly. But short of making such a stipulation, it will be hard to justify an attitude of hostility peculiarly to propositions.

words. But it is the linguistic expression of thinkables which we are bound to focus on, if we are to find anything of a systematic sort to say about them. One aim of theories of meaning is to show the significance of sentences as systematically dependent on properties of the words that make them up: theories of meaning, one might say, treat of thinkables' composition. The productivity of language, which can be revealed in its theory of meaning, then points towards another reason for using a modal notion, and speaking of think*ables*. Someone in possession of a theory of meaning for some language can say what was expressed in the use of any of the sentences on some list, composed from some stock of words; and is in a position to see that there are other things that would be expressed in the use of other sentences, not on the list, but composed only from words in the same stock. A theory of meaning, though its data are uses of actual sentences, is a theory which speaks to potential uses—to what would be said if some hitherto unused sentence of the language were used. There are actually unused sentences, which, just like the sentences we have given voice to or heard or read, express thinkables.

This suggests the place to look if we want to expand on the notion of a thinkable. We cannot postulate meanings in the mind or correspondents in the world. But we can look to the actual practices of language users. And we shall be reminded here of an idea first recommended by Donald Davidson—that we might put to work, as a theory of meaning of the language of some speakers, a definition of truth for the language which enables the interpretation of those speakers. Davidson's claim that a definition of truth for a language can serve as its theory of meaning depended in part on his thinking that Tarski had shown a way of displaying the recurrent significance of words—by treating words as having characteristics which affect the truth of sentences they come into.[11] In the present context, much of the importance of the idea of deploying such a definition of truth

11. Davidson 1967. I use '*definition* of truth' here as Davidson did there; and this allows me to avoid using 'theory of truth' ambiguously. (It seems impossible to avoid all possible ambiguity, however. Where a theory of truth [in the only sense of that phrase I use here] purports to give a definition, it purports to give a definition of truth; but of course what it purports to give is not the sort of language-relativized thing that Tarski showed one how to construct.)

One makes no assumptions about Tarski's own intentions in saying that Tarski in fact showed us a way to construct a definition of truth for L that can be used to do something that a theory of meaning for L has to do. (Etchemendy 1988 has an understanding of Tarski's purpose which leads to a view of a definition of truth for a language which encourages the deflationist attitude discussed in §III below.)

for a language is the view of predications of thinkables it affords. Where an account of a language's workings is interpretive of its speakers, it enables the theorist to give expression, in the case of any sentence in the language and any speaker of it, to the thinkable expressed by the speaker using that sentence. It thus gives the theorist the resources to say what speakers are doing when they use their language.[12]

An interpretive account of speakers is not narrowly linguistic. For speakers' productions of sentences cannot be seen as intelligible expressions of thinkables except as speakers are seen to have some purpose in producing the sentences. And any hypothesis about the purpose of a person who uses words on some occasion goes hand in hand not only with a hypothesis about the thinkable then expressed but also with hypotheses about her mental states—about how *belief* and *desire* and the other attitudes relate her to thinkables—and with hypotheses also about the states of mind of audiences to her speech, and of all the others who use the language on other occasions.

The imaginary theorist, who compiles the facts about words that could put one in a position to understand foreign speakers, would be involved not only in making attributions to speakers of psychological attitudes and speech acts towards thinkables, but also, and inevitably, in taking a view of the truth of the thinkables to which speakers are then taken to be related. One cannot generally take a view about what someone's purposes are without having some view of which of those purpose are achieved; people intentionally do what they try to do to the extent that the beliefs which explain their doing what they do are true (are believings of true thinkables, that is). Of course the word 'true' does not have to be dragged in in order to see someone's taking an attitude towards a thinkable as working as it does. One can just as well say 'She believed that the 'plane took off at 9, and the plane took off at 9' as one can say 'She believes that the 'plane took off at 9 and that is true'. But insofar as an interpretive account requires more than the idea of people's relations to thinkables, and more than the idea of interconnections between those relations, it requires grasp of the

12. I cannot here do more than take for granted a vast body of literature which shows the workability of definitions of truth for languages having natural languages' features. See, e.g., further papers in Davidson 1980. Davidson's idea has been endorsed by many others, of whom, in the present connection, McDowell should be mentioned; see, for example, his 1976.

distinction involved in assessments of thinkables as true or false. The view of thinkables that emerges, then, in trying to expand on the notion, is one in which some thinkables are taken to be (the same as) facts.

The study of interpretive accounts affords a distinctive perspective on the application of 'is true' to thinkables. 'True' can be treated as having a role alongside a variety of psychological predicates; but it is not itself treated as a psychological predicate, of course.[13]

II. 4   Discussions of coming to understand a foreign language sometimes assume its speakers to be more ignorant than the theorist: the facts at the theorist's disposal go beyond any of which the interpreted people are apprised. But this assumption is not essential to the idea of an interpretive account. Contemplating interpretive accounts shows the acceptability of a conception of potential uses of language expressive of thinkables outside one's ken, and some of which are facts.

One might think inductively here. Over the centuries, human knowledge, at least in some spheres, has expanded, and its expansion has been assisted by the introduction of new concepts, for instance in the formulation of scientific theories. If one believes that human knowledge will continue to expand, one is entitled to predict that thinkables which none of us here and now is capable of thinking will come to be known. One may envisage a theorist interpreting a language of the future: its speakers would think things, and the theorist, in coming to understand them, would learn from them. She could come to have access to facts, which in her present situation she is not even equipped to express.

Here one thinks of thinkables in connection with expanding knowledge. And it might then be supposed that the facts are to be

---

13. Cp. Davidson 1990, p. 287: 'the concept of truth has essential connections with the concepts of belief and meaning'; and 'what Tarski has done for us is to show in detail how to describe the kind of pattern truth must make'. Davidson himself thinks that the empirical evidence we need in order to identify the pattern must avoid, in the first instance 'states with (as one says) a propositional object'. Davidson, then, would not be happy with the introduction of, 'as one says', propositional objects (i.e. thinkables) at the outset. This explains why his objections to Paul Horwich begin at an earlier point than my own do (see n. 19). For his part, Davidson has a theory of verbal interpretation to elaborate: see 1990. To question the need for this would take me too far afield. But I can try to state Davidson's view in my own terms: such a theory of verbal interpretation has to be understood from the standpoint of someone contemplating an interpretive account in order that such contemplation should ensure that a philosophically adequate conception of truth is elicited.

circumscribed by reference to what is known by an ideal knower, at the limit, as it were, of an inductive series of more and more knowledgeable beings. But acceptance of unthought thinkables, some of which are facts, requires no such supposition. The supposition requires an understanding of the ideal situation for arriving at knowledge. And this can only be a situation in which all sources of error are eliminated or taken account of—a situation, that is to say, in which one is sure to believe what is *true*. Perhaps we can gesture towards such an ideal. But since we can explain it at best in terms of an antecedent notion of truth, the style of thinking used here to uncover a conception of facts can lend no support to an epistemic theory of truth.[14]

The conception of unthought thinkables elicited here does not depend upon any settled opinion about human ambitions or limitations, but only upon an idea of intelligible others from whom one could learn. It evidently yields a generous conception of facts, to which an identity theorist is entitled. I hope, then, that the identity theory emerges as a defensible theory of truth, in keeping with our commonsensically realist view about the extent of facts independent of us.[15]

---

14. Here I am thinking of, for example, the theory which seems to be endorsed in Putnam's 1981, which says that truth is an idealization of rational acceptability. In later writings (e.g. 1990), Putnam asks us to read the remarks he makes in supporting his Internal Realism as meant only to convey a picture, rather than as a theory of truth.

15. The remarks of this section are intended to go further than those of McDowell (reported in §I.1)—further towards showing that it is not a difficulty for the identity theory that it circumscribes the world using the notion of a thinkable. Although offered in defence of the claim that an identity theorist has a commonsensically realist conception of facts, they are not offered as a defence of any 'Realism' meriting a capital 'R'. In defending his 'Internal Realism' (see n. 14), Putnam's target was 'Metaphysical Realism', a doctrine which the identity theory is evidently also opposed to.

Of course it is possible to think that a defence even of commonsense realism is required: Michael Dummett has long urged this. In his 1990, Dummett thinks of the 'tacit acquisition of the concept [of truth]' as involving 'a conceptual leap;... just because this is so, it is open to challenge' (p. 200, in 1993 reprinted version). The leap, Dummett says, is one 'we all [made] at an early stage in our acquisition of our mother tongues': it involves a transition from the 'justifiability condition of an assertion to the truth-condition of the statement asserted' (p. 198). Now Dummett's own understanding of the conceptual leap is shown in his speaking of the notion of justification as 'cruder' and of truth as 'more refined'. But Dummett's opponent may resist any picture of the concept of truth as got from something cruder—as if there were something which might be added to justifiability to get truth, so that the child at some stage had to acquire the added extra. (The identity theorist seems bound to resist this, since she cannot allow *truth*'s applicability to be separated from *thinkability*.) Against Dummett, it may be said that the child who comes to belong to a community of speakers (a systematic account of whose uses of sentences deploys the concept of truth) is drawn into practices in which the concept already has a place. Evidently in saying this, one still does not supply the defence which Dummett seeks. But perhaps it helps to make it clear that one can reject Dummett's story about the acquisition of the concept of truth while acknowledging that truth is indeed in an obvious sense more demanding than justification.

III

III. 1   However defensible the identity theory of truth might be
made out to be, it might seem that there is an alternative to it—in
the minimal theory of truth.

The minimal theory is advanced by Paul Horwich (1990, pp. 6–7).

> [I]t contains no more than what is expressed by uncontroversial
> instances of the equivalence schema:
>
> (E)   It is true *that p* if and only if p.

Horwich calls this 'the deflationary point of view'. In advocating
a minimal theory, he means us to think that those who have waxed
philosophical about truth in the past have tried to say too much and
overshot the mark. He believes that we are apt to have an
erroneously inflated conception of truth.

There has been so much writing under the head of 'minimalism'
and 'deflationism' that in order that something should be fixed, I
shall use Horwich's position to define 'a minimalist theory'.
Deflationism, on the other hand, I shall treat as an attitude towards
truth which a minimalist theorist takes, but which is also taken by
others—disquotationalists, and, it seems, Richard Rorty.[16] In an
attempt to make out the identity theory's superiority to the minimal
theory, I start by suggesting that, despite what they have in
common, there has to be a genuine difference in their conceptions
of truth. Then I suggest that to the extent that the minimal theorist
wants to convey a deflationary message about truth, which is not
already conveyed in the identity theorist's opposition to correspondence, the message has to be resisted.

16. Disquotationalists differ from Horwich in taking the truth of *sentences* to be primary, so
that I have taken a stand against their position already (see n. 3 above). For criticisms of
disquotationalism as such, see David 1994. Many of these criticisms have versions applicable
to Horwich's theory: in connection with Horwich they would start from asking what is
involved in the acceptance of propositions—which is the question that I press below.
    For Rorty's deflationism, see n. 21.
    The characterization of deflationism here is deliberately vague (it is meant to be as
vague as the statements used to convey the deflationary message, see §III.3). But I should
note that, with Horwich's minimalist theory used as the paradigm of a theory provoking the
deflationist attitude, it is *not* a characteristic thesis of deflationism to deny that truth is a
predicate. Brandom 1994 takes his treatment of '... is true' as a prosentence-forming
operator to secure one of deflationism's characteristic theses. But I think that the identity
theorist's opposition to the deflationist attitude that Horwich means to provoke might
survive arguments about the correctness of pro-sententialism. (From Brandom's position,
one would see these issues in a different light. I cannot speak to it here, but I make a further
remark about it at n. 23 below.)

III. 2   One thing that the identity theorist and minimal theorist agree about shows up in connection with a point that Dummett once made (1958/9). Dummett famously said that an advocate of a minimal theory is ill-placed to tell us that *truth* can be used to explain *meaning*.[17] The point relies on two features of the minimal theorist's conception. On the one hand, *truth* is not a notion of substance, which can be utilized in accounting for something else; on the other hand, *meaningfulness* is simply taken for granted when one predicates truth. We find parallel features in the identity theorist's conception: On the one hand, facts are thinkables, so that there is nothing external to thought and meaning in terms of which truth can be understood; on the other hand, thinkables are what facts are, so that *thinkability* is presupposed when one talks about truth. These features of truth presented the obstacle that we initially saw to giving any account of thinkables (see §II.2). And they explain the lack of illumination which is felt at the point at which the identity theorist resorts to the word 'fact' (cp. n. 5).

To the apparent obstacle as it presents itself to the identity theorist, I have responded with the idea of an interpretive account of a group of language users. Taking the perspective that such an account provides, one does not purport to *explain* either meaning or truth. (Of course not: Dummett's point is well taken.) But one is in a position to elicit features of one's conception of truth. By turning to interpretive accounts, one can shed light simultaneously on truth and thinkability (where an account of linguistic meaning is situated in an account of thinkables). One does so by contemplating the use of definitions of truth which are such as to contain all the instances of the schema found in Tarski's Convention T (the analogue, as it were, for sentences, of Horwich's Schema (E)). But it is here that a real disagreement with the minimal theory is revealed. For the idea of an interpretive account is alien to the conception of truth that Horwich means us to take away from his theory. Horwich for his part defends not only a minimal theory of truth, but also minimalism about meaning; and he defends minimalism about meaning by doing his best to show that the concept of truth is not needed in the explication of meaning. It is supposed to be a consequence of a

---

17. Dummett was actually talking about the redundancy theory of truth. For the purposes of considering his argument, we may think of this as a species of minimalist theory. Dummett himself has called Horwich's theory (which Horwich calls 'minimal') 'redundancy'. (The name 'redundancy theory', however, is *sometimes* reserved for a theory in which predicate-hood is denied of 'is true', i.e. for a species of a kind of theory mentioned at nn. 16 & 23.)

minimal theory, that 'true', being deflated and shown to have no substance, could not play a crucial part in something as interesting as an interpretive account is thought by its defenders to be.[18]

Pressure can be put upon the minimal theorist, by showing that his conception of truth will be found wanting unless it is supplemented at least with some idea of interpretability. The minimal theorist hopes to say everything that needs to be said about truth by allusion to the Equivalence Schema. So he has said nothing about truth except insofar as the Schema is fully intelligible. When the Schema is used to give a theory of *truth*, it is taken for granted that the 'that p' construction within it is in good order. And this might be doubted.[19] But even when there are no doubts about the admissibility of the construction it uses, it must be a good question to ask of someone who advances the Schema what the intended range of its instances is. If one wrote the left hand side of the Schema 'The thinkable that p is true', then it would be clear that the 'that p' construction employed in it is just that which is employed when any of 'believes', 'hopes', 'states' *et cetera* are used. Making out the Schema's intelligibility, or revealing its range, then, would be a matter of showing how 'that p' and related constructions work, as it were, in the large. One would then be drawn to the idea of an interpretive account.[20]

18. On this reading, Horwich's argument to deflationism about *meaning* is indirect. (Truth has no substance, so meaning doesn't either.) But Horwich sometimes defends minimalism about meaning more directly, by reference to his own idea of semantic compositionality, which is 'minimal' and is supposedly superior to a so-called truth-conditional idea (i.e. one which portrays a language's structure in a definition of truth for its sentences.) This other style of defence suggests that Horwich's own deflationist attitude may rely on more than the thought that one says everything a philosopher could have any reason to say about truth by writing (E) down. Horwich seems sometimes to side with Rorty, see n. 21.

There are other ways of encouraging a generally deflationist attitude than Horwich's. Sometimes it is encouraged by the thought that 'true' having been shown (supposedly) to have no substance, we cannot be 'factualists' about the semantical. (Paul Boghossian, 1990, points out that it is hard to make sense of this except by supposing that we are factualists sometimes; but if we are factualists sometimes, then we cannot actually sustain the wholesale deflationary attitude to truth. Boghossian's thought suggests a difficulty for the move that Horwich makes on my reading—from 'Truth has no substance' to 'Meaning doesn't either'. The move seems to require connections between truth and meaning, which should, it would seem, have been officially renounced.)

19. Davidson doubts it: see n. 13. Davidson's objections to the minimal theory which were made in his Jacobsen Lectures (University of London, 1995) began from an objection to the use of 'that p' in the theorist's Schema.

20. Such an account, of course, treats utterances of sentences which are not appropriate substitutes for 'p' in Schema (E). (The treatment does not fall within the scope of the definition of truth for a language which it contains, but makes connections with the definition. Consider non-indicatives.) Horwich acknowledges that not all sentences are fit for substitution in (E) at the point at which he glibly dismisses the semantic paradoxes (pp. 41–2).

The place to which one turns to answer questions about the minimal theorist's Equivalence Schema, then, is exactly the place where the identity theorist finds the resources to demonstrate her theory's consonance with commonsense. It is not, however, that the allusion to interpretive accounts enables the identity theorist to understand the 'that p' construction in terms of something more primitive. Like the minimal theorist, the identity theorist takes the 'that p' construction for granted in the statement of a theory of truth. Both theorists assume that thinkables are the primary bearers of truth, and give priority to 'It is true that p' over 'sentence s is true' (see n. 3). The identity theorist nonetheless sees a particular point in the use of 'true in L' applied to sentences. As we saw, an interpretive account of a particular language L contains a definition of truth in L which speaks to *potential* uses of the sentences of L— to what would be said if one were used by an L-speaker (see §II.3). Within such an account, we find, for instance 'sentence s is true in L iff p'; and where this assists in interpretation, the place of 'p' is taken by a sentence in a theorist's language, fitted for the expression of a thinkable that a speaker would express if, as a speaker of L, she used the sentence s. (The thinkable that p is true if and only if it is a fact that p, which of course is exactly the condition for s's being true in L.) An interpretive account enables thinkables which might be expressed by speakers to be matched with thinkables that theorists can express. The idea of such an account would fill the lacuna in the minimal theorist's development of his conception of truth. With the lacuna filled, deflationary impulses go away.[21]

---

21. To subdue the deflationist impulse, it is not enough to acknowledge that definitions of truth for languages play a role in interpretive accounts: the exact role needs to be understood. Rorty promotes a kind of deflationism from the position of a pragmatist, rather than a minimalist. The basis for his dismissive remarks about truth are not the Equivalence Schema, but glosses on truth of the kind that Putnam gives in defending Internal Realism (see n. 14). Speaking of a definition of truth for a language playing the role to which Davidson wishes to put it, Rorty says: 'I should think that an empirical theory which entails T-sentences could as well be called "a theory of complex behaviour" as "a theory of truth"' (1995, p. 286). Well, of course a definition of truth for a language (often enough called 'a theory of truth', which Rorty here expresses a dislike for calling it) is not a theory of truth in the sense in which the correspondence theory, or identity theory, or epistemic theory, or whatever, claim to be. (It is because of the ambiguity in 'theory of truth' that I have here reserved *'definition'* for the Tarskian theories whose role is at issue between identity theorists and minimal theorists: see n. 11.) But Rorty's thought that it could 'just as well be called "a theory of complex behaviour"' does not depend upon any ambiguity in 'theory of truth'. It depends upon Rorty's failure to appreciate that a definition of truth for some speakers' language is [a] only a component in any account of their behaviour, but [b] a component in which 'true' plays a crucial role.

Where Horwich would have us think that the presence of 'true' ensures that the definition participates in nothing with any substance, Rorty, with the focus on 'behaviour', would prevent us from seeing 'true' as playing its normal, normative role there (cp. McDowell 1994, p. 150).

III. 3   The identity theorist, unlike the minimal theorist, is willing
to look to accounts of interpretation to elicit our conception of truth.
But the identity theorist accepts the idea which the minimal
theorist's Schema E may be taken to encapsulate. This is the idea
that in introducing a word for *truth* into a language not containing
such a word, one introduces nothing which is new (so to speak).[22]
For sure, the identity theorist introduces the word 'facts'; but that
is only in order to find a way of saying that the facts are the same
as what is true, and thus to be quite explicit about her opposition to
a correspondence theory of truth. By using the correspondence
theorists' own vocabulary of 'fact', the identity theorist sets herself
apart from the correspondence theorist's conception of truth. We
may ask what the minimal theory is supposed to be set apart from.
What might one have wanted to say about truth which it becomes
impossible to say when one's conception of truth has been deflated
sufficiently to conform to the conception that a minimal theorist
recommends?

Well, there are three popular statements of the deflationary idea.
First, it is said that truth has no underlying nature. Secondly, it is
said that in using the predicate 'true' we cannot get at any more facts
than we had access to already. Thirdly, it is said that there is no more
to truth than its serving a logical need.

The first claim, that truth has no underlying nature, is Horwich's
favourite. But if we try to read it in a distinctively deflationary way,
then it may seem to suggest that truth is not a predicate of thinkables
with any application independent of other predicates of thinkables.
And that is surely wrong.[23]

The second claim, that we cannot get at any more facts than we
already have access to, is correct if it makes a point about what the

22. Not only is nothing new introduced; nothing is excluded. This point may be used to
dispute the title of 'minimal' to the minimal theory. As Gupta 1993 points out, the ideology
of the theory is, in one obvious sense, maximal: cp. Frege's remark quoted at n. 7.

23. Truth's lack of 'an underlying nature' seems sometimes to amount to the impossibility
of analyzing or defining it. Such impossibility, of course, is acknowledged by the identity
theory: see n. 5.
    Horwich sometimes tells us that the predicate 'lacks substance'. But again I find a
difficulty. It seems as if *truth* can have any of the features of any property predicated in a
true thinkable (cp. nn. 7 & 22). But in that case 'true' is exactly as substantial as, and exactly
as insubstantial as, any predicate in the language; which would seem to ensure that we
actually cannot make sense of the claim that truth lacks substance. (This peculiarity of 'true'
might be used to motivate a treatment in which 'is true' is not a predicate. I do not think that
someone with the identity theorist's motivation has to be opposed to such treatment. The
kind of deflationism to which it leads need not be assimilated to Horwich's: see n. 16.)

word 'true' enables us to say or to think. (The identity theory shows what is correct about this. When we say or think that p is true, we say or think that it is a fact that p [and it *is* a fact that p if we are right]; but the fact that p which we may take ourselves now to have access to is the same as the thinkable that we say or think when we say or think that p: there is then no new fact to which we have access.) When a distinctively deflationary understanding of this claim is sought, however, it becomes all too easy to construe it as saying something incorrect. It could be understood as saying that the facts are exhausted by the thinkables to which we already have access. But then it would be suggested that we here now are not entitled to our view that there are facts which no-one here now can actually think. That suggestion is incompatible with the part of commonsense realism whose compatibility with an identity theory I have tried to show.

What, then, about the deflationist's third claim, that there is no more to truth than its serving a certain logical need? This is a claim about the point of having a word which functions as the English word 'true' does. Understood as such, it is correct. But a philosopher who thought to ask 'What is *truth*?' may not be satisfied by being told what sort of device the truth predicate is: she wants to know what sort of distinction it records.

We saw that a grasp of the distinction involved in assessments of thinkables as true or false is required in order to be in a position to make psychological predications of them (§II.3).[24] This is quite compatible with the truth predicate's being the sort of device that the deflationist says it is. And it ensures that there is no new mode of evaluation for thinkables which is brought onto the scene when the word 'true' is introduced. Yet a minimal theorist purports to advance a deflationary claim in using the Equivalence Schema (E) to tell us what sort of device 'true' is. How could he deflate truth further—beyond what is necessary to restore it to the uninflated condition in which the identity theory finds it? It seems that he must either take the distinction involved in assessments of thinkables as true or false to be implicit in some gloss on (E) that he might offer,

24. There could be debate about whether this suffices to ensure that truth is 'explanatory'. But however that debate might go, truth will not turn out to have the kind of 'causal explanatory role' that e.g. Hartry Field associates with assignments of truth-conditions which count as correspondence truth-conditions. (I touched on some of the issues about truth's role in my 1989.)

or he must deny that there is any such distinction. But of course there is a distinction between what is true and what is false. And unless a gloss on (E) has the sort of platitudinous ring that 'fact' carries, it will be bound to spoil the deflationary message.[25]

We have found no positively deflationary and correct thesis about truth for a minimal theorist to advance.

III. 4   The conception of truth which the identity theory brings with it allows truth to be a *sui generis* norm, in play where there are rational beings who may go right or wrong in their thought and speech. This is enough to let us shun correspondence theories, and it leaves us well-placed to make out our title to commonsense realism (if that should seem necessary). To the extent that advocates of a minimal theory say distinctively and genuinely deflationary things, they deny us that title; and then they lead us astray.

Answers to philosophers' questions about the relation between language and the world have traditionally taken a form which we now call theories of truth. I have not meant to develop any new theory here. Indeed I do not think that we need any theory of truth save insofar as we may go astray without one. I have promoted the identity theory, because I think that we have to find a position from which to avoid the false dilemmas that the theories currently on offer present us with.[26] I hope that reflection on the identity theory shows that antagonism towards correspondence theories, and indeed towards all theories which purport to analyze truth, is independent of the deflationary attitude. The identity theory provides a perspective from which many other theories will appear indefensible.[27]

Department of Philosophy
Birkbeck College
Malet Street
London WC1E 7HX

25. Wright 1992, Ch.1 §III, argues, in effect, that the deflationist's position is not made out until such a gloss is allowed, but that any such gloss must be inflationary by the deflationist's own lights.

26. David furnishes a good example of the false dilemma: the reader of David 1994 is invited to accept a correspondence theory of truth on the basis of a demonstration of the untenability of disquotationalism. The dilemmas are sometimes subtler: 'robustness', for instance, is sometimes taken to accrue to truth, or 'factualism' to a discourse which is 'truth apt' as soon as minimalism is denied; and correspondence conceptions may enter with talk of robustness and factualism.

REFERENCES

Blackburn, S. 1984: *Spreading the Word*, Oxford: Clarendon Press.

Boghossian, P. 1990: 'The Status of Content', *Philosophical Review* 99, pp. 157–84.

Brandom, R. 1994: *Making it Explicit*, Cambridge Mass.: Harvard University Press.

Candlish, S. 1995: 'Resurrecting the Identity Theory of Truth', *Bradley Studies*, 1, pp. 116–124.

David, M. 1994: *Correspondence and Disquotation*, Oxford: University Press.

Davidson, D. 1967: 'Truth and Meaning', reprinted as Essay 2 in Davidson 1984.

Davidson, D. 1969: 'True to the Facts', reprinted as Essay 3 in Davidson 1984.

Davidson, D. 1984: *Inquiries into Truth and Interpretation*, Oxford: Clarendon Press.

Davidson, D. 1990: 'The Structure and Content of Truth', *Journal of Philosophy* 87, pp. 279–329.

Davies, M. 1981: *Meaning, Quantification, Necessity*, London: Routledge and Kegan Paul.

Dodd, J. 1995: 'McDowell and Identity Theories of Truth', *Analysis* 55, pp. 160–165.

Dodd, J. & Hornsby, J. 1992: 'The Identity Theory of Truth: Reply to Baldwin', *Mind* 101, pp. 319–322.

Dummett, M. 1958/9: 'Truth', *Proceedings of the Aristotelian Society* 59, pp.141–162.

Dummett, M. 1976: 'What is a Theory of Meaning? II', in *Truth and Meaning: Essays in Semantics*, edd. G. Evans & J. McDowell, Oxford: Clarendon Press.

Dummett, M. 1990: 'The Source of the Concept of Truth', in George Boolos (ed.) *Meaning and Method: Essays in Honour of Hilary Putnam*, Cambridge: University Press.

[Page references are to the version reprinted in Michael Dummett, *The Seas of Language*, Oxford: University Press, 1993].

Etchemendy, J. 1988: 'Tarski on Truth and Logical Consequence', *Journal of Symbolic Logic* 53, pp. 51–79.

Field, H. 1986: 'The Deflationary Conception of Truth', in G. MacDonald and C. Wright (eds.) Fact, *Science and Morality: Essays on A. J. Ayer's Language, Truth and Logic*, Oxford: Blackwell.

Frege, G. 1918: 'The Thought'.

[Quotations are taken from the translation by A.M. and Marcelle Quinton, as reprinted in *Philosophical Logic*, ed. P.F. Strawson Oxford: Oxford University Press, 1967.]

Grover, D. 1992: *A Prosentential Theory of Truth*, Princeton N.J.: Princeton University Press.

Gupta, A. 1993: 'Minimalism', *Philosophical Perspectives* 7, pp. 359–369.

Hornsby, J. 1989: 'Semantic Innocence and Psychological Understanding', *Philosophical Perspectives*, 3, pp. 549–574.

Horwich, P. 1990: *Truth*, Oxford: Blackwell.

27. A visit to Monash University in 1991 provided me with some time for thought about truth: for that and more, including a useful discussion of this paper's first ancestor, I thank the Philosophy Department there. Both before and after that visit, I had helpful conversations with Julian Dodd; I can now reciprocate the generous acknowledgement of me in his doctoral thesis. I am grateful both to the members of a discussion group in Oxford which David Charles convenes, and to the Centro de Studie sulla Filosofia Contemporanea for sponsorship of a conference in Genoa in November 1995. My final thanks are to John Collins and David Wiggins, for comments on what was necessarily the final draft.

Jackson, F., Oppy G. & Smith, M. 1994: 'Minimalism and Truth Aptness', *Mind* 103, pp. 287–302.

McDowell, J. 1994: *Mind and World* (Cambridge Mass.: Harvard University Press).

McDowell, J. 1976: 'Bivalence and Verificationism', in Gareth Evans and John McDowell (eds.) *Truth and Meaning: Essays in Semantics*, Oxford: Clarendon Press.

Neale, S. 1995: 'The Philosophical Significance of Gödel's Slingshot', *Mind* 104, pp. 761–825.

Putnam, H. 1981: *Reason Truth and History*, Cambridge: University Press.

Putnam, H. 1990: 'A Defense of Internal Realism', in *Realism with a Human Face*, Cambridge Mass.: Harvard University Press.

Quine, W.V. 1960: *Word and Object*, Cambridge, Mass.: The M.I.T. Press.

Quine, W.V. 1970: *Philosophy of Logic*, Englewood Cliffs: Prentice-Hall.

Rorty, R. 1995: 'Is Truth a Goal of Enquiry? Davidson vs Wright', *Philosophical Quarterly* 45, pp. 281–300.

Rumfitt, I. 1993: 'Content and Context: The Paratactic Theory Revisited and Revised', *Mind* 102, pp. 429–454.

Russell, B. 1940: *An Inquiry into Meaning and Truth*, London: Allen and Unwin.

Wright, C. 1992: *Truth and Objectivity*, Cambridge Mass.: Harvard University Press.

II*—THE SANCTIONS OF THE CRIMINAL LAW

by Michael Clark

I

' All punishment', said Bentham, 'is a mischief. If it ought at all to be imposed it ought only to be imposed in so far as it promises to exclude some greater evil.' (*Introduction to the Principles of Morals and Legislation*, 12.) The punishment of adults within the penal system is prima facie a mischief, since when it is imposed by legal authorities for criminal offences it is intended to be unpleasant and inflicted without consent. Hart[1] and others have sought to defend the utilitarian justification of punishment by placing constraints on its distribution to avoid the punishment of innocents (as involved, for example, in vicarious and collective punishments) and inflicting excessive penalties on the guilty. The questions who should be punished, and how much, are held to be separate ones the answers to which are not necessarily dictated by the overall point of the practice.

> Much confusing shadow-fighting between utilitarians and their opponents may be avoided if it is recognized that it is perfectly consistent to assert *both* that the General Justifying Aim of the practice of punishment is its beneficial consequences *and* that the pursuit of this General Aim should be qualified or restricted out of deference to principles of Distribution which require that punishment should be only of an offender for an offence. Conversely it does not in the least follow from the admission of the latter principle of retribution in Distribution that the General Justifying Aim of punishment is retribution.... (*Op. cit.*, p. 9.)

By analogy we might say that the effort and expense of providing medical services is justified by the human benefit they bring, but that does not wholly determine answers to questions about the

---

1. 'Prolegomenon to the Principles of Punishment', in H. L. A. Hart, *Punishment and Responsibility*, Oxford: Clarendon Press, 1968.

*Meeting of the Aristotelian Society, held in the Senior Common Room, Birkbeck College, London, on Monday, 28th October, 1996 at 8.15 p.m.

distribution of those services. There will, presumably, be general agreement about the aim of medical treatment among those who disagree about its distribution: who disagree on whether it should depend on ability to pay, for example, or whether the young should have priority over the old.

I propose to defend Hart's approach against some major criticisms it has received. Although my own view is that this compromise approach is essentially correct, and I shall recommend it in a modified form, it is also important for its opponents not to dismiss it for unsound reasons. Even those who think that punishment for crime is to be justified as retribution, reform, education or penitence, for example, have an interest in attacking the view in its strongest version.

I begin by sketching the criticisms I wish to meet.

(1) Consequentialist justifications have notoriously been open to the Kantian complaint that they endorse treating those punished *solely as means* to secure the benefits for the rest of us.

(2) Secondly, there is a problem about the way Hart underwrites the prohibition on punishing the innocent. Hart claims that the prohibition respects our autonomy. We should treat everyone 'alike as persons by attaching special importance to voluntary action', says Hart. Society gives us a fair chance of choosing (i) to obey the law required for its protection or (ii) suffering the penalty. If we were liable to sanctions when we had not committed offences ourselves, then we could not be sure of avoiding the sanctions by refraining from crime, and in that way our autonomy would be reduced. One of the merits of confining punishment to the personally guilty, claims Hart, is that it protects our autonomy by increasing our 'power to identify beforehand periods when the law's punishments will not interfere with [us] and to plan [our] lives accordingly' (p. 23).

The trouble is that in restricting sanctions in this way we may well be exposing ourselves to more crime. The extra crime might limit our freedom and confound our expectations more than the incidence of unjust sanctions would. If collective punishment, vicarious punishment (or, indeed, excessive punishment of the guilty) would lead to less crime, then our greater freedom from crime might exceed the loss of autonomy involved in our being liable to such punishments. A principal standard objection to the pure utilitarian approach now seems to threaten Hart's position too.

(3) The compromise approach, it has been said, is inconsistent and uneconomic. It is inconsistent because the constraints which require only those personally guilty to be subject to punishment, and then not with disproportionate severity, may undermine the end of minimizing crime. 'How can something like the prevention of crime or the maximizing of utility be the overall goal of the institution, if punishment is distributed by standards that are not attuned to the promotion of the goal?' ask Braithwaite and Pettit in their recent book *Not Just Deserts* (Oxford: Clarendon Press, 1990, p. 167). It is uneconomic because a justification, like that offered by Braithwaite and Pettit in terms of what they call *dominion*, can yield complete answers to questions of liability and amount, and give a simpler, and therefore better, theory.

(4) Fourthly, and finally, it has been claimed that to admit what Hart calls 'retributive' constraints on liability and amount commits you to retribution as at least part of the justifying aim of punishment. For, it is argued, to admit retributive considerations at all is to admit that people *deserve* to be punished; and, in insisting that only the personally guilty deserve punishment and that they should not be punished more severely than they deserve, we are conceding that punishment is merited by the guilty, and consequently that the state *should* punish them. But then, it is argued, it should punish them even when it would not be justified by the consequences. You cannot consistently admit retributive considerations at all without letting them into the justification. 'Hart cannot introduce what is meant to be a restrictive principle of liability and simply style it a "retributive" principle without admitting the rest of the retributive approach' (John Morison, 'Hart's Excuses', in Philip Leith and Peter Ingram, eds., *The Jurisprudence of Orthodoxy*, London: Routledge, 1988, p. 127).

II

Using criminals solely as means. The objection that punishing offenders for social benefit uses them solely as means is an overstatement, since the offenders themselves, whether free or in detention, have an interest in being protected from crime on the part of others. Moreover, it is arguable that the constraints on distribution, if they are respected, do reflect some respect for people as ends in themselves. But even if punishing criminals technically avoids infringing Kant's principle, it seems to go against its spirit, particularly in the case of those sentenced to long prison terms: they are being used largely, even if not solely, as means.

By contrast, if the point of punishment is a retributive one, it is not a matter of *using* the person who is punished to exact the supposedly desired retribution, since punishing *is* exacting retribution. The problem here is to show that retribution is a good, and moreover one that the state should bring about. The only alternative, if punishment is still to be regarded as capable of justification yet entirely faithful to the Kantian principle, is to claim that it is inflicted for the benefit of its recipients, say by reforming them or enabling them to repent of their crimes. But unless the reform or penitence are sought in order to prevent further crime, which returns us to a consequentialist justification, the proponent of such a view has to explain why it is a matter for the state to take such expensive and paternalistic measures. In any case, if we are to be realistic we shall recognize that it is only rarely that the recipients themselves benefit overall from penal sanctions. It is much easier to see why the state should be concerned with preventing crime.

We are surely as justified in defending ourselves against crime when necessary by threatening penal sanctions against those who might be responsible for offending as we are in defending ourselves with force where necessary when others voluntarily attack us. The threat of punishment can be regarded as a form of self-defence; though when the punishment is inflicted it is no longer self-defence, since the offence has already been committed. But threats would be idle if they were never carried out; at which point the proponent of a consequentialist justification must say that, to the extent that penalising criminal offenders defies the Kantian principle, so much the worse for that principle. Like most moral principles it will be subject to an exception.[2]

On the view I am defending, sanctions are threatened principally in order to defend us from crime by deterring potential offenders from committing criminal acts. It is inconceivable, at any rate in

2. Braithwaite and Pettit, *op. cit.*, p. 174, claim that a virtue of their republican theory is that it makes us confront the fact that we cannot administer the penal system without treating people as means rather than ends-in-themselves. This 'invites a posture of moral reluctance rather than moral smugness, and that is surely a strength'. The same could be said for the compromise view defended here.

the societies we live in, that such threats should prove effective if they were never carried out. Sham punishments[3] just would not work, and an open society precludes them anyway.

R. A. Duff demurs:

> The proper aim of a system of law is to secure not merely obedience, but the citizen's acceptance of obligations which are justified to him by relevant reasons which show the law to serve the common good..., a condition which must be met if the law is to treat the citizen as an autonomous agent. Now a system of deterrent punishment abandons that ideal aim. (*Proceedings of the Aristotelian Society*, Supplementary Volume LXII, 1988, p. 158.)

If rational persuasion worked well enough, there would be no need to threaten punishment. Equally, if there were every prospect that I could protect life and limb against an aggressive assailant by rational persuasion, I would not be justified in using violence to defend myself; but, if persuasion fails or is not feasible, then may I not use physical force, at least when the assailant is responsible for attacking me, having chosen to do so? And if we seek to confine punishment to those personally responsible for breaking the criminal law we shall be respecting the autonomy of those subject to that law.

Of course it is a further question whether and to what extent punitive measures are likely to prevent crime which cannot be prevented by acceptable non-punitive measures. The consequentialist approach permits punishment for crime only when the benefits are likely to be great enough to merit the cost, and respects Bentham's principle of frugality, endorsing only as much punishment as seems necessary to achieve the benefits.[4]

3. Cf. Braithwaite and Pettit: 'A penalty could breach [uncontroversial] limits without incurring any utilitarian cost: say, if it involved extended imprisonment with drugs administered regularly to ensure euphoria' (p. 53). How do they imagine such a practice could be kept secret?.

4. *Pace* Braithwaite and Pettit, *op. cit.*, p. 206. The compromise theory is said to be uncritical in assuming that punishment rather than non-punitive varieties of reprobation is the proper response to crime. Not so: if we postulate a utilitarian end, then it is implicit that this must be pursued most economically, and that where it can be achieved more cheaply by non-punitive methods it should be. Although I recognise below that the end should not be construed in a purely utilitarian way and that we may be justified in punishing when the crime prevented is not a *greater* evil, this does not mean we have to abandon the requirement of economy of cost. After all, I may be justified in killing two assailants to save one life (my own), and other things being equal an act utilitarian would regard the two deaths as a greater evil than one. But I would not be justified in killing anyone if (at least in the circumstances as I understood them) it were evident to me that I could save my life by mere threats or flight.

There is, however, a need to modify the utilitarian justification. Is it always necessary to be confident that *greater* evil is likely to be excluded, at any rate if we equate evil with suffering or loss? I may justly inflict greater harm than I prevent in self-defence: for example, an old man may be justified in killing two young assailants to protect his own life. And are vindictive satisfactions to count as good consequences except in so far as they are means of preventing vigilante action? The justification will still be consequentialist, even when it fails to satisfy the Benthamite condition; moreover, not all the consequences regarded as good by a Benthamite utilitarian will count as beneficial, and not all those which are beneficial will always be available as justifications. In particular, I think we should distinguish between those beneficial consequences for which we can justifiably impose punishment and those for which we cannot but which are welcome none the less. Exclusion may sometimes be of the latter sort. Duff says:

> As to defence, we cannot just say that punishment prevents the criminal from committing future crimes; for if defensive coercion is to be consistent with a due respect for the person coerced, it must be a response to an attack in which he is *now* engaged. A preemptive strike to prevent an attack on which he *might* embark infringes his autonomy, by pre-empting his choices. Preventive punishments likewise infringe the autonomy of those who are punished. (*Op. cit.*, p. 161.)

But offenders like the Yorkshire Ripper have shown how dangerous they are; and, *pace* Duff, we cannot responsibly leave them free to continue their offences. In other cases Duff is right that exclusion is not *justified* on the basis of the prior offence. Suppose that only one in five hundred domestic murderers would have murdered again during the years that followed if they had not been imprisoned during those years. Preventing those few murders might not itself *justify* their incarceration, welcome though that prevention would be. But imprisonment might still be justified as a deterrent. We could then welcome all the goods produced by the incarceration, the prevention of crime both through deterrence and excluding the offender from the general community for a period. The imprisonment does not *have* to be justified in terms of exclusion if it can be justified on deterrent grounds. These considerations no doubt apply to individual deterrence as well.

I do not say that defence against crime through deterrence and, to some extent, incapacitation and individual deterrence, exhaust the consequentialist justification I endorse: another consequence that has often been appealed to is the protection of suspects from vigilante action, since if there were no effective state penal system, people would in many cases inflict their own penalties. Such protection is in the interest even of guilty suspects.

III

Autonomy and protection from crime. The second objection concerns Hart's appeal to the value of autonomy to underpin the constraint which proscribes punishing the innocent. The problem is that respecting this constraint could mean that we were subject to more crime than we would be if it were not respected. And if we are subject to more crime we have less autonomy, and there is no guarantee that this loss is outweighed or even balanced by the increase in autonomy we would gain by freedom from certain unjust punishments (collective or vicarious, for example). In one respect we should be less free to plan our lives, because we would be less sure that penal sanctions would not interfere with our plans; on the other hand, we might have reason for greater confidence that the criminal activities of others would not interfere.[5]

Nevertheless, punishing the innocent remains unacceptable. It's a matter of how officials, the penal system, treat us. There is some hope of redress for criminal injury and loss of property, and although some innocents might gain redress for unjust punishments there would, for example, be none for penal sanctions against morally innocent offenders punished vicariously or as part of a collective penalty. Freedom from unfair sanctions imposed by officials of the state has a special value for us: if we tolerated unjust penal sanctions we would not be accorded respect as people even by those who were, in a decent régime, otherwise honest, trustworthy and acting officially in the public interest. We shall

---

5. 'We are more likely to be a victim of crime than an excusable defendant and so, if we are concerned to maximize the efficiency of individual choice inside the costing system, it might seem that this could be achieved better by eliminating excuses and making the law more effective' (Morison, *op. cit.*, p. 141). But the question should be: are we more likely to be victims of *crime that would not occur if excuses were not admitted* than we are to be excusable defendants? That is, would abolition of excuses make us more secure or less, increase or diminish predictability?.

always be at risk from criminal elements, but if we were unjustly at risk from the state as well we should be liable to be treated as means by anyone. Respecting the constraint on distribution is not a matter of maximising overall autonomy, since it may expose us to more crime; but if it does, it is the criminal offenders, not the state, who are primarily responsible for it. The state would not be responsible for the extra crime in the way it would be responsible if it punished personally innocent people.[6]

But why, it might be asked, should autonomy take precedence over social safety? After all, we think it proper to quarantine the infectious and lock up the insane to protect the public. (Cf. Morison, *op. cit.*, p. 135.) The answer is that the innocent do not endanger others by their freedom in the way that the infectious or the insane do; the innocent, unlike the infectious and some of the insane, are not threats to others.

IV

Inconsistent; uneconomic? The third objection concerns the structure of the compromise approach, the separation of the question about justification from the questions about distribution. At worst, it is claimed, the position is inconsistent, at best uneconomic.

First, the charge of inconsistency. The distribution of punishment, argue Braithwaite and Pettit, should be 'attuned to the promotion of [its] goal'. But we frequently, if not invariably, place constraints on the means by which we pursue ends. If we adopt philosophical research as a goal, for example, we do not regard that goal as undermined by our unwillingness to steal books or murder those who obstruct us. The end, we say, does not justify the means. Parents should try to give their children a good start in life, but not

6. Cf. Thomas Nagel in a recent paper: 'I would not be surprised if the rate of violent crime in the United States, for example, could be substantially reduced if the police and courts were free to use methods to control, arrest, and imprison suspects which carried a greater risk of violating people's rights than the methods now legally permitted. Violent crimes are also violations of people's rights, so the balance might be quite favourable. The average person's chance of being mugged or murdered might decrease much more than his chance of being beaten up by the police or falsely imprisoned would increase. Yet a believer in individual rights will reject what appears to be the lesser evil in this case, preferring to maintain strict protections against maltreatment and strict standards of evidence and procedural safeguards for suspected offenders, even at the cost of a higher crime rate and a higher total rate of rights violations.' ('Personal Rights and Public Space', *Philosophy and Public Affairs,* 24, 1995, pp. 90–91.).

by using corrupt methods like nepotism. The prosecution of a war may be justified as necessary for the defence of the nation, but although considerable violence may be condoned in the pursuit of this end we draw the line at war crimes, even though they might further the war effort.

Braithwaite and Pettit say: 'Whatever of a utilitarian goal, a preventionist goal can hardly be served by distributing punishment according to negative standards; refraining from punishing the innocent and refraining from punishing the guilty beyond the deserved level can hardly be construed as rules that prevent crime' (p. 167). But neither can refraining from nepotism serve the goal of giving your children a good start in life, nor may refraining from war crimes forward the war effort. (Even if it does, that is not the only or most important reason for refraining from them). However, the constraints are not presented as furthering the goal, nor do they need to be. They are moral restrictions on the pursuit of defensible or desirable goals, because the end does not justify the means, that is the end does not necessarily justify the use of any means whatsoever of achieving those goals. There must be few, if any, ends that do. It is absurd to imply that no goal can be recommended or justifiably pursued if the constraints on its pursuit do not flow directly from the goal itself.

Alleging a further incoherence in the compromise position, Braithwaite and Pettit say: 'If your goal is crime prevention or a relevant sub-goal such as deterrence then you are not given any reason why you should not think of going beyond uncontroversial bounds in order to try the better to achieve your objective' (p. 79). But it is equally true that, if your goal is giving your children a good start in life or the defence of your country, the mere identification of these goals does not give you any reason not to overstep the bounds in their pursuit. Yet it is surely wrong to infer from this that no reason can be given for restricting the means by which the goals may be pursued, or that these goals cannot be acceptable ones.

Next for the charge that a compromise position is uneconomic. Braithwaite and Pettit offer a more economic and unified justification of punishment in terms of what they call *dominion* (the Roman republican value of 'libertas'): a single value to generate answers to all three of Hart's questions (as well as ten other penal issues). In their own words:

A person enjoys full dominion, we say, if and only if

1. she enjoys no less a prospect of liberty than is available to other citizens

2. it is common knowledge among citizens that this condition obtains...

3. she enjoys no less a prospect of liberty than the best that is compatible with the same prospect for all citizens. (*Op. cit.*, pp. 64–5.)

In other words, everyone has an equal and optimal prospect of liberty, and everyone knows this.

Isn't protection from crime nevertheless the *primary* aim of criminal punishment? Consider a penal system conforming to Hart's principles in a totalitarian state: republican justification won't extend to non-democratic régimes. Protection from harm to the person, from damage to or loss of property, etc., are to be welcomed even in an authoritarian state whose citizens have little hope of enjoying freedom. Such protection has a value independently of the contribution it might make to political freedom. No doubt freedom from criminal harm is a *component* of dominion, and the notion of dominion may well underpin a political ideology which admits punishment consistent with that allowed by the compromise position, just as a basic theory of atomic physics may yield a theory about the behaviour of molecules in gases. But the latter is hardly discredited thereby.

Dominion is unlikely to be achieved in a society that does not have a penal system to control crime, does not have reasonable medical services nor adequate educational provision. Is it therefore wrong to say that the aim of a health service is the alleviation of illness, or that the goals of an education service are personal self-development and nourishment of the economy? Braithwaite and Pettit offer us an all-embracing political ideology which seeks to accommodate these essential institutions and practices in a coherent manner, and they engage in a valuable philosophical enterprise. However, just because of its more comprehensive reach, such an ideology is likely to be more vulnerable to criticism and more difficult to defend. Moreover it needs to be tested by examining its consequences for the institutions and practices it recommends. To preclude justification of punishment in Hart's terms frustrates such evaluation. It is as if we could not properly investigate the behaviour of gases and formulate a theory of the behaviour of molecules in gases without first establishing a basic theory of atomic physics and deriving the specific theory about gases from that. Either the dominion theory has the right consequences for punishment (if the compromise theory is correct, it licences punishment when necessary to curb crime provided side-constraints are respected), or it does not. If it does not then it is at least in need of amendment; but, if it does, far from excluding the more specific theory of punishment, it entails it.

Furthermore, there is a decisive objection to the approach of Braithwaite and Pettit. If the justifying aim of punishment is, or includes,[7] the protection of autonomy, this does not remove the need for side-constraints which prohibit the punishment of innocents, because, as I have conceded, observing the constraints may not maximise autonomy. Even though we do not know whether they increase or diminish our overall autonomy, we still want our autonomy to be respected by the state. Including autonomy among the aims of punishment is not guaranteed to generate the constraints. The compromise approach, with its separation of the question of justifying aim from questions of distribution, cannot defensibly be displaced by a unitary consequentialist account which generates satisfactory answers to all of these questions at the same time.

It might be suggested that the values the compromise position seeks to protect, including the importance it should attach to the state's respect for the autonomy of individuals, could be built into the goal of punishment. The notion of dominion might perhaps be characterised in a way that is sensitive to that importance, and the independent value of protection of the person and property included in a portmanteau goal. But this is not a genuine alternative, because the issues discussed under the headings of justification, liability and amount will now arise under the single heading of general justifying aim, and the various components of the goal which generate the constraints will still need individual defence. Any apparent gain in economy and coherence would be spurious.

V

Retribution in liability and amount. The final objection concerns the legitimacy of so-called retributive constraints on a consequentialist justification. Retributive constraints on distribution, it seems, require not punishing people who don't deserve it, and not punishing people more than they deserve. But desert, we are told, implies they *should* to be punished, even if no end is served. 'When retribution as a value is invoked anywhere in the theory of punishment it brings with it the whole retributive apparatus' (Morison, p. 127; cf. Ted Honderich, *Punishment: the supposed justifications*, London: Hutchinson, 1976, pp. 152–3).

However, the compromise theorist can continue with logical impunity to say that the innocent do not deserve punishment and that there are limits to what true offenders deserve which should be respected in applying sanctions. For you can deserve something without its being the case that you ought to get it or must get it since to deserve x is simply to be *worthy* of x. Suppose that two students are each trustworthy as babysitters, but that I need only one babysitter. Both of them can be trusted to babysit for me tonight, but I need trust only one of them. I do not have to trust the other, since her services are not needed if I employ the first. Entrusting someone who was not trustworthy with my baby would be wrong, but there is nothing wrong with not entrusting someone who is. Similarly, it is wrong to drive an unroadworthy car on the public highway, but not wrong to refrain from taking out a roadworthy one. This gives us the asymmetry needed for the compromise position, since it condemns the punishment of someone who is not worthy of it without requiring the punishment of someone who is if no good end would be served by it.

If penal desert increases with guilt, what punishments do perpetrators of horrendous genocide like Hitler and Eichmann, or war criminals like Mengele, deserve? If an ordinary murderer deserves extended imprisonment, would they not deserve the most excruciating and prolonged torture possible? But what decent civilised person could say that it was binding on the penal authorities to inflict such a penalty? Even if they are worthy of it barbaric torture would be a moral outrage: it cannot be a moral imperative that we meet barbarism with barbarism. This shows, nothing else does, that we cannot claim that a deserved penalty is always morally required.

So it is arguable that, even if offenders *do* merit suffering, it is not the job of the state to inflict it if it does not also serve an end the state should properly embrace, any more than it is required that the state should reward the meritorious. (Cf. Braithwaite and Pettit, p. 165.) To the extent that it does reward the meritorious (by a system of honours, for example) that is not morally objectionable in the same way, since we are expressing our gratitude by means of rewards acceptable to the recipients.

By way of comparison, consider medical services again. It is internal to the idea of medical practice that its point is the prevention and alleviation of illness. But agreement about the point does not require agreement about the distribution of those services. Some people (though I am not among them) favour taking patients' responsibility for their own medical condition into account in the distribution. Those who smoke or drink to excess, for example, and become ill as a consequence would be given lower priority than those who could not be held responsible for their illness in the same way. But the people who hold this view are surely not committed to a retributive theory of medical treatment, to the view that the point of health services is a retributive one, or even that this retribution is *part* of its point. They would give lower priority to those who were ill through their own irresponsible unhealthy living, on the grounds that they were not worthy, or less deserving, of treatment. But this does not entail that the (or one) *point* of medical services is to reward the responsible (and thereby penalise the irresponsible).

Nevertheless, it may still be felt that talk of desert concedes too much to the idea of retribution. That someone deserves something is arguably always a reason for seeing that he or she gets it; it is just that in some cases there are overriding reasons against doing so. Someone deserves promotion but there is only one vacancy at the higher rank and a competitor is more deserving; or the company cannot afford to promote anyone. An offender deserves a severe penalty but its infliction would be inhumane or pointless.

However, there is no need to state the compromise theory in terms of desert anyway: Hart himself did not do so. It is a negative notion of retribution that Hart employs, and this is very different from the positive retribution required by the Kantian. Even the word *retribution* can be avoided and simply replaced by the terms in which it is characterised: punishments should be confined to those found guilty of responsibly offending and should not be disproportionately high.

VI

Amount. But how exactly are we to underwrite the prohibition on excessive punishments? Severe punishments for minor transgressions would often be ruled out because the cost of the relatively minor benefits is too high. But (a) they will not always be ruled out (possibly only one or two long prison sentences for parking offences would be enough virtually to eliminate anti-social parking, a considerable social benefit) and (b) I have conceded that the evil which punishment promises to exclude need not always be greater than that of the punishment. Hart deals with excuses and mitigating factors by appeal to autonomy. But what of excessive punishments for offences where there is no excuse or mitigating factor: there is a lacuna in Hart's account, because he does not give an adequate rationale for proscribing these. Barbaric penalties[8]—torture, bodily mutilation and the like—can be excluded by appeal to the civilised values of human dignity; not simply the dignity of the victims of punishment but of the community which authorises and inflicts the penalty. (Cf. the constitutional prohibition on 'cruel and unusual punishment' in the United States.) But what of excessive punishments which are not barbaric in that way? If a punishment is too severe it is out of proportion with the gravity of the offence. I shall not rehearse the difficulties in applying this idea; sufficient to say that there are undoubtedly cases in which it is uncontroversial that a punishment is excessive in this way, and that we try to deal with other cases by comparison and ranking. Even if the punishment contravenes the Kantian principle of ends I have insisted that where offenders have had the opportunity to avoid the penalty by refraining from crime we are justified in so using them in the war against crime if there seems no cheaper way of procuring the same effect. But I suggest that *excessive* punishment is too egregious a use of offenders to be morally acceptable. In limiting

8. Whether or not excessive.

punishment to those who had a fair opportunity of avoiding it there is some residual respect for them as ends which would be gravely reduced if people were liable to severe penalties for relatively minor offences. The total benefit might, in utilitarian terms, be great enough to outweigh the punishments (as in the imagined example of draconian penalties for parking offences) but it would be thinly spread and no individual beneficiary could decently demand the severe penalty even if it need only rarely be inflicted. [9]

VII

My modifications of Hart. Finally, let me reiterate the modifications to Hart's position that I consider necessary.

1. The General Justifying Aim, though consequentialist, need not be utilitarian in the sense of requiring in every case that the suffering to be excluded is likely to be greater than that involved in the punishment. Nor may *all* the benefits which may accrue from punishing offenders be appealed to as justification.

2. Restricting punishment to the guilty may not make it easier to plan our lives; for although we can generally avoid the interference of penal sanctions by refraining from crime, the constraints on punishment may expose us to more crime, the occurrence of which we shall not be able to predict. Thus our overall autonomy may not be enhanced by the constraint. However, freedom from unjust sanctions imposed by officials of the state has a value of special importance for us.

I have argued that, with these modifications, the compromise position is defensible against four major criticisms that have been made of it.

Department of Philosophy
University of Nottingham
University Park
Nottingham NG7 2RD

Michael.Clark@nottingham.ac.uk

9. This is only a gesture towards a possible way of filling the lacuna, and needs to be worked out in detail. I make it to pre-empt the further objection that the lacuna is fatal to the compromise position because it cannot be filled within it.

III*—CONDITIONS ON UNDERSTANDING LANGUAGE[1]

by Ernest Lepore

I

Philosophers in general are uncomfortable, if not downright sceptical, about attributing semantic knowledge, particularly of a semantic *theory*, to ordinary speakers.[2] Those who do not feel the pinch often adopt a two-pronged defence: they rebut sceptics with an array of distinctions (and hedges), contending that the sceptics' confusions arise because they ignore such distinctions,[3] and, at the same time, argue that attributing such knowledge provides the best available working *empirical* hypothesis to account for linguistic comprehension.[4] Though sceptical arguments abound about the relevance of semantics in explicating linguistic comprehension,[5] a more acute challenge issues from Fodor and Schiffer: each offers an account of language understanding that *excludes* metalinguistic (semantic) knowledge, and therefore, knowledge of semantic *theory*.[6]

Both Fodor and Schiffer deny that there is any more to mastering a language than coming to have a capacity to go from what is heard to what is said:

> A theory of understanding for a language L would explain how one could have an auditory perception of the utterance of a novel

1. I would like to thank Herman Cappelen, Donald Davidson, Ray Elugardo, Lou Goble, John Heil, Kirk Ludwig, Stephen Schiffer and especially Jerry Fodor and Barry Smith for comments on earlier drafts of this paper.

2. See, e.g., Quine 1970, Thomason 1974, Hacking 1975; Dummett 1974, Foster 1975; Devitt 1981, Evans 1981, Baker and Hacker 1984, Schiffer 1987, Wright 1986.

3. See, e.g., Davies 1981; Lepore 1982; Higginbotham 1983, 1987; George 1989.

4. See, e.g., Partee 1975, 1979; Evans 1981; Higginbotham 1988, 1995; Larson and Segal 1995; Segal 1994.

5. See, e.g., Chomsky 1986; Fodor 1975, 1987; Hornstein 1984; Stich 1983; Schiffer 1987; Soames 1989.

6. See, e.g., Fodor 1984, 1989; Schiffer 1987, 1995; see, also, Harman 1975.

*Meeting of the Aristotelian Society, held in the Senior Common Room, Birkbeck College, London, on Monday, 11th November, 1996 at 8.15 p.m.

sentence of L and know what was said in the utterance of that
sentence [Schiffer 1987, p. 113, cf., also, p. 262].

I assume that language perception is constituted by non-
demonstrative inferences from representations of certain effects of
the speaker's behavior (sounds that he produces, marks that he
makes) to representations of certain of his intentional states, [in
particular] a canonical representation of what the speaker said
[Fodor 1984, pp. 5–6].

Fodor and Schiffer deny that knowledge (or any other kind of
epistemic/doxastic/psychological attitude) about the semantics of
one's spoken language is causally relevant for effecting these
transitions.

[W]hen we understand the utterance of a sentence we do not first
come to the belief that it means such-and-such and then have that
as our basis for thinking that the utterer was saying such-and-such
[Schiffer 1987, my emphasis, p. 262].

What really matters is this: For any perceptually analyzable
linguistic token there is a canonical description (DT) such that for
some mental state there is a canonical description (DM) such that
'DTs cause DM's' is true and counterfactual supporting [Fodor
1989, p. 8].

On this view, understanding consists in being a template for a
causal network between the perceived linguistic sounds and
shapes, and subsequent internal mental states. Understanding,
adverting to jargon, consists in having a linguistic module in the
mind. This module works (however it works) to set up a certain
law-like covariation between instantiations of categories in the
world and concepts in the mind.

The translation algorithm [from English into Mentalese] might well
consist of operations that deliver Mentalese expressions under
syntactic descriptions as output given English expressions under
syntactic descriptions as input with *no semantics* coming in
anywhere except, of course, that if it's a good translation, then
semantic properties will be preserved [Fodor 1990, my emphasis,
pp. 187–8].

Schiffer concurs: no internally represented semantics is required
for the use of a public language *even if* it has a semantics [Schiffer
1987, p. 116]. This is the lesson of Schiffer's Harvey counter-
example [Schiffer 1987, pp. 192–207].

> Harvey thinks in Mentalese… and his language processing uses
> not an internally represented [meaning theory] of English but rather
> an internally represented *translation manual* from English to
> Mentalese… Such a theory assigns no semantic values to the
> expressions of either language and in no sense determines a
> grammar (i.e., a meaning theory) for either language [Schiffer
> 1987, emphasis in the original, p. 192f; p. 262; cf., also, Schiffer
> 1994, p. 304].

Since Schiffer contests the need for an internally represented
compositional semantics, whether *any* epistemic relationship
between a speaker and this semantics need exist cannot even arise.
So, if the Fodor/Schiffer account, *translationism,* merely to label
it,[7] is correct, then the semanticist's is not, as Fodor likes to say,
the only game in town.[8]

But how could translationism be right? Isn't it obvious speakers
of Italian, for example, know semantic facts like (1)?

1. 'Sta nevicando' means that it's snowing.

Translationists *can* agree that (1) is a truth Italian speakers know.
But why, they wonder, *must* such knowledge be invoked in order
to understand Italian? (1) is true only because speakers of Italian
use 'Sta nevicando' to communicate ('encode' or 'express') the
thought that it's snowing [Schiffer, 1993, 1994, pp. 303–04].[9] So,
if someone knows that (1), this must be because he knows his words
can express this thought. From this it does *not* follow that such
knowledge is (or need be) utilized in understanding 'Sta
nevicando'. This is *all* Fodor means when he writes he is 'Gricean
in spirit though certainly not in detail' [Fodor 1975, pp. 103–104;
see, also, 1987, p. 50; and Schiffer 1982, p. 120; 1994, p. 323].
Fodor—and even Schiffer now—are Gricean *only* inasmuch as
both hold that whatever semantic properties natural language
expressions have they inherent from (a language of) thought,

---

7. Actually, 'transductionism' might be a better label since it suggests an analogy with
perception and since the notion of translation that Schiffer and Fodor are employing bears
little resemblance to what we ordinarily call 'translation' [cf., Fodor 1984].

8. Hornstein [1984], travelling a different route, arrives at a position similar to
translationism.

9. I am going to circumvent the debate between Dummett [1993] and McDowell [1988]
about the relationship between thought and language; whether language is a code or an
expression of thought. As far as I can see, even if it were true that there is no having thoughts
without having the words to express them, nothing follows about the causal efficacy of
semantic knowledge in linguistic comprehension.

Mentalese. So, contra Dummett [1978, p. 97], translationists maintain that semantic knowledge about language is *inconsequential*; it plays no causal (and therefore, no rationalizing) role in linguistic competence.[10]

Still, aren't translationists postponing the inevitable? Suppose, as Harman believes, English speakers think 'in English'. Wouldn't it follow that understanding requires invoking knowledge about the semantics for English expressions? It would not. Even if one's *lingua mentis* is one's own public language, *pace* Fodor [1975, p. 79ff] and Schiffer [1987, p. 187], understanding still involves only the capacity to make transitions from what is heard to what is said, regardless of which language we think in. As Harman puts it, '[w]ords are used to communicate thoughts that would ordinarily be thought in those or similar words' [Harman 1975, p. 271]. So, if we think 'in English', then when someone who understands English hears an individual A utter 'It's snowing', into her 'belief-box' will go an English sentence to the effect 'A said that it's snowing'.[11] No assumptions about the semantic properties of A's words need be invoked, much less knowledge about these properties?

But, one might wonder, how can merely tokening an English *sentence* in one's belief-box suffice for understanding? Mustn't we understand these internalized English sentences as well? Harman replies that we don't understand thoughts; we merely have or entertain them. Schiffer puts the point this way: '...understanding a [language of] thought is simply a matter of thinking in it' [Schiffer, 1994, p. 322]. We don't say he's thinking it's raining but doesn't understand his thought. This could only mean he is unclear in his *conception* of rain or some such thing. So, nothing *need* be

10. I also won't address what has become a rather large rift between Fodor and Schiffer, namely, whether there must be a compositional semantic theory for Mentalese itself. Fodor argues that thought is productive and systematic because Mentalese is productive and systematic and this is best accounted for by assuming that there is an internalized compositional semantic-theory for Mentalese [Fodor 1987, 1991]. Schiffer, to the contrary, argues first that any language rich enough to express propositional attitudes lacks a compositional semantic-theory and so Mentalese lacks a compositional semantic-theory and secondly that he can show how productivity and systematicity could be otherwise explained [Schiffer 1987, 1991]. These issues, though important, are irrelevant to the topic of this paper, I hope.

11. *Pace* Segal [1994, p. 115], there is no need to view this function as mapping structural descriptions of representations of natural language expressions into structural descriptions of representations of a language of thought (cf., fn 7). If I'm right, then there is no way for Segal to run a translation-style argument à la Davidson against translationism (see below).

known in order to understand thought. Translationism, in short, maintains:

i. Understanding a natural language involves nothing more than having a (perceptual) capacity to hook up the natural language expressions with symbols of (the language of) thought.

ii. This skill requires no metalinguistic (semantic) knowledge.

My aim in this paper is to refute (i) and (ii).[12] Before embarking, I'd like to say more than a few words about how the challenge of translationism illuminates anew what most philosophers argued was a misguided research program.

II

Structural Semantics—A Misguided Research Program? In the 1960's and early 1970's, Fodor (along with Katz and Postal) practised structural semantics (hereafter SS). SS theorists countenance properties and relations like synonymy, antonymy, meaningfulness, anomaly, logical entailment and equivalence, redundancy and ambiguity as a good initial conception of the range of semantics. Shunning details, SS theorists proceed by translating (or mapping) natural language expressions into (sequences or a set of) expressions of another language. There is no uniformity among them about the nature of this language or about how these translations or mappings are to be effected, but I beg no interesting questions by restricting attention to Katz and Fodor's SS proposal [1963]. The culmination of the various mapping rules and other apparatus within the Katz/Fodor framework results in theorems like (2):

2. 'Sta nevicando' in Italian translates (or is mapped) into the language Semantic Markerese as S.

Mappings like (2) are constrained, and this is the raison d'être for them as well as for semantic markers, such that synonymous expressions of a language L translate into the same (sequence or

---

12. There's lots to fuss about here. For example, Fodor and Schiffer are committed to the view that thought is (logically) prior to public language. So, I could write a paper detailing why this language of thought hypothesis is wrong, but I won't. Besides, I agree with Fodor, and Loewer and Rey that the supposition that there is a language of thought, Mentalese, 'is best viewed as simply the claim that the brain has logically structured, causally efficacious states' [Loewer, and Rey, 1991, p. xxxiii)].

set of) expressions of Semantic Markerese, ambiguous expressions
of L translate into different expressions of Semantic Markerese,
anomalous expressions of L translate into no expression of
Semantic Markerese at all and so on.

Once they surmised what SS was about, dissenting semanticists
could not get into print fast enough to explain to Fodor and Katz
just how confused they were about semantics. Davidson [1967,
1973], Vermazen [1967], Lewis [1972], Cresswell [1978], Partee
[1975], among many others, each argued that since SS theories do
not articulate relations between expressions and the world they
cannot provide an account of the truth conditions for such
sentences, and therefore, SS theories are not really semantic.
Critics charged that the phenomena SS concerns itself with
represent only a small portion of the full domain of semantics and,
SS, they argued, cannot accommodate this full domain. As David
Lewis put it:

> ...we can know the Markerese translation of an English sentence
> without knowing the first thing about the meaning of the English
> sentence; namely, the conditions under which it would be true.
> Semantics with no truth conditions is no semantics [1972, pp. 169–
> 170].

Critics protested that even if an SS for Italian assigned an
interpretation to every Italian sentence it would not specify what
any expression of Italian means. On a Davidsonian conception, an
adequate semantic theory for L must not only ascribe meanings to
expressions of L, it must also ascribe them in a way that enables
someone who knows the theory to understand these expressions.
SS fails on this account because in the overall picture of SS there
are three languages: the natural language, the language of Semantic
Markers, and the translating (or mapping) language, which may be
Semantic Markerese, the natural language, or some other language
[Davidson 1973, p. 129]. Since SS proceeds by correlating the first
two languages using the third, one can understand its mappings, for
example (2), knowing only the translating (or mapping) language
and not the other two. We can know that (2), perhaps on the basis
of what Katz and Fodor tell us, without knowing what either 'Sta
nevicando' or its Semantic Markerese translation S means.

If someone understands Semantic Markerese, he no doubt can
utilize (2) to understand the Italian sentence; but this is because he

brings to bear two things he knows (2) does not state, namely, that Semantic Markerese is a language he understands and whatever information he has in virtue of which he understands S. It is this latter information an adequate semantics must characterize.

III

Fodor's Revenge. Shortly after the assault on SS by practically the entire philosophical community, Fodor ceased doing semantics. Most philosophers thought, certainly I did, he had acceded to his critics. However, in 1975, Fodor wrote he saw little difference, if any, between specifying meaning by translation and specifying it with truth-conditions:

> We're all in Sweeney's boat; we've all gotta use words when we talk. Since words are not, as it were, self-illuminating like globes on a Christmas tree, there is no way in which a semantic theory can guarantee that a given individual will find its formulas intelligible... So the sense in which we can 'know the Markerese translation of an English sentence without knowing... the conditions under which it would be true' is pretty uninteresting [Fodor 1975, pp. 120–21].

In a critical response, I argued either Fodor misunderstood Lewis' objection against SS or the nature of truth-conditional semantics [Lepore & Loewer 1981]. I took Fodor to be misconstruing Lewis as saying that one must understand the language in which the canonical representation is expressed before one can utilize a semantic theory to determine what the represented sentences means and that's a problem every semanticist faces. This certainly is correct, but Lewis' point is not this obvious one. Instead, he is arguing that someone who understands a translation and knows it to be true *need not* understand the sentence of the translated language. We cannot understand (3) or (1) unless we understand English. But knowledge that (1), unlike knowledge that (3), requires no familiarity with English. Simply note that whereas (1) and (3) are grammatical, (4) is not:

3. 'Sta nevicando' in Italian translates 'It is snowing' in English.

*4. 'Sta nevicando' in Italian means that it is snowing *in English.*

One need know no more English to know that (1) than Galileo knew for us truthfully to say that he said the earth moves.

With respect to the question whether language mastery requires semantic knowledge, none of this shows any more than that a semantics that specifies truth-conditions for sentences of a language L may serve to characterize (at least partially) knowledge sufficient for understanding L, while a semantics that specifies translation from L into another language by mapping structural descriptions of L into structural descriptions of the latter cannot (unless we add the assumption that the latter language is known). The conjectural inference from knowledge of truth conditions (partly) *suffices* to understand L to knowledge of truth conditions (partly) *constitutes* this understanding may seem natural, perhaps even good science, but Fodor, for one, balks. What's wrong with translationism, he asks?

Fodor's current scepticism about the utility of semantics for natural languages to account for linguistic comprehension is more than congenial with his early commitment to SS. He has repudiated much of the original SS program: its commitment to an analytic/ synthetic distinction [Fodor and Lepore 1992]; its commitment to certain views about lexical decomposition [Fodor, Fodor, and Garrett 1975; Fodor, Garrett, Walker, and Parkes 1980]. But his early commitment to SS is of a piece with his denying the cogency of semantics for natural languages, at least *qua* theory of understanding.

Once Fodor gave up on the idea that understanding requires knowledge of a semantic theory, he began to see the semanticist's emphasis on natural language as sweeping all the interesting philosophical questions about content under the rug. For example, what bestows intentional (i.e., contentful) states on a cognitive system. Semantic theories, whether of the SS or truth-conditional variety, are useless here. Since natural languages, according to Fodor, merely *shadow* real intentionality, (philosophical) explication of semantic properties must focus on the mind, in fact, on the semantic properties of symbols of the mind. But explicating the semantic properties of thought, according to Fodor, is a metaphysical enterprise. Metaphysical questions merit metaphysical answers; not epistemic or psychological ones.

How does this make Fodor unrepentant? A truth-conditional account is *no better* than the original SS translation account not because both employ language, but rather *because* both leave unanswered interesting metaphysical questions about intentionality. Philosophers *qua* semanticists for natural language need not, nor should they be expected to, answer these questions. Fodor concurs. He concludes that semantics for natural languages, worse than boring, is worthless. This is his real challenge. Translationists challenge semanticists to supply a purpose for their endeavour. The rest of this paper assumes this challenge by advancing considerations that incline me to conclude that (a) and (b):

a. Understanding a natural language requires metalinguistic knowledge.

b. This metalinguistic knowledge must be semantic, and so cannot be merely translational.

IV

Understanding and Rationalization. Maria utters to Massimo 'Sta nevicando'. Because translationism is *compatible* with Massimo believing Maria said it's snowing without his believing anything about the (causal) connection between what he heard and what he believes she said, it seems equally compatible with Massimo believing Maria said that it's snowing that Massimo foster only *false* beliefs about what Maria's words mean. But how, then, can the capacity to make correct transitions from what is heard to what is said alone suffice for linguistic competence? How can someone who has *only* false beliefs about what the expressions of a language L mean be linguistically competent with L? At least one author seems to think it's possible. Richard writes that someone 'might hold a false theory about competence, but still himself count as competent' [1992, p. 45]. If 'false theory' means false beliefs about what words mean, then I disagree unless by 'count' Richard means that the individual might never be exposed, something of no philosophical significance. So, is semantic scepticism compatible with translationism?

Translationists, because going Gricean is an option, can say it is not. By virtue of being linguistically competent in their sense and by virtue of knowing what thoughts words express or encode, translationism can frustrate semantic scepticism. But this concedes nothing to those who insist semantic knowledge is partly *constitutive* of linguistic competence, since semantic knowledge, on this account, is of no *consequence*. So, even if it were *impossible* to be linguistically competent without having true beliefs about what one's words mean, nothing follows about the causal efficacy of these beliefs in rendering the transitions translationists identify as constitutive of understanding. Even if intuition inclines one toward authority about what one's words mean (perhaps because we have authority about what our thoughts are, according to translationism), no one is inclined to endow speakers with authority about the causal ancestry of their beliefs, in particular, their beliefs about what another says when he speaks (or even the causal history of beliefs about what their words mean). This, unfortunately, is really bad news for philosophers/cognitive scientists who hope to frustrate translationism on empirical grounds [e.g., Segal 1994, pp. 116–17]. Even if the best psychological account available of linguistic comprehension attributes rich semantic knowledge to competent speakers, this cannot establish that translationism is false, since it too can attribute such knowledge. To defeat translationism, we must establish that semantic information has *repercussions* for understanding. Neither the impossibility of semantic scepticism nor empirical science can establish anything so strong. I will take a different tack.

What I want to argue is that translationism is *inconsistent* with Massimo having *reasons for* his new belief. Like Dummett, I want to maintain that 'any adequate account of language must describe it as a *rational* activity' [1978, p. 104, my emphasis]. Though Dummett's target is 'a causal theory such as Quine appears to envisage, representing [language mastery] as a complex of conditioned responses' [1978, p. 104], I want to cast my net wider to encompass translationism, a position, unlike Quine's, that is thoroughly cognitive. To this end I must show that the rationalizations speakers *qua* speakers have *cannot* be underwritten by translationism.

Why should the sort of rationalizing linguistic comprehension carries require ascribing metalinguistic (semantic) knowledge to speakers? Why isn't it secured already by the *reliable* connections between heard utterances and beliefs about what is said translationism presumes? The capacity for language comprehension produces correct internal states on the basis of what is heard; so, why aren't such states justified on this basis alone?

Someone's belief being justified and his having another belief which rationalizes his belief are distinct. Many perceptual beliefs are justified directly by experiences on which they are based, and in principle a belief can be justified simply by being the result of a reliable belief forming mechanism. One's belief that one is currently in pain is clearly not justified on the basis of other beliefs one has. The only explanatory story we are in a position to give is one which invokes a mechanism that connects reliably one's being in pain with one's believing one is. Translationists see linguistic comprehension in the same light [Fodor 1984].[13]

What's on offer is reliabilism [Dretske 1981; Goldman 1986; Nozick 1981]. Beliefs about what's said count as justified just in case processes that produce them tend, in the 'relevant' set of counterfactuals, to be truth inducing. There is indeed a lawlike correlation between an Italian speaker's beliefs about what is said and the heard utterances that bring them about.

Also, no 'KK principle' is invoked; being justified that p does not entail being justified that you are justified that p. This reliabilist feature serves translationism well. If someone's belief fixation processes may be reliable and constitute justification even though he does not realize they do, then translationists can deny speakers require special metalinguistic knowledge about the connection between what's uttered and what's said in order to secure whatever justification linguistic comprehension requires.

Much has been written, pro and con, about reliabilism, but in this context its viability is not relevant. We want to know Massimo's reason for his belief that Maria said it's snowing when he heard her utter 'Sta nevicando'. That he has a certain faculty that, *ceteris paribus*, delivers him from heard Italian utterances to true beliefs about what is said fails to reveal his reason. If Massimo knew he was so constituted, by virtue of learning Italian, that he reliably acquires true beliefs about what's said when he hears Italian utterances, then Massimo would have a reason for his belief.

---

13. Of course, nothing comes easy. If perception requires propositional knowledge, any appeal to an analogy with perception will not bolster translationism [cf., Fodor 1989, pp. 9ff; Fodor 1984, and Bruner 1957].

But drawing on such knowledge here is illegitimate. It undercuts reliabilism's appeal by resurrecting the KK principle.[14]

So, does Massimo have a reason for his belief *even* if he lacks beliefs about Italian? Imagine, as is consistent with translationism, that Massimo is *clueless* about why he believes (correctly, let's suppose) that p when he hears Maria utter something Italian. Nothing *in his head* justifies his belief. Massimo's condition is mildly pathological. Poor dupe, running around the world telling all he meets what others said but always lacking reasons for such attributions. Massimo *can* no better explain his belief that Maria said it's snowing than to say 'I don't know why I believe this. I just do. Didn't Maria say "Sta nevicando"?' But someone who understood not one word of Italian and happened to find himself believing Maria said that it's raining could make the same case for himself. Massimo is not unlike someone who perpetuates ghastly deeds, but literally has (or should I say, *can* have) no idea why he persists. No degree of prodding or assistance *could* bring him to reconstruct reasons for his behaviour. Just as we would withhold agency from him, we should withhold linguistic comprehension from clueless Massimo.

Diagnoses: Even if reliabilism secures some sort of justification, it does not secure one sufficient to underwrite linguistic comprehension. If Massimo believes Maria said it's snowing when he hears her utter 'Sta nevicando', we expect him to have beliefs about Maria's utterance that *play* a *rationalizing* role. If such rationalization is integral to language understanding, where could it spring from if not from knowledge (or belief or other propositional attitudes) about the sounds and shapes of the language itself.[15]

---

14. Reliabilism is not committed to our *never* knowing we know certain things, only that we need not always know we do. So, if Massimo knows he's reliable, why doesn't this provide a robust reason for his belief that Maria said it's snowing when he heard her utter 'Sta nevicando'? Massimo's reason, then, is that he knows he's a reliable disquoter of Italian utterances. His justification is, I suppose, something like: people tell him he's very good; he has no trouble communicating with Italian speakers, and so on.

Despite any apparent initial plausibility, this view is absurd. I do not come to believe I understand my first language because I see others treat me as though I'm correctly disquoting them. Any such discovery comes long after I'm proficient in my mother tongue.

15. What about adults who lack expressions for meaning and quotation (or anything like them). Am I claiming that because they are unable to *consciously* construct a metalinguistic justification for their transitions from what they hear to what is said, it follows that they don't understand their language? No.

Massimo, in our imagined scenario, really is clueless. He has no idea why he believes Maria said it's snowing when he heard her utter 'Sta nevicando'. So, even though he makes the transition, he has no reason—*conscious, unconscious, tacit, explicit, implicit*, or any other sort. I am claiming that if one understands a language, he must have reasons that rationalize his transitions. To echo Davidson, 'nothing can count as a *reason* for holding a belief except another belief' [1986, my emphasis, p. 123]. I know no argument that defends this position *tout court*, but it seems right in the case of language comprehension. What about linguistic comprehension provides reason for the belief that it's snowing when this understanding combines with the belief that Maria uttered 'Sta nevicando'? Additional beliefs or knowledge Massimo has about Maria's utterance that non-speakers lack. In short, if translationism is right, it behooves us to ask about another's reason for what he believes on the basis of linguistic shapes and sounds (he believes) he perceives. But then *nothing less than appeal to* other mental states *about* what he perceives can rationalize the belief.

Suppose I'm right both about the failure of reliabilism to deliver required rationalizations for beliefs about what's said and suppose even further that such rationalizations require intervening attitudes about words heard. Question: why can't the translationist rebut, 'OK, but why isn't this just the denial of semantical scepticism, something I've already conceded?' Answer: what I'm assuming is that rationalizations for beliefs parallel rationalizations for actions, that is, both require causally efficacious intervening attitudes. So, a belief that p (partly) rationalizes a belief that q only if the belief that p is (partly) causally responsible for the belief that q. Needless to say, this isn't uncontroversial.[16]

There is an important feature of my discussion I have not flagged. Not all that long ago, Chomsky spent too much time defending the psychological/epistemic status of grammatical theories he postulated to account for linguistic comprehension. My argument against translationism circumvents these hairy issues. It's insignificant for the purposes of this debate what the nature of the

16. Looking back to note 13, if linguistic comprehension is more like thinking than sensing, it may very well be that the best account for it posits causally relevant intervening internal states. But this is, obviously, something I can do no more than mention, much less settle, in this paper.

relationship is between a speaker and whatever metalinguistic information is essential for understanding. If I'm right, then there *must* be a relationship. Whether it amounts to tacit or implicit or explicit knowledge, or whether the relationship is not knowing but 'cognizing', or whether it is a completely different doxastic relationship is irrelevant. What's essential is, if I'm right, there must be some such epistemic/psychological/doxastic relationship toward semantic information that stands between the heard utterance and the acquired belief about what is said if the latter is not be an unrationalized psychological state. We can leave open its nature.[17]

V

*Why **Semantic** Knowledge?* Suppose translationism is wrong. It doesn't follow that knowledge about *meaning* must be invoked to account for transitions from heard utterances to beliefs about what's said. Take Schiffer's story. Why doesn't it suffice to say that what underwrites Harvey's understanding his language is his knowing a *translation* manual from his public language into his language of thought?

> A translation manual from L to L´ is a finitely axiomatizable theory that correlates words and structures of L with words and structures of L´ so as to entail theorems that correlate L sentences with their synonyms in L´. Such a theory assigns no semantic values to the expressions of either language and in no sense determines [a meaning theory] for either language... Harvey works in the following way. His internally represented translation manual determines a function that maps each English sentence onto its Mentalese synonym, and he is so 'programmed' that when he has an auditory perception of an utterance of a, then straight-away there enters his belief box the Mentalese translation of 'The speaker in uttering "a" said that a'... [Schiffer, 1993, p. 244].

It's easy to get snowed by Schiffer's technical jargon and by what appear to be merely heuristic devices, for example, appeals to Mentalese, translation manuals, the belief-box, talk about translating public language sentences into Mentalese. We want to know Massimo's reason for his belief that Maria said it's snowing when he believes she utters 'Sta nevicando'. According to Schiffer, Massimo understands Maria's utterance if he is caused to believe

17. So, here I depart from Smith [1992].

Maria said that it's snowing (i.e., token in his belief-box a sentence of Mentalese which expresses what 'Maria said that it's snowing' does in English) when he hears her utter 'Sta nevicando'. If an epistemic relationship toward some internal psychological state is required for linguistic comprehension, why can't it be knowledge of the correct mapping from the Mentalese counterpart of 'Maria uttered "Sta nevicando"' to a Mentalese counterpart of 'Maria said that it's snowing'?

If this is possible, using L does not require knowing anything about an internally represented *meaning* theory for L. So, the inference that knowledge of meaning is required for language comprehension is still not sanctioned. However, elevating Schiffer's suggestion to an object of knowledge doesn't work; seeing that it doesn't shows why an adequate account of linguistic comprehension requires reference to connections between language mentioned and language used, i.e., *semantic* information.

Schiffer's choices are between a function that maps structural descriptions of Italian expressions into structural descriptions of Mentalese expressions, in which case it is a translation manual (and Davidson's translation argument kicks in); *or* a function that maps structural descriptions of Italian expressions, that is, language mentioned, e.g., Maria uttered 'Sta nevicando', into language *used*, that is, that Maria said that it's snowing. Everything turns on how we understand the locution a certain sentence is tokened in Massimo's belief-box.[18]

Massimo hears Maria utter a certain sentence; he knows what she uttered translates into a certain Mentalese sentence; whatever corresponds in his *lingua mentis* to 'Maria said that' concatenates with this translation and the entire product goes in his belief-box. That suffices for him to understand Maria's language. What I'm doubting is that we can specify this knowledge in a way that both avoids the standard translation argument and does not itself draw upon semantic information, i.e., meaning, truth, or satisfaction conditions.

The standard Fodorian reply that, for Mentalese, questions about understanding cannot arise won't work here. It may be illegitimate

---

18. So, I'm disagreeing with Segal [1994, pp. 114–115]. Nothing about translationism requires that the function from heard language into the language of thought map structural descriptions onto structural descriptions.

to ask in virtue of knowing what does someone understand one's
mentalese? [Cf., Lycan 1984, p. 237f.] But that is not our question.
We're asking, in virtue of what knowledge does one understand his
public language? The suggestion that it is in virtue of knowing a
translation manual from, say, Italian, into Mentalese won't work if
the mapping is from structural descriptions into structural
descriptions. But suppose it maps structural descriptions into, say,
well, what? It cannot be propositions or states of affairs. That
would be entirely useless to Massimo; what about a sentence used
in the language of thought or a *sentence-in-use* in the language of
thought. I want to argue that a 'translation manual' in this sense
determines a meaning theory, that is, a semantic theory.

Suppose a function F in effect maps a set S of structural
descriptions of sentences of L into a set P of *sentences* (not
structural descriptions) of L´ such that $F(s)$ (in S) = p (in P) iff (if
X assertively utters s in L, then X says that p). Then F determines
a semantic theory for L.[19]

T is a truth theory for a language L in a metalanguage L´ iff for
every structural description s of a sentence of L, T implies a true
sentence of L´ such that:

s is true in L iff p

(where p is replaced by a sentence of L´, and each s translates
whatever replaces p). F determines an adequate truth theory T for
L in L´ iff for any structural descriptions s_1 and s_2 of sentences of
L, $F(s_1) = F(s_2)$ only if T implies (for some sentence p of L´) (a)
and (b):

a. s_1 is true in L iff p
b. s_2 is true in L iff p

But $F(s_1) = F(s_2)$ only if there is some p in L´ such that both s_1 and
s_2 'translate' p. But this establishes that some truth theory for L
implies (a) and (b).

If F were merely a translation manual in a traditional sense, this
result could not follow. That's what Davidson's translation
argument establishes. That 'Sta necicando' translates 'It's
snowing' cannot determine that 'Sta nevicando' is true iff it's
snowing. The disquotation principle behind this inference is not

19. I'll couch my discussion in truth theories, but nothing hangs on this.

innocent. It assumes that 'It's snowing' is true iff it's snowing. In the current context that assumption is question begging since it's exactly what I'm trying to defend.

None of this establishes, of course, that knowledge of F provides the rationalization I claim (partly) constitutes linguistic comprehension, merely that it *determines* something that could provide this warrant. That I know p, and p determines something q such that if I knew that q, my belief that r would be rationalized does not imply that knowing p alone rationalizes my belief that r. Moreover, even if knowledge of a semantic theory for L suffices for understanding L, it's still open whether knowledge of non-semantic mechanisms might suffice for understanding L as well. So, I have not established that semantic knowledge is necessary. And, so I have not established that semantic theoretical knowledge is necessary since it is consistent with what I argued that one need not know any more than the meaning theorems that issue from an adequate semantic theory. Massimo's belief that Maria said it's snowing is justified if he merely believes 'Sta nevicando' means that it's snowing and Maria assertively uttered 'Sta nevicando'. That he need also know that *an object a satisfies 'neve' iff it's snow* in order for the transition to be justified requires further argument. These are rather significant loose ends; I believe they can be tied up. I'll leave that for another occasion.

VI

Conclusion. So, where are we? We began with what I still think is the greatest challenge to those of us who find semantics for natural language not only interesting but valuable, *viz.*, how to refute translationism? To this end I argued that translationism leaves speaker's beliefs about what others say unrationalized. Going externalist about rationalization, as reliabilism recommends, seems misguided, at least to me. Internalist accounts both invoke attitudes about the words we hear and treats those attitudes as causally responsible in effecting beliefs about what's said. Traditional translation manuals mapping structural descriptions into structural descriptions are no help here; and any 'translation' manual that takes words mentioned into words used (or words-in-use) sneaks in just the semantic information we are trying to redeem. There are obviously many missing steps and many of the steps taken lack anything like an ironclad defence, but I hope, at least, the dialectic is sufficiently precise. Let me end on a different note.

The most common reason for resisting the idea that speakers have semantic (theoretical) knowledge is that such knowledge is not 'within the ken of plain folk' [Schiffer 1987, pp. 255–261]; not something of which we have 'conscious access' [Foster 1975, p. 2]; not something we can 'literally credit' to speakers [Dummett 1974, p. 110]. Nothing I'm recommending requires Massimo to have *explicit* representations or be able to consciously reconstruct pieces of practical reasoning from perceived sounds to extra-linguistic belief [Lepore 1982; Higginbotham 1983; 1987; George 1989]. Massimo may be unequipped, incapable, or unskilled. But if his beliefs about what's said are rationalized, it makes sense for us to articulate his reasons. My argument, if any good, establishes that some relationship toward metalinguistic states or information about one's language is required for linguistic comprehension. I don't have a clue what the psychological make-up of this relationship must be like; but no one should take a critical stance on these issues without, at least, having a fairly developed account of concepts against which to evaluate such attributions.

Center for Cognitive Science
Rutgers University
New Brunswick
New Jersey 08903
USA

BIBLIOGRAPHY

Baker, G.P. and P.M.S. Hacker, *Language, Sense and Nonsense*, Basil Blackwell, Oxford, 1984.
Bruner, J., 'On Perceptual Readiness', *Psychological Review*, 65, 1957:14–21.
Chomsky, Noam, *Knowledge of Language*, Praeger, 1986.
Cresswell, M.J., 'Semantic Competence', in M. Guenthner Ruetter and F. Guenthner (eds.), *Meaning and Translation*, Duckworth, London, 1978:9–27.
Davidson, D., 'Truth and Meaning', *Synthese* 17, 1967. Reprinted in Davidson 1984.
Davidson, D., 'Radical Interpretation', *Dialectica*, 27, 1973. Reprinted in Davidson 1984.
Davidson, *Inquiries into Truth & Interpretation*, Oxford University Press, Oxford, 1984.
Davidson, D., 'A Coherence Theory of Truth and Knowledge', in *Truth and Interpretation*, 1986:141–154.

Davies, Martin, *Meaning, Quantification, Necessity,* Routledge and Kegan Paul, London, 1981.

Devitt, M., *Designation,* Columbia University Press, New York, 1981.

Dretske, F., *Knowledge and the Flow of Information,* MIT Press, Cambridge, MA, 1981.

Dummett, Michael, 'What is a Theory of Meaning (I)?', *Mind and Language,* ed., S. Guttenplan, Clarendon Press, Oxford, 1974:97–138.

Dummett, Michael, 'What do I Know When I Know a Language?' (1978), reprinted in *The Seas of Language.*

Dummett, Michael, *The Seas of Language,* Clarendon Press, Oxford, 1993.

Evans, G., 'Semantic Theory and Tacit Knowledge', in S.H. Holtzman and C.M. Leich, eds., *Wittgenstein: To Follow a Rule,* Routledge and Kegan Paul, London, 1981.

Evans, G. and J. McDowell, eds., *Truth and Meaning,* Duckworth, Oxford, 1975.

Fodor, J, *The Language of Thought,* Crowell, New York, 1975.

Fodor, J.A., *The Modularity of Mind,* MIT Press, Cambridge, MA, 1984.

Fodor, J.A., *Psychosemantics,* MIT Press, Cambridge, MA, 1987.

Fodor, J.A., 'Why Must the Mind be Modular', in *Reflections on Chomsky,* ed. A. George, Basil Blackwell, Oxford, 1989.

Fodor, J.A., 'Review of Stephen Schiffers's *Remnants of Meaning*', in *A Theory of Content and Other Essays,* MIT Press, Cambridge, MA, 1990.

Fodor, J.A., 'Reply to Schiffer', in *Meaning and Mind,* eds. B. Loewer and G. Rey, Basil Blackwell, Oxford, 1991.

Fodor, J.A., Fodor, J.D., and Garrett, M. 'The Psychological Unreality of Semantic Representations', *Linguistic Inquiry,* 6, 1975:515–531.

Fodor, J.A., M. Garrett, Walker, and Parkes, 'Against Definitions', *Cognition,* 8, 1980:263–367.

Fodor, J.A. and E. Lepore, *Holism: A Shopper's Guide,* Basil Blackwell, Oxford, 1992.

Foster, J., 'Meaning and Truth Theory', in Evans and McDowell, 1975.

George, A., 1989, 'How not to become confused about linguistics' in *Reflections on Chomsky,* A. George, ed., Basil Blackwell, Oxford, 1989:90–110.

Goldman, A., *Epistemology and Cognition,* Harvard University Press, Cambridge, MA, 1986.

Hacking, Ian, *Why does Language Matter to Philosophy?,* Cambridge University Press, Cambridge, 1975.

Harman, G., 'Language, Thought, and Communication', in *Minnesota Studies in the Philosophy of Science,* vol. 7, ed. K. Gunderson, University of Minnesota Press, Minneapolis, 1975.

Higginbotham, J., 'Is Grammar Psychological?' in L. Cauman, et al. (eds), *How Many Questions? Essays in Honor of Sidney Morgenbesser,* Hackett Publishing, Cambridge, MA, 1983.

Higginbotham, J., 'The Autonomy of Syntax and Semantics', in J. Garfield, ed., *Modularity in Knowledge Representation and Natural Language Understanding,* MIT Press, Cambridge, MA, 1987.

Higginbotham, J., 'Is Semantics Necessary?', *Proceedings of the Aristotelian Society,* 87, 1988:219–241.

Higginbotham, J., 'The Place of Natural Language', 1995, in *On Quine,* Leonardi, P and Santambrogio, M., eds., Cambridge University Press, Cambridge, 1995.

Hornstein, N., *Logic as Grammar,* MIT Press, Cambridge, MA, 1984

Katz, J. & J. Fodor, 'The Structure of a Semantic Theory', *Language,* 39, 1963:170–210.

Larson, R. and P. Ludlow, 'Interpreted Logical Forms', *Synthese* 95, 1993:305–356.

Larson, R., and G. Segal, *Knowledge of Meaning*, MIT Press, Cambridge, MA, 1995.

Lepore, E, 'What Model Theoretic Semantics Cannot Do', *Synthese*, 54, 1983:167–187

Lepore, E. 'In Defense of Davidson', *Linguistics and Philosophy* 5, 1982:277–294.

Lepore, E., ed., *Truth and Interpretation: Perspectives on the Philosophy of Donald Davidson*, Basil Blackwell Press, Oxford, 1986.

Lepore, E., and B. Loewer, 'Translational semantics', *Synthese*, 48, 1981:121–133.

Lewis, David, 'General Semantics', *Synthese*, 22, 1970:18–67.

Loewer, B. and G. Rey, eds., *Meaning and Mind: Fodor and his Critics*, Basil Blackwell, Oxford, 1992.

Lycan, W.G., *Logical Form in Natural Language*, MIT Press, Cambridge, 1984.

McDowell, J., 'In Defense of Modesty', in Barry Taylor, ed., *Michael Dummett: Contributions to Philosophy*, Martinus Nihjof, 1988.

Nozick, R., *Philosophical Explanations*, Harvard University Press, Cambridge, MA, 1981.

Partee, B., 'Montague Grammar and Transformational Grammar', *Linguistic Inquiry*, 6, 1975:203–300.

Partee, B., 'Semantics: Mathematics or Psychology?' in Bäurle, R., and E. Egli, eds., *Semantics from Different Points of View*, 1979, 1–14.

Quine, W.V.O., 'Methodological Reflections on Linguistic Theory', in *Semantics of Natural Language*, D. Davidson and G. Harman, eds., D. Reidel, Dordecht, 1972: 442–454.

Richard, Mark, 'Semantic Competence and Disquotational Knowledge', *Philosophical Studies*, 65, 1992:37–52.

Schiffer, Stephen, 'Intention-Based Semantics', *Notre Dame Journal of Formal Logic*, vol 23, no. 2, 1982:119–156.

Schiffer, Stephen, *Remnants of Meaning*, MIT Press, Cambridge, 1987.

Schiffer, Stephen, 'Actual-Language Relations', *Philosophical Perspectives* 7, 1993:231–258.

Schiffer, Stephen, 'A Paradox of Meaning', *Nous* 28, 3, 1994:279–324.

Segal, G., 'Priorities in the Philosophy of Thought', *Proceedings of Aristotelian Society, Supplementary Volume,* 1994:107–30.

Smith, Barry C., 'Understanding Language', *Proceedings of Aristotelian Society* CII, 1992:109–141.

Soames, S., 'Semantics and Semantic Competence', *Philosophical Perspectives*, 3, *Philosophy of Mind and Action Theory*, ed. J. Tomberlin, Atrascadero, Ridgeview Publishing Company, 1989:185–207.

Stich, S., *From Folk Psychology to Cognitive Science*, MIT Press, Cambridge, 1983.

Thomason, R. (ed.), *Formal Philosophy: Selected Papers of Richard Montague*, Yale University Press, New Haven, CT, 1974.

Vermazen, Bruce, 'Review of Jerrold J. Katz and Paul M. Postal, *An Integrated Theory of Linguistic Description*, and Jerrold J. Katz, *The Philosophy of Language, Synthese*', 17, 3, 1967:350–65.

Wright, Crispin, 'Theories of Meaning and Speaker's Knowledge', in *Philosophy in Britain Today*, ed., S.G. Shanker, State University of NY Press, Albany, 1986:267–307.

IV*—VALUES, REASONS AND PERSPECTIVES

by Alan Thomas

I

The aims of this paper are threefold. First, I want to explain away an apparent inconsistency that presents a challenge to both moral cognitivism and an impartial conception of moral reasons. Secondly, in drawing on Amartya Sen's concept of evaluator relativity to solve the problem, I want significantly to amend Sen's proposal. I will suggest that it runs together two different ideas, that its proper location is in the theory of practical reasoning, not the theory of value, and that it is illuminating to connect his analysis to wider discussions in metaphysics of perspectival and absolute representations.[1] Thirdly, I want to connect the account I present to recent investigations into the puzzling status of deontic constraints, with the aim of supporting Thomas Nagel's suggestion that there is an intimate connection between such constraints and the relation of agent and victim.

The problem I want to discuss is the following. Could two moral agents be confronted with the same situation, acknowledge that the values in that situation are the same for both of them, but come to different 'all things considered' judgements about what they ought to do? Our first response must be that they cannot. An agent's reasons for action cannot be detached from the values that he or she judges a situation to exemplify. Values and reasons must stand in some relation of determination or supervenience, such that the

---

1. Sen has already initiated this wider discussion, in 'Positional Objectivity', *Philosophy and Public Affairs*, Vol. 22, No. 2 (1993), pp. 127–145. Sen discusses in this paper a range of perspectival representations, but does not deploy the distinction between different kinds of perspectivalness which I will argue is crucial in the application of his general theory to moral reasons.

---

*Meeting of the Aristotelian Society, held in the Senior Common Room, Birkbeck College, London, on Monday, 25th November, 1996 at 8.15 p.m.

evaluative 'shapes' of situations ground an agent's judgement about what he or she ought to do.[2] Thus, a situation meeting the characterisation I have outlined would be, if not a formal paradox, inconsistent in a problematic way.

I have three commitments which make this apparent inconsistency a troubling prospect for me. The first is that I believe that situations which seem to meet this description are part of our moral experience. The second commitment that makes this apparent inconsistency in our judgements problematic is that I am a moral cognitivist, and believe that our moral beliefs can constitute knowledge of values. The third element of my position is that I believe moral reasons are impartial. Before expanding on these three points, I will describe a scenario which I take to be a plausible exemplification of the problem.

I will adapt for my own purposes the example discussed by Peter Winch in the course of his subtle paper, 'The Universalisability of Moral Judgements'.[3] Winch presented an interpretation of Melville's *Billy Budd: Foretopman,* which I will adapt in two ways. First, it will become important to eliminate the special problems of the fact that both Winch and I are writing about fiction. Secondly, it is unclear in Winch's presentation whether Winch and Vere make their respective judgements about the narrative on the same evaluative basis. My interest is in examples where this is so; where the parties broadly agree on the relevant range of evaluative considerations.

The protagonist of Melville's narrative, Captain Vere, unjustly condemns the innocent Billy Budd to death. Winch commented that while he, Winch, could not have acted in the way Vere did, there was a sense in which Vere had acted rightly for a person viewing the situation from his involved participant's perspective. In an important paragraph, Winch observed:

2. I take the useful expression 'evaluative shape' from Jonathan Dancy, *Moral Reasons* (Oxford: Basil Blackwells, 1993), pp. 111–116. The idea is that evaluative properties are ordered according to a moral 'Gestalt' in which some considerations are viewed as more salient compared to others.

3. Winch's discussion was focused on the usefulness of universalisability as an instrument of practical reason, as his title indicates: 'The Universalisability of Moral Judgement', *The Monist,* vol. 49, no. 2 (April, 1965), pp. 196–214. I believe that on this point Winch was perfectly correct, and his results harmonise with other sceptical accounts of the usefulness of universalisablity, such as that of J.L. Mackie in *Ethics: Inventing Right and Wrong* (London: Penguin, 1977), pp. 83–102.

> If A says, 'X is the right thing for me to do', and if B in a situation not relevantly different says 'X is the wrong thing for me to do', it can be that both are correct.... It may be that neither what each says, nor anything entailed by what each says, contradicts anything said or implied by the other....This certainly does not mean that if A believes that X is the right thing for him to do, then X is made the right thing to do by the mere fact that he thinks it is....[4]

Winch seems to have described the type of inconsistent situation that threatens cognitivism and impartialism and it is easy to see how one could construct from such a case both anti-cognitivist and anti-impartialist arguments. For example, a non-cognitivist could argue that the best way of explaining the apparent inconsistency is by denying that the two protagonists possess the same basis of moral knowledge. If their moral judgements are essentially practical, with a 'direction of fit' from world to mind, then the inconsistency in the judgements involved is easily explained. Some form of non-cognitivism would be the more appropriate diagnosis and indeed a more ambitious argument could conclude that moral cognitivism had been demonstrated to be false.

The second claim apparently threatened by the case Winch describes is that of the impartiality of moral reasons. A line of argument diametrically opposed to the above accepts that the agents cognise value, and looks for the source of the different practical verdicts in the particular character and personality of the individual agent. This explanation of the Winch/Vere scenario argues that it casts light on the personal nature of ethics, a sense of 'the personal' intrinsically opposed to the idea that moral reasons are impartial.[5]

The cognitivist or impartialist could, of course, just deny that our moral experience ever presents us with such cases. However, this seems to me unacceptable; the case is phenomenologically plausible and Winch's description of it compelling. Furthermore, at least one influential theory of practical reasons has been developed in response to it.[6] I hope to demonstrate that the description of the

---

4. Winch, 'Universalisability', p. 209.

5. See for example, R. Gaita, 'The Personal In Ethics', in *Wittgenstein: Attention to Particulars*, edited by Peter Winch and D.Z. Phillips (London: Macmillan, 1989), pp. 124–50. My very different view of the relation between the impartial and the personal is indebted to Adrian Piper's 'Moral Theory and Moral Alienation', *Journal of Philosophy*, 84, 1987 pp. 102–118.

6. The theory of practical reasons is that of David Wiggins, which I will discuss below. Wiggins wrote of Winch's argument, 'I, for one, am prepared to salute [it] as deeply interesting'.

case harmonises with independently plausible accounts of the
nature of deontic constraints. Given my prior commitments to both
cognitivism and impartialism it is incumbent on me to find an
alternative diagnosis of the problem posed by the apparent
inconsistency in the case Winch describes.

II

The first step towards a plausible solution of the problem I have
outlined was made by David Wiggins. Wiggins's reconciliation of
the kind of agency phenomena Winch has drawn attention to with
moral cognitivism proceeds by making a crucial distinction
between an axiological account of what Wiggins calls 'specific
evaluations' and a separable account of moral reasons, the latter
being located within the theory of practical reasoning.[7] 'Specific
evaluations' are judgements that objects, persons or states of affairs
exemplify certain evaluative properties.[8] An evaluation, when
expressed, is straightforwardly assessable as true or false.
However, to take up a practical attitude is to be disposed to perform
an action, and that is not a cognitive exercise.[9] Wiggins is more
inclined to compare practical reasoning to constructivist mathematics, involving 'the compossibility of objectivity, discovery, *and*
invention'.[10] Wiggins proceeds to build on this distinction an
alternative approach to the initial problem, which for reasons of
space I will not discuss in full here. The essence of his alternative
solution is to appeal to 'cognitive underdetermination', value
pluralism and value incommensurability in order to claim that
reasons only weakly, not strongly, supervene on the 'weightings' of
values.[11] My alternative argument, on the contrary, takes as its
starting point Samuel Guttenplan's critique of Wiggins on precisely
this point. I want to develop a solution to the problem that is still

7. David Wiggins, *Needs, Values, Truth,* Second Edition (Oxford: Basil Blackwell, 1991),
especially the essays, 'Truth, Invention and the Meaning of Life' and 'Truth as Predicated
of Moral Judgements'. Wiggins was soon to change his mind on this key point, claiming in
'What Would Be a Substantial Theory of Truth?' in Z. van Straaten (ed.), *Philosophical
Subjects: Essays Presented to P.F. Strawson* (Oxford University Press, 1990), that the space
of practical reasons sustained all the marks of plain truth. I will not be addressing this later
position here.

8. Wiggins, *Needs, Values, Truth*, pp. 95–96.

9. Wiggins, *Needs, Values, Truth*, pp. 95–96.

10. Wiggins, *Needs, Values, Truth*, p. 130.

available to the cognitivist even if reasons *strongly* supervene on values.[12]

This distinction between the axiological and the practical dimensions of moral judgement is, in my view, a crucial first step towards solving the problem. The task is to see if combining this distinction with the acceptance of the determination of reasons by the evaluative shapes of situations allows any scope for the claim that two competent judgers can nevertheless reach different 'all things considered' verdicts about what one has most reason to do. I apply the axiology/practical reasoning distinction to different aspects of one and the same moral content—a 'dual aspect' view. According to this view, moral reasons have a double aspect. Viewed under one aspect, they are belief states, the proper objects of moral knowledge. However, under another aspect they are the conceptualisations of a situation which an agent would employ in their final deliberative verdict as to what they had most reason to do, 'all things considered'—his or her 'maxim'. Corresponding to each aspect is a different governing norm. Qua cognitive states, moral reasons are answerable to truth in their dimension as specific evaluations. Qua 'maxims', moral reasons are answerable to the formal constraint of impartial acceptability. A single content can be responsive to these two demands since in my view they are compatible.

In outline, my solution is to use the distinction between the two aspects of moral content to describe two different ways in which such contents are perspectival. I take this term from general metaphysics, and argue that as objects of knowledge moral judgements exhibit a weak form of perspectivalness that arises when a judgement is indexed to our metaphysical 'point of view'.

11. That is, that there can be no change in the supervening practical reasons without a change in the *weighted* subvening values (weak supervenience) as opposed to the claim that there can be no change in the subvening values without a change in the supervening practical reasons (strong supervenience). I claim only that this is a useful way of viewing Wiggins's argument, not that he would approve of the terminology—I suspect he would not!

12. The problem, as identified by Guttenplan, is that Wiggins's strategy involves claiming that judgements about specific evaluations are robustly cognitive, whereas comparative judgements about these values are not. Guttenplan argues that Wiggins's twin theses of value pluralism and incommensurability cannot prevent this transfer of robust 'factuality' from evaluation to judgement, and hence he is committed to a strong supervenience claim. The issue is controversial, but I am sufficiently persuaded by Guttenplan's argument to try an alternative tack on behalf of cognitivism. See Samuel Guttenplan, 'Moral Realism and Moral Dilemmas', *Proceedings of the Aristotelian Society*, New Series, vol. LXXX (1979/80), pp. 61–80.

By contrast, as maxims for an agent, moral judgements are perspectival in a stronger sense, in so far they directly map proposed actions under a description on to practical reasons.[13] Thus, the two aspects of moral content are to be related separately to the phenomenon of *perspectivalness*.[14] It is necessary to explain the various ways in which truth evaluable contents *per se* can exhibit perspectivalness. That is the task of the next section.

III

I take the terms 'absolute' and 'perspectival' to be predicates of modes of presentation of contents, not predicates of contents. One way to motivate this distinction would be via the theory of concepts: thus *perspectival* representations are made up of components that are only graspable from a perspectival point of view. The idea of a representation that can be grasped from any point of view corresponds to the metaphysical idea of an *absolute* representation.[15]

This contrast between perspectival and absolute representations can be used to illuminate a wide range of metaphysical disputes, centrally debates over objectivity. However, the terminology must be handled with care if the distinctive features of particular cases are to be respected. For the purposes of this argument I need to make two distinctions: between the genuinely perspectival and the merely observer relative and a related distinction within the class of perspectival phenomena.

My first distinction sets aside an irrelevant issue. The perspectival is defined in terms of the *peculiarities* of the concepts

13. I thus match Sen's characterisation of the 'narrow deontologist' at the end of 'Evaluator Relativity and Consequential Evaluation', *Philosophy and Public Affairs*, 12, no.2 (Spring, 1983), p.130.

14. I have already noted that the wider connection between Sen's view of moral reasons and the general metaphysical category of the perspectival has been made by Sen himself, though not, I will argue, in exactly the right way in the case of deontic constraints. However, there is an intriguing comment on page x of Sen's *Inequality Re-examined* (Oxford: Oxford University Press, 1992), Sen writes: 'Willard Quine has recently suggested to me that I should explore the comparison between [a] classificatory principle for the ethics of social arrangements based on the equalities that are preserved [....] and [....] the classificatory principles used in Felix Klein's attempted synthesis of geometry [...] in terms of the property of a space that are invariant with respect to a given group of transformations. I think there is an important general connection here, which can prove to be quite illuminating....'. My aim is to illuminate the character of this general connection.

15. Adrian Moore, 'Points of View', *The Philosophical Quarterly* (1987), pp. 1–20.

deployed by particular classes of judgers. Thus, there is a distinction between the perspectival and the merely relational. Consider the fact that in our best physical theory, relativity theory, ideas such as that of measurement become relativised to a framework of observer cum apparatus. Does this make physics perspectival? Not at all. Acknowledging this relativity is quite compatible with robust realism about the physical phenomena measured by the theory. Observer relativity is a contingent epistemic constraint on our access to the facts and does not condition them in any way. Furthermore, it does not rest on any of our peculiarities qua knowers. Thus the observer relative is not the perspectival.[16]

Matters are complicated, however, by the fact that a related distinction can be drawn *within* the general class of the perspectival. This second contrast I have in mind is the following: there is a contrast between cases where we accept that perspectivalness in representation is compatible with the objectivity of the facts represented, and cases where acknowledgement of perspectivalness seems to move us towards a denial of objectivity about the relevant range of facts.

Here are a couple of admittedly controversial examples. Take the perspectivalness of our colour judgements. Our colour concepts are conditioned by the peculiar character of our perceptual sensibilities; it is possible to imagine other makers of judgements with a different set of colour concepts. However, this does not seem, on reflection, to destabilise the objectivity of our judgements that the physical world is coloured. This is a case where we acknowledge perspectivalness and yet accept that colour judgements are objective judgements.

The matter is different when we turn to, say, qualia. Qualia, if there are any, are the contents of our subjective experience. They are 'what it is like' to experience sensations. However, they are philosophically controversial since they seem to introduce the dubious category of a perspectival fact whose nature is *exhausted* by the subject's perspective on it. In cases such as these it is difficult

16. This is denied by Hilary Putnam, who takes the observer relativity of physics to be an argument for 'internal realism', for example in 'Realism' in *Realism With a Human Face*, Cambridge MA.: Harvard University Press, 1990), pp. 5–11. Since Putnamian dialectic takes internal and external realism to be exhaustive, and external realism to be identical to the 'absolute conception of the world', one can infer that Putnam takes observer relativity to be an argument for perspectivalness.

to detach the content of the judgement from the subject's epistemic grasp of it, and I take it this lies behind our impulse to deny the objectivity of judgements about qualia.

My proposal is to take this distinction within the class of the perspectival and apply it to the two aspects of moral judgements I have already distinguished. However, to do so I am going to suggest a criterion for discriminating between the two cases. The criterion is whether or not it is possible systematically to transform judgements across different points of view. If we can systematically perform such transformations, this suggest to us that the perspective is, as it were, all in the epistemology. In such a case, perspective is conditioning our access to objective fact. However, if such transformation fails, we seem to have a phenomenon that is perspectival 'through and through'. This criterion seems intuitively plausible.

To apply it, we must ascend from the egocentric perspective of individual judgers and take up the standpoint of an intersubjective group of judgers so that we have a means of defining co-ordinates across which we can apply the transformation test. Take the twin cases of colours and qualia: one reason, I suggest, why we are happy to be objectivists about colours while admitting our colour concepts are perspectival is that colour judgements are stable across a whole class of judgers. However, qualia are not even stable across individuals. Picked out as they are epistemologically, as essentially captured by one's first person access to them, the asymmetry between their first and third personal characterisations makes us quite rightly sceptical of their aspiration to objectivity.

Another way of making the same point has been presented by Adrian Moore, to whose discussions of this issue I am indebted. Moore uses the idea of an 'external counterpart' for perspectival representations, in which we separate out the perspectival element of a judgement from its objective content.[17] The availability, or otherwise, of such a counterpart is another way of drawing the distinction I have made within the class of perspectival pheno-

17. The central metaphysical problem surrounding perspectival contents concerns their eliminability: whether it is possible, for any given perspectival content, to construct what Moore calls an 'external counterpart' of that content. This construction of an external counterpart allows one to separate the 'vehicle' and the 'content' of a perspectival representation, and to restrict the perspectival element to the former. See Adrian Moore, 'Points of View', p. 5.

mena. I suggest that the transformation test is a useful criterion for the availability of such an external counterpart.

I need some terminology to pick out these two different kinds of perspectival phenomena. I will refer to the first class, those which are stable across transformations, as 'perspectivally invariant'. I will refer to the latter class, those which do not systematically transform across an inter-subjective group of judgers, as 'perspective dependent'. Finally, I will call my epistemological criterion the 'transformation test'.

IV

The basis of my proposed solution is that the theory of value is only perspectivally invariant; its deep metaphysical relativity is quite compatible with robust cognitivism at the level of its content for the makers of evaluative judgements. However, a judger's proposed maxim of action is perspective dependent. Such maxims fail systematically to transform across different frames of description. Maxims only function as practical reasons relative to the individual agent's location within the intersubjective framework of reasons. Thus, the structure of practical reasons is perspective dependent, in that it displays the phenomenon which Amartya Sen has called 'evaluator relativity'. My resolution of the initial problem is that *reasons* vary according to one's 'location' within the space of reasons, whereas *values* do not vary at all. However, to preserve my commitment to the impartiality of moral reasons, I further argue that reasons do *not* vary according to individual character or one's moral personality.

My argument takes a crucial distinction from Sen's account of evaluator relativity, and applies it not at the level of values, nor of agents, but at the level of the intersubjective structure of reasons. Sen's concerns are not those of the present paper. His interest lies in formulating a defensible version of consequentialism, but I take from his discussions two ideas.[18] The first is that the reasons that individual agents discern in states of affairs may vary with their relative 'location' *vis-à-vis* these states of affairs when the latter are viewed as potential outcomes of their agency. The second is

18. Amartya Sen, 'Rights and Agency', *Philosophy and Public Affairs,* 11, No. 1 (Winter, 1982), pp. 3–39; 'Evaluator Relativity and Consequential Evaluation' and 'Positional Objectivity'.

that this result is not relativistic: that this move is perfectly compatible with the content of the agent's reasons remaining 'objective'.[19]

I want to detach a structural proposal from the details of Sen's actual argument about the nature of value. Sen points out that classical consequentialism sees the values of outcomes as the same for all agents, whereas he argues that this is not so. For example, the state of affairs where Othello has murdered Desdemona is, in Sen's opinion, worse from Othello's point of view than from that of a non-involved spectator, since Othello is responsible for bringing about the state of affairs. His argument for evaluator relativity is centrally that the 'evaluator may be morally involved in the state of affairs he is evaluating, and the evaluation of the state may have to take note of that involvement'.[20] This intuition motivates Sen's basic thesis that, 'the goodness of a state of affairs[....]depends intrinsically (not just instrumentally)[....]on the position of the evaluator in relation to the state'.[21] Sen remarks that this position relativity need not be marked in ordinary language and that it is not up to the agent which location *vis-à-vis* an outcome he or she occupies:

> The fact of 'relativisation' does not in any way rule out the peculiar relevance of a particular value of a variable with respect to which the function is relativised....one of these roles is his own, and that specification 'closes' the relativised system and determines the 'solution'.[22]

The terminology of 'locations' and 'roles' in relation to outcomes is equivalent. They bear no more of a theoretical load than this: an agent can stand in the relation of 'doer' or 'viewer' of a potential act. I will return to this important point below.

I would argue that this distinction can be put to productive use in a different theoretical framework. This alternative strategy offers a solution to the current problem which preserves

19. Sen, 'Evaluator Relativity', p. 117. My theory hinges on the point that Sen's notion of 'objectivity' covers two different forms of perspectivalness in objective judgements. The view is not relativistic since it introduces the *relational* and not the *relative*, in order to preserve Winch's important point that he is not trying to resurrect Protagoreanism. Practical reasons are indexed to a location, but not constituted by that location.

20. Sen, 'Evaluator Relativity', p. 114.

21. Sen, 'Evaluator Relativity', p. 114.

22. Sen, 'Evaluator Relativity', p. 124. See also 'Rights and Agency', p. 37.

cognitivism and impartialism while also respecting Guttenplan's 'strong supervenience' claim. It does so by deploying the structure Sen has focused on within the theory of practical reasoning, not the theory of value. The failure of transformation that Sen has pinpointed should not be further explained by invoking different values, but should rather be explained by the status of these contents as practical reasons for an agent.

Sen's 'framework' for evaluator relativity is a special instance of the phenomenon of the perspectival. Explaining how it relates to the two perspectival aspects of moral content I have already classified resolves the problem posed by the initial problem, and does so in a unified theoretical context. The further, crucially important, distinction I wish to draw may be clarified by examining the following remark of Sen's:

> It is possible to get trans-positional statements from positional ones. Further a state could happen to be good from every position. This does not make the goodness nonpositional, but only indicates that there is interpositional invariance.[23]

An ambiguity lies in the phrase 'it is possible to get trans-positional statements from positional ones'. Applying the criteria I described above it will be clear that they yield different results when applied to the two different aspects of moral content. The crucial issue in distinguishing between the two kinds of perspectival phenomena I have called the 'perspectivally invariant' and the 'perspective dependent' depended on how one applied the transformation test across classes of makers of judgements.

Applied to the present case, my claim is that values in a situation are the same for all agents, no matter how they are located *vis-à-vis* those values. Evaluative judgements systematically transform across viewpoints and are thus merely perspectivally invariant. While in the deepest metaphysical sense they are perspectival, in that the categories they deploy are anthropocentric, this is no more of a barrier to cognitivism about value than it is to cognitivism about colours. However, there is a different result when one examines the second aspect of moral judgements, their status as proposed actions under a description, or 'maxims', for an agent. This does not systematically transform across viewpoints: reasons

23. Sen, 'Evaluator Relativity', p. 115.

for an agent are sensitive to their 'location' in relation to outcomes and are thus perspective dependent, not perspectivally invariant. The former dimension of the judgements is systematically invariant across transformations, whereas the latter dimension is not.

This failure of systematic transformation expresses Williams's point that in understanding the use of 'role-reversal' tests in ethical thinking, where moral observers imaginatively occupy the 'location' in the space of reasons in fact occupied by another, imaginative empathy is not total identification. Thus, in one important sense, by the exercise of imagination the position of Captain Vere is intersubjectively accessible to us. However, this accessibility is constrained in two quite distinct ways, reflecting two different failures of transformation across viewpoints.

The first constraint, much stressed by Winch, is that the our third-personal access to the character of the deliberating agent can take that character as an 'object' for judgement, whereas for the agent him or herself it is what they deliberate *from*. This is quite correct, and is central to those arguments for grounding deontic options which are based on the importance of the 'personal point of view'. However, these arguments are not my central concern since in my view they implicitly draw on certain values. The inconsistent situation which is my main concern requires a shared evaluative basis.[24]

My focus is on the metaphysical impossibility of actually *being* Vere, occupying exactly his 'location', and hence accessing the 'all things considered' reason indexed to that location. This point is crucial to my argument, so it is worthy of further clarification. My argument is that it *does* make a difference to the reasons an agent has whether or not he or she is the agent that would carry out a particular act. This insight is well expressed by Solzhenitsyn's principle that even if evil will come into the world when one does not act, it is better that one's agency is not the instrument of such evil.[25] One can explore, deploying imagination at the service of

24. The 'personal point of view' simply gives rise to an inappropriate set of considerations in the case of Billy Budd. Consider two representative values correctly stressed by proponents of the 'personal point of view', namely, an agent's 'ground projects' or his or her 'integrity'. Neither value is threatened in the Billy Budd case and if they were introduced as the basis for practical reasons the charge of moral narcissism would be well placed.

25. The principle is discussed by Jonathan Glover in, 'It Makes No Difference Whether Or Not I Do It', *Proceedings of the Aristotelian Society, Supplementary Volume*, 49 (1975), pp. 171–190. Glover quotes Solzhenitsyn from his Nobel acceptance lecture: 'Let the lie come into the world, even dominate the world, but not through me'.

practical reasoning, what it would be to face such a choice. One can imaginatively occupy the standpoint of the agent preparing to act. But this 'role reversal' test does not involve the fantasy of actually becoming the other person: sympathy is not identification or psychological fusion. The resulting amalgam of viewpoints would have little psychological plausibility as a model of a collective psyche.[26]

My account is quite compatible with meeting the requirement that the reason indexed to that location be impartially acceptable. Both Vere's (the agent's) and Winch's (the observer's) reasons are acceptable from an impartial standpoint that accepts the perspective dependence of deontic reasons, provided this standpoint also acknowledges the crucial 'viewer'/'doer' distinction. One steers the correct middle course by noting that while one cannot be Vere, and hence occupy his location, it is not by *virtue of being Vere* that he occupies his location. This would be to confuse accident with essence. I will return to a related point—that unless the reason is indexed to the location not the individual, one is open to the charge of moral narcissism.

V

The previous section has set out the basic elements of my resolution of the problem. However, I need further to specify how it is compatible with the initial constraints I assumed of cognitivism about value, and impartialism about moral reasons. I will clarify each of these points in turn.

First, the metaphysical status of value. The deep metaphysical relativity of value means that moral values, like secondary qualities, are anthropocentric. However, just as in the case of secondary properties, their explanatory indispensability indicates that anthropocentricity does not debar these properties from figuring in knowledge claims.[27] In order to pass the test of reflective stability, one may have to concede an even more 'local' form of perspectivalness tying such properties to culturally local categories, but again this is no obstacle to their figuring in

---

26. A point made by Bernard Williams in his rejection of Hare's 'World Agent' model for practical decision, as presented in *Moral Thinking: Its Levels, Method and Point* (Oxford: Oxford University Press, 1981). Williams writes, 'Any one agent who had projects as conflicting, competitive and diversely based as the World Agent's would be (to put it mildly) in bad shape', Williams, *Ethics and the Limits of Philosophy* (London: Fontana, 1985), p. 88.

27. David Wiggins, *Needs*, pp. 155–60, also my *Value and Context* (forthcoming) chapter four.

knowledge claims.[28] Thus, these concessions that moral contents are, while cognitive, also perspectival does not take one further than *perspectival invariance*.

Secondly, I will clarify the different form of perspectivalness exemplified by deontic maxims. An emphasis on the personal nature of ethics is quite compatible with the impartiality of moral reasons. The confusion between taking moral reasons to be impartial and to be impersonal is widespread, but it must be admitted that it is fostered by some of the terminology in this area.[29] Critics of impartialism argue that the position ignores the personal dimension of ethics, such as character, integrity and individuality. This is quite mistaken. The objection runs together the claim that ethics is impartial with the claim that ethics is impersonal: impartialism is perfectly compatible with the personal, but not with the partial. Impartialism requires that personal values and reasons should be represented from the impartial point of view, but has no objection to them *per se*.[30]

The exact test involved in determining the impartial acceptability of reasons cannot be fully specified here, but I would argue that impartiality is a norm implicit in reason-giving practice which is internal to our moral outlook.[31] Much of the criticism directed against the norm of impartiality takes it to be a constraint derivable from the nature of practical reasons as such, and thus implicated in the Neo-Kantian project of an a priori derivation of substantive ethical constraints from a 'pure' and thus formal account of reason. This is not my understanding of the norm of impartiality.[32] I view it as a moral norm internal to our practice

28. Contra the claim of Williams, *Ethics and the Limits of Philosophy*, chapters eight and nine. I argue for this claim in *Value and Context*, chapter two.

29. Such as the equation of 'objective' and 'impersonal' in Nagel, *The Possibility of Altruism* (Oxford: Oxford University Press, 1970), in the key chapters XI and XII.

30. Adrian M. Piper, 'Moral Theory and Alienation'. My use of the term 'represent' is deliberate, following Rawls's use of the idea of the original position as a 'device of representation'. The impartial point of view is in my view merely a heuristic standpoint, and should not be metaphysically interpreted as a special, non-perspectival view of our reasons from some Archimedean standpoint. The point of the impartial point of view is to endorse reasons we are already committed to, not to generate reasons itself.

31. I take this conception of an impartial reason from Nagel, *Possibility*, chapters X–XIII; I take it to be separable from that work's commitment to *external* reasons. The later *View From Nowhere* (Oxford: Oxford University Press, 1986) is much clearer about the status of the norm of impartiality as I would understand that term, clearly adopting the position described in footnote 30.

32. This is another point of agreement between myself and Winch; Winch's target was the stronger claim that a substantive moral norm of impartiality was derivable from the meaning of the word 'ought'.

which shapes 'how we go on' in moral argument. It is best expressed, in my view, in Scanlon's contractualist commitment to grounding moral reasons on considerations that an agent will not reasonably reject, in so far, I would add, as that agent is rational.[33] Partial reasons are not reasons we can put before other agents, at the 'tribunal of their reason', without rejection by a perfectly reasonable interlocutor.[34] This transposition of the norm of impartiality to a perspective within, rather than external to, moral practice, weakens its demands, but does not make them negligible.

VI

It is useful to compare my treatment of the Billy Budd case with those of both Wiggins and Winch. Wiggins's treatment of the example of Winch and Vere making incompatible judgements concerning the fate of Billy Budd is as follows: given the plurality of values in play, there is no incompatibility between the observer Peter Winch arriving at a different 'all things considered' judgement about what he ought to do from that of the involved agent, Vere. Both parties were making the same judgements as to a panoply of values displayed by the apparently inconsistent scenario, but their respective 'weightings' or emphases led to the situation presenting them with a different evaluative 'shape'. Hence the differential finding. But my response, following Guttenplan, is that this line of argument is quite compatible with there being, in fact, a *single* best 'all things considered judgement' as to what one ought to do in this situation.

My view is that Wiggins's value pluralism must be supplemented by an agency dimension which allows a wider range of 'perspective relative' judgements about what one may do in the envisaged scenario. Unlike Sen, I do not take this to be a judgement about the values in play in the situation: values are the same for all agents. It is deontic space rather than evaluative space which is 'curved', moulded relative to the agency dimension introduced by

33. I take this important qualification from Christine Korsgaard's paper, 'Scepticism about Practical Reason', *Journal of Philosophy* (January, 1986), pp. 5–25.

34. I borrow the phrase 'tribunal of reason' from Jeremy Waldron's 'Theoretical Foundations of Liberalism', *The Philosophical Quarterly,* 37 (1987) pp. 127–50. The essentials of Scanlon's contractualism is presented in 'Contractualism and Utilitarianism', in Sen and Williams, *Utilitarianism and Beyond* (Cambridge: Cambridge University Press, 1982).

considering oneself as a potential agent in the situation. The individual moral agent is located in a system of intersubjective reasons whereby his or her relative 'location' is a parameter within his or her decision making. The strong supervenience of reasons on values is compatible with different reasons being indexed to different 'locations' within a single, inter-subjective framework of practical reasons.

Thus, in my solution, the respective judgements of Vere and Winch contain hidden indexicals which indicate their relative location *vis-à-vis* the envisaged outcomes: this perspectivalness is the perspective dependence of maxims. This form of perspectivalness follows from the fact that such maxims are indexically tied to the location from which they are made, and hence perspective *exhausts this aspect of their content*. This is compatible with the cognitive content of the reason exhibiting only perspectival invariance, since the evaluation of a content as a reason for action and its evaluation as an object of cognition focus on different aspects of one and the same state. Furthermore, this is compatible with the agent's proposed maxim conforming with the formal constraint of impartial acceptability.

The comparison with Winch's position is also of interest. The central difference between my argument and the line of enquiry Winch inaugurated is my undemanding use of the metaphor of 'location'. I use it simply to draw the viewer/doer distinction. In explaining this distinction, this is the point at which I must set aside the special problem that Winch is writing about a fictional case. One can hardly apply a viewer/doer relation to such a case since Winch is not going to intervene in a fictional narrative.[35] So let me restrict my account to actual cases, where 'viewer' and 'doer' are both in a position to assume either role.[36] A similar point is that it is irrelevant that Vere is 'involved in' while Winch is 'detached from' Billy Budd's case; if I switch to a non-fictional example I can take 'involved' and 'detached' as a distinction between practice and reflection that is accessible to both protagonists. This is obscured by the fictional case, and the terminology of 'viewer' and 'doer' carries these overtones too. But my argument is intended to apply to cases where both protagonists could act, if they decided to, and

35. Unlike, for example, in Woody Allen's 'The Kugelmass Episode', in which Professor Kugelmass gets trapped in the text of *Madam Bovary*.

36. This also allows for the possibility of giving true moral advice in 'if I were you form'.

both can reflect on the difference it makes to be the person who actually brings the outcome about.

Unlike Winch and those influenced by him I do not take Captain Vere's character, defined by the moral capacities and incapacities revealed to him in deliberation, as a determinant of his 'location'. I regard this line of argument as misguidedly psychologistic, and would draw a distinction between a theory of an agent's reasons and a theory of reasons for an agent. The account I have presented here takes it that the reason available to Vere is determined by the evaluative shape of the situation, his 'role' as potential agent, and the constraint of impartiality. It is thus a theory of an agent's reasons. Whether Vere has the psychological capacity to 'access' this reason is a separate matter located in moral psychology. There is a great deal we can say in appraising Vere's reasoning, obviously relevant to our appraisal of his virtues and vices of character. This, however, is a theory of reasons for an agent and does not determine what the normative content of his reason should be.

I can agree with Winch that moral decisions such as Vere's can be instruments of self-knowledge. As such, they blur the line between 'deciding' what to do and 'finding out' about oneself. I can also agree to the epistemological claim that as a consequence of the link between moral decision and self-knowledge, one can only understand Vere's decision by imaginative empathy with his deliberative process, which deploys his first personal deliberative vocabulary. However, I would still press a distinction between the evaluation of the psychological *process* leading to Vere's decision and its *product*. Ignoring this distinction lapses into psychologism and reduces the normative force of the content of Vere's conclusion to the psychological processes that generated it.[37]

VII

The use of Sen's distinctions certainly offers insight into how one can defuse the challenge with which this paper began. But it might

37. I find a connection here between Winch's discussion of Vere and his view of the methodology of the human sciences more generally, in *On the Idea of a Social Science* (London: Routledge and Kegan Paul, 1958).There is a mistaken slide from the correct and important view that hermeneutic understanding begins with the 'agent's point of view' to the error of taking the first personal point of view as incorrigible. For a penetrating discussion of a position called 'vulgar Wittgensteinianism' that may, or may not, be Winch's, see Charles Taylor's 'Evaluative Realism and the Geisteswissenschaften' in Holtzmann, S. and Leich, C., (eds.) *Wittgenstein: To Follow a Rule* (London: Routledge and Kegan Paul 1981).

seem to leave the key question open: why should there be the phenomenon of evaluator relativity, or in my terms an ineliminably perspectival dimension to the intersubjective structure of reasons? I believe this point can be satisfactorily addressed by focusing on the dimension which introduces the relativity, namely, the dimension of potential agency. Different maxims are consequent upon viewing oneself as the potential author of an act.

The key question, however, is why the agency dimension alone should be the focus of the problem. The assumption I have worked with throughout is that the values exhibited in a situation are the same for all judgers. Thus, I cannot avail myself of Sen's explanation that being the agent of an outcome makes that outcome evaluatively *worse* than an alternative. Nor am I identifying 'maxims' with intuitively known deontic constraints that offer an independent constraint on action functioning separately from the evaluative dimension—a 'dual source' view.

To address the issue, it is useful to reflect on the example mentioned above which Sen uses to express his intuition: that when Othello kills Desdemona, the resulting situation is worse from the point of view of Othello than from that of an observer. I want to set alongside this the equally powerful intuition that from the perspective of evaluation alone, the badness of the state of affairs resulting from the action can be judged to be the same by anyone. The agency dimension introduces, in my view, a special reason indexed to the location Othello occupies *vis-à-vis* the outcome, namely that of potential agent. But there seems no reason to infer from this that the value of the outcome varies relative to 'location'.

In my account, this special reason is to be located in the agency perspective, but that is a special perspective on the facts—not a special kind of perspectival fact, as Sen's alternative diagnosis would have it. Here, as in more general metaphysical discussion, one can object to 'perspectival facts' on the grounds of 'double counting'. If alongside every absolute fact we must place a perspectival one to accommodate the perspective of the observer/judger, the same state of affairs is being counted twice. It is thus hardly surprising that Sen can accommodate his view within a consequentialist framework: in Sen's theory the disvalue of an evil act counts twice when we take the perspective of its author into account. This is implausible.

My argument against Sen is a straightforward one: he can offer a theoretical backing for his intuition about the 'authorship' of acts and value, whereas I can accommodate both this intuition and the intuition most directly opposed to it. There is indeed something special about the reasons agents have for viewing outcomes as potential effects of their agency, but this special status of such maxims need not be further explained by a difference in the values involved. We have the countervailing intuition that the evil Othello brings into the world is not *more* evil when judged from any particular point of view—including Othello's own. Thus, by conceiving of moral contents under two aspects and taking the special status of maxims as an explanatorily primitive idea, both intuitions are satisfactorily reconciled.

However, placing this much theoretical emphasis on the agency perspective may seem *morally* problematic. If the peculiar character of deontic constraints is explained by the special relation into which agent and victim are placed, does this not invite agents to become morally narcissistic or self-indulgent? I would address this concern by noting that if an agent declares 'I just cannot do it', simply on the basis of the Solzhenitsyn principle, the special reason is indexed to their 'location'—it is not indexed to them. They are not excusing just on the grounds of being the particular person they are. Their remark is not mere autobiography, although it is that as well.[38]

This emphasis on the agency perspective converges with other recent work on the topic of justifying deontic constraints as opposed to deontic options. More than one commentator has drawn out the connections between the distinctive character of deontic constraints and agency. Nagel's and Korsgaard's recent work on grounding deontology has focused on personal relatedness, and has located deontic reasons as supervenient on such relations as victimhood and acting as the agent of another's suffering.[39] I should emphasise that while Nagel's and Korsgaard's discussion of deontic maxims are compatible with the account presented here, their account of values is not. Both write within a contemporary

38. It would not mark a slide from the 'critical' to the 'clinical', as Cavell has nicely put it. I should re-iterate at this point that my focus in this paper is on deontic options, not constraints. In the case of deontic options, it *would* be relevant to cite the indexical link between having the personal projects one has, and being the person one is.

39. Thomas Nagel, *The View From Nowhere*, p. 139; Christine Korsgaard, 'The Reasons We Can Share', in Paul, E.F., Miller, F.D. and Paul, J. (eds.) *Altruism* (Cambridge: Cambridge University Press, 1993), pp. 24–51.

discussion shaped decisively by Scheffler's work, in which deontic constraints appear more problematic than deontic options. They both, quite independently, look to the agent/victim relationship to explain the puzzling status of deontic constraints and to use this relationship to elucidate the Kantian injunction to treat persons as ends and never as means.

Korsgaard further emphasises the inter-subjective nature of the collective structure of deontic reasons.[40] However, both Nagel and Korsgaard offer a direct equivalence of reasons and values, which leads them to overlook the distinction between the two kinds of perspectivalness moral reasons exhibit. Thus, Korsgaard maintains that the ontological status of values is that they are 'inter-subjective' as opposed to 'objective' or 'subjective', on the grounds that this is the status of the corresponding reasons.[41] This seems to me clearly mistaken, even if read as 'transcendentally inter-subjective', which would be equivalent in my argument to the idea of the perspective dependent. Evaluative discourse has stronger cognitive credentials than this. To adapt one of Wiggins's remarks it would be 'false or senseless' to judge that the cruelty of an act could not be an object of knowledge. There seems to be no sense, not even a transcendental one, in which 'we' give it this cognitive status. This single content, however, can also be deliberated over as a maxim, under which deontic aspect both Nagel's and Korsgaard's accounts of its special status as a reason are supportive of the argument I have developed.[42]

Department of Philosophy
Kings College London
The Strand
London WC2R 2LS

40. Korsgaard, 'Reasons We Can Share', p. 25.

41. Korsgaard, 'Reasons We Can Share', p. 25; 'I have assumed an equivalence or at least a direct correspondence between values and practical reasons.... In this I follow Thomas Nagel'.

42. Let me anticipate two 'matters arising': first, the position set out in this paper is intended to be a contribution to 'descriptive' rather than 'revisionary' ethics. Any proposal to revise or eliminate the structures I have described arise, in my view, at this later stage. A second, connected, point is that while I have located Sen's relativity within the theory of practical reasoning, not the theory of value, I have left it open whether or not there is an indirect link between the agency dimension and the theory of value—for example, the proposal that persons be treated as ends and never as means because of their capacity for 'endorsing' themselves as valuable. These issues seem to me to be open to further consideration.

Finally, thanks for helpful comments and criticisms to Adrian Moore, Martin Stone, Roger Crisp, Anthony Savile and Jo Wolff. Special thanks are due to Kathryn Brown.

V*—FIRST PERSON PLURAL ONTOLOGY AND PRAXIS

by Andrew Chitty

I

What am I? More exactly, what kind of thing am I? This is not intended as a classificatory question. It is not like asking 'what kind of butterfly is this?', where answering the question is just a matter of identifying the butterfly in question as belonging to one type or another: for example, as a cabbage white. If the question was intended as a classificatory question, then the obvious answer would be 'a human being'. Here, though, it is intended as an ontological question. I know that there are several basic kinds of things in the world: inanimate things, plants, animals. It seems to me when I think about myself that I am a basically different kind of thing from any of these, or to put it more formally, that I belong to a different basic kind from them. More generally, it seems to me that this is true of all of us human beings. We are a basically different kind of thing from plants or animals,[1] while at the same time, we are basically the same kind of thing as each other. Furthermore it seems possible in principle that there could be, or could have been, non-human creatures, in unexplored forests or on other planets, that are basically the same kind of thing as we are. After all, there are many species of animals and of plants, so why could there not be several species of the basic kind of thing that we are? Now the question as intended is, what is the 'nature' of this kind[2] of thing that I am, or (to reformulate it in the plural) that we are? That is, what is the fundamental characteristic, or combination of characteristics, that we all have that *makes* each of us this kind of thing, and accordingly sets us apart from other kinds of thing? I call this the first person plural ontological question.

1. I am using 'animals' in the sense that excludes human beings.
2. From here on I use 'kind' as a shorthand for 'basic kind'.

*Meeting of the Aristotelian Society, held in the Senior Common Room, Birkbeck College, London, on Monday, 9th December, 1996 at 8.15 p.m.

If we could identify this fundamental characteristic then we would be able to put a name to the kind of thing that we are. In fact, putting a name to this kind of thing is a shorthand way of identifying the fundamental characteristic in question. For example, traditional Christian theology says that we are immortal souls, so it is our having an immortal soul that makes us each the kind of thing that we all are and sets us apart from any other kind of thing. Descartes said that we are thinking things, so what makes us the kind of thing that we are is our capacity to think. Kant said that we are rational beings, with rationality understood as a matter of subordinating intuitions and inclinations under universal rules, so possessing this capacity for rational cognition and action is what makes us the kind of thing that we are. Heidegger said that we are Dasein, which as I understand it is a way of saying that it is the capacity to construe (or misconstrue) things, including ourselves, as being one kind of thing or another that makes us the kind of thing that we are. This capacity is what enables us to ask the first person plural ontological question itself, so here our ability to ask the question provides the clue to its answer.

II

The question of what kind of thing we are is not a question that can be isolated. Answering it in one way or another generally goes hand in hand with not only a metaphysics but also an epistemology, and even an ethical and political outlook. In other words, an answer to the question forms a crucial component of any basic philosophical 'world view'. In fact philosophical world views can almost be individuated by their answers to the question. Even those that typically involve an explicit rejection of the question usually assume an implicit answer to it.

For example, someone who inhabits a 'scientific naturalist' philosophical world view, one based on the natural sciences, would probably say that the question presupposes for its sense the idea that human beings have a special ontological status that separates them off from the rest of the physical universe, that this idea is nothing but a remnant of the idea of the soul, and that it has no place in a scientific account of the world. The only large-scale distinctions to be made between things in the world are those made in terms of their degree of internal complexity or integration. However, although this looks like a rejection of the question, it is actually the rejection of a different question, a question in which those posing the question stand outside the human race as a whole and ask 'what is the fundamental characteristic that makes *them* what they are and sets them apart from other kinds of thing?' This is a third person ontological question. In fact for us human beings it is an impossible question since we cannot stand outside the human race as a whole. We (that is, some of us) can stand outside any one human being, but not outside all human beings at once. Meanwhile the inhabitant of the naturalist world view does assume an answer to the first person plural ontological question, an answer that is implicit in the usage of 'we' in scientific journals. What characterises this 'we' and sets it apart from other kinds of thing is simply 'our' capacity to know how everything in the universe works.

The difficulty for the scientific naturalist world view is that this 'we' has to refer to the very human beings who are also being thought of from the third person perspective as simply animal organisms of a particularly complex and integrated sort. Yet it looks impossible to conceive ourselves in both of these ways at once. In particular, it looks impossible to conceive our own knowledge in both ways at once. From one point of view this knowledge is a representation of reality, rationally derived from our encounter with it, which we can take seriously. From the other point of view it is just a part of reality, simply a set of neuro-chemical patterns in human brains, causally produced by the operation of the laws of nature, which we cannot take seriously. The result is a contradictory conception of ourselves.

Scientific naturalists usually avoid this difficulty by tacitly assuming that the knowing 'we' is always a different set of individuals from those who are currently being discussed from the third person point of view. This suggests an invidious distinction within the human race between the 'knowers' and the 'knowables', and anyway it cannot resolve the difficulty, since it can hardly be denied that the 'knowers' are also complex animal organisms, so that the contradiction in the scientific naturalist's answer to the first person plural ontological question recurs with respect to us 'knowers'.

To take another example, the inhabitant of the currently popular postmodern philosophical world view would probably also reject the ontological question, this time on the grounds that to pose the question assumes that there is an objective truth, waiting to be discovered, about the kind of thing that we are. Instead, the postmodernist would argue, all such 'truths' are only ever our own inventions or constructions, usually furthermore inventions in the unacknowledged service of some personal or political end. Here again, though, an implicit answer to the question is being assumed even while overtly the question is rejected. For surely in the postmodern outlook it is exactly the capacity to further our ends by inventing and sustaining a conception of the world, while thinking that what we are doing is discovering the truth about the world, that characterises and distinguishes us. At least, I have never heard this capacity attributed to animals. In short, we are 'motivated truth-inventors'.

The result is a difficulty analogous to that of scientific naturalism. For postmodernists are human beings too. So on their own account their own ideas of how the world is must also be motivated inventions. Yet it is hard to see how one can ever apply this view to one's own ideas of how the world is while continuing to take them seriously.

The issue comes to a head if we focus on the postmodernist's idea that human beings are motivated truth-inventors. For this idea cannot, on their own account, express an objective truth about human beings that obtained before they pointed it out. It can itself only be another motivated invention, and it seems impossible to acknowledge it as such without ceasing to take it seriously.

Postmodernists sometimes try to avoid this difficulty by trying to present their accounts of how other human beings invent truths without making any positive truth-claims themselves. But the fact remains that the accounts make no sense unless they are understood as descriptions of how things are, and how things already were before the postmodernists pointed them out. Alternatively, sometimes postmodernists are willing to proclaim frankly that the account being given is a motivated invention as much as any other account humans give of their world is, while justifying it pragmatically, as a liberating invention. The argument is that once we have seen that every conception of the world is a motivated invention rather than a reflection of the way that the world objectively is, this will give us the courage to reinterpret the world freely, no longer inhibited by a sense of obligation to make our conceptions match a pre-given reality. Furthermore, the idea that all our conceptions are just motivated inventions can give us that courage even if we see that idea itself as nothing but a motivated invention. Yet, again, this last claim looks false. If we feel inhibited from inventing conceptions freely because we feel that there is an objective reality and that a conception of reality is an attempt to describe that reality, then we will only lose that inhibition if we come to feel that this is not the case, and that it is not the case independently of whether we decide to think that it is not the case. A claim to the effect that it is not the case which is itself a self-acknowledged invention is one that we cannot take seriously enough for it to disinhibit us.

I have tried to show through these examples that the first person plural ontological question is not as escapable as it may seem to be. I have also tried to show that in both examples the answer to the question runs into difficulties, and in somewhat parallel ways. In each case, the answer to the question is a highly 'cognitivist' one; that is, the characteristic that is said to make us the kind of thing that we are is in each case based on our capacity to form an idea about how the world is. And in each case, difficulties arise in making this cognitivist way of conceiving ourselves work both when looking at ourselves from the 'inside', i.e. adopting the point of view of the cognising subject, and from the 'outside', i.e. adopting a point of view external to that of the cognising subject.

Thus the scientific naturalist answer to the question, that we are knowers, makes sense when we think of ourselves from the point of view of the cognising subject, but not when we think of ourselves from a point of view external to it, since from the external point of view we just look to the naturalist like complex physical structures. Conversely, the postmodern answer to the question, that we are motivated truth-inventors, makes sense if we think of ourselves from the external standpoint, but not from that of the cognising subject itself, since from that standpoint our cognition only makes sense as an attempt to describe the way the world is, independently of that attempt.

Maybe, then, there is a general problem with cognitivist answers to the ontological question. Maybe cognitivist self-characterisations will always lead to a contradiction when we try to apply them both from the 'outside' and from the 'inside', because from the inside we have to take our cognitions seriously as portrayals of reality, whereas from the outside they collapse into mere products, whether of neuro-chemical mechanisms or of our own ulterior motivations.

III

This kind of criticism of cognitivist answers to the question is an immanent one, in that it tries to show that cognitivist answers lead to an internal contradiction in our self-characterisation. In addition, though, cognitivist self-characterisations have been criticised by appealing to an external standard, specifically the standard of our own ordinary experience of ourselves: our ordinary sense of what we are. The criticism goes that understanding ourselves simply as cognitive beings fails to accord with this self-experience, for in it we don't just experience ourselves as cognisers, but also as, for example, as living organisms, as agents, as language-users, and as emotional beings. That is, we have a sense that these features of ourselves make us what we are as much as our cognitive capacities do, that without them we would not be the kind of thing that we are.[3]

This criticism, appealing as it does to our own sense of what we are, in order to criticise cognitivist answers to the ontological question, implies that such an appeal to self-experience should also be the way in which to find a better answer to the question. Such an approach to the ontological question raises two difficult issues and two associated objections.

The first is that it seems to address the question by looking for those characteristics without which we wouldn't be the kind of thing that we are, rather than those characteristics that distinguish us from other kinds of thing. From this point of view being alive and having emotions can count as characteristics that partly make us the kind of thing we are regardless of whether animals or plants

---

3. This criticism can be supplemented with a political one. Marxists can argue that a cognitivist conception of what makes us the kind of thing that we are expresses the self-conception of those who do not produce, and reinforces their rule over the producing classes. Similarly, feminists can argue that it expresses a specifically male self-conception and is complicit in the maintenance of men's power over women, and ecologists can argue that it expresses a conception of humans as set above the rest of nature and helps to legitimate the treatment of nature as a mere resource to be exploited for human ends. However in all these cases there must be an uneasy relation between the political criticism and the criticism that simply appeals to ordinary self-experience, in so far as the political outlook in question sees our ordinary self-experience as already estranged or distorted by the kind of society that it criticises.

have them. In objection to this it could be said that if we want to find out what makes us the kind of thing that we are, and not an animal or a plant, we should be looking for our *differentia specifica*, for the characteristics that *distinguish* us as a kind from every other kind. Such an objection seems to push us back towards a cognitivist answer to the question, for if we address the question by looking for the distinguishing marks that differentiate us from animals and plants, then our cognitive capacity does seem to provide one of the most obvious.

There seems to be a danger here that we may be dealing with two separate questions rather than one: one question about the characteristics that makes us the kind of thing that we are and another about the characteristics that distinguish us from other kinds of thing. Is the ontological question really two such questions rolled into one?

I do not think that it is. As I formulated the question, it was: 'What is the fundamental characteristic, or combination of characteristics, that we all have that makes each of us the kind of thing that we all are, and accordingly sets us apart from other kinds of thing?' If there is a combination of characteristics that makes us the kind of thing that we are, then for a thing to have that combination of characteristics must be enough to make it that kind of thing. Since if it is that kind of thing it cannot be any other kind of thing, it follows that for it to have that combination of characteristics is also enough to distinguish it from any other kind of thing. Any one of those characteristics may be shared with some other kinds of thing,[4] but only that kind of thing will have that particular combination of them. The question simply asks for that combination of characteristics. This is a unitary question.

However it is true that the question is closely connected to a specific question about our distinctiveness. Let us follow tradition and call the characteristics that in combination make something a certain kind of thing (so that without any one of them it would not be that kind of thing) the *essential* characteristics of that kind. Then the first person plural ontological question asks us for the essential characteristics of our own kind, just as our sense of what we are is our sense of those essential characteristics. Now if we were able to establish the essential characteristics of both our own kind and of

4. In fact every one of them may be.

all other kinds, then we could answer the question, 'which, if any, of the essential characteristics of our kind is unique to that kind?' Furthermore if we were able to answer this question, which I shall call the first person plural uniqueness question, we would certainly have established *some* of the essential characteristics of our kind, and so gone part of the way to answering the ontological question. It is even true that if our interest in answering the ontological question arose from an interest in discovering what distinguishes us from other kinds—and it was this interest that I used to introduce the question—then answering the uniqueness question might give us as much of the answer to the ontological question as we want.[5] In addition, if it turned out that each kind had just one essential characteristic, then the answers to the ontological question and the uniqueness question would be the same. So the uniqueness question is closely connected to the ontological question, to the point that they may sometimes be confused. Nevertheless, it is a distinct question, and the fact that it exists and is closely connected with the ontological question does not undermine the unity of the ontological question itself.

I conclude that if the appeal to our sense of what we are in order to answer the ontological question leads to an answer that counts characteristics which we share with animals or plants as essential to our kind, then this fact does not as such constitute an objection to the answer, as long as the full combination of characteristics listed in the answer is not shared by any other kind. To object to the inclusion of a particular characteristic in a proposed answer to the ontological question on the grounds that it is a characteristic we share with some other kind is to confuse the ontological question with the uniqueness question.

The second issue raised by the appeal to self-experience in answering the ontological question is that of whether such an appeal is in fact a legitimate way of answering the question. For it could be argued that our own pre-philosophical sense of what we are may well be misleading, both as a guide in trying to answer the question, and as a standard by which to assess answers that have already been proposed to it. Quite possibly our essential characteristics, the

---

5. Of course if our kind had no unique essential characteristics and was distinguished from all other kinds only by its particular combination of essential characteristics, then the answer to the uniqueness question, namely 'None', would not help in discovering what distinguishes us.

essential characteristics of our kind, are such that we cannot derive them, or verify them, from our self-experience at all.

A short response to this objection is to say that we must have some pre-philosophical sense of our basic kind in order to be able to pose the first person plural ontological question in the first place. It is true that we lack an everyday term for this basic kind, so that we may only be able to express this sense by talking about 'what makes us human', but we are quite aware when we do so that we are using 'human' in a weightier sense than when, for example, we talk about human beings as a particular biological species, *Homo Sapiens*, set apart from others by merely physiological distinguishing marks. In speech we even emphasise the word 'human' slightly when we use it in this weightier sense. We must therefore have some pre-philosophical sense of which of our characteristics are essential, and any philosophical answer to the ontological question will have to be broadly compatible with that sense. At the same time, consulting our own intuitions on the matter of what makes us what we are is unlikely to take us very far, if only because those intuitions are often uncertain. If they were not, we would not be asking ourselves the ontological question; its answer would be obvious to us.

IV

I conclude that the self-experiential approach to the ontological question is not defeated by those two kinds of objection. What I shall go on to do now is look at an argument that combines a version of the self-experiential criticism of cognitivist self-characterisations with the immanent criticism.

In this version the self-experiential criticism does not appeal directly to our sense of which characteristics are essential to us. Instead it appeals to our sense of which *ways of relating* to other things are essential to us. Specifically, it argues that cognitivist self-characterisations result from the idea that the essential way in which we relate to other things is by 'representing' them, whether this representing takes the form of simply looking at them or of creating a theoretical 'picture' of their internal structure, conceiving this as if it were something that could be looked at. The criticism is that we do not in fact experience representing as the essential way, or perhaps even as one of the essential ways, in which we relate to other things.

The argument then goes on to claim that such a 'representationalist' conception of our essential way of relating to things leads on the one hand to a conception of those things as 'representables', beings that can be represented, and therefore as fundamentally inert, and on the other to a conception of ourselves as 'representers', beings capable of representing such inertness—the cognitivist self-characterisation. Representer and represented become two basically different kinds of things. When the 'other thing' to which we relate in this representationalist way is another human being, we have to think of this thing as simultaneously a representable and a representer—a knowable and a knower. Yet, as argued above, we cannot conceive ourselves in both of these ways at once without contradiction.

Here, then, the immanent criticism supplements a version of the experiential criticism. The argument is that we misconceive our essential way of relating to things in a way that does not fit our actual experience of ourselves, and that this then leads to a contra-dictory account of ourselves. Accordingly, there must be a further, implicit, suggestion here: that if we were to conceive our essential way of relating to things in a way that did fit our experience we would not fall into such a contradictory account of ourselves.[6]

V

How else, then, should we conceive our essential way of relating to things? There are several options here: we could *substitute* the representationalist way of relating by a completely different one, thinking of that one instead as essential; we could *supplement* it by adding in other ways of relating as equally essential; or we could *subordinate* it as a subsidiary element within another way of relating to things which we think of as essential. I will leave aside the substitution option because it does not seem plausible to argue that we could cease altogether to relate to things representationally while remaining the kind of thing that we are. I will also leave aside the supplementing option, on the grounds that it would be more satis-factory if we could discover a unitary conception of our essential way of relating to things rather than seeing ourselves as having several unconnected but equally essential ways of relating.

6. I leave aside the question of why, in principle, a failure to match self-experience should lead to a contradiction in the resulting self-characterisation.

This leaves the subordination option. I shall look at one candidate for a unitary essential way of relating to things in which representation could be a subsidiary element. This is the one that Marx suggests in the first of the *Theses on Feuerbach*, 'praxis'.[7] I shall assume that what Marx has in mind by praxis is not physical activity in general but something like 'producing things for each other', where 'producing' is a matter of making something into something else which other members of our kind can use.[8]

If we conceive production for each other as our essential way of relating to things and to each other, this seems to lead to a conception of the things concerned as 'usables', as useful things. For this is how they figure from the point of view of production. The things we produce are useful to members of our kind, the things we use as raw materials are useful for turning into products, and the things we use as tools are useful for acting on those raw materials in order to turn them into products.

At the same time, this view gives us a conception of ourselves as producers and users of each other's products. What makes us members of our kind is now that we produce for others of our kind and use what others of our kind have produced for us. It follows that this is a rather peculiar kind. Each member of it is constituted as a member of the kind by virtue of the relations of producing-for and using-the-product-of (production relations[9]) that obtain between that individual and other members of the kind, who in turn are constituted as members of the kind in the same way. We all maintain each other as members of this kind by virtue of the production relations that we engage in with each other. I think that this is what Marx means when he says that the human essence is 'no *Abstraktum* inherent in each particular individual' but is in its actuality the 'ensemble of social relations'.[10] Production relations are 'interconstitutive'.[11] Their different forms then constitute not just different forms of society, but different ways of being the kind

7. K. Marx and F. Engels, *Collected Works*, London: Lawrence and Wishart, 1975–, vol. 5, p. 6.

8. I understand production in this sense to include transporting a product to its user. Here and below I use the term 'use' to mean 'employ either in order to achieve some end, or else as part of an activity pursued for its own sake'. In this sense one uses a bicycle when one gets to somewhere on it, but also when one just goes for a ride on it.

9. In defining a term of Marx's in this way, I am in effect claiming that this is what he too meant by the term.

10. Marx and Engels, op. cit., p. 7. Marx always conceives 'society' as a plurality of human beings bound together by producing things for each other.

of thing that we are: in Marx's terminology, different ways of being human.[12]

What we have, then, is a 'productionist' view of our essential way of relating to things, a productionist self-characterisation, and correlatively a functionalist characterisation of other things. On this account representing must remain a way of relating to things that is essential to our kind, for it is difficult to see how we could engage in producing from, or with, things, or in using the finished products, without at least on occasion representing these things to ourselves. Such representation, though, would be essential only in so far as it is a subordinate element in the relationship of producing things for each other and using those things. That is, what now counts as an essential way of relating to things is not representing things as such but 'representing things as part of the process of using them'.[13]

VI

Does this account of what makes us the kind of thing that we are match up with our self-experience? If we ask ourselves this question individually, then the answer seems to be no. It is true that producing and using each other's products are activities that saturate our lives—we go to work, cook, write, wear clothes, live in buildings, get to places by road, and so on. Yet it does not seem to me that I would cease to be the basic kind of thing that I am simply by ceasing to produce and use human products. To put it intuitively, if I was shipwrecked on a deserted island with nothing at all I would have a very uncomfortable time there, but I would

11. The idea of interconstitutive relations can be traced back via Feuerbach and Hegel to Fichte, for whom we are only rational and free in virtue of relations of mutual recognition between each other. See J.G. Fichte, *The Science of Rights*, tr. A.E. Kroeger, London: Truebner, 1889, §§1–4, pp. 31–83. It is at least foreshadowed in Rousseau's account of the social genesis of humanity in the *Discourse on Inequality*.

12. Marx does not make much of the distinction between humanity and the basic kind, defined by production relations, to which humans belong. He does have a distinct term for that kind, though: 'species-being'. The kind species-being is the kind whose members belong to it by virtue of producing for, and being produced for by, other members of that kind: by virtue of engaging in 'species-activity'. See Marx and Engels, *Collected Works*, vol. 3, pp. 216, 219, 275–6. The term 'species-being' comes from Feuerbach, but I think it is Fichte who first uses term 'species' (*Gattung*) to designate a kind the relations between whose members are interconstitutive. See Fichte, op. cit., p. 61.

13. In trying above to develop the connections between a productionist view of ourselves and a correlative view of other things from Marx's sketchy remarks in the *Theses on Feuerbach*, I have drawn on Heidegger's conceptions of *Vorhandenheit* (presence-at-hand) and *Zuhandenheit* (readiness-to-hand) in *Being and Time*, tr. J. Macquarrie and E. Robinson, Oxford: Blackwell, 1962.

still be a human being (emphasised). So on an individual level I do not seem to experience producing and using human products as essential to being the kind of thing that I am.

On the other hand, if we ask the question on a collective level then the match with experience looks much better. Suppose that for some reason we *all* stopped producing for each other, perhaps because for some reason we just lost any interest in using human products.[14] It seems plausible not only that, for those of us who survived, our existence would return to a pre-stone-age level, but that we would cease to have anything to say to each other. We might well then lose our capacity for language and with it our capacity for linguistically formulated thoughts, hence our cognitive capacities and even our capacity for differentiated emotions, in so far as that differentiation depends on conceptual content. We would become distinguishable from animals (or rather now from other animals) only physiologically. In short, it could plausibly be argued that all those individual characteristics which we experience as essential and unique to our kind are characteristics that depend on our belonging to a society of mutual production.

Admittedly, all that has been argued here is that belonging to a society of mutual production is necessary for having those characteristics. To demonstrate a full match with experience we would need to show that belonging to a society of mutual production is also sufficient for having those characteristics, but here too a plausible argument might be constructed.[15]

In the light of this, perhaps the productionist self-characterisation should be formulated as follows. What makes any *group* of things members of our basic kind is that they produce things for each other,

14. Admittedly it is difficult to imagine circumstances in which, being the kind of thing that we are, we could lose this interest. This difficulty makes it hard to carry out the thought experiment I am proposing here, but at bottom I think it strengthens the productionist case.

15. Even so, to show that production for each other is necessary and sufficient for our having the individual characteristics that we feel to be essential to us is not the same thing as showing that we feel such production itself to be essential to us, although as I have presented it the productionist account began with an appeal to the latter rather than the former aspect of our self-experience. In moving to the collective level, I have in effect used the former as an indicator of the latter. More seriously, it could be argued that to show in the way I have suggested that production for each other is necessary and sufficient for our having the characteristics we experience as essential is only to show that it 'makes us what we experience ourselves to be' in the consequential sense of 'makes' (as when we ask what it is that makes a dog bark) rather than in the constitutive sense (as when we ask what it is that makes a plant a vegetable—in virtue of what it counts as one), and that it is in the constitutive sense that we need a match with experience. I think that the productionist response to this would have to be that in the context of the ontological question no clear distinction between the two senses of 'make' can be maintained, but I cannot take this further here.

and so individually possess the characteristics that follow from such mutual production.[16] What makes any *individual* thing a member of that kind is that it has acquired those characteristics by virtue of participation in such a group.[17]

VII

Still, the productionist account, with its particular answer to the first person plural ontological question, is open to some obvious criticisms. I will mention four, and then conclude by raising the question of whether this account avoids giving rise to contradictory self-characterisation.

Firstly, there is an asymmetry in the way that I have characterised things of our own kind and other things. Our own kind is characterised by the fact that its members actually engage in production for each other. The other kind is characterised by the fact its members *could* in principle be used by members of our kind. By means of this characterisation, it is possible to include all the physical things we can ever encounter in the second kind, since it is always possible that any of them could serve in some way in production or use. We have used the stars for navigation, for example. Nevertheless, the asymmetry is worrying.[18]

Secondly, as in the case of the 'representer/represented' conception, we end up with just two types of things in the world: human beings (and whatever undiscovered creatures there may be of the same kind as us) and everything else. Animal and plants have just the same status in this division as inanimate objects. This seems inadequate. Surely the differences between animals and inanimate things, for example, are in their way as fundamental as the differences between animals and human beings?

Thirdly, this division of the universe into two kinds of things, things of our own kind and things that are potentially useful for our

16. They would not need to produce things for all members of their kind, or even of their biological species (although Marx does seem to think that the latter is necessary for humans to fully realise their nature as species -beings). So groups of beings completely isolated from each other, even by having quite different physiologies and needs, could still belong to this same kind.

17. A wolf-child, then, would not count as belonging to this kind, though of course it would still belong to the biological species *Homo Sapiens*.

18. It could be removed by characterising our own kind as things that are *capable* of producing for each other, but this would eliminate the idea of interconstitutive relations and instead reduce what makes us the kind of thing we are back to an '*Abstraktum* inherent in each particular individual'.

kind, looks profoundly anthropocentric, or at least 'our-kind-centric'. To put the point metaphorically, by what right can we throw everything in the universe, apart from our selves and any others of our particular kind, into a single kind and label it 'things that may possibly be useful to us'? Don't things have their own species and genera, independently of whether or not they could be of any use to us? A response to this criticism might be that it betrays an underlying account of things as 'representables', which is just what is being contested, but I shall not try to pursue this here.

Fourthly, if producing for each other is what makes a group of things members of our kind, then it would seem that ants, for example, must count as members. To avoid this, we would have to make it explicit that producing-for (and perhaps also using-the-product-of) is an intentional relation, that is, one that involves actions in which the other parties, and the things produced, figure as intentional objects. Unless an account of such actions can be given which does not involve representation, this reintroduces representation at the ground level of the account of our essential relations.

It may well be possible to overcome these criticisms, but from the point of view of this paper I think there is a more urgent question about the productionist account: does it give us a self-characterisation that is not contradictory in the way that I have suggested that cognitivist ones are? If it does not then it cannot rely on the immanent criticism of cognitivist accounts as part of the argument in its favour, since it will be susceptible to the same kind of criticism itself.

The contradiction arose because we had to conceive ourselves at once as 'representables' and as 'representers'. Yet in so far as we conceived ourselves as representables it was difficult to take our own representations of the world seriously. Now the productionist account of our essential relations has a basic difference from the representationalist one that I have associated with cognitivist self-characterisations. In it our essential way of relating is not a two-way but a three-way one, between individual human beings as producers, things, and individual human beings as users of products. Thus this way of relating has built into its structure a distinction between two different kinds of thing to which one relates: the thing that one uses in production (or as a product) and the fellow member of one's own kind for whom one produces (or whose product one uses). The representationalist way of relating only occurs within this relation as a subsidiary way of relating to the things that one uses, whether as raw materials, tools, or products. It is these things that are conceived as 'representables'. Therefore it could be said that the contradiction that results from characterising human beings as both representers and representables cannot arise, since human beings do not figure at all as representables in our essential way of relating to things and each other.

Nevertheless, even if in this way of thinking things only figure as representables in the context of figuring as 'usables', surely we are quite capable of treating our fellow human beings as usables, and thus also as representables, so the original problem seems to arise again.

Perhaps the best response to this from the productionist point of view is to agree that this does happen, in fact it happens all the time. Class society is precisely a society in which one section of society treats another as usables. Yet on the productionist account such treatment is at odds with the essential character of our kind. It is the practical equivalent of a category mistake. If we adopt the productionist way of thinking about ourselves, though, we do not have to repeat this mistake on the theoretical plane, and as long as we avoid doing so we will not run into contradiction.

To summarise: I have suggested that cognitivist answers to the first person plural ontological question lead to a contradiction in our self-characterisation, and also that they can be attacked for failing to match up to our ordinary sense of what we are. I have tried to connect these criticisms through an argument according to which it is a representationalist conception of our essential way of relating to things, one at odds with our ordinary self-experience, that is responsible for both cognitivist self-characterisations and their internal contradiction. Finally I have looked briefly at an alternative productionist conception of our essential way of relating to things, derived from Marx, to see how well it matches our sense of what we are and avoids the same internal contradiction. My conclusion is that the productionist conception has problems, but that, as we say, it deserves further research.

School of English and American Studies
University of Sussex
Falmer
Brighton BN1 9QN

DISCUSSIONS

CRANE ON MENTAL CAUSATION

by William Child

I

It is often held that the mental is in some way constituted by, composed of, realized by, or supervenient on, the physical. In a recent paper Tim Crane argues that this view (or family of views), which he calls *orthodox physicalism*, is either unstable or unmotivated.[1] It is unstable if it lacks the resources to show that mental causes 'have their effects in virtue of their mental properties'. It is unmotivated if it tries to accommodate the causal relevance of mental properties in one of the standard ways; for the standard accounts undermine the usual motivations for orthodox physicalism.

II

Crane's account of the motivation for orthodox physicalism can be summarized thus. 'We want to say (i) that mental properties of causes are causally responsible for their effects and (ii) that physical features of causes completely suffice for all physical effects. But we also think (iii) that effects that have both mental and physical causes are not overdetermined by those mental and physical causes. The apparent conflict between (i)–(iii) can be resolved if we conclude that a cause's (possession of) mental features is constituted by its (possession of) physical features.'

Crane's next point is that, in giving an account of the causal relevance of mental properties, orthodox physicalists standardly say something like the following: for a mental property to be causally responsible for an effect is for it to be constituted by physical properties that are causally responsible for that effect. He cites a number of accounts that take this general form.[2]

1. Crane 1995; all page references in the text are to this article, unless stated otherwise. Crane introduces orthodox physicalism as the view that 'there is some... relation of "constitution" between the mental and the physical' (211). He mentions the other notions (composition, realization, supervenience) along the way, taking them either to be inter-changeable with 'constitution' or to be ways of describing the constitution theory (212, 220, 229, 235).

2. Crane (233–4) mentions Kim's 1993 account of mental causation as supervenient causation, as well as the accounts offered by Block 1990, Papineau 1993 and Yablo 1992.

But, Crane argues, such accounts undermine the original motivation for orthodox physicalism. If we explain the causal relevance of mental properties in the way just suggested, then mental causation 'cannot be the same relation as physical causation' (233). But, Crane claims, the original motivation for physicalism depended on the idea that mental and physical causation *are* the same relation—that they are 'homogeneous' (219, 235). If homogeneity is denied, then the fact that an event has both mental and physical causes will not even appear to show that that event is overdetermined; for an event is overdetermined only if it is produced by distinct causes in the very same sense. And if there is not even the appearance of overdetermination, there is nothing to be resolved by appeal to the idea that mental causes are constituted by physical causes. So the standard defence of the causal relevance of mental properties undermines the usual motivation for orthodox physicalism.[3]

III

I think Crane's argument fails to show that orthodox physicalism is unmotivated.

In the first place, there is something odd about Crane's reading of the dialectical position. The orthodox physicalist will see things in the following way. We start off with a worry about overdetermination. The constitution view, with its account of mental causation as supervenient causation, then shows that mental causation is a different kind of causation from physical causation; the theory thereby shows how it is possible for an effect to have both mental and physical causes without being overdetermined by them. Now Crane suggests that we can detach this conclusion from the theory. He thinks we could simply have asserted at the outset that mental and physical causation are different kinds of causation; so we could have seen at the outset that there is no problem about overdetermination, without ever needing the constitution theory. But this seems evidently fallacious. If an apparent problem is shown to be illusory given the acceptance of a certain theory, we cannot simply help ourselves to the conclusion that the problem is illusory without accepting the theory.

To answer this defence of orthodox physicalism, Crane would need to show that we can make sense of the idea that mental and physical causes produce their effects in different ways in advance of having any account,

---

3. I follow Crane's way of setting things up: first, in allowing causation to be a relation between *properties*, or a relation that holds *in virtue of* this or that property of a cause; second, in raising questions about which properties of causes are *causally relevant*; and third, in considering whether or not mental and physical causation are the *same kind of causation*. My own preference would be to see causation as a relation between events, and to pose the other questions in terms of causal explanation. (See my 1994, ch. 3 §2 and ch. 6 §§2–6.).

like the constitution view, that gives us a way of understanding *how* mental and physical causation are different relations. Unless he does so, the orthodox physicalist is entitled to reject Crane's criticism, for the reasons just given.

We can put the point like this. Consider the following claims:

(I)   Mental and physical causes produce their effects in the same sense,

(II)   Effects are not overdetermined by mental and physical causes,

(III) Mental causes are not identical with physical causes.

In Crane's account, the argument for orthodox physicalism accepts all of (I)–(III); it then invokes the idea that mental causes are constituted by physical causes in order to show how it is possible for (II) to be true, given (I) and (III). Given that understanding of the argument, it is not surprising that, in Crane's view, the argument collapses if we drop (I); for (I) is an essential premise. I am suggesting a different way of seeing the argument, in which it does not have (I) as a premise. In this view, the appeal to the constitution view explains how (II) can be true by giving an account in which mental and physical causes produce their effects in different senses, an account that therefore shows that (I) is false.

Both versions of the argument aim to show that it is not the case that effects are produced in the same sense by distinct mental and physical causes. But the two versions avoid overdetermination in different ways. In Crane's version, we avoid overdetermination by showing that effects *are* produced in the same sense by their mental and physical causes, but that those causes are not distinct. In the version I am suggesting, we avoid overdetermination by showing that effects are *not* produced in the same sense by their mental and physical causes.

This first response to Crane accepts his characterization of the worry about overdetermination, but gives a different account of the way the constitution view resolves it. A different response would be to reject Crane's account of the original overdetermination worry altogether.

There are cases in which an effect is overdetermined by two independently operating causes. Crane gives an example: 'Suppose a man is killed by being simultaneously shot and stabbed. Both the stabbing and the shooting kill him, but either would have done so if the other hadn't' (215). According to the second response to Crane, the physicalist's point in insisting that effects are not overdetermined by mental and physical causes is that mental and physical causes are not related like that; unlike the shooting and the stabbing, they do not operate independently. More specifically, if the mental causes of an effect were absent, the effect would not have occurred nonetheless, brought about by its physical causes; nor can a physical effect be produced by the operation of mental causes alone, in the absence of any physical causes. The argument for a constitution view is then that we need an account of what makes it true that, if a cause had not had the mental properties it did, it would not have produced the effect it did; and the constitution view is the best account available. Understood in this way, the argument has nothing to do with the homogeneity of mental and physical causation; even if we started with the assertion that mental and physical causation are not homogeneous, we would still need to say something about the relation between mental and physical causes to make intelligible the fact that effects are not overdetermined by mental and physical causes in the way just specified. So, once more, Crane's main point fails to undermine the motivation for orthodox physicalism.

However, a new question arises at this point. In the current view, the motivation for orthodox physicalism comes from an argument to the best explanation, where the *explanandum* is the fact that, if a cause had not had the mental properties it did, it would not have produced the effect it did. To show that orthodox physicalism does indeed provide the best explanation, we would need to show that there is no better account of the truth of the counterfactual claim. And Crane canvasses a rival account.

IV

At one stage in his paper, Crane briefly describes a 'non-physicalist' view which, he thinks, is 'plausible' though 'unpopular' (232).[4] The idea is that a mental cause and a physical cause can bring about the same effect, though the mental cause is neither identical with, nor constituted by, the physical cause. This view recognizes that it would be 'implausible [to] claim that in putative cases of mental causation, if the mental phenomenon had not been there, the physical effects would still have happened' (231). And it recognizes the need to say something about the relation between mental and physical properties, which will ground the appropriate counterfactual claim. What it appeals to is a psychophysical law: 'Suppose I have a pain which causes me to go to the cupboard and get an aspirin. The pain and the brain state are both actual causes of my going to the cupboard, and since they are linked by a psychophysical law it is not a coincidence that both causes result in me going to the cupboard' (232). As Crane says, this has the desired consequence for the relevant counterfactual: 'it wouldn't be true that if I hadn't had the pain, I would still have gone to the cupboard. The reason is that because the pain and the brain state are linked by a psychophysical law, the closest worlds in

4. Crane actually describes two non-physicalist views. It is unclear to me that they really differ; and unclear that the principle of the completeness of physics said to be rejected by the first view (231) is the same as the principle that is endorsed by orthodox physicalism (217)

which I didn't have the pain are worlds in which I didn't have the brain state either' (232).

The difference between orthodox physicalism and Crane's alternative[5] lies in what they conceive as grounding the claim that, if a mental cause had not occurred, or been present, its effect would not have occurred anyway, produced by its physical causes: orthodox physicalism grounds the counterfactual in the thesis that mental causes are constituted by physical causes; Crane's alternative grounds it in the thesis that there are psychophysical laws linking mental and physical causes. What can be said to adjudicate between these views?

If the psychophysical laws envisaged by Crane's alternative are laws linking particular propositional attitudes with particular brain states, I myself would reject this alternative; following Davidson, I would argue that the role of rationality in our understanding of mental phenomena rules out the possibility that particular physical properties of a person could be matched up, even on an occasion, with particular mental properties.[6] But that is not an argument open to the orthodox physicalist, who himself holds that particular mental properties are constituted by particular physical properties.

What, then, could an orthodox physicalist say against Crane's alternative? The question for him to press is how we are to make sense of the relevant psychophysical laws obtaining. If some actual mental property of mine and some actual brain property are linked by a psychophysical law then, as Crane notes, the closest non-actual worlds in which I don't have the mental property are worlds in which I don't have the brain property either (232). But why is this so? What accounts for the link? The orthodox physicalist has an answer to that question; if my wanting to break the window is constituted by my being in a given physical state it follows naturally that, had I not wanted to break the window then, *ceteris paribus*, I would not have been in that physical state. Crane's alternative, by contrast, has nothing to say about why the worlds in which I do not have the desire are worlds in which I do not have the associated brain property either—other than to repeat that the two states, or properties, are linked by law.

Does this matter? There will always be some sets of properties, linked by law, for which there is no story to tell about why, in nearby worlds in which something lacks one property, it also lacks another. Some laws, that is, are barely true. But there is no good reason to take a given law as barely true if an account of why it obtains is actually available, or looks to be available. If there were no such account then perhaps we would have to

5. 'Crane's alternative' is just a label for the position. I do not mean to suggest that it is Crane's own view.

6. See my 1994, ch. 2.

acknowledge that the psychophysical law was a matter of brute correlation. But, the orthodox physicalist says, we can see a way of explaining the correlation; and it is more rational to accept that explanation than to insist that this is just a brute psychophysical correlation.

To resist this thought, we would need some positive argument, from the advocate of Crane's alternative, for thinking that a person's possession of a mental property *could not* be constituted by her possession of a physical property, an argument compatible with saying that the two properties are linked by a psychophysical law. If there is such a reason, Crane does not give it.[7]

V

For my own part, I disagree with the orthodox physicalist about the level at which we can explain why a person's mental properties depend on her physical properties: the orthodox physicalist thinks we can match up particular mental and physical properties; I think we can say only that a person's mental properties as a whole are determined, given the context, by her overall physical constitution. So I do not, in the end, want to defend the precise form of constitution view that Crane attacks. Nonetheless, I agree with the orthodox physicalist's general line of argument: an appropriate constitution view is to be preferred to the acceptance of brute correlations; and there is, contrary to Crane's doubts (235–6), adequate motivation for a kind of physicalism that is stronger than the denial of Cartesian dualism but weaker than a psychophysical identity theory.[8]

University College
Oxford
OX1 4BH

BIBLIOGRAPHY

Block, Ned 1990: 'Can the Mind Change the World?', in G. Boolos (ed.), *Meaning and Method* (Cambridge: Cambridge University Press).
Child, William 1994: *Causality, Interpretation and the Mind* (Oxford: Clarendon Press).
Crane, Tim 1995: 'The Mental Causation Debate', *Aristotelian Society Supplementary Volume*, 69 (1995), 211–36.
Kim, Jaegwon 1993: 'Epiphenomenal and Supervenient Causation', in his *Supervenience and Mind* (Cambridge: Cambridge University Press).
Papineau, David 1993: *Philosophical Naturalism* (Oxford: Basil Blackwell).
Yablo, Stephen 1992: 'Mental Causation', *Philosophical Review*, 101, pp. 245–80.

7. Nor, to be fair, did he aim to. His purpose was to attack the motivation for the constitution view, not its coherence.

8. For my positive views about the relation between the mental and the physical, and between psychological and non-psychological causal explanations, see my 1994 *passim*, but especially ch. 2, ch. 3 §3 and ch. 6.

REPLY TO CHILD

by Tim Crane

In 'The Mental Causation Debate' (1995), I pointed out the parallel between the premises in some traditional arguments for physicalism and the assumptions which give rise to the problem of mental causation. I argued that the dominant contemporary version of physicalism finds mental causation problematic because it accepts the main premises of the traditional arguments, but rejects their conclusion: the identification of mental with physical causes. Moreover, the orthodox way of responding to this problem (which I call the 'constitution view') implicitly rejects an assumption hidden in the original argument for physicalism: the assumption that mental and physical causation are the same kind of relation ('homogeneity'). The conclusion of my paper was that if you reject homogeneity, then there is no obvious need for an account of the relation between mental and physical properties.

William Child challenges this conclusion on two grounds. First, he challenges the idea that the constitution view has no motivation once homogeneity is denied. And second, he claims that the constitution view's solution to the mental causation problem is preferable to one of the non-physicalist solutions I describe in section IX of my 1995 paper. I shall take each point in turn.

Child's first point is that the constitution view can be seen as a way of explaining how the denial of an identity theory of mental and physical causes is consistent with the completeness of physics and the denial of overdetermination. He proposes two ways of construing this sort of argument for the constitution view. The first argument does not assume homogeneity, but rather, in explaining why it is that mental and physical causes do not overdetermine their effects, it constructs a theory which delivers the consequence that homogeneity is false. The second argument says that even if we start off with a rejection of homogeneity, we still need to explain why overdetermination is false, and the constitution view is the best explanation of this.

I agree with Child that the constitution view should not argue from the premise that homogeneity is true, to a conclusion which denies homogeneity. But I did not present the argument for the constitution view in this way. That is, I did not say that the constitution view presents its own motivation in terms of the rejection of homogeneity. I said that the arguments for the *identity* theories must assume homogeneity. I did not discuss distinct arguments for the constitution view, since it seemed to me that the view is normally defended on the basis of a general commitment to physicalism, plus a recoil from the identity theory, rather than on the basis of a specific argument for constitution. My claim was then that given the need to avoid both the identity theory and overdetermination, the best way to make sense of the constitution view's solutions to the mental causation problem is to see it as rejecting homogeneity.

Since Child seems to agree with this last claim, the question which divides us is whether denying homogeneity removes any motivation for the constitution view. Child thinks that it does not. The essence of his objection is that 'even if we started with the assertion that mental and physical causation are not homogeneous, we would still need to say something about the relation between mental and physical causes to make intelligible the fact that effects are not overdetermined by mental and physical causes'. And the point of the constitution view is to make this intelligible.

The situation Child asks us to envisage is one where it seems that a mental cause produces a certain effect E, and a distinct physical cause produces E, but there is no commitment to the idea that the causes produce E in the same sense. And this situation is supposed to create apparent overdetermination, to be resolved by the postulation of a constitution relation between the mental and the physical cause.

How should we make sense of the idea of two distinct causes 'producing' the same effect in different senses? And if we can make sense of it, would the situation described be an apparently problematic case of overdetermination? I shall argue that we cannot make sense of this idea independently of the specific theories of mental causation advanced in this context; and that once we look at the issue in this light, there is no further problem of overdetermination for the constitution view to resolve.

In the context of contemporary theories of causation, the question of whether mental and physical causation are homogeneous is not one which would necessarily occur to someone independently of thinking about this particular problem of mental causation. Why should someone worry about whether these kinds of causation are distinct, prior to any consideration of whether mental causation is compatible with physicalism? Someone might have a thesis about physical causation—for instance, that it is the transfer of energy—and then worry about how there can be mental causation, given this view. Or someone might think, with Papineau (1993), that all physical effects have their chances fixed by prior physical causes, and then worry about what role the mental can play in fixing the chances of physical effects. Aside from these sorts of considerations, it is hard to see why anyone should raise the question of homogeneity.

So to understand what it really means to deny homogeneity, we would need to look at the specific accounts of mental causation which rely on its denial: Jackson and Pettit's (1988) account of mental causes as programming for their effects; Dretske's (1988) account of mental causes as structuring causes rather than triggering causes; Kim's (1993) theory of supervenient causation; and Yablo's (1992) account of mental causation. I will take it, then, that this is the sort of thing one means by denying homogeneity. My aim here is not to dispute the coherence of these accounts, but to raise the following question. Suppose we had one of these accounts in mind when denying homogeneity—would the worry about overdetermination still arise?

As Child says, a genuine case of overdetermination of a physical effect by a mental and a physical cause, is a case where the following counterfactuals are true:

(M) If the mental cause had not occurred, then the physical effect would still have occurred;

(P) If the physical cause had not occurred, then the physical effect would still have occurred.

The guiding idea of the accounts of mental causation just mentioned is that the 'higher-level' mental cause ensures (e.g. by structuring or programming mental causation) the occurrence of the physical effect by ensuring that some physical effect or other brings about (e.g. by process or triggering physical causation) the physical effect. So on this kind of view, (P) is true: the closest worlds where the particular physical cause does not occur are worlds where the effect still occurs, because the mental cause would have 'ensured' that some other physical cause would step in and do its job.

But (M) is false, on these views of mental causation. For once we have accepted the two-causation picture of mental and physical causation, it just isn't true that if the mental cause had been absent, the physical effect would still have occurred. The whole point of the two-causation picture is to explain the sense in which 'higher-level' properties *make it the case* that some 'lower-level' property will produce the effect. For example: Jackson and Pettit (1990, p. 114) consider an explanation of why a piece of uranium emitted radiation over a certain period in terms of the fact that some of its atoms were decaying. Their account of this explanation is that the piece of uranium's property of having some of its atoms decaying 'programmes for' the emission of radiation. The existence of this property means

> that there would be a suitably efficacious property available, perhaps that involving such and such particular atoms, perhaps one

involving others. And so the property was causally relevant to the radiation, under a perfectly ordinary sense of relevance, though it was not efficacious. (1990 p. 114)

If the higher-level explanation is indispensable, as Jackson and Pettit argue it often is, then the lower level property will not produce the effect unless the higher-order property also programmes for the effect. On this view, then, it is obvious that the closest worlds where the programming cause does not exist will therefore be ones where the lower-level efficacious property does not exist. So (M) is false and there is no problem of overdetermination.[1]

I disagree with Child, then, that one can formulate a genuine worry about overdetermination even if one has denied homogeneity, since to make real sense of denying homogeneity, one has to have some account of the ways in which the distinct kinds of causation *are* distinct. But once such an account is in place, overdetermination will not be an issue. I conclude, against Child, that homogeneity is essential to formulating the worry about overdetermination.

Child may respond here that this concedes one of his critical points: that it is only in the context of a constitution view that one has a motive for denying homogeneity. So, he may say, one cannot just assert the denial of homogeneity without bringing to bear the theory which supports this denial: this would be to 'detach the conclusion [the denial of homogeneity] from the theory [the constitution view]'.

But there are two kinds of theory under discussion: the theory of causation, and the constitution view. And what the discussion above reveals is that the question of how to spell out the denial of homogeneity is distinct from the question of constitution. For consider: one could accept the distinction between two kinds of causation even if one were not a physicalist of any kind at all. A parallelist dualist might think that mental causation was one kind of thing, physical causation another. And someone could, I suppose, accept the idea that the mental is constituted by the physical even if they accept homogeneity (though they would probably be forced into accepting epiphenomenalism about mental properties).

My original claim was not over whether there is any motive for denying *homogeneity*. Although I would accept homogeneity myself, I think that its denial is a live option. My claim was rather about whether there is any motive for the idea that the mental is *constituted* by the physical once homogeneity is denied (and presumably, once some theory such as

1. Here I have illustrated my point using Jackson and Pettit's account, for simplicity of exposition. But it would be a simple matter to show how the point applies to Dretkse's and Yablo's accounts too. The situation with Kim's account is complicated by the fact that he treats supervenient causation as 'epiphenomenal causation'.

programming, structuring or supervenient causation is accepted in its place).[2] Of course, many theories of mental causation are also theories of constitution (Yablo 1992 is a case in point). But this does not mean that the issues are not distinct.

Putting the question of motivation to one side, I now turn to Child's second criticism of my paper. The burden of this criticism is that the constitution view can be seen as offering the best explanation of why certain effects are not overdetermined by mental and physical causes. But this defence will work only if there are no better explanations available. This is why Child argues in section 4 of his paper that the non-physicalist view I described in my paper compares unfavourably to the constitution view.

The non-physicalist alternative solves the problem of over-determination not by denying homogeneity, but by saying that the mental and physical causes are linked by psychophysical law. Child's criticism of this alternative is that, unlike the constitution view, it can provide no account of why this law is true: it must accept that the law is barely true. 'And there is no good reason to take a law as barely true if an account of why it obtains is actually available.'

But a defender of the non-physicalist alternative is not obliged to say that there is nothing more to say about why these laws hold. The claim that there are psychophysical laws is supposed to be an empirical speculation, albeit one which has some support in our own experience of the mind (see Crane and Mellor 1990). But nothing in this claim rules out the possibility that there are other laws which give some explanation of why these laws hold. There is no need for the non-physicalist to take a stand on this issue merely by making the claim about psychophysical laws.[3]

Child may say that to explain the holding of psychophysical laws in terms of other laws will not satisfy a defender of the constitution view. For statements of these laws will—like any law-statements—be contingent, and the fact that the laws hold, and their relations to the psycho-physical laws, may well be 'brute'. What the constitution view requires is a more

2. Perhaps Child's conflation of these two distinct ideas is revealed when he talks about 'the constitution view, *with its account of mental causation as supervenient causation*' (my emphasis). My present point is that the constitution view is one thing, the account of mental causation another. Similarly, Child claims that to make my criticism stick, I need to explain how homogeneity is denied 'in advance of having any account, *like the constitution view*, that gives us a way of understanding *how* mental and physical causation are different relations' (my emphasis). I agree that to understand how homogeneity might be denied, we need to have some account of this. But the relevant account will be an account of causation, not of constitution.

3. Child himself would reject the claim that the existence of psychophysical laws is an empirical issue (see his 1994, chapter 2). But this question is orthogonal to the dispute between the constitution view and me.

illuminating account of how mental and physical properties are related. But what justification can be provided for this requirement? After all, we cannot expect the truth of every law-statement to be explicable in terms of the truth of some other statement: Child himself accepts that some law-statements will be barely true. What *a priori* reasons are there for thinking that we know, prior to any empirical investigation, which kinds of laws these will be? Neither Child nor any defender of the constitution view has provided such a reason.

My two responses to Child have something in common. Both responses express scepticism about the extent to which we need a distinctively *metaphysical* account—like 'constitution'—of the relation between mind and body, once considerations about dualism or over-determination are out of the picture. On this way of looking at things, the non-physicalist alternative is metaphysically cautious: within the naturalistic context of contemporary discussions of physicalism, it should be an open empirical question which laws apply to the mind, and therefore it should be an open question whether certain psychophysical laws are barely true. Given the adequacy of my first response to Child, his objection to the non-physicalist alternative appears to amount to a metaphysical objection to 'brute' nomic correlations involving mental properties. But without some further motivation for the constitution view, physicalists are not entitled to this objection.

Department of Philosophy
University College London
Gower Street
London WC1E 6BT
tim.crane@ucl.ac.uk

REFERENCES

W. Child (1994), *Causality, Interpretation and the Mind* Oxford: Clarendon Press.
W. Child (1997), 'Crane on Mental Causation' *Proceedings of the Aristotelian Society,* Vol. XCVII, 1997.
T. Crane and D.H. Mellor (1990), 'There is no Question of Physicalism' *Mind* 99 pp. 185–206.
F. Dretske (1988), *Explaining Behaviour* Cambridge, Mass.: MIT Press.
F. Jackson and P. Pettit (1988), 'Functionalism and Broad Content' *Mind* 97 pp. 381–400.
F. Jackson and P. Pettit (1990), 'Program Explanation: a General Perspective' *Analysis* 50 pp. 107–117.
J. Kim (1993), 'Epiphenomenal and Supervenient Causation' in *Supervenience and Mind* Cambridge: Cambridge University Press.
D. Papineau (1993), *Philosophical Naturalism* Oxford: Blackwell.
S. Yablo (1992) 'Mental Causation' *Philosophical Review* 101 pp. 245–280.

VI*—SUFFICIENT REASON

by Ralph Walker

L eibniz presents the Principle of Sufficient Reason as holding universally within the created world. He gives us various formulations of it; examples are 'Nothing is without a reason', and 'Nothing takes place without a sufficient reason, that is, nothing happens without its being possible, for someone who knew enough about things, to give a reason which would suffice to determine why it is thus and not otherwise'.[1] Ultimately, he thinks, this leads us to seek a sufficient reason for the existence of the world itself, and to find it in God's choice of the best. For any particular object or event, there will be a less ultimate explanation to be found as well: the sun is shining because there is a gap in the clouds. But any such explanation is incomplete. Filling it out leads us in due course to fundamental statements about the world we live in, and the question becomes why that world (a world governed by these laws, and with those initial conditions) exists. The answer is that the actual world has been chosen by God because it is the best of all possible worlds.

This naturally raises the question what sufficient reason there is for God's choice, or for the existence of God himself. Leibniz recognizes the danger of this regress.[2] He has to show that the regress *must* terminate here, or at least that there is nothing arbitrary about our stopping the quest for reasons here. Most people think there is no way of satisfying this ideal of an absolutely complete explanation, in which the regress is terminated. I want to show that there is nothing wrong in principle with the idea that the regress can terminate, and terminate with God. Whether it can be made to do

---

1. When referring to the works of Leibniz available in the translation by R. Ariew and D. Garber, *G.W. Leibniz: Philosophical Essays* (Indianapolis: Hackett, 1989), I shall give page references to that translation, though I have not always followed it. I shall abbreviate it AG. These two quotations are from 'First Truths', AG p. 30, and 'Principles of Nature and Grace', sect. 7, AG p. 210.

2. 'Principles of Nature and Grace', sect. 8, AG p. 210.

*Meeting of the Aristotelian Society, held in the Senior Common Room, Birkbeck College, London, on Monday, 13th January, 1997 at 8.15 p.m.

so in practice is another matter, and on that I shall do no more than indicate where an argument lies.

I

First, however, more needs to be said about the Principle of Sufficient Reason itself, because it may seem to be just an outdated metaphysical assumption. It cannot be outdated altogether, because what it says is that whatever happens has an explanation, and an explanation which we could in principle recognize as such. As a methodological assumption this is as indispensable now as it was to Leibniz, though we may have lost his confidence that there will always be an explanation to be found. In assuming that whatever explanations we do find are recognizable as such, we inevitably rely on criteria of simplicity or neatness, criteria which determine what constitutes a best, or an adequate, explanation in any particular case. What is more (and just as vital), we cannot satisfy ourselves with a mere exhortation to look for such explanations. We may not agree with Leibniz that such explanations are always to be found, but we think not only that they are always to be sought: we agree with him also in believing that where we *do* find them, they give us the truth about the world. We rely on that assumption every time we judge that something before us continues to exist when we are not perceiving it; we rely on it in every inductive inference. From the observation that grass has always been green in the past we move to the prediction that it will be green tomorrow, but what mediates that is the idea that this is the simplest hypothesis; the prediction that grass is in general green (within our part of the universe at any rate) is the best explanation for the observed uniformity, and it entails the prediction.

It is worth noticing how large an assumption we are making here. Our preferences for mathematical simplicity and for neatness of overall theory are, after all, *our* preferences, and the fact that 'green' seems to us a simpler predicate than 'grue' is likewise a fact about us. To suppose that these preferences of ours yield truth about the world is to suppose something rather remarkable: that there is some kind of built-in correspondence between the way we think and the way the world works. Our considerable success in explaining things, and in basing on our explanations predictions that turn out accurate, might be thought to provide a justification for expecting that success to continue. But that justification would be inductive, and our inductive practices themselves depend on just those preferences the success of which seems so remarkable. The inductive principle is only a special case of the general tendency to choose simple hypotheses, by projecting the continuance of a uniformity, and in applying it we employ an assessment of simplicity which is inevitably our own—as the 'green'/'grue' example shows. So the remarkable fact remains.

The difference between scientific realists and instrumentalists is a difference over the way in which our explanations relate to the world, within certain fields (deemed 'scientific'). Scientific realists think that if we can get the best possible overall explanation of a phenomenon, that explanation will itself be true. Instrumentalists deny this, holding rather that the explanation's value lies in its predictive power and its capacity to suggest new lines to explore. It need not, and should not, be taken itself to be claiming truth. For our present purposes this dispute need not concern us. Whichever view one takes, the remarkable fact remains: the explanations that meet our criteria for simplicity and neatness are the ones that yield predictions that turn out true. Moreover, even instrumentalists agree that in everyday (as opposed to 'scientific') matters we take the explanations to be true themselves.[3] The footprints at the window and the body in the library serve not only to predict the butler's confession; they tell us that he murdered the colonel.

Of course, the more our explanations try to explain, and the closer they come to pretending completeness, the more likely it is that their claims to truth will need to be qualified in any case. As more evidence turns up, and as more reflection goes on, the account that seemed to be the simplest overall may be superseded by another, as Newtonian mechanics has been superseded. It may be sensible, therefore, for even the most committed scientific realist to claim only approximate truth in such cases, while no doubt also observing that it would be highly mysterious if Newtonian mechanics could have yielded so many accurate predictions without being even close to the truth. Thus the explanation that seems to us best at a given time may not be the exact truth, because it may need subsequent revision; but the subsequent revision would take the form of showing some alternative explanation more fully

3. Thus B.C. van Fraassen, *The Scientific Image* (Oxford: Clarendon Press, 1980), pp. 19 f.

to satisfy our criteria of overall simplicity, and these are not in any way undermined as guides to truth.

So we, like Leibniz, accept not only the methodological requirement to search for sufficient reasons, or best explanations, wherever they can be found; we also share his assumption that when we find them these explanations yield us truth about the world, or approximate truth anyway. None of this tells us what an explanation is, and Leibniz is no clearer on that than most other writers. The criteria that determine which explanations are best are, as we have seen, our criteria, but if an explanation is true it must tell us something about how the world is. It must give us some condition on which the *explanandum* depends. At least, it must if it is to be an explanation in the ordinary sense—an explanation of why something is or comes to be. The term 'Principle of Sufficient Reason' suggests the condition should be a sufficient condition, and no doubt Leibniz thought this. He rejects the idea of an indeterministic universe because the Principle would not be universally true within it. We might think, on the contrary, that the universe may be indeterministic, containing events which lack sufficient conditions of the required sort, but that these events can still be given explanations, perhaps of a statistical kind. However here our difference from Leibniz is less great than it may appear, and consists only in his believing, and our rejecting, that everything that happens can be explained *fully*. No difference in the conception of explanation is involved, for we can readily agree with him that events which lack sufficient conditions (of the required sort) cannot be explained fully. Instead of explaining them fully we may be able to cite factors that explain them partially, increasing their probability, while at the same time we continue to feel the desirability of getting a full explanation if one is possible. These factors that increase probability are again conditions of the events they explain.

What matters more is to have some idea of the kind of conditions we are talking about, for evidently not all conditions are explanatory. Logical sufficiency is not what is required: we cannot say that the presence of a sheep in the room is explained by the fact that there are two sheep in the room. Not just any non-logical sufficient condition will do either. The condition must be responsible for the event's occurrence, or for the thing's being as it is. In some circumstances the presence of certain track-marks will be a sufficient condition of a lion's having passed by a day earlier, but one would explain the tracks by reference to the lion's passing and not the lion's passing by reference to the tracks. The tracks may be a sufficient condition of the lion's having passed but they are not responsible for it. I shall say that they are not a *determining* sufficient condition. A determining sufficient condition is a condition which is responsible for that thing or productive of it. Without it, the effect might perhaps have come about in some other way, but it would not have come about *anyway*—if it would have come about anyway, the condition we are concerned with would not have been responsible for it.

I doubt if the notion of a determining condition can be further analysed, but for our present purposes that does not matter. What matters is that the Principle of Sufficient Reason enjoins us to seek determining sufficient conditions for whatever is or comes to be; and tells us that by seeking for explanations that meet our criteria of simplicity and the like, we shall come to the truth or at any rate close to it. Thus far we can agree with Leibniz. Where we disagree with him is in his confidence that for everything that exists, and for everything that happens, there is a sufficient reason to be found. This however is relatively unimportant. The agreement is enough to carry us along to Leibniz's cosmological argument.

II

In part Leibniz's cosmological argument is a version of the standard cosmological argument for the existence of God. Discussion on this has become threadbare on both sides, and I shall make only one observation about it. Many people feel they would be content to give up the search for further explanations once they had reached basic scientific laws. It seems to them gratuitous, inappropriate, or even incoherent to seek, as Leibniz does, for a sufficient reason why these laws should hold. However this is an odd position to take, because it is arbitrary. We are all normally committed to the search for explanations wherever they can be found, and differ from Leibniz only in our lack of confidence that they always can be. To refuse even to search in this particular instance is in conflict with our ordinary, and scientific, procedure. And if someone came up with an explanation which met our criteria—whether a theistic explanation or an explanation of some other kind—to refuse to accept it as true would again conflict with our ordinary procedure, and (at least on a scientific realist account of the matter) our scientific procedure as well.

The reason people are so inclined to give up at this point cannot be that any cosmological explanation would be bound to take us beyond the limits of what we can verify experimentally, since scientific explanations do that all the time (and so do our everyday claims about the continuing existence of unobserved objects). It is rather, I think, that they fear an unstoppable infinite regress in the search for explanations. People often take it for granted that the regress must be unstoppable. What is important about Leibniz's account is that he shows this is not so.

So far as I know Leibniz is the only philosopher to have pointed out how the regress might successfully be halted, though of course he is by no means unusual in claiming that it can be. Spinoza makes an interesting attempt, from a point of view that is not in any ordinary sense theistic; I shall return to Spinoza in a moment. An alternative strategy is the neo-Platonic attempt to account for everything in terms of the Good or the Best. On this view, whatever exists does so because it is best that it should, and that includes God, if he exists. The Good itself does not exist and so does not require explanation; it is beyond being and non-being; but it is by reference to it that everything else can be explained.[4] No doubt there is something attractive about this line of thought, but it is far from clear why the Good should be thought to explain anything at all. It may be a first step towards explaining the existence of something to show that it is best that it should exist, but only if that fact can be connected with something else—like there being a powerful God who chooses to create it for that reason. In exactly the same way, it might be a first step towards explaining the existence of something to point out that it is red, if one could connect that with there being an artist around who creates as many red things as possible. The attraction of the neo-Platonic view is not that it explains things in a way that meets our criteria for adequacy in explanation; it does not do that at all. The attraction of it is that it encourages us to feel at home in the universe, to feel

4. For a vigorous defence of an approach of this kind see J. Leslie, *Universes* (London: Routledge, 1989), ch. 8.

that all is for the best. But that reflects a moral ideal (or a religious one), and has no direct connection with explanation.

Leibniz thinks we can meet the moral ideal and the ideal of adequate explanation together, but only because there exists a creator God who chooses to bring into existence the best of all possible worlds. So the fact that this world is the best does not *directly* explain its existence. And Leibniz certainly does not think God's existence is to be explained by saying it is best he should exist, or anything of the sort. According to Leibniz God's existence is not to be explained at all. He makes two different suggestions about that. One is that God's existence requires no explanation because God exists necessarily—by no means an original idea. The other is that it requires no explanation because without God there would be no logical truths; there would not even be any possibilities.[5]

What is meant by saying that God exists necessarily? Not that it is (in Kant's terminology) analytic. Leibniz did not think we could show anything interesting about God by building things into the meaning of the word 'God', and although he makes use of the ontological argument he never thought it worked just by the analysis of a concept which might be no more than a fictional construction. Conceptual analysis matters to Leibniz only if it reflects the real natures of things, and when he says that God exists necessarily what he means is that it belongs to God's essence that he exist. Sometimes he seems to think it is enough to say that. However it is not enough, and for that reason this first of Leibniz's two suggestions will not work. Sugar is necessarily soluble, in the sense that to be soluble is part of its essence, but it is still reasonable to ask why it is; in that case we are in a position to answer the question, by explaining how molecules of different forms interact. So we do not stop the demand for explanations by observing that sugar is necessarily soluble, and for the same reason we do not stop the demand for explanations why God exists by observing that existence is part of his essence. Nor would that observation help with the ontological argument, which still does not work, even if we add that existence is a predicate or property. The objection that existence is not a predicate was made by Gassendi, against

5. 'Monadology', sects. 43–4, AG p. 218; *Theodicy* sect. 184; 'On the Ultimate Origin of Things', AG p. 152.

Descartes' form of the argument, and it has been popular ever since, but like so many of Gassendi's contributions it seems hardly relevant.[6] We can hold, with Aquinas, that existence is an essential property of God, without supposing, any more than Aquinas did, that this commits us to God's existing. It would commit us only to holding that if God does exist he does so necessarily, just as if sugar dissolves in water it does so necessarily. There cannot be sugar which does not dissolve, and likewise there cannot be a God which does not exist—though to say this is not to say much.

At any rate, to show that something is necessarily so is not to show that we cannot properly ask why it is. Fortunately Leibniz also has another, and quite different, argument to stop the regress. He says that God 'carries the reason of his existence in himself', but it is unclear what this means.[7] It may help to look first at Spinoza.

Spinoza describes his one substance, 'God or Nature', as 'cause of itself', but in order to indicate what he is getting at he amends the traditional definition of substance as 'that which is in itself', adding 'and is conceived through itself'. He follows this up with what sounds like a very rationalistic axiom concerning causation: 'The knowledge of an effect depends upon, and involves, the knowledge of its cause'.[8] This sounds even more obscure, and rather antiquated, but only because he is using the word 'knowledge' (cognitio) not in any of those modern ways that are so exhaustively discussed, but in the older fashion that goes back at least to Plato and equates knowledge with understanding. So he is saying that understanding the effect involves understanding the cause, that is, knowing what explains it in its turn. Far from being a mysterious and outdated point, this amounts to the perfectly defensible observation that a full and complete explanation of any effect would involve not only knowing its immediate preconditions but also their preconditions in turn; a complete explanation of why the kettle boils ultimately involves the whole of physics, and whatever else there is to be known about the world.

6. Gassendi, 'Rebuttals to Meditation V', Doubt II, Article 1; in The Selected Works of Pierre Gassendi, ed. and tr. C.B. Brush (New York: Johnson Reprint Co., 1972), p. 258.

7. 'Principles of Nature and Grace', sect. 8, AG p. 210.

8. Spinoza, Ethics, Part I, Df. 3 and Axiom 4; following the translation in E. Curley, The Collected Works of Spinoza, Vol. 1 (Princeton NJ.: Princeton University Press, 1985).

When Spinoza says that God or Nature is 'conceived through itself' what he means is that a full understanding of God does not involve anything beyond God. Since in Spinoza's conception of things God or Nature includes all that there is, there is nothing else that could be a sufficient condition of its existence. Its own existence is sufficient for itself, no doubt, but only in the empty and irrelevant logical sense. Thus it is misleading to say that God or Nature explains itself; nothing could be a determining sufficient condition of itself, or render itself intelligible in the appropriate way. But we can see (Spinoza thinks) that it would be futile to ask for a further explanation, since nothing could qualify as one. Here, then, the search for further explanations comes to a stop.

If this were so, it would only be because God or Nature is understood so very broadly, as including all that exists. That leaves us unsatisfied: we wanted to know why things are as they are and not otherwise. On this Spinoza has nothing to add to the unsatisfactory thought that they are so of necessity. Moreover his position rests in any case on an undefended assumption. This is, that what exists cannot be explained by reference to what does not exist.[9] It may seem a plausible assumption, but it is not self-evident. Someone could try to explain things as coming into existence in order to promote the good, without supposing that the good already exists prior to their coming into existence. So it is not absurd for Leibniz to ask the question Spinoza here seeks to disallow: why does there exist something rather than nothing? There can be no answer to that question if it demands a sufficient condition which itself exists, but there can be if it does not.

Although Leibniz poses the question, he does not think God's existence requires an explanation. That is partly because he thinks it necessary, but he has a better reason, that without God, nothing would even be possible. This is not because possibilities are the result of God's free choice (as Descartes thought), but because elementary logical laws and possibilities have their being in God's *intellect*. His argument for this is not compelling; it starts from the premise that what is possible and what is necessary must be 'grounded in' what is actual, but it is not clear why we should concede this for any sense of 'grounded in' which gets us anywhere near Leibniz's conclusion. He firmly rejects the modal realism of

9. Cf. *Ethics*, Part II, Prop. 10, second Scholium, which is unargued.

Plato or of David Lewis, for example, but gives little argument for the rejection.[10] However, supposing his argument were successful, and nothing would even be possible unless there were a God: would that show that the existence of God requires no explanation?

The answer to this is yes. The existence of Leibniz's God cannot be explained by reference to something that is merely possible, since what is possible depends upon God—possibilities and necessities have God as their determining sufficient condition. Now Leibniz, unlike Spinoza, does not include within God all that exists, so at first sight there would appear to be room to explain God's existence by reference to something else that exists: God's parents, perhaps, who owe their existence to God's grandparents. However, to explain something involves finding a determining sufficient condition for it, and Leibniz does have a reason for thinking there can be no determining sufficient condition for the existence of God, though he does not spell it out very clearly. Whatever else can be said about it, a determining sufficient condition must at least be a condition: to say that A is a determining sufficient condition of B is to say something about possibilities. It is to rule out the possibility that A might have obtained without B. For Leibniz a world without God would be a world without modality, and therefore a world without determining sufficient conditions; a world without sufficient conditions of any sort, except for materially sufficient conditions, where P counts as materially sufficient for Q wherever P is false and wherever Q is true. Material conditionals do not express conditions in anything but a trivial sense. Proper conditions require modality, and modality (according to Leibniz) requires God. The existence of God cannot depend upon any condition, because the existence of the condition depends upon God.

Because Leibniz does not properly establish that what is possible must be grounded in what is actual, his argument is incomplete; and he would have to show, further, that it must be grounded in the intellect of God. Still, the idea of an explanation or a sufficient reason does seem to be inherently modal, and if God is the source of modality in the way Leibniz thinks, he must be right to point out

10. See R.M. Adams, *Leibniz: Determinist, Theist, Idealist* (New York: Oxford University Press, 1994), ch. 7 sect. 1. In this chapter Adams provides much the best discussion I know of Leibniz' argument about eternal truths, though without seeing that it really does provide a way to stop the regress.

that there is no room to ask for an explanation of God. So he has found a way in which the demand for further explanations could be stopped.

At least, there would be no place for an explanation of the *existence* of God. It would remain possible to ask why God *chooses* as he does. Spinoza dismisses the question; God does not go in for anything so human as choice. The eternal and infinite essence of God determines everything that happens in the world.[11] Leibniz does ascribe choice to God. God chooses the best, and his choice is free; but it seems to be fixed by his nature all the same.[12] What exactly Leibniz can mean by calling God's choice free is a tricky matter, but unless he is prepared to admit something which cannot be fully explained he cannot be ascribing genuine unpredictability to God. It cannot be that (in any ordinary sense) God could have done otherwise. If he could, there would be something left over as unexplained in the account of God's choice, for although he chooses this world because it is the best there remains room to ask why, on this occasion, he did choose the best. Since that would violate the demands of the Principle of Sufficient Reason it is not surprising that he firmly rejects the idea, describing it as 'falling back into the loose indifference, which I have amply refuted, and shown to be absolutely chimerical'.[13] Leibniz's view is that God chooses the best, because he prefers the best, and because his nature guarantees that he will do so. That it is the best is also determined by God's own nature, though not by God's will. The eternal truths are truths about God's intellect, and it is an eternal truth that A is better than B.[14] Hence if there is no room to ask for an explanation of the existence of God, there is no room either to ask for an explanation of God's choice, for it would in effect be to ask why God has the nature he does; or, to put the same thing another way, why this God (rather than some alternative God) exists.

Since both Leibniz and Spinoza both hold that God's nature determines what happens in the world the difference between them may now appear to be rather small. However at least three

11. *Ethics*, Part I, Props. 29 and 32.

12. See (amongst many others) the paper 'On Contingency', AG pp. 28 ff. How Leibniz can say both these things, and why he has to, is much discussed; see note 15 below.

13. Leibniz's third letter to Clarke, sect. 7, AG p. 325.

14. *Theodicy*, sect. 20.

important differences remain. The first is just that Spinoza's God or Nature includes all that there is; Leibniz's God does not. The second is more problematic, but important: Leibniz ascribes choice to God, even if God's choice is predictable. This is not empty. What it means is that there are numerous counterfactuals true about how things would have been if God had chosen differently. Securing the truth of these counterfactuals is one of Leibniz's most important objectives. It is in this way that he can find room for his alternative possible worlds, and give a sense to talking of divine and human freedom, though a vindication of the coherence of his position here would require a separate paper.[15] Thirdly, and for our purposes most importantly of all, Leibniz is able to stop the regress where Spinoza failed to. To the question why God has the nature he (or it) does, Spinoza could only say that it was so of necessity, and that since God included everything that exists his nature could not be explained by reference to anything else that exists. Leibniz leaves nothing at all, existent or merely possible, by reference to which God or his nature could be explained, and provides a reason for thinking that nothing could count as explaining them. For if anything is a condition or reason for anything it owes that status to God, and would lack it without him. God is prior to everything in the order of explanation, since without God nothing can be an explanation of anything.

This is the line I think we shall have to pursue if we want to find an ultimately sufficient reason for things, capable of stopping the regress of repeated demands for explanation. Leibniz's attempt fails, because (or to the extent that) he does not convince us of the reality of his God whose intellect is the locus of eternal truths and the source of modality. However, the attempt is enough to show that the demand for an ultimate explanation is not in principle unsatisfiable.

III

I think the Principle of Sufficient Reason pushes us towards something like Leibniz's account of things, even if we disagree with him over the nature of modality. We are committed to the Principle of Sufficient Reason in the sense that we are committed

---

15. On these issues see esp. R.M. Adams, *op. cit.*, Part I, and D. Wiggins, 'The Concept of the Subject Contains the Concept of the Predicate', in J.J. Thomson, ed., *On Being and Saying* (Cambridge, Mass.: Bradford Press, 1987).

to the search for reasons, and committed to thinking that our best explanations give us truth—or approximate truth—about the world. But because our best explanations encapsulate standards and criteria that are our own, there is something lacking from them, unless they can say something about why these standards should give truth about the world. We constantly and unavoidably assume that they do, and this assumption has often led us to make the right predictions in the past, but its continued success itself requires explanation. It is something the Principle of Sufficient Reason in its methodological form requires us to search out. It is arguable—and I have tried to argue it elsewhere—that the only adequate explanation is that there is a God who ensures that the world must accommodate itself to our ways of thinking about it.[16] If that is right (and of course it does need some hard arguing) the Principle of Sufficient Reason leads us to postulate such a God. Whether or not it is right, the Principle of Sufficient Reason urgently requires us to do something to explain the match between the way the world is and the standards that govern our thought. Otherwise none of our explanations would really be adequate; they are all incomplete until an account has been given of this match between the world itself and the simple and systematic theories we construct in accordance with our own standards and values.

If we do provide such an account, whether in theistic terms or in some other way, can our explanations now be complete? There is one obvious sense in which they cannot, since any account we offer of the match between the world and our theories must itself be an *explanation*, which recommends itself to us in virtue of those very same standards whose match with the world we were seeking to explain. This however is inevitable, for there is nothing else it could be. There are no other standards for us to use. This sort of circularity in any attempt to explain their adequacy is entirely unavoidable. But the Principle of Sufficient Reason does not demand the impossible. What it demands is a *reason* which is *sufficient*; and what we should have here would be a reason which is as sufficient as it is in the nature of a reason to be; an explanation which is as complete as it is in the nature of an explanation to be.

16. See my *The Coherence Theory of Truth* (London: Routledge, 1989), ch. XI. And for the problem it solves, see T. Nagel, *The View from Nowhere* (New York: Oxford University Press, 1986), ch. V.

At any rate, it would if we adopted the theistic hypothesis. Whether any other hypothesis could play the same role, and leave us with an explanation which was similarly complete, I very much doubt. Another way of saying that is, that it seems to me the Principle of Sufficient Reason pushes us towards the theistic hypothesis, as the only hypothesis which will fully satisfy its demands. If that is right, it is important, since the Principle guides all of our thought in science and in everyday life.

But it may seem that the theistic hypothesis is still evidently *not* complete, because nothing has ruled out the possibility that there may be some cause of God's coming into existence. Perhaps he emanates from the One, as Plotinus thought, or is the child of Kronos and Rhea. But even if God does have a cause, I think we can still learn from Leibniz how to stop the regress of explanations.

Let us suppose God's existence does have a cause, and that this cause is a determining sufficient condition. To explain something is not just to point to a determining sufficient condition which does in fact obtain. It is to do so in a way that conforms to our standards of explanation, and which thereby gives us something we can recognize as a reason for thinking that this condition obtains. It is only by reference to our standards for explanation that we could ever have reason for thinking a hypothesis true; without them it might actually be true, but we could never have reason to think so, for it is these standards of ours which enable us to determine which explanations to adopt and which to reject. Leibniz argued that the idea of a determining sufficient condition for God was incoherent, because if anything is a condition for anything it owes that status to God, and would lack it without him. I do not want to go so far: I am prepared to concede that something could be a condition, and a determining sufficient condition, for God's existence. But if anything is to be an *explanation* for anything—to meet, in a reliable way, the epistemological condition on explanation and thus to render intelligible what it explains—then it owes *this* status to God, who is responsible for the match between our standards and the way the world is. So the counterfactual conditionals associated with *A*'s being a condition of God's existence may in fact be true, e.g. that God would not have come into existence *anyway*, whether or not *A*. But these counterfactual conditionals could not be the content of any hypothesis we might reasonably frame, because at this point there is no longer any reason to suppose our standards for hypothesis-formation will match the way the world is. Since nothing can be an explanation without God, nothing can be an *explanation* of God.

Thus Leibniz's argument seems to me to be right in principle, and capable of being rescued from its questionable assumptions about modality. The Principle of Sufficient Reason demands that we should always look for reasons; but we have here come to a place where nothing that could count as a reason—nothing that could match the epistemological requirements on an explanation—could ever, in principle, be found. Not everyone will agree with my way of stopping the regress, any more than everyone will agree with Leibniz's; certainly not without much further argument. But at least everyone should agree that it is not impossible in principle to stop the regress.[17]

Magdalen College,
Oxford OX1 4AU.
ralph.walker@magd.ox.ac.uk

17. I am extremely grateful to David Wiggins for stimulating me to think about these issues and helping to clarify my mind on them. We continue to disagree on most of the contentious matters.

VII*—ON THE NOTION OF CAUSE 'PHILOSOPHICALLY SPEAKING'

by Helen Steward

Sometimes in philosophy, an orthodoxy is seriously challenged and yet things carry on as though nothing had happened. There are circumstances which can make this understandable—the relevant arguments might be complex and difficult, or buried deep in some journal that few read, or formulated by a little-known philosopher whose work fails to attract the attention it deserves. But it is puzzling when the challenge is presented by a world-famous philosopher, in a widely-read essay, the main thrust of which a competent undergraduate might reckon herself to have understood, and yet still, seemingly, no one takes any notice—sometimes not even the world-famous philosopher himself. What I am speaking of is Davidson's critique, in his widely-read paper, 'Causal Relations', of Mill's account of causation.[1] I regard Davidson's comments about Mill as an attack on an orthodoxy because it seems to me that in various significant respects, many—perhaps most—philosophers are still unreconstructed Millians when it comes to causation. But how has it been possible for these Millian views to remain so prevalent, given the force of the points made by Davidson, which, so far as I am aware, have never been successfully met, and which paradoxically, indeed, have encountered a kind of silent acceptance, even as their hugely radical consequences for our ways of thinking about a number of central philosophical issues have been ignored?

I think the conclusion must be that it has never been properly understood just how far-reaching are the repercussions of Davidson's criticisms of Mill. As I have already mentioned, there is evidence to suggest that even Davidson has failed to see how damaging they are for a certain conception of the relationship

1. *Journal of Philosophy* 64 (1967), 691–703, repr. in D. Davidson *Essays on Actions and Events* (Oxford: OUP, 1980), 149–62.

*Meeting of the Aristotelian Society, held in the Senior Common Room, Birkbeck College, London, on Monday, 27th January, 1997 at 8.15 p.m.

between causes and their effects.[2] In this paper, I want to attempt to show why Davidson's criticisms of Mill, taken to what I regard as their logical conclusion, show that we must give up a conception or picture of causation which I call the network model of causation, a model which dominates contemporary philosophy of mind (as well as many accounts of the nature of causation in general) and shapes prevailing ideas about the form of some of its most important questions.

I shall begin, in §I, by trying to characterise the network model of causation. I hope and expect that this characterisation will be readily recognised as an expression of an idea which has had a highly significant influence on several areas of philosophical debate, particularly on recent theories of the mind-body relation. Then in §II, I shall move on to discuss Davidson's argument against Mill in 'Causal Relations'. I shall initially focus on a particular example which is used by Mill to elucidate his conception of the cause of an effect, before going on to discuss Davidson's response, in 'Causal Relations', to the case Mill describes. Davidson's remarks about this example, I shall suggest, ought to seem deeply puzzling to a proponent of the network model of causation. In §III, I shall explain how the distinction made by Davidson between particular causes, on the one hand, and (necessary and sufficient) conditions,[3] on the other, underlies his response to Mill and will draw out two further premises which we seem to need to attribute to Davidson, if we are to understand his conclusion about Mill's example. Then in §IV, I shall argue that the two premises are true. Their truth, I believe, is a matter of great consequence, not only for Mill, but also for an assumption which is utterly central to the network model—the idea that the causation of any particular effect is typically a matter of a number of simultaneously existing causally efficacious particulars, usually conceived of as a mix of

2. See 'The Material Mind', in Davidson, *Essays on Actions and Events*, 254–5, for evidence of commitment to what I shall below call the network model of causation.

3. Davidson speaks of 'necessary and sufficient' conditions. In what follows, I shall continue, for ease of exposition, to speak often of necessary and sufficient conditions; but it is not part of my view that the causal relevance of a condition to some effect consists in its being either necessary or sufficient for that effect. I should have no objection, therefore, if someone wished to substitute, e.g., 'condition which raises the chance of its effect', or some other probabilistic formulation. I shall not be concerned, in this paper, with the distinction between conditions which necessitate their effects and those which merely make their effects more probable; what is crucially important, for my purposes, is the contrast between particular causes and causes which are conditions of *any* sort.

events and so-called 'token' states—combining together to produce a resultant consequence which can be conceived of as part-caused by each separate causal factor. Only the sum of all the factors taken together, on this view, can really be regarded, 'philosophically speaking' (to use Mill's now rather notorious expression), as the 'whole' cause of the relevant effect. I shall argue that once we have properly understood Davidson's distinction between particular causes and causal factors which are conditions, and have accepted the two premises, Mill's conception of the 'whole' cause of an effect—a conception which I believe has not lost its hold on our imagination when it comes to thinking about causation—no longer makes any sense. There will not be space explicitly to draw out the consequences for philosophy of mind, but I hope it will be easy to see how radical they are, if I am right.

I

It is obviously true that we can usually invoke a number of different factors in connection with the causal explanation of any particular event or circumstance. A car might crash, for example, because of a faulty braking system, but it might be clear that even given the faulty brakes, the car would not have crashed if there hadn't been a blind corner and an icy road, and if its driver's reactions hadn't been slowed by alcohol—so we naturally conclude that these, too, were considerations which must be taken into account in giving a good causal explanation of the crash.[4] Philosophers have made use of a range of models and metaphors to describe the ontological reality in which the influence of such multiplicities of causal factors is envisaged as grounded, but perhaps the most prominent has been the concept of a causal network. The idea of a network is an almost irresistible resource in the attempt to visualise and make manageable our understanding of the highly complicated causal relationships which seem to be revealed by the wealth of alternative, equally true causal explanations we can offer of any event or circumstance. It is an obvious refinement of another exceptionally compelling image by means of which we often encode our understanding of the temporal relations which causally related events bear to one another: the image of a causal chain. But

---

4. The example is adapted from David Lewis, 'Causal Explanation', *Philosophical Papers*, Vol. II (Oxford: OUP, 1986), 214.

while chains are linear, each link being related only to (at most) two others—its two neighbours in the chain—networks are branching and so they have a kind of complexity which chains lack, complexity which makes them seem well-suited to the representation of the intricate systems of causal relations to which our multifarious causal explanations seem to point. In a network, two or more different chains can come together and, in doing so, they can create new effects, effects which would not have resulted from any single chain alone. At the nodes of causal networks, different causes 'add' together, the effect which results being conceived of as part-caused by each separate causal factor.

Thinking of causal relations in terms of network imagery obviously raises the question: what are the entities which are linked by the various interconnected chains? What are the causes and effects which exist, as it were, at the nodes of the network? One tempting line of thought which is often found in the literature on causation goes as follows. First, events must be included in causal networks, for events are needed to bring about other events—states alone cannot cause change. For example, the dryness of the ground, the density of the foliage and the wind's being strong may all be causally relevant to the explanation of a forest fire, but these conditions might persist for ever and the forest fire never occur without an event to trigger it off—someone's lighting a match, say, or dropping a lighted cigarette into the bushes. But, second, it is imperative that states be included alongside events. The cigarette's being dropped into the bushes would never have caused the forest fire had the ground not been so dry, the wind so strong, the foliage so dense—and so these factors must also be included in the causal network that describes the causal provenance of the effect-event. Events occur against the background of standing conditions, combining with those conditions to produce effects in such a way that each relevant event and state can be considered a part of the cause of the effect-event. And these states, like the events with which they are thought of as combining, are to be conceived of as particular, causally efficacious entities, rather than general conditions which might obtain at numerous different places and times—perhaps we might therefore call them 'token' states. The ontology of a causal network, it is concluded, is thus a two-fold ontology of events and token states.

There are doubtless other ways of thinking about the ontology of causal networks. In particular, some philosophers have supposed that the relata of the causal relation fall into the category of *trope* or *property instance*, rather than that of *event* and *state*. But I intend to focus, for the purposes of this paper, only on the particular version of the network model which utilises an event/state ontology. I firmly believe that the category of property instance offers no real escape from the arguments to come; indeed, it seems to me that the category is usually introduced into causal contexts only because the distinction between particular causes and causes which are conditions has not been properly understood. But I shall not attempt to show this here. I shall restrict myself, for the purposes of this paper, to arguing explicitly only against the event/state version, which is what I shall mean henceforth by speaking of the 'network model of causation'.

Understandings of causation which conform to the network model are very widely invoked in a number of different areas of philosophy where the notion of causation is to the fore. In particular, the influence of the model on the formulation of questions and theories to do with the relation between the psychological and the neurophysiological causation of human behaviour has been immensely significant. Talk of systems or structures or patterns of causally interrelated psychological events and states is all over the place in recent literature in philosophy of mind. The prevalence of the idea is perhaps most obvious in characterisations of functionalism, functionalists being standardly said to believe that between perceptual input and behavioural output is a huge network of causally efficacious events and states, whose place in the causal web (their 'causal role') is the feature which determines their mental or psychological type—a picture of the causation of human actions by psychological factors which is obviously inspired by the network model. But it is not only functionalists who speak of mental events and states in ways which reveal commitment to the network model; it would not be an exaggeration to say that the idea provides the framework in terms of which much recent writing on mental causation must be understood.

I am convinced that the network model of causation is utterly unsustainable. In the rest of the paper, I want to try to show why we ought to regard it as a casualty of the line of thought which Davidson deploys against Mill in 'Causal Relations'.

II

In his discussion of causation in *A System of Logic*, Mill speaks of the 'invariable sequence' that we find in nature between antecedents and consequents of certain sorts. He appears to have in mind the thought that certain kinds of circumstance or event are always followed by an effect of a certain type. But Mill goes on to note that it is seldom, if ever, that this 'invariable sequence' subsists between a consequent and a single antecedent:

> It is usually between a consequent and the sum of several antecedents; the concurrence of them all being requisite to produce, that is, to be certain of being followed by the consequent. In such cases it is very common to single out only one of the antecedents under the denomination of Cause, calling the others merely Conditions. ...The real Cause is the whole of these antecedents; and we have, philosophically speaking, no right to give the name of cause to one of them exclusively of the others.[5]

The antecedents which may 'concur' in the production of particular effects, according to Mill, are a mixture of events and states. One of Mill's examples concerns a man—let us call him S— who dies through eating a particular dish; Mill asks whether it would be correct to say that S's eating of the dish was the cause of his death, even though eating from the dish was not alone a sufficient condition for death, there being a number of factors (Mill mentions 'a particular bodily constitution, a particular state of present health and perhaps even a certain state of the atmosphere')[6] which were also causally relevant to the fact that S died. He concludes that it would not be correct, and writes that:

> What in the case we have supposed disguises the incorrectness of the expression is this: that the various conditions, except the single one of eating the food, were not *events* (that is, instantaneous changes or successions of instantaneous changes) but *states* possessing more or less of permanency; and might therefore have preceded the effect by an indefinite length of duration, for want of

5. *A System of Logic*, 8th edn. (London: Longmans, 1873; 1st edn., 1843), 214.
6. *A System of Logic*, 214.

the event which was requisite to complete the required concurrence of conditions...[7]

It is usually more natural, according to Mill, to single out an event than a state as a cause, but it is illusory to suppose that the connection between the event and the effect is any closer than that between any of the individually necessary standing conditions and that same effect. In Mill's words, 'All the conditions were equally indispensable to the production of the consequent; and the statement of the cause is incomplete unless in some shape or other we introduce them all'.[8]

In 'Causal Relations', Davidson disputes Mill's verdict about the case of S. It is not true, according to Davidson, that S's eating of the dish in question was not the 'whole' cause of his death. The reason we are urged by Mill to deny the status of whole cause to S's eating of the dish is that the connection between someone's eating from that dish and their subsequently dying is not entirely 'invariable'—perhaps only the weak and ill succumb to the poison contained in it, for example. But this, according to Davidson, cannot be a reason for refusing to allow that S's eating of the dish was, in this particular case, the cause of his death. For S *did* die— as a result, let us say, of the fact that he *was* weak—which means that this particular dish-eating can be described as a dish-eating by a man who was weak. The fact that we do not mention S's weakness in saying that his eating of the dish was the cause of his death does not imply, according to Davidson, that the dish-eating was not its whole cause:

> Mill ...was wrong in thinking we have not specified the whole cause of an event when we have not wholly specified it. And there is not ...anything elliptical in the claim that a certain man's death was caused by his eating a particular dish, even though death resulted only because the man had a particular bodily constitution, a particular state of present health, and so on ... Mill's critics are no doubt justified in contending that we may correctly give the cause without saying enough about it to demonstrate that it was sufficient; but they share Mill's confusion if they think every deletion from the description of an event represents something deleted from the event described.[9]

7. *A System of Logic*, 214.
8. *A System of Logic*, 214.
9. 'Causal Relations', 156–7.

I think Davidson's conclusion here should seem bewildering to a proponent of the network model of causation. An advocate of the network model surely ought to want to ask Davidson how the dish-eating event could have been the *whole* cause of S's death, when it was only in combination with certain other causal factors, amongst them the notable circumstance that S was weak, that it brought about his death. Surely we have to accept that S's state of weakness (something the proponent of the network model is likely to be inclined to think of as a token state, or perhaps more plausibly, a conjunction of such states) was one of the causes of his death—but if it was, how can the dish-eating be its whole cause? Davidson seems inclined to suppose that the fact that S was weak is simply one of the features which we might hit on in order to describe more fully the event which was his eating of the dish, and that therefore it does not need to be considered as a separate particular cause; and of course it is true that the dish-eating *can* be described as an eating of a poisoned dish by a man who was weak. But might we not as well argue that S's state of weakness was the 'whole' cause of his death, on the grounds that we can describe it as a state of a man who ate a poisoned dish?

Davidson is not as explicit as he might be, in 'Causal Relations', about the source of the asymmetry between event and state which his account appears to imply. But there are indications early in the paper that his disagreement with Mill centres around Mill's confusion about the distinction between what Davidson calls 'particular causes' and 'necessary and sufficient conditions'. I want next, therefore, to say something about that distinction, and to try to explain how it might underlie Davidson's insistence that the exclusion of S's state of weakness from an account of the cause of his death would be a deletion only from the *description* of the cause, not from something which we might sensibly think of as the 'whole' cause of the death itself.

III

Davidson's distinction between particular causes and necessary and sufficient conditions is mooted in the first section of 'Causal Relations', when Davidson discusses a range of views which take it for granted that 'the notion of cause may be at least partly characterised in terms of necessary and sufficient conditions', and charges that 'we do not understand how such characterisations are to be applied to particular causes'.[10] It becomes clear, in this section of the paper, that the entities which Davidson calls 'particular causes' are individual events—things which may be referred to by singular terms such as names, definite descriptions and demonstratives. Conditions, on the other hand, for Davidson, correspond to whole sentences. It needs to be said that we are likely, of course, to nominalise, in one way or another, if we are looking for something which we can *call* a condition; sentences will not comfortably fill the frame '... is a (causally necessary or sufficient) condition of... '. 'The match was struck with a sufficient degree of force is a necessary condition of the match lit', for example, is bad English; we would need either to preface our sentences by the phrase 'the fact that', or perhaps just 'that' (e.g., 'The fact that the match was struck with a sufficient degree of force (*or* 'That the match was struck with a sufficient degree of force) was a necessary condition of the fact that the match lit') or to produce gerundive nominalisations (e.g., 'the match's being struck with a sufficient degree of force was a necessary condition of the match's lighting'). But these are merely minor grammatical adjustments which produce expressions which preserve a basically sentential structure. Neither 'the fact that the match was struck with a sufficient degree of force' nor 'the match's being struck with a sufficient degree of force' are genuine definite descriptions, though they bear a superficial resemblance to some such descriptions. They are not singular terms; they are essentially propositional constructions.

How might a distinction between particular causes and causal factors which are expressed sententially bear on Davidson's discussion of Mill's example? Davidson is clearly reluctant to allow the term 'cause' to have application to causal factors which are other than particular,[11] and one can see, in this idea that conditions ought not to be *called* causes, the beginnings of a story which might explain why Davidson feels able to exclude such

10. 'Causal Relations', 150.

11. It needs to be said, I think, that this is pretty obviously at variance with ordinary usage, which permits us to speak of causally relevant conditions as 'causes' (e.g., 'The room's being full of methane was the cause of the explosion'; 'The fact that the picture was missing was the cause of much frustration amongst the gallery's visitors'.) I have therefore not followed Davidson in his restrictive usage.

things as *the fact that S was weak*, together with a range of other putative causally relevant conditions, from being each regarded as part of some large conjunction which we might think of as the 'whole' cause of his death. But this linguistic policy alone is clearly not enough to justify Davidson's conclusion that we may regard S's eating of a poisoned dish (an event) as the whole cause of S's death. There seem to be two difficulties. First, just as we might suppose that, though a refusal to call a causally relevant condition a cause excludes our accounting *the fact that S ate a poisoned dish* part of the cause of S's death, it does not prevent us from regarding *S's eating of the poisoned dish*, a particular event, as its cause, or at least as part of its cause, so we might likewise suppose that though it excludes our accounting *the fact that S was weak* part of the cause, it does not prevent us from thinking that *S's state of weakness*, also conceived of as a particular cause, or as a collection of such causes, was part of the cause of his death. The distinction between particular causes and necessary and sufficient conditions cannot prevent the exclusion of token states from an account of 'the whole cause' of an effect from seeming to be unjustified, unless it can be shown that there is something wrong with the supposition that our regarding S's being weak as part of the causal explanation of his death necessarily involves the existence of a 'token state' of weakness (or perhaps the existence of a range of 'token states', which together might be thought of as constituting a token state of weakness), a state which participates as a particular cause in the bringing about of S's death. And second, even if this could be done, it would still need to be shown why the exclusion of conditions, as opposed to particular causes, from an account of 'the whole cause' of some event was anything more than a trivial and uninteresting consequence of the restrictive linguistic policy, whereby Davidson permits only particular causes to be accounted 'causes' at all. For it might be asked why particular causes and conditions could not still both be regarded as parts of something which it made sense to think of as the 'whole' cause of a phenomenon; why the heterogeneity amongst different sorts of causal factor, if indeed it exists, should be so damaging to the network model.

It looks, then, as though the following two premises are in need of defence, if Davidson's conclusion about Mill's example is to be justified:

(i) There are no particular 'token states' (whether states of weakness or anything else) which need to figure in any complete account of the particular causes which led to S's death.

(ii) There is something wrong with the idea that particular causes and causes which are conditions can be conceived of as things which could be added together, one to another, in order to give 'the whole cause' of some phenomenon.

In the final section of the paper, I shall try to explain why I believe both premises are true, and why I think this has such important consequences for the network model of causation.[12]

IV

One of the points which emerges from 'Causal Relations' is that it is a distinctive feature of a certain kind of causal statement—the kind Davidson calls a singular causal claim, in which two singular terms are linked by the two-place predicate 'cause'—that such claims are non-committal about which particular property, or properties, of the particular cause which is in question, were causally relevant to the effect it brings about. What a singular causal claim tells us is simply that the particular in question was somehow involved; it leaves it unspecified which precise features of that particular were the ones which really mattered causally to the effect. This is clear from Davidson's emphasis on the distinction between 'causes and the features we hit on for describing them'[13]; it is essential to Davidson's view that the truth of a singular causal claim does not depend on the way in which cause and effect are singled out. For example, take the singular causal claim: 'S's eating of a poisoned dish caused his death'.[14] This could perfectly well be true and yet it be false that S died because he ate from a poisoned

---

12. The arguments I offer can really be no more than sketches in a paper of this length—and there are lines of objection which I cannot deal with here. I present a much more thorough defence of my views on causation and ontology in *The Ontology of Mind: Events, Processes and States*, forthcoming (Oxford: OUP, 1997).

13. 'Causal Relations', 155.

14. The potential for event/fact ambiguity in nominal phrases like 'S's eating of a poisoned dish' has been well documented (see Z. Vendler, 'Effects, Results and Consequences', in R.J. Butler (ed.) *Analytical Philosophy* (New York: Barnes and Noble, 1962), for a good account). It is essential, of course, for making sense of what I say here, that the nominal phrase 'S's eating of a poisoned dish' be understood as referring to a particular event, not to the fact that S ate a poisoned dish.

dish. Suppose, for instance, that the situation is as follows: S knows that the dish from which he is eating is poisoned, but has a perfectly reliable, fast-acting antidote to the poison in his possession, which he consumes afterwards, in the sure and certain knowledge that it will prevent the poison from harming him in any way. Unfortunately for him, the dish also contains a fragment of sharp glass, which punctures S's stomach some hours later, leading to his eventual death. In such a situation, it is true that S's eating of a poisoned dish—an event which happened also to be describable as S's eating of a dish which contained a tiny fragment of glass— caused his death. But it is not true that S died because he ate from a poisoned dish. He died because of the fact that he ate from a dish that contained a tiny fragment of sharp glass—that the dish was poisoned was irrelevant.

Now, if this really is a correct account of the way in which reference to particular causes figures in singular causal claims (as I believe it is), it ought to apply equally to 'token states', if they are indeed particular causes, no less than to events. It ought not simply to *follow*, for example, from that fact that someone's state of weakness caused their death that the death occurred because the person was weak; the claim that the state of weakness caused the person's death ought, similarly, to be non-committal about which particular properties of the 'token' state of weakness were the causally relevant ones. For particulars, at any rate on the view of them which I share with Davidson, are many-propertied entities, and the claim that a particular is the cause of something, as we have just seen, does not entail that the property, if any, by means of which it is singled out, was causally relevant to the effects which that particular causes. But is it conceivable that a man's state of weakness might have caused his death, though it was not true that his death occurred because he was weak? It seems to me that this conjunction of claims is very difficult to make coherent, and that this throws grave doubt on the idea that we really succeed, in speaking of 'S's state of weakness', in referring to a many-propertied entity of the sort which deserves the designation 'particular cause'. I should say, indeed, that what one would normally mean, in saying that someone's state of weakness caused his death, simply *is* that it was causally relevant to his death *that he was weak*—i.e., what is being invoked is really a causally relevant condition, not a particular cause. There is no proper space for a logical gap between the two claims of the kind which one would expect if S's state of weakness really were a particular entity. To all intents and purposes, the two assertions make the same claim.[15]

It seems to me, then, that in the case of Mill's example, we have no reason to suppose that there is any true causal claim to be made concerning the relation between S's state of weakness and his death which is genuinely distinct from the claim that S died because of the fact that he was weak, no true causal claim to be made in which the causal factor cited is not a condition. And this is surely equivalent to saying that there is no reason for believing in any particular 'token state' of weakness, any many-propertied entity, which needs to figure in an account of the etiology of S's death. More generally, indeed, I should maintain that the introduction of 'token states' into the metaphysics of causality is always an attempt to respond to the recognition of the causal relevance of a condition to some effect, and that it is always misguided. Normally, what we mean to assert, when we make a claim about the causal relevance, to some effect, of someone's or something's being in a certain state, is something which could be equally well said by means of a claim that it mattered that that person or thing had a certain property, and this is the kind of claim that requires the causally relevant factor to be expressed by means of a 'that' clause or a whole sentence. Fears about how such things as facts or truths could possibly be the sorts of things which might have efficacy have doubtless been

15. One might perhaps think there could be circumstances which might justify someone's saying that S died, not because he was weak, but because he was weak in a certain particular way (because his weakness was so extreme, say, or because it was of a certain particular kind) and this might make us suppose we had found circumstances in which it was correct to say that S's state of weakness caused his death, though it was not true that he died because he was weak. But the reason for the failure of implication here, if there is one, does not stem from the fact that the so-called 'state' of weakness here is a genuinely particular cause. 'S's state of weakness' here is just standing in for some more exact description of the degree to, and manner in which he was weak, not for a particular entity. What is being said, when it is asserted that his state of weakness caused his death, yet denied that he died because he was weak, is simply that it is not the condition *that he was weak* that was causally crucial, but rather that it was some unspecified, but in principle more fully specifiable, condition involving weakness, *that he was extremely weak*, say, or *that he had a weak liver*, that really mattered. The failure of entailment is not a result of the fact that S's state of weakness is a many-propertied particular entity, but rather to the fact that we are using the phrase 'S's state of weakness' as a kind of place-holder for a more complete description of the precise weakness-involving condition (which, note, remains a *condition*, however precisely it is specified) which we consider to have been causally relevant to his death.

the source of a widespread reluctance to regard causal explanations in which the causal factor is expressed sententially as revelatory of any basic causal relations in what we like to think of as 'the world', thus encouraging a search for the real, particular entities whose efficacy lies behind and explains the truth of the puzzling sentence-functional constructions in which we conduct most of our causal talk. But these are misplaced fears, based on the failure to recognise that not everything which it may be appropriate to call a cause has to be literally *efficacious*, failure, indeed, to recognise the existence of the category of causes which are conditions, causes which are counterfactually relevant to their effects rather than efficacious in their production, causes which are facts, not things.[16]

I have argued, then, that premise (i) is true.[17] It remains to be explained why (ii) is also true. For it needs to be shown why the network model could not be adapted to the recognition that we often invoke causally relevant conditions as well as particular causes; why we could not simply free the model from the assumption that the causes which interact at the nodes of causal networks are all particular, while retaining the idea that every particular event or circumstance is produced by a conjunction both of particulars and conditions, hence holding on, in essence, to Mill's notion of the cause 'philosophically speaking'.

Why should recognising the distinction between particular causes and causally relevant conditions prevent us from being able

---

16. In philosophy of mind, one notable example of what can go wrong as a result of this failure is the mess which results from the frequent deployment of 'token states' of belief and desire as a means of understanding the causal explanations by way of which we make it intelligible why some agent did what he or she did by adverting to what they believed or wanted. But to offer an explanation of the form: 'S ø-ed because she believed that *p*', is to advert to a causal factor which is properly conceived of as a condition, not a particular. *That S believed that p* is what mattered; had S not believed that p, either she would not have ø-ed, or would have been less likely to ø. If we introduce 'token states' of belief and desire, which we go on to conceive of as genuine, many-propertied particulars, we just create for ourselves a spurious problem about how we can be sure that the token state's *being a belief that p* or *being a desire that q* were properties of that token state which mattered causally to the effect in question—a version of the worry about the epiphenomenality of mental properties which has dogged anomalous monism. But the solution to this problem is obvious, once the distinction between causes which are conditions and particular causes is in view. Since the difficulty stems from the mistaken attempt to treat an explanation which adverts to a causally relevant fact as grounded in the causal efficacy of a particular thing, we should just refuse the move which tells us that we have to invoke 'token states' of belief and desire to understand these explanations in the first place.

17. Though more really needs to be said than I have been able to say here about the concept of a state; for the term is used in a number of different ways. See *The Ontology of Mind*, Ch. 4, for a more thorough discussion than I have provided here.

to talk sensibly of the 'whole' cause of some effect, just conceived of as a giant conjunction of all the causes, both particulars *and* conditions, which we regard as having a place in its etiology? The difficulty is that once we have satisfied ourselves that conditions are definitely going to have to figure in causal 'networks', whether alone, or in combination with particular causes, the idea that there is some total combination of causal factors which, at any given time, together constitutes the 'whole' cause of any given effect starts to look as though it might be senseless. For there does not seem to be any reason why there should be a definite limit to the number of conditions which, at any given point in time, might have been relevant to the occurrence of some particular effect. The right of a condition to a place in a causal story depends not just on the actual circumstances in which an effect is brought about, but also on counterfactual matters; to decide whether a condition was relevant to the occurrence of some effect, we have to ask ourselves such questions as 'Would the effect still have occurred if *p* hadn't been true?' or perhaps 'Would the effect have been as likely to occur if *p* hadn't been true?' And the number of possible different substituends for *p* which might generate a negative answer to whichever of these questions we decide is the relevant one, thus grounding *p*'s claim to be considered a causally relevant condition, looks as though it must be potentially limitless. This becomes particularly clear when one reflects that conditions can be negative as well as positive. In the case of Mill's example, for instance, we might regard it as causally crucial to S's death that no ambulance was called, that no antibiotics were available, that no stomach pump was applied—and so all these conditions might be regarded as necessary conditions of (or conditions which made more probable) the final death. But it seems obvious that there is no clear end to the number of alternative scenarios which might conceivably have resulted in survival rather than death, and so no clear limit to the causally relevant conditions which might be generated by consideration of such scenarios. Pragmatics, of course, is what limits us for practical purposes; we would not normally account it causally relevant to S's death from food poisoning, for example, that he was not suffering from gastro-enteritis at the time (a condition which, we can imagine, would have saved him by expelling the poison from his body before it could be absorbed).[18] But the prospect of offering an account of the causal relevance of causes which are conditions, which sets determinate, non-pragmatically-based limits to what is and is not to be accounted part of the whole cause of some phenomenon looks exceedingly dim. The idea that there is some completely determinate 'web' of causal factors waiting to be extracted from our everyday causal explanations of particular effects is a myth, based on the false idea that every such explanation works by adverting somehow to a causally efficacious particular.

The conclusion I believe we ought to draw from 'Causal Relations' is that the notion of the cause 'philosophically speaking' of any particular event or circumstance is incoherent. There is simply no such thing as 'the whole cause' of anything, in the sense Mill imagined—no such thing as a determinate network of causally interacting events and 'token states' which precedes and produces every individual occurrence, no such thing as a complete, pragmatically unconstrained list, even in principle, of all the events and standing conditions which participated in the production of each effect. And this implies, in turn, that we must jettison the network model of causation. Our causal claims are vastly heterogeneous in their logical form (the distinction between singular causal claims and explanations which advert to causes by means of sentential constructions is, I believe, the most important dimension of heterogeneity, but there are many others); and this heterogeneity, I believe, puts an insurmountable obstacle in the way of acceptance of the network model. The things we call causes lie on both sides of the divide between facts and particulars—one of the most important ontological divides there is. And the consequences of this truth need to be faced, not ignored whenever they threaten to become an inconvenient impediment to the unproblematic application of the metaphors we find it tempting to deploy in connection with causation.

Balliol College
Oxford
OX4 3AY

---

18. At any rate, we would not account it causally relevant unless we had some antecedent reason for thinking that S might well have had gastro-enteritis, had things gone only very slightly differently—e.g., if S's family all had gastro-enteritis, or if S had had gastro-enteritis only a week before.

VIII*—THE ANALYSIS OF POSSIBILITY AND THE POSSIBILITY OF ANALYSIS

by John Divers

I

The quantificational treatment of (unrestricted) possibility is based on the principle that propositions of the form ◊P are equivalent to propositions that report P's being the case at some world—let that principle be represented by the equivalence (E):

(E) $\Diamond P \leftrightarrow \exists x(Wx \ \& \ P^*x)$[1]

Comparable quantification over worlds yields equivalences dealing with other modal notions such as unrestricted necessity, variously restricted notions of possibility and necessity, strict entailment, counterfactual conditionals etc., but let us take (E) as the basic case. The advantages of the quantificational treatment of modalities are widely supposed to be these. Firstly, substituting explicitly modal expressions by their 'worldly' equivalents allows us to do modal logic by proxy in a first-order logic; thus we simplify the logical resources that we need to handle modality, no longer requiring special axioms or rules of inference to handle the modal operators as we would if these were treated as primitive. Secondly, we can get a semantics by proxy for the modal operator language by providing a semantics (involving suitably rich models) directly for the worldly language; such a semantics may be fully extensional rather than intensional as would normally be required if the modal operators were treated as primitive. Thirdly, a variety of (not always appropriately discriminated) expressive advantages are supposed

---

1. I hope that nothing in the ensuing discussion depends on concentrating on this object-linguistic articulation of the equivalence rather than its metalinguistic analogue: (E*) '◊P' is true iff. ∃x(Wx & P*x). But it would be foolhardy to be entirely confident that this is so. Also, the equivalence could be expressed more neatly by using a special sort of variable for worlds—i.e. (E**) ◊P ↔ ∃wP*w—but it facilitates the discussion to make explicit the semantic role of the world predicate that is implicit in the use of special world variables.

*Meeting of the Aristotelian Society, held in the Senior Common Room, Birkbeck College, London, on Monday, 10th February, 1997 at 8.15 p.m.

to ensue, namely: that we can articulate more modal concepts by quantifying over a domain of worlds and their parts than we can if restricted to the use of sentential modal operators and 'actualist' quantifiers; that we can represent modal content in a more comprehensible and user-friendly way when we use equivalent worldly expressions (e.g. by exchanging iterated modality for multiple quantificational generality and accessibility relations); and that use of the worldly language brings a significant gain in expressive power over standard modal operator languages, since the former takes fewer logical resources as primitive and offers a greater range of expression. Those who endorse (E) equivalences typically regard them as analytic, and perhaps no weaker attitude will square with the conception of the equivalences as licensing the listed advantages. Among those who endorse the analyticity of (E) equivalences, genuine modal realists are distinctive in claiming that the (E) equivalences can properly be viewed as articulating an analysis of possibility by way of right-sides that contain no primitive modal element. That (E) equivalences afford such an extra-modal analysis of possibility is rejected by most, if not all, of the other major characters in the field of contemporary modal metaphysics including ersatz realists (presently represented by Lycan (1988, 1991a & 1991b), modalists (Forbes 1989, Shalkowski 1994), modal fictionalists (Armstrong 1989, Rosen 1990) and modal quasi-realists (Blackburn 1986)). Predictably, the ambitious claim to have provided an extra-modal analysis of possibility is confronted by various paradoxes of analysis. By a paradox of analysis, I mean any argument that purports to show that successful analysis, in a given sense, is required to satisfy conditions which are subsequently shown not to be co-satisfiable. The two main paradoxes that I will discuss in this paper focus on the condition of non-circularity in analysis or reduction. My aim will be to try to bolster these paradoxes by discriminating conceptions of circularity and indicating how suitably discriminated conceptions bear on the substantive question of whether an extra-modal analysis or reduction of possibility is possible. But to orientate the discussion I will begin by reflecting briefly on another, venerable, paradox of analysis.

II

Insofar as genuine modal realist analyses are conceived as giving the meanings of modal expressions in extra-modal terms (see e.g. Lewis 1973, p. 1) they are threatened by a Moorean paradox of analysis.[2] This paradox has it that such analyses cannot succeed because they are required both to issue synonyms of the statements that are up for analysis, and to be informative. The argument is that these requirements cannot both be met since synonymy requires a pair of statements to be psychologically or cognitively equivalent —broadly, an understanding subject could not sensibly take different cognitive attitudes (belief, disbelief, not believing) to the contents of such a pair—yet, if a pair of statements is psychologically equivalent, one who already held any particular cognitive attitude to one would, if only she took the trouble to think about it, already (be in a position to) form the same attitude to the other. Thus, no synonym-generating analysis is also informative. In light of this Moorean paradox either of the following two lines of response may appeal to the genuine modal realist. Firstly, he might maintain a conception of synonym-generating analytic reduction, but reject the conception of synonymy that requires such psychological equivalence. Secondly, he might retreat to the position of advocating a metaphysical reduction, the success of which is held not to require the analyticity of equivalences. The former response seems in keeping with Lewis's own conception of the reducibility of possibility, and it has already been emphasised that the linguistic benefits associated with the quantificational treatment of modality may depend on maintaining such a view.[3] For the purposes of this paper I will presume that there are available to the analytic reductionist legitimate notions of synonymy and analyticity that do not allow the Moorean paradox to take hold. Concerning the latter response, I take such a claim of metaphysical reducibility to entail (i) that true modal statements are made true by (are true in virtue of) the existence and properties of the worlds quantified over in the right-sides of (E) equivalences where (ii) the truth-making state of affairs is, in some appropriate sense, extra-modal. So, all

2. I claim no more than that such a paradox is suggested by some of Moore's work on analysis. See Baldwin (1990, p. 88)

3. In Lewis (1973) there is more talk of giving the meanings of modal expressions, but that gives way to more general talk of analyses in Lewis (1986)

that I want to take from the brief engagement with the Moorean paradox is that it leaves undefeated two such further versions of the thesis that possibility is reducible to the extra-modal. Further, I believe that we attain the best view of the landscape of the relevant issues on the basis of the following proposal. There are conditions—basic conditions—that may reasonably be taken to be individually necessary for a successful metaphysical reduction of possibility to the extra-modal, and these basic conditions are also individually necessary for a successful analytic reduction of possibility to the extra-modal. So the conditions that will be discussed concern the success of either kind of reduction, and so for the most part the term 'reduction' can be used as neutral between the two projects. The conditions that I have in mind and which feature in the paradoxes due to Lycan (discussed in III) and Shalkowski (discussed in IV) are conditions of material adequacy, non-circularity and non-arbitrariness.

III

Lewis holds that genuine modal realism is superior to rival theories of modality because only genuine modal realism yields a specification of the truth-conditions of modal sentences that is materially adequate and non-circular (Lewis 1973, p. 85). Lycan's paradox—as I'll say—has it that a successful genuine modal realist reduction of possibility to the extra-modal would have to be, but cannot be, both materially adequate and non-circular. Before discussing Lycan's paradox directly, I will attempt to provide what the debate so far lacks, that is general formulations of the relevant conditions.

Even in the case of material adequacy, the formulation and subsequent evaluation of satisfaction of an appropriate condition is not an entirely straightforward matter. Consider, as a general formulation of a necessary condition of material adequacy, (MA):

(MA) A proposed reduction is materially adequate only if it associates each statement in the given class with some statement in the reducing class that has the same truth-value.

There are two noteworthy features of (MA). Firstly, (MA) does not compel the would-be reductionist to acquiesce in prior consensus about left-side truth-values. The proponent and opponent of the proposed reduction might agree that (MA) is satisfied despite disagreeing about left-side truth-values, so long as they have matching disagreement about right-side truth-values. Thus, to take an example from the broad family of modal statements, a genuine modal realist and an actualist may both endorse the material equivalence (1):

(1) $\forall y$Actually $\exists x(x=y) \leftrightarrow \forall y(y$ is spatiotemporally related to us)

The genuine modal realist endorses (1) since he takes both sides to be false, while an actualist may endorse (1) since she takes both sides to be true. It seems right that we ought not to exert the stronger requirement that the reductionist should be bound, in the name of material adequacy, to assign invariably to left-side statements the truth-values determined by pre-reductive consensus. Of course, there comes a point when an analytic proposal that engages in large scale revision of left-side truth-values risks the charge of irrelevance to the concepts that are circumscribed by our prior uses of the given vocabulary. But the case for tolerating a measure of revision is that since the point of reduction is to illuminate some aspect of the class of left-side statements as a whole, it seems appropriate to allow for some revision of opinions about truth-values in light of such illumination. Certainly, the plausibility of an analytic reduction is inversely proportional to the degree of disturbance of opinion about truth-values, but some such disturbance is tolerable if 'reflective equilibrium' between prior consensus about truth-values and philosophical illumination through the provision of analysis is thereby maximised. Secondly, whether (MA) is satisfied will predictably be disputed in a case where the proponent and opponent of reduction disagree about the very existence of the kinds of states of affairs in which the truth of right-side statements is supposed to consist. Note that the opponent of analysis typically does not have that reason for rejecting the truth of the relevant biconditionals, since the right-side typically enjoys relative ontological security: cf. reductions of the mental to the physical (idealism notwithstanding), the moral to the psycho-logical, secondary to primary properties etc. But the present case is atypical in this respect. While all parties may hold it true that it is possible that there are talking donkeys, the genuine modal realist proponent of the reduction stands alone in believing that there is a non-actual, concrete world at which there are talking donkeys. Moreover, the dialectic is further complicated in this case because the very success of the reduction in question is presented as a salient reason for accepting the existence of the ontology that constitutes the reductive base—an ontology which we have no pre-reductive disposition to recognise. These considerations underline that we cannot long ignore the question from whose standpoint it is that it is dialectically appropriate to judge whether (MA) is satisfied. In answering that question, I think that it is appropriate to offer further leeway to the would-be reductionist. It is obvious, at least, that little illumination will be gained if we simply insist that the pre-reductive opinion must hold sway and thereby deem that the reductionist falls at the first hurdle. This is especially so insofar as the judgement of material inadequacy is informed only by the prima facie incredibility of that ontology whose credibility the success of the reduction is supposed to establish.[4] So the suggestion is that (MA) is viable as a necessary condition of material adequacy, especially when allied to a conception of how its satisfaction should be judged that is tolerant to the reductionist.

It seems appropriate, and especially in light of Lycan's paradox, that an adequate non-circularity condition on reduction should be non-trivial with respect to the condition of material adequacy: that is, a condition of non-circularity is unacceptable which deems a proposed reduction to have failed simply because the condition of material adequacy is satisfied. To put the point otherwise there can be no appropriate material conception of circularity—circularity in extension—since to require non-circularity in that sense is simply to require that the condition of material adequacy should not be satisfied. So, we cannot deem a supposedly extra-modal reduction of possibility objectionably circular for no reason other than that (by reductionist lights) the truth-values of the right-sides of the (E) match those of the left-sides. But what feature is it, then, of the left-side sentences that should be ruled out from re-emerging on the right? Even though such a condition is being entertained as necessary for success in both analytic and metaphysical reduction, the first suggestion that will be developed here is that a non-circularity condition is most appropriately conceived as a condition on the concepts associated with right-side vocabulary—more

4. cf. the 'incredulous stare' at genuine possibilia, Lewis (1986), 133ff.

specifically, a condition on right-side vocabulary and how such vocabulary could be understood.

Firstly, it seems obvious that an adequate non-circularity condition of this character must be able to rule out the use of typical left-side vocabulary in the right-side of a proposed reductive equivalence. Imagine that a prior list of explicitly modal terms has been agreed by all parties to be proscribed from appearance in the right-side of a proper, non-circular, extra-modal reduction. Taking a straw case, then, if someone were to propose as a suitable instance of a reductive equivalence, (2):

(2) $\lozenge$(There are talking donkeys) $\leftrightarrow$ It could be conceived that there are talking donkeys

we should expect this to fail a condition on circularity that draws on any reasonably informed proscribed list of modal vocabulary in virtue of the presence on the right-side of 'could'. The introduction of a tougher condition is motivated by the need to deal with cases of 'new' and potentially contentious theoretical vocabulary that the reductionist may wish to introduce. An especially blatant, and easily anticipated, kind of case occurs when the would-be reductionist tries to meet the basic vocabulary condition by simply introducing a new item of vocabulary that isn't on the proscribed list, but which turns out to have a sense which can be adequately conveyed only by using already proscribed vocabulary. For example, we would have such a case if it turned out that we could only understand the genuine modal realist world predicate 'W_' via an explanation that involved the use of explicitly modal vocabulary, e.g. 'possible'. So any intuitively adequate non-circularity condition, stated in terms of constraints on right-side vocabulary, would have to rule out both such essential appeal, whether explicit or implicit, to distinctive left-side concepts in conveying the meanings of right-side expressions. It seems then, that these two considerations give rise to at least a necessary condition on non-circularity, thus (NC1):

(NC1)   A proposed reduction is non-circular only if the right-sides of equivalences involve the use of neither: (i) vocabulary from the proscribed class; nor (ii) vocabulary the sense of which could be conveyed adequately only by using vocabulary from the proscribed class.

I shall consider in due course whether there is more to objectionable circularity than is allowed for in (NC1). But (NC1) merits attention in the first instance since, as we shall see, Lycan presents his paradox precisely as arising from considerations about the senses of right-side expressions in (E) instances.

Lycan's paradox is the form of the argument presented below that is suggested in Lycan (1988, 1991a, 1991b)—thus:

(L1) The material adequacy of the proposed reduction is established only if the genuine modal realist rules out impossible worlds from the extension of the world predicate 'W_'.

(L2) Impossible worlds are ruled out from the extension of 'W_' only if the proposed reduction is circular.

(LP) The proposed reduction is materially adequate only if it is circular.

The uncontroversial background to this argument is an observation about the material adequacy of equivalences in which the left-sides are assertions of the possibility of the impossible—typically, '$\Diamond(P \ \& \ -P)$'. In such cases, material adequacy requires the association of such a false statement with a false statement that there is a world at which the non-modal content sentence holds, i.e. '$\exists x(Wx \ \& \ (P \ \& \ -P)^*x)$'. This much is in line with the formulation (MA) and with the genuine modal realist view of truth-values. Premise (L1), however, articulates more than this uncontroversial background observation, imposing on the genuine modal realist the burden of establishing material adequacy by ruling out the scenario—the existence of impossible worlds—in which the right-side sentence would be true. Naturally, the genuine modal realist may take issue with this location of the burden of proof, and this much is evident (more shown than stated) in the response of Miller (1993, p. 159): since there are no impossible worlds, what's to rule out? But to take the dispute into potentially more fertile territory, let us assume that the burden of ruling out impossible worlds does lie with the genuine modal realist, so that premise (L1) is accepted. Let us turn our attention, then, to (L2) and the case for ensuing circularity.

Firstly, let us note, following Miller (1993, p. 160), that the 'ruling out' of impossible worlds that is involved in (L1) and (L2) might be construed epistemically, so that the proponent of reduction is being challenged to justify his belief that there are no impossible worlds. In that light, the genuine modal realist's salient justification is that we don't need to believe in impossible worlds in order to express impossibility claims. But more important than the specific content of the justification is the consideration that there is no immediate or obvious connection between (NC1)—a condition on right-side vocabulary and its sense—and the demand that the proponent of reduction should justify his beliefs about the extension of an item of right-side vocabulary, viz. 'W_'. So there is a significant gap to be filled if the manner of genuine realist justification for disbelief in impossible worlds is to form the basis of an indictment of circularity in light of (NC1). More generally, it is potentially an important part of the reductionist's defence against circularity charges that he should distinguish: specifications of sense for right-side expressions; the extensions of such expressions; and justifications for beliefs about the extensions of such expressions. The point bears expansion.

The genuine modal realist may opt to proceed as follows. Let the 'definition' (W) (cf. Miller 1991, p. 477) be taken to give the sense of 'world' (and its formal analogue 'W_'):

(W) (1) Individuals are worldmates if they are spatio-temporally related.

(2) A world is a mereological sum of worldmates.

Then, assume that the sense of the unrestricted existential quantifier is specified in whatever way is deemed to be appropriate independently of any consideration of whether there are non-actual possibilia or impossibilia—perhaps by citing (*inter alia*) appropriate introduction and elimination rules.

A strong point against the allegation of (NC1)-circularity, then, is that even those who were wholly innocent of modal concepts would appear to be in a position to grasp the senses of right-side expressions as conveyed by these specifications. Moreover, on that account of the senses of the key expressions, we are entitled to maintain the natural view that disputes about non-actual ontology can be regarded as genuine ontological disputes—i.e. disputes among those who use the same concepts, who attach univocal senses to key items of vocabulary, but disagree about the associated extensions. Thus, the actualist believes that there is (at most) one world, no non-actual possibilia and no impossibilia; the genuine modal realist believes that there are many worlds, non-actual possibilia but no impossibilia; and the impossibilist believes that, in addition to the worlds that the genuine modal realist believes in, there are others worlds containing impossibilia such as round, square cupolas and the like. In doing so, they disagree: they do not talk at cross purposes.

So far, then, there are insufficient grounds to convict the genuine modal realist of circularity in light of (NC1). But the discussion so far has followed the observation that the reductionist might argue that the epistemic 'ruling out' of impossible worlds involves no circularity. Let us suppose now that a non-epistemic reading of 'ruling out' in (L1) and (L2) is required, and see whether is more to be said in defence of the reductionist in response to Lycan's supporting argument for (L2). The following are the key passages from each of Lycan's presentations of his paradox that speak to the effects of 'ruling out' impossible worlds:

> ... but Lewis mobilizes a modal primitive nonetheless. It is 'world'. 'World' for him has to mean 'possible world', since the very flesh-and-bloodiness of worlds prevents him from admitting impossibilia. (1988, p. 46)

> ... a Concretist is hard put to imagine how a physical flesh-and-blood world could have logically incompatible constituents. Lewis himself simply refuses to countenance impossible worlds. For him, 'world' just means '*possible* world'. Thus it is itself a modal primitive even though it is not spelled like one. Insofar as the Concretist needs or wants to rule out impossibilia by fiat, the Concretist is stuck with a modal primitive. (1991a, p. 224)

> [Lewis] is forced to stipulate the nonexistence of impossible worlds in order to distribute truth-values correctly over modal sentences, 'world' for him means 'possible world' and to mean 'possible' as opposed to 'impossible' is to be a modal term.' (1991b, p. 212)

The direction of argument that is suggested throughout is from a premise concerning the genuine modal realist's (concretist) account of the nature of worlds to the conclusion that 'world' must thereby be taken to mean 'possible world'. As such, further lines of resistance to the charge of circularity are available.

Firstly, even if it is accepted that concreteness prevents worlds from being impossible, this need not be a matter of analytic prevention. It might be held to be a matter of absolute but non-analytic necessity that whatever is concrete is not impossible, so that even if an impossible world were a metaphysical impossibility, it would not yet follow that 'world' must *mean* 'possible world' (any more than—on the received view—it follows from the impossibility of water being other than H_2O that 'water' means H_2O).[5] Now, regardless of the merits of this response, it is to be emphasised that the genuine modal realist who pins his hopes on it will be taking on a heavy burden of explanation. For to maintain that (E) equivalences were—even if absolutely necessary—non-analytic, would be to jettison the basis on which the claims about the various semantic and logical benefits afforded by the equivalences (and outlined at the outset) would naturally be justified. I do not say that no justification can be recovered on that basis for the claims on the various benefits, but in view of the risk involved the genuine modal realist would be well advised to look into options that do not involve jettisoning the analyticity of (E) equivalences.

One such response would involve conceding that the genuine modal realist is entitled to regard (E) equivalences as materially adequate only if he also accepts that 'world' means 'possible world'. Crucially, this concession does not amount to an admission of circularity by the standard of (NC1). For even given synonymy of left and right-sides, and no less a claim than that 'world' means 'possible world', circularity by the (NC1) standard ensues (in the absence of the right-side use of the given vocabulary) only if conceptual priority, as it were, attaches to the explicit vocabulary of the left-side—i.e. only if one could only grasp the senses of right-side expressions through explanations that involved appeal to explicitly modal vocabulary. But even given synonymy, the conceptual priority of left-side vocabulary in this case cannot simply be taken for granted. For, eminently, it may be that we have analytic biconditionals, connecting synonyms, because we are to take the possibility operator as defined, 'by fiat', by its overt syntactic role and the content channelled into it from the right-side

5. I postpone until IV discussion of the entitlement of the would-be reductionist to modalise about the instances of (E).

sentences that feature existential quantification and the notion of a concrete world. This move, it should be emphasised, is one that the proponent of an analysis of possibility may well be compelled to make on adjacent grounds anyway. For it is arguable that in addition to other necessary conditions on successful reduction, justification is required in face of the equivalences for assigning appropriate—conceptual or metaphysical—priority to one side of the equivalences rather than the other. Why do we have a reduction rather than a neutral monism of states or of content differently referred to or expressed? In that light it is a relevant and compelling thought that relatively familiar and better understood modes of presentation of content are bound to hold explanatory or conceptual priority over modes of presentation that are relatively unfamiliar and less well understood. Applying that thought to the case at hand, it is tempting to make the observation that extensional, first-order objectual quantification is among the most semantically perspicuous of all the modes of presentation of content that we deploy, while deployment of intensional sentential operators is among the least perspicuous. To lend the point metaphysical emphasis, we seem to have a relatively secure grip on the category of truthmakers that is introduced by existential quantifiers and associated singular terms (i.e. the category of objects and its paradigm instances) while our understanding of what category of entity—if any—corresponds to the semantic contribution to sentences of intensional sentential operators seems, to say the least, relatively insecure. Of course if the proposal is, in effect, to define the operator, '$\Diamond$', some appeal will be necessary to prior practice with the use of 'possible' and its cognates, in order to judge whether the proposal is successful or even relevant to possibility as we know it. But such considerations are available to the would-be reductionist. Salient among these will be that the validity of uncontroversially valid modal inferences is faithfully represented under the first-order 'definition' of the modal operators, and perhaps even that we now have an explanation—in terms of different constraints on accessibility relations—of why the question of validity for other inferences involving modal operators has seemed controversial or at least underdetermined by prior practice. Indeed the definition of the modal operators in terms of objectual quantification may be justified in terms of an appeal to the fruitfulness of the definition in generating the 'laws of modal logic' in a fashion that is roughly analogous to the Fregean justification for fixing the senses of numerical identity statements in terms of the fruitfulness of such definitions in generating the laws of number.[6] But there is no scope for expanding these brief remarks here. The fundamental point is this, 'world' may mean 'possible world' because the latter is defined in terms of the former via appeal to the conceptual priority of right-side over left-sides in (E) equivalences. Lycan addresses no such questions of priority and far less does he establish the left over right conceptual priority that (NC1) circularity requires.

The foregoing defence of the reductionist in face of Lycan's paradox is, however, vulnerable at least two points.

Firstly, since we have considered only (NC1), and since (NC1) states only a necessary and not a sufficient condition for non-circularity, an obvious anti-reductionist rejoinder will be to insist that there is more to circularity than has been allowed for in (NC1). To consider one obvious expansion of the conception of circularity, in light of the earlier discussion, it may be thought that objectionable circularity may otherwise attach to a reductionist proposal in the way proscribed by (NC2):

> (NC2) A reductionist proposal is non-circular only if the reductionist can adequately express, without using proscribed vocabulary, whatever other claims he is committed to expressing in defence of his proposal.

(NC2) is motivated by the thought that the reductionist is committed to clarifying his proposal, not only by specifying the senses of right-side expressions, but further, by expressing his beliefs about their extensions. In that light Lycan's point might be taken to be that the reductionist can distinguish his beliefs about what worlds (or spatiotemporal relations) there are from those of the impossibilist only by stating explicitly that those that he believes in are those that are possible. Now if the appeal to a conception of circularity so expanded is to be persuasive, that conception has to be motivated independently of the consideration that it looks likely to cause trouble for the reductionist in the present case. Moreover, even if the expanded conception of circularity can be established as proper, it has yet to be established

6. Frege (1953) §70, 81

that the genuine modal realist falls foul of it. Crucially, though, there is, as far as I can see, nothing in Lycan's discussion of circularity that allows us to distinguish between the conditions (NC1) and (NC2), and nothing that can be discerned as argument that genuine modal realism falls foul of the latter, as opposed to the former. The moral is that a successful argument against the reductionist needs a properly motivated and formulated condition of non-circularity: insofar as (NC1) alone is at issue the reductionist is not guilty, and the case has yet to be made that the further condition (NC2) is both justified and effective in establishing guilt.[7]

The second point of vulnerability in the defence of reductionism is that the appeal to right-side conceptual priority that was made in face of (NC1) is open to the objection that even if such a stipulation is adequate to secure the required logical properties of '$\Diamond$', there remains scope for the charge that such a reduction is yet arbitrary.

These two vulnerable points in the reductionist defence merit further attention in light of Shalkowski's paradox.

IV

Shalkowski (1994) argues that a successful genuine modal realist metaphysical reduction of modality to an extra-modal domain of objects would have to be, but cannot be, both non-circular and non-arbitrary. The central argument—Shalkowski's paradox—may be represented as follows:

(S1)   Either the set of objects meets the prior modal conditions of being all and only the objects that there could be, or it does not.

(S2)   If the set of objects meets the prior modal conditions, then the proposed reduction is circular.

(S3)   If the set of objects does not meet the prior modal conditions then the reduction is arbitrary.

7. To underline the point that there is work to be done here, anyone who is tempted towards the expanded conception of circularity should consider the following question. Why should the genuine modal realist not be thought to have discharged his theoretical obligations by expressing either belief or disbelief when confronted with any given ontological claim, rather than requiring—as it were—an informative characterisation of his intended domain of quantification as a whole. Are actualists in possession of such a characterisation, or are their existential beliefs best and adequately expressed in terms of belief in these and disbelief in those?

(SP) The proposed reduction is either arbitrary or circular.

p. 675–80)

Clearly, the idea that the right-sides of (E) equivalences being subject to *prior* modal conditions is crucial to this argument. But prior in what sense, and what senses of priority import circularity? To recapitulate, I claimed that metaphysical reductions are constrained to be non-circular in just whatever sense analytic reductions are constrained to be non-circular. The notion of circularity in extension is of no avail to the anti-reductionist, since to insist, in the name of non-circularity, that the two sides of a proposed equivalence cannot be extensionally equivalent is simply to trivialise the issue by demanding in the name of non-circularity the failure of the condition of material adequacy. Subsequently I formulated two necessary conditions on non-circularity that involved, respectively, considerations about the senses of right-side expressions, and the terms in which reductionist commitments are expressible. With these conditions, one can see how circularity is constituted by a certain kind of priority attaching to primitive modal language: circularity is constituted, in light of (NC1) by appeal to prior understanding of primitive modal vocabulary in conveying senses for right-side expressions, and in light of (NC2) by appeal to the expressive priority of explicitly modal vocabulary.

My suggestion will be that we can bolster Shalkowski's paradox by allying observations about priority that are contained in his supporting arguments to the (NC2) condition on non-circularity.

Shalkowski observes that if there exist impossible objects (cf. Lycan) or fewer objects than there could be (Shalkowski's further observation), (E) equivalences would fail the condition of material adequacy in virtue of the extension of the existential quantifier.[8] He then argues that a reduction may be arbitrary which involves a stipulative definition of the possibility operator that is (by stipulation) materially adequate and logically adequate in generating the 'laws of modal logic'. For such a reduction may be based on right-side quantification over a domain of objects (pencils in a drawer, the bottletops in Hackensack) that bears no relation to our pre-theoretical concept of possibility (ibid, 675–80). Against

---

8. The point is really about kinds of object rather than objects per se since. e.g., material adequacy is unaffected by the existence of indiscernible possibilia.

this background, Shalkowski might be taken to be making the point—and thereby bringing (NC2) into play—that it is only if the reductionist can provide an appropriate expression of his beliefs about the objects in the range of the right-side quantifier that he can convince us that we are not faced with an arbitrary reduction. There is another strand in Shalkowski's discussion that can be teased out to suggest an adjacent worry about the reductionist's expressive commitments.

In support of his paradox, Shalkowski articulates what seems to be intended as a strictly metaphysical notion of priority—thus:

> The need for the restriction [that the domain should be all and only the objects there could be] shows that the most basic facts of existence are not the nonmodal facts involving the existence of worlds but the modal facts that restrict the entities there are. (p. 678)

> These conditions determine which objects may be admitted to the reductive base, and as admission conditions they are not subject to the prior existence and nature of possibilia. (p. 680)

But what is there in the notion of metaphysical priority that is here suggested? There are aspects of these remarks that raise suspicions that a crucial question is being begged against the reductionist, in that the impression is given that we are dealing with two kinds of fact that might stand in relations of relative priority—the existence of a suitably rich plurality of worlds being one set of facts, the totality of possibilities being another. The question that seems thereby to be begged is precisely that two sets of facts are involved—two distinct sets of truthmakers corresponding to the different sides of (E) equivalences—where the reductionist hypothesis is that there is but one set of facts that suffices for the truth of each side of the equivalence. But, equally it is fair to raise the question of what it is that the reductionist has to do to convince us that, even if there does exists a suitably rich totality of worlds and other objects, the set of facts so constituted does suffice as truthmakers for left-side as well as right-side sentences. The anti-reductionist might reason, following reflection on arbitrary cases of material equivalence, that to get beyond material equivalence to identity of truthmakers, we need the supplementary hypothesis that the equivalences are also, at least metaphysically, necessary. Let us entertain as a hypothesis about metaphysical modality the S5 principle that whatever is possible is necessarily possible, so that

(E) left-sides are metaphysically necessary.[9] It would remain to be established then, that it is not merely a metaphysically contingent fact—even given that it is a fact—that all possibilities are realised (cf. Lewis) across a multiverse of spatiotemporally isolated worlds.[10] But if a commitment thereby falls to the reductionist to assert that the set of objects constituting the multiverse has a certain modal status, it is not just the commitment that they should be all and only the (kinds of) objects that there could be. That much is insufficient to meet the requirement that is being urged since it might be regarded as a metaphysically contingent fact that such plenitude obtains. What needs to be added is that the relevant plenitude obtains as a matter of metaphysical necessity—that all and only the possible objects exist *and* necessarily this is so. For only then would the metaphysical necessity of left-side statements be matched by a set of existential assertions that are also metaphysically necessary.[11] This further development of Shalkowski's theme might be viewed as generating further reductionist commitments. For, in sum there are now three modal conditions, in the form of commitments to three kinds of modal assertion, on the success (qua demonstrable non-arbitrariness) of reduction: commitments to assert (i) that the objects that exist are all and only the objects there could be; (ii) the necessitations of (E) instances; and (iii) that necessarily, what exists are all and only the objects there could be. Now given that the reductionist is committed to these assertions, circularity, as determined by the notion of expressive priority of unreduced modal vocabulary captured in (NC2), still remains to be established by showing that the reductionist is unable to express the contents of these claims in the worldly, non-modal mode of presentation that he favours. After all, and for example, the commitment on the part of the would-be reducer of numbers to sets to assert that the empty set has exactly

9. In support of the hypothesis, remember that '◊' is being supposed to represent absolute, unrestricted possibility.

10. This, I take to be a relevant expansion of Shalkowski's point that what makes true possibility claims true—their truthmakers—cannot be identified with a set of objects that '*just happens to be* "lying around"' (ibid 677, my emphasis).

11. Of course, the metaphysical necessity of (E) equivalences is at best a necessary and not a sufficient condition of the envisaged reduction being non-arbitrary since the reductionist, intuitively, gets the matter badly wrong even if he succeeds in correlating possibilities (about donkeys, Socrates etc.) with metaphysically necessary truths about the necessarily existing real numbers.

one subset, imports no damaging circularity so long as the numerical mode of expression can be exchanged for the set-theoretic. So what are the prospects of securing a conviction of circularity in the present case on this basis?

In the case (ii), the (metaphysical) necessitation of (E) equivalences, the reductionist may be inclined to propose that he can satisfy (NC2) by asserting that (E) instances hold true at every world—thus, (NE):

(NE) $\forall y(Wy \rightarrow (\Diamond P \leftrightarrow \exists x(Wx \ \& \ P^*x))^*y)$

The problem in this case, as the recent modal fictionalism debate has shown, is that the genuine modal realist has to find a way of distinguishing between the desired claim that truths about many worlds hold at each world, and the undesired claim that many worlds exist in each world.[12] If that distinction can successfully be drawn, the same tactic will be available for application in case (iii) to express, as required, the necessitation of the output of case (i). But case (i), requiring expression of the claim that the objects that exist are all and only those there could be, raises difficulties of its own. Intuitively the difficulty is this. When the genuine modal realist seeks to express that there could not be certain things, his mode of expression is that (unrestrictedly) there are no such things. In case (i), what needs expressing is that there could not be more than there is—not that there could not be more than there actually is, but that there could not be more than there unrestrictedly is. As such what seems to be required is that a first order language should be able to express that its own unrestricted quantifier is *the* absolutely unrestricted quantifier, and that is the problem. Of course, in any first-order language we can express that there is no more in the domain of quantification than there is in the domain of quantification—all that there is, is all that there is—along the following lines:

(T) $-\exists y \forall x -(y=x)$

But that does not seem to meet the requirement which, it is currently being suggested, that the genuine modal realist must meet.

12. See Brock (1993), Rosen (1993), Menzies & Pettit (1994), Noonan (1994).

So we have here a prima facie case that the genuine realist's proposed reduction does indeed fall foul of expressively determined circularity arising from commitments to make certain assertions in order to demonstrate the non-arbitrary character of the proposed reductions. I say only that we have a prima facie case, and I certainly do not want to claim that the point is decisive. But there is one bluff rejoinder that might be made on behalf of the genuine modal realist here that deserves immediately to be quelled. It might be thought relevant to point out that whatever expressive deficiencies attach to the worldly mode of presentation of modal content are more than matched by the expressive deficiencies of modal operator languages (cf. Lewis 1986, pp 13–17). Now even if there are such expressive deficiencies, that is of little significance in the present context. It might indeed be taken as a disadvantage of modal operator languages that they can be rendered expressively adequate only by deploying the (theoretically unsatisfactory) tactic of adding primitive modal devices. But there is an enormous qualitative gap between the impact on those who accept some modality as primitive of having to admit further primitive modal devices in order to attain expressive completeness with respect to ordinarily formulable modal claims, and the impact on the would-be extra-modal reductionist about modality who is forced into the acceptance of some primitive modality, rather than none, in order to achieve that result. For if the latter case obtains we have a refutation of reductionism not an embarrassing amendment. So if, as I have suggested, Shalkowski's paradox may be allied to the (NC2) condition to strengthen the anti-reductionist case, the resulting difficulty for the reductionist is not offset by appeal to expressive deficiencies in standard modal operator languages.

V

My aim has been to develop the challenge to the would-be reductionist of possibility to the extra-modal by presenting an explicit formulation of non-circularity and other relevant conditions. I do not claim that these formulations have been so adequately motivated, and their consequences so tightly argued, that we are in a position to say that the reductionist project has failed. But I hope that we have some more clues as to what failure or success would consist in.[13]

Department of Philosophy
University of Leeds
Leeds LS2 9JT
England
j.divers@leeds.ac.uk

REFERENCES

Armstrong, D.A. (1989) *A Combinatorial Theory of Possibility* (Cambridge University Press, Cambridge)

Baldwin, T. (1990) *G. E. Moore* (Routledge, London)

Blackburn, S. (1986) 'Morals and Modals' in G. MacDonald and C. Wright (eds.) *Fact Science and Morality: Essays in honour of A.J. Ayer* (Blackwell, Oxford), 119–41.

Brock, S. (1993) 'Modal fictionalism: A Reply to Rosen' *Mind* 102, 147–50.

Forbes, G. (1989) *Languages of Possibility* (Blackwell, Oxford)

Frege, G. (1953) *The Foundations of Arithmetic*, Trans. J.L. Austin (2nd edition, (Blackwell, Oxford)

Lewis, D. (1973) *Counterfactuals* (Blackwell, Oxford)

Lewis, D. (1986) *On The Plurality of Worlds* (Blackwell, Oxford)

Lycan, W. (1988) Review of Lewis (1986) *Journal of Philosophy*, 85, 42–7

Lycan, W. (1991a) 'Two—No, Three—Concepts of Possible Worlds' *Proceedings of the Aristotelian Society* 91, 215–27

Lycan, W. (1991b) 'Pot Bites Kettle' *Australasian Journal of Philosophy* 69, 212–13.

Menzies, P. & Pettit, P. (1994) 'In Defense of Modal Fictionalism' *Analysis* 54, 27–36.

Miller, R.B. (1989) 'Dog Bites Man: A Defence of Modal Realism' *Australasian Journal of Philosophy*, 67, 476–8.

Miller, R.B. (1993) 'Genuine Modal Realism: Still the Only Non-Circular Game in Town' *Australasian Journal of Philosophy*, 71, 60–1.

Noonan, H. (1994) 'In Defense of The Letter of Modal Fictionalism' *Analysis* 53, 133–9.

Rosen, G. (1990) 'Modal Fictionalism' *Mind* 99, 327–54.

Rosen, G. (1993) 'A Problem for Fictionalism About Possible Worlds' *Analysis*, 71–81.

Shalkowski, S. (1994) 'The Ontological Ground of The Alethic Modality' *Philosophical Review* 103, 669–688.

13. Thanks to members of the Dept. of Philosophy, at St. David's College, University of Wales (especially Bernhard Weiss) and to Mike Beaney, Darren Brierton, Jim Edwards, Joe Melia, Alex Miller, Peter Mott, Stephen Mumford, Scott Shalkowski, Alan Weir and Roger White.

IX*—WHAT THE EXTERNALIST CAN KNOW A PRIORI[1]

by Paul A. Boghossian

Even after much discussion, it remains controversial whether an externalism about mental content is compatible with a traditional doctrine of privileged self-knowledge. By an externalism about mental content, I mean the view that what concepts our thoughts involve may depend not only on facts that are internal to us, but on facts about our environment. It is worth emphasizing, if only because it is still occasionally misperceived, that this thesis is supposed to apply at the level of sense and not merely at that of reference: what *concepts* we think in terms of— and not just what they happen to pick out—is said by the externalist to depend upon environmental facts. By a traditional doctrine of privileged self-knowledge, I mean the view that we are able to know, without the benefit of empirical investigation, what our thoughts are in our own case. Suppose I entertain a thought that I would express with the sentence 'Water is wet'. According to the traditional doctrine, I can know without empirical investigation (a) that I am entertaining a thought; (b) that it has a particular conceptual content, and (c) that its content is <u>that water is wet</u>.

Let us call someone who combines an externalist view of mental content with a doctrine of privileged self-knowledge a *compatibilist.* In this paper, I will present a *reductio* of compatibilism; in particular, I intend to argue that, if compatibilism were true, we would be in a position to know certain facts about the world a priori, facts that no one can reasonably believe are knowable a

1. Earlier versions of the argument of this paper were presented to my seminar on 'Self-Knowledge' at Princeton in the Spring of 1991, to my seminar on 'Mental Content' at the University of Michigan in the Spring of 1992, and to the plenary session of the Conference on Self-Knowledge at the University of St. Andrews in August of 1995. I am grateful to those audiences for helpful comments and reactions. I am especially grateful to Anthony Brueckner and Stephen Schiffer for detailed comments on a previous draft and to John Gibbons and Christopher Peacocke for numerous helpful conversations on the general topic.

*Meeting of the Aristotelian Society, held in the Senior Common Room, Birkbeck College, London, on Monday, 24th February, 1997 at 8.15 p.m.

priori. Whether this should be taken to cast doubt on externalism or on privileged self-knowledge is not an issue I will attempt to settle in this paper. Anti-compatibilist arguments with this general form have been attempted in the past, but I believe that those earlier efforts have misstated the case that needs to be made.[2] Before we get into the details, however, it will be useful to outline certain semantical preliminaries.

I

Semantical Preliminaries. In the case of a general term—for instance 'water'—I recognize a three-fold distinction between its extension, its referent, and its meaning. A term's extension is just the set of actual things to which it correctly applies. In the case of 'water,' it is all the bits of water existing anywhere in the universe. Since we know that those bits of water are just aggregates of H_2O molecules, we may also say that the extension of 'water' consists in the set of all aggregates of H_2O molecules that exist anywhere (including those aggregates that we may never encounter).

By a term's referent, I mean the property that it denotes. In the case of 'water' it will be natural to say that its referent is the property of being water. It is possible to wonder whether it would be equally correct to say that it is the property of being H_2O. That depends on whether the property of being water may be identified with the property of being H_2O, an example of an interesting question in the theory of properties, but not one that I need to settle for present purposes. What is important here is to be able to distinguish between a term's extension and its referent, so that we are able to say that a term may express a property that nothing actually has. I think of a sentence's *truth condition* as the proposition it expresses; and I think of the proposition it expresses as composed out of the referents denoted by its terms. Thus, the truth condition of the sentence 'Water is wet' is the proposition made up out of the property of being water and the property of being wet and which says that anything that has the one has the other.

2. See, for example, Michael McKinsey, 'Anti-Individualism and Privileged Access', *Analysis* 51 (1991), pp. 9–16, and the effective response by Anthony Brueckner, 'What an anti-individualist Knows A priori', *Analysis* 52 (1992) pp. 111–118. This style of anti-compatibilist argument is to be distinguished from the 'traveling case' arguments discussed in my 'Content and Self-Knowledge', *Philosophical Topics* 17 (1989), pp. 5–26.

I distinguish between the property that the term 'water' denotes and its *meaning*. The terms 'water' and 'H_2O' may have the same referent, but they do not have the same meaning. What do I mean by the meaning of a term? I wish to be as neutral about this as possible and not to presuppose any particular view. I will let the reader decide to what extent I have succeeded in my neutrality.

Finally, I identify a word's meaning with the concept it expresses, and so I take the meaning of the sentence 'Water is wet' to give the content of the belief that a literal assertoric use of the sentence would express. I use quotes to name words and underlining to name the concept those words express: thus, water is the concept expressed by 'water'. Now, for the argument.

II

Externalism and Twin Earth. Abstractly speaking, externalism is easily enough defined. It is simply the view that facts external to a thinker's skin are relevant to the individuation of (certain of) his mental contents. So stated, externalism does not commit one to any specific form of dependence of mental contents on external facts, just to some form of dependence or other.

However, philosophers who embrace externalism don't do so because they regard it as a self-evident truth. They embrace it, rather, because their intuitive responses to a certain kind of thought experiment—Putnamian Twin Earth fantasies—appear to leave them little choice.[3] And that sort of thought experiment motivates externalism only by motivating a specific form of dependence of mental contents on external facts. In particular, it underwrites the claim that, in the case of an atomic, natural kind concept C, the substance actually picked out by C enters into the individuation of C. To put the claim another way: the substances with which a person actually interacts help determine what atomic, natural kind concepts, if any, that person has.[4]

3. In this paper, I will be restricting myself to externalist theses that are motivated by Putnamian Twin Earth experiments concerning natural kind concepts. In particular, I want to put aside for present purposes externalist theses that are motivated by the influential Burge-style thought experiments involving deference to the usage of linguistic communities. I believe that an argument parallel to the one given in this paper can be mounted for those sorts of externalism as well, but will not argue for this here.

4. By the schema 'x individuates y', I just mean that if the value of 'x' had been different, the value of 'y' would have been different, too. By itself, this doesn't tell us anything about what the value of 'y' is for any particular value of 'x'. More on this below.

To see this, let us remind ourselves how the Putnam thought experiment is supposed to work. Whereas Oscar, an ordinary English speaker, lives on Earth, his molecular and functional duplicate, Toscar, lives on Twin Earth, a planet just like Earth except that the liquid that fills its lakes and oceans, while indistinguishable from Earthly water in all ordinary circumstances, is not H_2O but some other substance with a different chemical composition—call it XYZ. Going by whatever criteria are relevant to such matters, water and twin water are distinct kinds of substance, even though a chemically ignorant person would be unable to tell them apart. Now, widespread intuition appears to have it that, whereas Oscar's tokens of 'water' apply exclusively to H_2O, Toscar's tokens of 'water' apply exclusively to XYZ. Widespread intuition appears to have it, in other words, that Oscar's and Toscar's 'water' tokens have distinct extensions. If this intuition is sustained, then that implies either that their 'water' concepts are not individuated individualistically or that they are not individuated in terms of their referents. For Oscar and Toscar are molecular and functional duplicates of each other: they are alike in all internal respects (up to intentional description). Yet the referents of their concepts differ. Hence, either those concepts don't determine what they refer to in some context-independent way (they are not individuated in terms of their referents) or they do determine what they refer to and so are not individuated individualistically.

It is worth emphasizing that a Twin Earth experiment by itself does not get you all the way to an externalism about concepts; it only gets you as far as this disjunction. It is possible to respond to the experiment, and to the intuitions it generates, by opting for the individualistic disjunct and abandoning the idea that concepts are individuated in terms of their referents. That is the response favoured by so-called 'narrow content' theorists. To get an argument for concept externalism you need not only Twin Earth intuitions, you also need to insist that any notion of mental content deserving of the name has to be individuated in terms of its truth conditions, has to determine the conditions for its truth or satisfaction in some context-independent way. Given this further assumption, there is then no option but to say that Earthly and Twin Earthly tokens of 'water' express distinct concepts—water in the case of the former, and let us say, twater in the case of the latter.

Let us make explicit, then, the various presuppositions involved in using the TE thought experiment as a basis for concept externalism. First, and least controversially, water and twater have to be thought of as distinct substances, distinct natural kinds; otherwise, it won't be true that Oscar's word 'water' and Toscar's word 'water' have distinct extensions and referents. Second, the word 'water'—whether on Earth or on Twin Earth—must be thought of as aiming to express a natural kind concept; otherwise, the fact that water and twater are distinct natural kinds will not be semantically relevant. Third, Oscar and Toscar have to be thought of as chemically indifferent, as having no views about the chemical composition of the liquid kinds around them; otherwise, they won't end up as functional duplicates of each other in the way that the experiment requires. Fourth, the concepts expressed by the Earthly and Twearthly tokens of 'water' have to be thought of as atomic concepts, not compound concepts that are compositionally built up out of other concepts in well-defined ways. For example, the experiment presupposes that <u>water</u> can't be thought of as capable of being defined as: <u>A tasteless, odourless liquid that flows in the rivers and faucets</u>. For if it were a compositional concept of that sort, its extension would be determined by the extension of its ingredient parts. Hence, a conclusion to the effect that <u>water</u> and <u>twater</u> have different extensions would have to proceed differently than it does in Putnam's original experiment, by showing that one of the *ingredients* of water—the concept expressed by 'liquid', for example—has a different extension from that expressed by its Twin counterpart. Finally, and as I have recently noted, concepts must be thought of as individuated in terms of their referents.

III

The Argument. Now, let us suppose that Oscar—our prototypical Twin Earth subject—is a compatibilist. I claim that Oscar is in a position to argue, purely a priori, as follows:

1. If I have the concept <u>water</u>, then water exists.

2. I have the concept <u>water</u>.

Therefore,

3. Water exists.

Since the conclusion is clearly not knowable a priori, one of the premises in Oscar's evidently valid reasoning had better either be false or not knowable a priori. The question is: Can Oscar, qua compatibilist, safely count on one or the other claim? I shall argue that he cannot, that he is committed to both premises (1) and (2) and to their being knowable a priori. If I am right, then the compatibilist is committed to the manifestly absurd conclusion that we can know a priori that water exists.

Now, the a priori knowability of premise (2) just *is* the view that I have called the doctrine of privileged self-knowledge, so we don't have to spend any time debating its dispensability for compatibilism. The only real question concerns premise (1), to an extended discussion of which I now turn.

IV

Perhaps: Water is not required for Water. Two possible objections need to be considered. On the one hand, an opponent might wish to reject the first premise out of hand, on the grounds that it isn't necessary, on an externalist view, that water exist for someone to have the concept water. On the other, he might wish to argue that, although it is true that water is required for water on an externalist view, that fact is not knowable a priori. Which, if any, of these two alternative strategies is available to the compatibilist? Let us begin with a discussion of the first.

How might Oscar have acquired the concept water without actually interacting with some water, according to a Twin Earth externalist? He couldn't have acquired it merely by virtue of its internal functional role, for his duplicate shares that functional role and yet is said not to have the concept water. And he couldn't have acquired it by theorizing that the liquid around him is H_2O, for it is stipulated that Oscar is no chemist and has no specific views about the microstructure of water.

An externalist could claim that Oscar might have acquired water from other speakers who have the concept. This suggestion harbours a number of difficulties which limitations of space prevent me from discussing here.[5] Even if it were ultimately sustained,

---

5. Part of what I have in mind here is that not all speakers could reason in this way, for some of them must have acquired the concept without any help from others. But it would be a needless distraction to go into this now.

however, its impact on the argument I'm pursuing would be minimal—it would simply force us to slightly complicate the absurd conclusion that I have claimed the compatibilist is in a position to derive a priori. Instead of (3), we would now have the equally unpalatable disjunction:

3′. Either water exists or other speakers who have the concept water exist.[6]

For now, however, I propose to set aside this complication and say, simply, that if Twin Earth externalism is true, then contact with water is required for possession of the concept water.

V

Water is required for water, but that fact is not a priori. The most important challenge to the line of argument I'm pursuing derives not from opposition to the truth of this claim, but from opposition to its alleged apriority. This opposition can be stated in a number of related ways; I shall present the strongest version I can think of.

According to the externalist, we know that water is required for possession of the concept water because we know, roughly, that 'water' is one of those words on which a Twin Earth experiment can be run. But doesn't our knowledge that a given word is Twin Earth-eligible rest on empirical information? Compatibilists are very fond of saying that it does;[7] however, it is rare to find their reasons explicitly spelled out. Where exactly do empirical elements intrude into the TE experiment? Let us look at this in some detail. What conditions does a word have to meet if it is to be TE-eligible?

As we have seen, it has to be a word that expresses an atomic concept. It also has to aim to name a natural kind. Furthermore, the user of the word must be indifferent about the essence of the kind that his word aims to name, he must be chemically indifferent.

---

6. It is interesting to note that here we are in agreement with Tyler Burge, if not on the apriority of the disjunction, then at least on its truth, as far as externalism is concerned:

   What seems incredible is to suppose that [Oscar], in his relative ignorance and indifference about the nature of water, holds beliefs whose contents involve the notion, even though neither water nor communal cohorts exist.

   See 'Other Bodies', in A. Woodfield (ed.) *Thought and Object* (Oxford: OUP 1982), p. 116.

7. Tyler Burge has urged this in conversation; for a statement in print, see Brueckner, *op. cit.*

But aren't all these conditions available a priori to the user of the word? More to the point, wouldn't a compatibilist have to hold that they are?

The answer is perfectly straightforward, it seems to me, in the case of the latter two conditions. Whether or not a person has beliefs about the microstructure of the kinds around him, and whether or not he intends one of his words to name one of those kinds, are matters that not only seem intuitively a priori, but that a believer in privileged access would have to hold are a priori. Notice that we are not asking whether the word actually names a natural kind, but only whether its user intends it to do so. And according to the doctrine of privileged access, the contents of one's intentions and beliefs are available to one a priori.

It might be thought, however, that the question about atomicity is somewhat more delicate. For is it so clear that facts about compositionality are a priori? Haven't we, as philosophers, often been in the unhappy position of assuming that a concept was compositional, investing a lot of effort in seeking its definition, only to conclude that it has none, that it must be deemed atomic after all?

It is important not to conflate apriority with ease. A fact may be a priori but very difficult to uncover, as the example of any number of mathematical or logical theorems might illustrate. We need not claim that facts about atomicity are easy, only that they are not empirical. And in fact it is hard to see how they could be otherwise. What sense can we make of the idea that knowledge of whether a concept is internally structured might depend on empirical information about the external world?

So far, then, we have not come across a TE-eligibility criterion that could plausibly be claimed not to be available a priori. We are now about to consider another criterion, however, which, if it really were a criterion, would definitely make TE-eligibility an empirical matter. The criterion is this: In addition to *aiming* to express a natural kind, a word must *actually* name a natural kind, if it is to be Twin Earth-eligible. One cannot run a TE thought experiment on a word that aims, but fails, to name a kind.[8]

---

8. I am grateful to my colleague John Gibbons for helping me see the need to confront this objection and the general line of argument that it opens up.

In support of this claim someone might offer the following. Putnam's original experiment is carried out on a term—'water'—in full knowledge that it does refer to a kind, namely, H_2O. That knowledge plays a central role in the experiment. Twin Earth by itself doesn't speak to what we should say about a term that doesn't name a natural kind. So, for all that Twin Earth overtly commits us to, actually naming a natural kind is a condition on TE-eligibility and that is certainly not a condition that is available a priori. True, Twin Earth teaches us that water is required for the word 'water' to express the concept water, such an objector would concede; but we only learn this because we know—empirically—that water is the kind actually named by 'water'. Hence, TE-eligibility is not a priori.

Now, I think that this objection, as stated, isn't correct; buried within it, however, is another objection that is considerably more challenging. The reason this particular objection doesn't succeed is that it is quite clear that we *can* run a TE experiment on a word that doesn't actually name a natural kind. Suppose we had such a word, W, on Earth. Then, to get a successful TE experiment, all you need to do is describe a Twin situation in which, although the users of the word type W are functional and molecular duplicates of their counterparts on Earth, W does name a kind in the Twin situation. Provided intuition still has it that the extension of Earthly tokens of W are different from the extension of the Twin tokens of W—which of course they will be since the extension of the former will be empty and the extension of the latter won't be—the experiment will succeed.

Now, however, the objector would appear to be in a position to pose a more difficult challenge. For if this is in fact right, and we can run TE experiments even on terms that fail to refer, then how do we know a priori that water is required for 'water' to express water? We can't infer that claim merely from the fact that 'water' is TE-eligible, for we have established that even empty terms are TE-eligible. Maybe water is the concept that 'water' expresses when it fails to name a natural kind, when there is no water for it to name. If we can be said to know that water is required for water, we know that only by virtue of our knowledge that 'water' does name a natural kind, namely, water. And that, of course, is something that we could only have come to know empirically.

Hence, our knowledge that water is required for <u>water</u> is not a priori.

Here, finally, we come across the most important challenge to the line of argument I've been pursuing. It will be interesting to uncover the reason why it doesn't ultimately protect compatibilism from the charge of absurdity.

VI

The Empty Case. I want to approach a response to this objection somewhat indirectly, by focusing on the following question: What should a Twin Earth externalist say about the case where a word aiming to name a natural kind fails to do so? Two sorts of scenario might lead to such an outcome. On the one hand, a word like 'water' may fail to name a natural kind because the liquids to which it is competently applied don't form a natural kind, but rather a heterogeneous motley. On the other hand, a term may fail to name a kind because there fails to be anything at all out there—motley or otherwise—to which it could correctly be said to apply. Here I want to concentrate on the second more extreme sort of case because it throws the issues of interest into sharper relief.

So let us imagine a planet just like ours in which, although it very much seems to its inhabitants that there is a clear, tasteless and colourless liquid flowing in their rivers and taps and to which they confidently take themselves to be applying the word 'water', these appearances are systematically false and constitute a sort of pervasive collective mirage. In point of actual fact, the lakes, rivers and taps on this particular Twin Earth run bone dry. All of this may seem very far-fetched, and no doubt it is. However, the scenario described is not substantially different—except in point of pervasiveness—from what has actually turned out to be true in the case of such terms as 'phlogiston' and 'caloric'; and, anyway, the point isn't to describe a genuine possibility. Rather, it is to inquire how a particular semantical theory proposes to treat cases of reference failure and whether it is committed to treating such cases in a particular way. What *concept*, if any, should a Twin Earth externalist say would be expressed by tokens of the word 'water' on this Dry Earth?

Some may think the answer to be obvious. Since externalism is the view that the concept expressed by a word is individuated in part by the referent of that word, then it follows, does it not, that if the word has no referent that it expresses no concept?

This reasoning would be far too hasty. It confuses the claim that a concept is individuated in terms of its referent, with the claim that the existence of the concept depends on the existence of a referent. To put matters in terms of a familiar technical vocabulary, it confuses externalist individuation with object-dependence. All that Twin Earth externalism is committed to, strictly speaking, is the claim that, if the referent of a given word were different, the concept it would then express would be different, too. And that is consistent with the claim that the word would express a concept in a case where it fails to refer, provided that the concept it would there express is different from any it would express in a case where it does refer. To say it again, externalist individuation, in the sense in which Twin Earth externalism is committed to it, is just the view that, if two words differ in their referents, then they also differ in the concepts they express; strictly speaking, that is consistent with a word's expressing some concept or other even when it fails to have a referent.

But what concept should we say 'water' expresses under the conditions described, in which there fails to be any natural kind for it to refer to? We may consider options under two main headings: compound and atomic.

We could try saying that under the envisioned dry conditions, 'water' expresses a suitable compound concept made up in the familiar way out of other available concepts. Which compound concept? Most plausibly, I suppose, something like: the clear, tasteless, colourless liquid that flows in the taps and the rivers around here and.... It won't matter much for the purposes of this argument how precisely this proposal is fleshed out. On any such view, the word 'water' will contribute a complex property to the proposition expressed by whole sentences involving it, one which, as a matter of contingent fact, nothing in that environment possesses.

Intuitively, this seems to me to be a plausible view of the matter. When I think of a group of people just like us, applying the word 'water' confidently to something that appears to them to be a clear, colourless, tasteless liquid in their environment, when in fact there is no such liquid in their environment, I feel tempted by the sort of error theory of their linguistic behaviour that the present proposal delivers. It seem plausible to me to say that what these people mean by the word 'water' is this clear, colourless, tasteless liquid etc., which, however and unfortunately, is not to be found in their environment.

The problem is that it is very difficult to see how such a view could be available to the Twin Earth externalist. Remember, the TE externalist is committed, for reasons detailed earlier, to holding that 'water' expresses an *atomic* concept under conditions where it has a non-empty extension, whether that extension be H_2O or XYZ or whatever. That is one of the presuppositions of the Twin Earth experiment. But, then, how can the very same word, with the very same functional role, express an atomic concept under one set of external conditions and a compound, decompositional concept under another set of external conditions? A concept's compositionality is exclusively a function its internal 'syntax' and can't be contingent upon external circumstances in the way that the present proposal would require.

Let me forestall a possible misunderstanding of this point. My argument here is not that, if the compatibilist were to embrace the compound notion, that would undermine his commitment to privileged access. For although it is true that embracing the compound option for 'water' on Dry Earth, while being committed to its atomicity on Earth, would have the effect of making facts about compositionality come out a posteriori, that would not flout any doctrine of privileged access that I have defined.

Nor is my argument here that the compound option is unacceptable because it runs into conflict with the independently plausible claim that facts about compositionality are a priori, although, as I noted above, that is something I believe and would be prepared to defend.

In fact, my argument here is not epistemic at all, but rather metaphysical. The compound option requires the externalist to say that one and the same word, with one and the same functional role, may express an atomic concept under one set of external circumstances and a compound decompositional concept under another set of external circumstances. But it is hard to see how the *compositionality* of a concept could be a function of its external circumstances in this way. Compositionality, as I understand it, can only be a function of the internal syntax of a concept; it can't supervene on external circumstances in the way that the compound proposal would require. (This is especially clear on a 'language of thought' picture of mental representation, but is independent of it.)

How do things look with the other main class of available options, that according to which the empty tokens of 'water' express an atomic concept? On this branch, too, we need to answer the question: Which atomic concept will that be, according to the TE externalist?

The externalist will know quite a lot about which concepts it cannot be: in particular, he will know that it cannot be identical with any of the concepts that are expressed by non-empty tokens of 'water'. To suppose otherwise would contradict his overriding commitment to individuating a concept in terms of its referent. But can he tell us, in line with his overriding commitment, what concept *is* expressed by the empty tokens of 'water'?

Unfortunately, there would appear to be a compelling argument showing that the externalist will not be able to say what atomic concept is expressed by the non-referring tokens of 'water', because by his own lights there can't be such a concept. Let me explain.

We have seen that one of the assumptions that is needed to transform a TE experiment into an argument for externalism is the assumption that concepts have context-independent conditions of satisfaction, or, in the case of thought contents, context-independent conditions of truth. So let us ask this: What are the satisfaction conditions for 'water' on Dry Earth, to what sorts of liquid does it apply? By assumption, of course, the actual extension of 'water' is empty on Dry Earth, so there is no liquid in its actual environment to which it applies. But the question I am asking is consistent with the word's actual extension being empty, and consistent even with its extension being empty in all worlds. What I want to know is: What proposition—what truth condition—is expressed by sentences of the form, 'Water is wet', for example, as uttered on Dry Earth? What is it that gets said? Never mind if such sentences are ruled false in the actual world, or even in all worlds.

On the line we are currently investigating, the answer has to be that there is no fact of the matter what truth condition is expressed by sentences involving 'water' on Dry Earth, for there is no fact of the matter what property is denoted by those tokens of 'water'. Since there is no natural kind at the end of the relevant causal chain leading up to uses of 'water' on Dry Earth, there is no fact of the matter what the referent of 'water' is and so no fact of the matter what proposition is expressed by sentences involving it.

But on an externalist view, this admission is fatal to the claim that there is a concept there in the first place, for an externalism about concepts is fuelled in part by the conviction that thought contents must possess context-invariant conditions of satisfaction or, as appropriate, of truth. If, in a given context, there is no fact of the matter what the referent of a given concept is, then to that extent there is also no fact of the matter what the concept is.

We have looked at two possible tacks that an externalist might take regarding empty tokens of 'water', and we have found them both to be irremediably problematic. Letting the empty tokens express a compound concept, while having the virtue of supplying the word with a property to refer to, runs directly into conflict with the externalist's commitment to the atomicity of 'water'. Evading this problem by letting the word express an atomic concept, on the other hand, runs into direct conflict with the externalist's commitment to the idea that concepts must possess determinate, context-independent, conditions of satisfaction.

What then is the externalist to say about the empty case? The answer would appear to be that he has to say just what the proponent of object-dependence said he should say all along—namely, that the empty tokens simply don't express a determinate concept. That turns out to be the right thing to say not because TE externalism is conceptually equivalent to object-dependence, but because TE externalism, in conjunction with its other commitments, entails object-dependence.

VII

The Argument Completed. If this is right, then the compatibilist is in a position to conclude—via purely a priori reasoning—that if a term expresses a concept in the first place, that it must have a non-empty extension. Moreover, privileged access assures him that he will be able to tell a priori whether or not a given term does express a concept, and indeed, if it does, which one. In particular, our friend

Oscar will be able to tell non-empirically that his term 'water' expresses a concept, and in particular that it expresses the concept water. Putting these two bits of information together, he is in a position to conclude, a priori, that water must have existed at some time. And that, we are all agreed, is not something he ought to be able to do.[9]

Department of Philosophy
New York University
New York
NY 10003

9. To generate our problem for the compatibilist we have had to assume that when Oscar reasons as we have described, his a priori warrant for the premises of his argument transmits, across the a priori known entailment, to the entailed conclusion. Recently, some philosophers have taken to questioning whether this principle is correct. Aren't there cases, they have asked, where although A is known a priori, and although A is known a priori to entail B, nevertheless B is not known a priori. See, for example, the interesting paper by Martin Davies, 'Externalism, Architecturalism and Epistemic Warrant', in MacDonald, Smith and Wright, *Knowing Our Own Minds* (Oxford: Oxford University Press, 1997). I have to say that I would be very surprised if there turned out to be any such cases that survived scrutiny. However, defending this claim in full generality is something that deserves separate treatment and will have to be left for another occasion. Here, I will settle for discussing one such case that has been suggested to me (by Stephen Schiffer). Consider the following inference:

If I have toothache, then teeth exist.

I have toothache.

Therefore,

Teeth exist.

I have defined 'a priori knowledge' as 'knowledge that is obtained without empirical investigation'. Relative to this (admittedly vague and informal) characterization, don't the premises of this argument come out a priori? Can't I know that I have toothache without empirical investigation? And, also, that if I have toothache then that I have teeth? However, the conclusion of this argument is clearly not a priori. Therefore, there must be something wrong with the transmission of warrant principle that we have been assuming.

My perhaps predictable reply is that it is not at all clear that the premises of the toothache argument are a priori, relative to the intended notion of 'a priori'. That we are in pain, and even that we are in a particular kind of phenomenologically classifiable pain (a 'toothachey' pain)—these matters seem clearly a priori. But there is no intuitive reason to believe, it seems to me, that we can know a priori that we have toothache, if that is supposed to mean, as it evidently does in the objection under consideration, that we have an ache *in a tooth*. Imagine a toothless person insisting that he has toothache; would we have to defer to his alleged a priori access to that fact?

X*—PICTURES AND BEAUTY

by Robert Hopkins

W hy do we care about pictures? There are many reasons for doing so. Much of what we value in a painting, drawing or photograph is the sort of thing we value in works of other kinds— in poems or operas, for example. But is there something aesthetically valuable in pictures that is not found in the other arts? Is there any distinctive reason to care about pictorial art? I want to explore one way to answer this question in the positive. It involves drawing a particularly intimate connection between pictures and beauty.

I

In the *Laocoon*, Lessing makes the striking claim that 'painting and painting alone can imitate material beauty'.[1] This, I think, points us towards an answer to our question. However, to follow that lead we will need first to interpret Lessing's claim, and then to reinterpret it quite radically, in the light of an obvious objection.

By 'material beauty' Lessing means simply the beauty of material objects, and it is clear that he restricts himself to beauty which can be seen. I don't know whether it makes sense to describe something as beautiful to some other sense, to touch perhaps, but whether it does or not, such properties were not Lessing's concern, and they will not be ours.[2] By 'painting' Lessing means either sculpture or pictorial art (*ibid.*, Preface), and the contrast he draws is with the literary arts, in particular with poetry. What I have to offer will also apply equally to pictures and sculpture. This leaves us, in interpreting the claim, with the notion of imitation.

1. G.E.Lessing *Laocoon* (1766), trans. E. A. McCormick (Indianapolis: Bobbs Merrill, 1962), p. 104.

2. Perhaps some readers will find the very notion of beauty obscure, or multiply ambiguous. Such people are often more at home with 'thicker' aesthetic concepts, such as *elegance* or *gracefulness*. I think that the argument which follows could be run for such concepts too, but I will not attempt to establish that.

*Meeting of the Aristotelian Society, held in the Senior Common Room, Birkbeck College, London, on Monday, 10th March, 1997 at 8.15 p.m.

Often when Lessing speaks of 'imitation', he seems to mean no more than what we would call representation, the power of a picture or poem to represent something else. However, so read, his claim faces an insuperable obstacle. It seems perfectly possible for the literary arts to represent beauty, at least if it suffices for representing beauty that something be represented as beautiful. Indeed, Lessing himself, in the very passage from which the claim comes, provides us with examples, noting that the *Iliad* describes Nereus as beautiful, and Achilles as yet more so. In the face of this compelling difficulty, I propose to put Lessing aside for the moment, and, unhampered by the demands of exegesis, to pursue a line of thought which leads in the same direction.

II

We can make progress by considering a striking claim about our epistemological situation when confronted with a picture, as opposed to a description. The claim is that pictures, but not words, let us judge whether or not what they represent is beautiful.

This needs clarifying. It might mean that pictures let us judge whether any actual objects represented are in fact beautiful. Alternatively, it might mean that pictures let us judge whether the thing represented, actual or not, is represented as beautiful. In other words, is the beauty we are considering in the world as represented or the real world?

The claim we should consider concerns represented beauty. Looking at a picture of, say, a mountain scene, I am able to judge whether that scene, as represented, is beautiful. I am able to say whether, with just those colours on the trees and just those shapes for the nearest crags, the scene is beautiful or not. In contrast, a description of such a scene does not allow me to judge whether the scene, so described, is beautiful. We should focus on this version of the claim because it promises to capture the deeper phenomenon. For if it is possible to learn from pictures whether real things are indeed beautiful, it is so because those pictures represent those things as having certain features, and are accurate in so representing them. The pictures' ability to let us judge the beauty of things as represented underpins their ability to let us judge the beauty things really have.

However, the claim also needs refining. We are concentrating on judgements about beauty in the world as represented. But what holds in the represented realm is dictated by the representation: if the latter represents that realm as containing something beautiful, it does so. And this is as true for descriptive representations as for pictorial ones. So to judge represented beauty in a description one merely needs to know whether it describes anything as beautiful. For example, reading that passage in the *Iliad* where Nereus is explicitly described as beautiful will let the reader know whether Nereus is, as represented, beautiful. The intended contrast has vanished.

The necessary refinement is this. Pictures are distinctive in letting us judge represented beauty *on the basis of other represented properties.* Confronted with the painting of the mountain landscape, I can form a reasonable belief, on the basis of the other properties ascribed to the mountain scene, about whether it is beautiful or not. Confronted with the description of Nereus, I can do no such thing. I can, indeed must, accept Homer's stipulation that the hero is beautiful, but that is not to make that judgement on the basis of the other properties ascribed to him. And if there is no such stipulation, I am at a loss as to whether Nereus is beautiful. (Indeed, it is simply indeterminate.)

Are there difficulties for the claim even in this refined form? I hope that its positive element, that pictures do indeed let us judge in the way described, will be uncontroversial. True, not all pictures allow us so to judge. Those which are sufficiently uninformative about the appearance of their objects, such as stick figure pictures, or some of Picasso's portraits, leave us unable to tell whether something with the properties ascribed would be beautiful. The claim is only that some pictures do let us judge in this way. This still leaves room for a strong contrast with literary art, for it might be that what some pictures actually do, no linguistic representation could.

It is this negative part of the claim, the denial of this power to descriptions, which is likely to raise suspicion. It may help dispel that doubt to expand our view a little. Seeing pictures is by no means the only way to judge beauty. One obvious alternative is to see things in the flesh—as when I judge the beauty of the piazza spreading below me. But there is yet a third way—visualising. If I

visualise this barren oak in full leaf, or how the vase would look
fired in a deep blue glaze, I may judge that the tree as I picture it
is beautiful, or that the pot so coloured would be. Of course,
visualising is something I do intentionally, and is at least usually
under my control. It is sometimes said that it is therefore not
possible to observe my visual imagery, or to learn from conjuring
it. This may seem to threaten the idea that visualising allows us to
judge the beauty of what is visualised. However, matters are the
other way round. It is quite plain that we can and do use visualising
to judge beauty, especially in deciding how to alter or arrange
things. Whatever the correct account of visualising's subjection to
the will, it should respect the phenomenon here noted, and cannot
justify rejecting it.[3]

Now, I don't deny that descriptions may let us judge beauty
through leading us to *visualise* the things described. My claim is
that they cannot do so in any other way. Pictures, in contrast, are
not similarly dependent on visualising. When I see the picture of
the mountain landscape, and grasp what it depicts, I am already in
a position to judge the mountain's beauty. I do not need to take the
further step of visualising the depicted mountain.[4]

This claim can certainly be questioned. Couldn't a description
which was sufficiently informative about the appearance of the
object described let me judge that thing's beauty, even without
visualising it? Candidate descriptions might do this in virtue of
their enormous length, or by using aesthetically loaded terms of
the 'thicker' variety, or simply by ascribing to the internal object
the precise appearance of something the beauty of which we have
already assessed. A full discussion would have to deal with all these
possible threats, perhaps refining the judgement claim further.
However, I will not pursue that discussion here, for three reasons.
First, I am about to use the contrast in terms of judgement to frame
a second contrast between pictures and literary works, one which
is both more compelling and of greater aesthetic significance. This

3. For the point about observation, see Sartre, *The Psychology of Imagination*, London:
Methuen 1972 (1940); and Wittgenstein, *Zettel*, Oxford: Blackwell. For some defence of
visualising as a route to aesthetic judgement, see P. Taylor 'Imagination and Information',
pp. 205–223, *Philosophy and Phenomenological Research*, vol.XLII (1981–2).

4. I am tempted by another claim: that when I do judge the beauty of what I visualise in
response to a description, what is visualised is always more determinate than what is
described. At the least, this disparity *often* holds.

second contrast has the greater claim on our attention. Second, there is some chance of using the second contrast to bolster the first. Although I will not carry this project through in what follows, I will at least sketch it in outline. Finally, contrasts do not have to be of the strong form considered hitherto in order to be aesthetically relevant. If literary art could, but in fact never did, let us judge represented beauty, whereas pictorial art made use of this power, this difference could still underpin differing reasons for caring about the two, as actually practised. If so, the hardest part of defending the contrast over judging represented beauty, showing that no description *could* let us so judge, is not something I need undertake.[5]

III

To frame the second contrast, we need to distinguish between judging beauty and savouring it. The notion of judging beauty is very thin. It amounts to no more than forming a belief that something is beautiful, on the basis of some of its other features. But, at least standardly, when we judge something to be beautiful we also respond to it in a more full-blooded way. Suppose I am confronting a beautiful thing in the flesh—perhaps I am looking at a mountainous panorama. In such a situation, I will do more than simply form the belief that the scenery is beautiful. It will also be the case that my sensibilities are engaged by that beauty. I will respond to it aesthetically, and that response will be the source of the pleasure I take in the scene. It is this further response that I call *savouring* something's beauty.

Now, we are not restricted to judging beauty that we see. As I have argued, we can also judge the beauty represented in pictures. This raises the question whether we can also savour that beauty, and I think it clear that we can. A picture of a mountain scene may evoke just the same responses, engage the same aesthetic

5. Some have denied that there are general conditions determining the applicability of any aesthetic concept (F. Sibley 'Aesthetic Concepts', *Philosophical Review* lxviii:4 (1959), pp. 421–450), or of beauty in particular (M. Mothersill, *Beauty Restored*, Oxford: OUP, 1986). My claim is different. For even if there are no general conditions governing beauty, a description could still *prima facie* let us deploy whatever resources are required to judge beauty—e.g. Sibley's 'taste' (p. 421). In fact, my denial that descriptions let us judge represented beauty implies the weakest claim such views involve, that there are no general conditions from which it follows that something is, *all things considered*, beautiful; but is independent of a stronger claim, that there are no conditions stating features which always contribute positively to a thing's beauty (Sibley pp. 428–30, Mothersill ch. III).

sensibilities, and in consequence elicit the same pleasures, as a mountain landscape itself.[6] And herein lies the second, and more important, contrast with the literary arts. For however evocative and masterful a description of such a scene, it could not enable us to savour the beauty attributed to the landscape. In reading it, our sensibilities might of course be engaged by the beauty of the description itself, but not by the beauty it represents. Pictures, but not descriptions, let us savour represented beauty. And I take it that this contrast is more obvious than that for the power of the two with respect to letting us *judge* represented beauty.

It would be useful to be able to link the two contrasts, so that the plausibility of that for savouring accrued to that for judging. The simplest way to do this would be to argue that, quite generally, judging beauty depends on savouring it—that we have no way to judge something's beauty save by letting it engage our sensibilities. I find this line plausible, but it requires a good deal of work. Part of what is needed is to clarify the notion of savouring. Independently of the desire to argue in the way just sketched, the notion can be open-ended. Provided that whatever might fall under it as it applies in seeing face-to-face also holds for seeing pictures of things, there is no need to clarify just what exactly savouring involves. And this is as well, since for all the obviousness and importance of the idea that to appreciate beauty is to do more than apply a concept, it is far from clear what else is involved. Linking the two contrasts, however, requires us to distinguish, within the various responses which might go by the name 'savouring', those which, plausibly, are essential to judging beauty from those which are not. Since I am unsure how to do this, and since this is not the only work the argument requires, I can do no more here than note the attraction of trying to connect the two contrasts in this way.[7]

---

6. This is not to say that the two might be indistinguishable from an aesthetic point of view. Indeed, some of what I say later (§§V,VI) suggests otherwise. The claim is only that the same broad sorts of response might be elicited by mountain scenery, or by pictures of such scenery.

7. Attempts to forge something like this link date from Kant (in the third critique) to Mothersill (*op.cit*), both of whom offer accounts of what savouring might involve. Some have built the link into the very notion of judging beauty. If they are right to do that, the thin notion of judging offered above cannot be of more than expository value. That is all I need, or want, to claim for it here.

IV

What explains this difference between pictures and words? How are the former able, as the latter are not, to let us savour the beauty represented in them? A first response might appeal to the differing power of each to represent *other* properties of the beautiful item. The thought would be that, although both pictures and words can represent beauty (§I), only pictures can represent other properties intimately related to beauty—either those properties which constitute it, or those on which it depends. So, for instance, one might say that the contrast is explained by the fact that something's beauty depends on how it looks, and that only pictures capture the looks of what they represent. This is too simple-minded as it stands, since descriptions are not wholly barred from representing features of an object's appearance, and we lack an explanation of why they can't do enough to allow for savouring beauty, whereas pictures can. But perhaps the account can be sharpened, and perhaps Lessing himself offers one way to do this. He states that beauty is the 'harmonious juxtaposition' of a thing's parts, and implies that pictures can represent something's parts in their juxtaposition, whereas descriptions can't.[8]

The problem with any explanation of this form is that it far better explains why pictures and words differ with respect to judging beauty than with respect to savouring it. Indeed, the explanation seems tailor-made for the former contrast. That concerned the relative ability of pictures and words to let us judge represented beauty *on the basis of other represented properties*. Explanations of the form proposed tell us which are the other properties on the basis of which, quite generally, judgements of beauty are made. They also claim that pictures can represent those properties, and that descriptions cannot. If so, it is hardly surprising that grasping that a picture depicts something with various determinates of those properties will allow one to judge whether the represented item is beautiful; while grasping the content of a description, which must be silent on the matter of those properties, will not.

Unfortunately, the prospects for explaining savouring are far worse. The explanation operates with a very thin notion of

8. *Op. cit.* p. 104. See also A. Savile *Aesthetic Reconstructions*, Oxford: Blackwell, 1987, ch. 2.

representation, thin enough to cover both pictures and words. This is perfectly adequate when what is at stake is conveying information—information that the conditions for beauty are met, or whatever other information is required to judge beauty. But savouring beauty is not a matter of receiving information, but of having one's aesthetic sensibilities engaged. It is not so much a cognitive achievement, as an affective response. This seems to require more substantial contact with the beauty savoured than representation, thinly conceived, can afford. Certainly representing a property does not, in general, involve instantiating it; and the presence of a representation does not guarantee the presence of (some instance of) the property itself. So when the beauty savoured is not that of something before one, but only beauty represented in a picture, how is it that one's sensibilities are engaged? It is no answer to be told that other properties, intimately related to beauty, are also represented. For the difficulty is precisely to see how the representation of properties, beauty or others, can allow for aesthetic engagement with them. Thus the explanation is useless. It does not help us see how any representation could let us savour represented beauty, and so leaves it mysterious how pictures can do this, while words cannot.

Of course, there is nothing perplexing about how a picture can *itself* engage our aesthetic sensibilities, if by 'the picture' we mean the marks on the canvas (or other surface). Those marks are as capable of beauty as any other visible item, and their beauty, and the engagement with them in which that embroils us, is neither more nor less puzzling than that of any material thing. But I have not argued that pictures engage our sensibilities by being beautifully marked surfaces, I have urged that they allow us to savour the beauty *they represent*. And this raises the question how they can do this.

One response might be to question the assumption that pictures *represent* at all, in the hope that abandoning that will remove the above obstacle to seeing how pictures let us savour beauty.[9] For myself, I cannot see how to begin to describe pictures and their significance without some such notion as representation. However

9. Although the terminology and motivation are rather different, one can perhaps find this suggestion in K. Walton 'Are Representations Symbols?', pp. 236–54, *Monist* 5 (1974). See also Susan Feagin 'Paintings and their Places' pp. 260–8, *Australasian Journal of Philosophy*, vol. 73, no. 2 (1995).

that may be, the proposal would anyway gain us nothing. For think again of the parallel between savouring the beauty of a mountain panorama seen in the flesh, and savouring the beauty of such a scene in a picture. All the same possibilities for affective response are there in the two cases, and they are even if the marks which make up the picture are not themselves in any way beautiful, and are thus not suitable objects of those various responses. Here beauty is savoured, but not that of the marks seen. Since no mountain is seen either, there is still the question what it is about the picture which allows our sensibilities to be engaged in this way. Whether or not we talk of what the picture represents, the fundamental problem stands.[10]

V

Perhaps the problem will not seem acute. To see a picture of a mountain scene is not to see, or to be in the presence of, a mountain; but there is surely a sense in which the picture makes such a scene present to one, as a description would not. After all, the thought goes, there is all the difference in the world between seeing the marks which compose the picture while making out the mountain scene in them, and seeing them without doing that—seeing them as just coloured patches. True, there is a partially analogous difference between reading a description with understanding, and seeing the words without knowing what they mean. However, there is also a crucial disanalogy here—in the picture case to see the marks with understanding is to have an experience of them in which, in some obscure but important way, one is shown a mountain.

10. The problem I have posed is roughly epistemological. It is to say what sort of access pictures offer us to represented beauty, such that we can savour it. A quite distinct, more metaphysical problem would be to ask how we can have any access to represented beauty when there is, quite possibly, no actual beauty represented, and thus is no beauty for us to savour. That the two are distinct is clear—the epistemological problem can be framed even for cases in which the beauty represented is present in the real world, i.e. accurate pictures of beautiful things (cf.§VI). Moreover, the metaphysical difficulty is irrelevant here. For whatever we say in response to it, we should not surrender the key phenomenon, that pictures let us savour represented beauty, whether real or not. In fact, the metaphysical problem is one of a set of puzzles concerning our responses to represented entities, and in each case we should not abandon the response in the face of metaphysical puzzlement. Solving these problems is a matter of showing how it is *the representation* that is responsible for our response, even though that response is directed at *what is represented*, and is so even if the real world contains no such thing. I am optimistic that some such solution is available, here as elsewhere; and that that solution will leave the epistemological problem untouched.

What is right about this is its seeking to explain the contrast between pictures and words by appeal not to *what* is represented, but to the *forms* of representation involved. We need to focus not on representation as something neutral between pictures and words, but on what is special about representation by pictures. The suggestion points us this way by ignoring the particular properties pictures can represent, and concentrating on our experience of them. For if pictures do indeed give rise to a special form of experience, one which in some sense presents whatever the picture represents, this fact can hardly be irrelevant to the nature of pictorial representation. The basic thought must be that representation by pictures essentially involves the arousal of such object-presenting experiences,[11] and that this is what enables it to sustain savouring the beauty represented. Since parallel claims are not at all plausible for representation in language, the contrast between words and pictures can be explained. However, the suggestion remains unacceptably obscure until we are offered a clearer characterization of the 'object-presenting' experience.

The simplest proposal is that the key experience of the picture, although not a case of seeing (e.g.) a mountain scene, is phenomenologically identical to such an experience. To see the picture with understanding is to be in an experiential state which exactly matches, in its phenomenology, the state of seeing a mountain of the shape, colour, etc. represented. Thus the experience of the picture is object-presenting in the most straightforward sense: there is no mountain, but the experience is *as of* one. If so, we can readily explain how pictures let us savour represented beauty. For we can certainly savour the beauty of a scene in seeing it in the flesh, and it seems inessential to this that the experience be veridical. Even if the experience is an hallucination, just the same sensibilities can be in play, just the same responses of contemplation and pleasure elicited, as would be if it were veridical. It is the character of the experience, not its etiology, which matters, and since the current proposal has it that pictures of scenes engender experiences of just the character which the scenes themselves would induce, there can be no difficulty in understanding how pictures enable us to savour

11. There would have to be more to pictorial representation than this. For what this extra might be, see R. Hopkins 'Explaining Depiction', *Philosophical Review* 104:3 (1995), pp. 421–455, esp. 444–6.

the beauty they represent. We might dub this approach to our experience of pictures *illusionism*.[12]

Unfortunately, this otherwise admirable proposal suffers from a fatal drawback: its characterization of our experience of pictures is simply false. The appearance of a mountain and that of a picture of one differ very greatly, at least in some respects, and these differences are manifest in our experience of the two. We see the picture for what it is, that is, at least in part, just coloured marks on a flat surface, perhaps clearly composed of oils, the texture reflecting the light, the glaze showing faint cracks; whereas the mountain is seen as the robustly three-dimensional, multi-faceted, and complex object it is. It would be desperate to say that such differences lie only in the beliefs formed on the basis of experiences which are intrinsically alike. Rather, the differing beliefs reflect the differing character of our experience in the two cases.

Of course, there are many ways in which the primitive account just rejected might be adapted. The problem is to adjust it so as to fulfil two demands: that the characterization be plausible, and that it enable us to explain how pictures let us savour represented beauty. To give a sense of the sharpness of this difficulty, consider a couple of possibilities.

One amendment would be to claim that although our experience of the picture is not *in toto* the match of the experience we would have of the mountain, it is so in part. That is, our experience of the picture is composite—in part experience of marks on a canvas, in part an experience exactly like that of a mountain scene. The idea might be that these components occur simultaneously, or that they occur one after another, in rapid and continual alternation. Whichever is preferred, this proposal retains the ability of the original account to explain savouring, but also its implausibility. For consider the difference between seeing the picture without making out the mountain in it, and seeing it in the way we are trying to capture. Sometimes we shift from the former experience to the latter. When we do, although the marks do not appear to have altered, they come to look quite different. They now appear organized in a special way. But on the current proposal, all that has changed is that a new component has been added to the earlier

12. See E.Gombrich *Art and Illusion*, 5th edition, Oxford: Phaidon, 1977. Note that the above makes no reference to the *beliefs* to which pictures give rise.

experience so that, as well as seeing the marks just as we did before, we now also have the illusion of seeing a mountain. This addition, of a new component to the old, could not possibly constitute a change in the way the marks themselves look; for that is dictated by the component of the experience which is, for all we have been told, intrinsically unchanged.

Suppose instead, then, that we try another way to weaken the account, claiming that our experience of the picture is not the exact match of that we would have of a mountain of the sort depicted, but that the former experience is merely phenomenologically *like* the latter. To my mind this doesn't get the phenomenology right either,[13] but the point I want to stress here is that it already threatens to fail in respect of the other desideratum, explaining savouring. For why should an experience merely akin to that of seeing a mountain allow us to savour the beauty the picture ascribes to the scene? Seeing red is a bit like seeing orange, but it doesn't follow that the one experience allows us to savour what the other one does—the richness of a deep vermilion, for example. In cases where the object seen is more complex, there is the further complication of what we might call the *fragility* of beauty—the fact that small differences in other features of an item (which, presumably, will be reflected in small differences in our experience of it) may have a major impact on whether or not we find it beautiful, i.e. find any beauty in it to savour. So even at this early stage in the retreat from full-blooded illusionism, the ability to explain savouring has slipped away.

Illusionism seeks to explain pictures' ability to let us savour beauty by assimilating our experience of pictures to the standard way to savour beauty—seeing things face-to-face. Another obvious approach would be to assimilate it instead to visualising, since, very plausibly, visualising provides the third and final way to savour beauty. Again, there are more or less sophisticated lines to take here. We could claim that seeing things in pictures is just like, presumably because it involves, visualising them; that it involves visualising them as a component; or merely that it bears some phenomenal similarity to visualising them. The possibilities here have proved less enticing than those on the illusionist side,[14]

13. For my own account, see 'Explaining Depiction', *loc.cit.*

14. Kendall Walton offers an account of pictorial experience in terms of imagining seeing (*Mimesis as Make-Believe,* Cambridge, Mass: Harvard, 1990, ch. 8), but is reluctant to construe the imagining as visualising (see his Reply to Reviewers, *Philosophy and Phenomenological Research*, vol.LI, 1991).

and perhaps for good reason. For it is hard to see how the imagination can provide a decent account of our experience of pictures, and is particularly difficult if the imagining in question is visualising. This is a view there is only space to record here,[15] along with the suspicion that the difficulty of simultaneously accommodating savouring while staying true to the phenomenology of our experience of pictures will be every bit as acute, and indeed will manifest itself in much the same dialectic, here as in the case of illusionism.

So how should we characterize our experience of pictures so as to meet the two demands? Frankly, I don't know. There are many accounts of that experience available, but none known to me promises to do what we here require.[16] Since this includes the account I favour, I consider the problem to be acute. We might seek to free ourselves of one of the two demands, either by rejecting the attempt to understand pictorial representation through our experience of it, or by trying to explain savouring without appeal to the nature of pictorial representation. However, there are good reasons for thinking that the former course cannot succeed,[17] and, aside from the alternative proposal rejected in §IV, I have no idea how one might pursue the latter course. My view is thus that the need to explain savouring presents a new constraint on the task of characterizing our experience of pictures, a task that has already proved challenging enough. But perhaps the need to explain savouring at all will seem of rather academic interest. In the hope of banishing any such impression, I close by returning to the implications of the above for the aesthetics of pictorial art.

VI

What has all this got to do with whether there is something distinctive to value in pictures? I have tried to argue that pictures let us savour the beauty they represent. That is, they allow represented beauty to engage our aesthetic sensibilities, and thus

15. I defend it in my review of *Mimesis as Make-Believe*, in *Philosophical Books* vol.33, no.2 (1992).

16. In addition to the accounts mentioned above, see R. Wollheim *Painting as an Art*, London: Thames & Hudson, 1987 ch. 2; F. Schier *Deeper Into Pictures* Cambridge: CUP, 1986 ch. 10; M. Budd 'How Pictures Look' in *Virtue and Taste*, eds. D. Knowles and J. Skorupski, Oxford: Blackwell, 1993.

17. See 'Explaining Depiction', *loc.cit.*

allow us to take pleasure in that beauty. This is not something that linguistic representations do. Since it is something aesthetically valuable, we have here a distinctive source of value for pictorial art.

To help clarify this position, I first return to an issue raised in §IV, how represented beauty relates to the beauty of the picture itself. It is no part of my thesis that representing beauty is necessary to being a beautiful picture. That claim, which Lessing found at least tempting,[18] is patently false. Pictures clearly have properties appropriate to make them, independently of what they represent, candidates for beauty. They are, for instance, distinctively coloured and patterned. Moreover, we are perfectly aware of those properties, even when seeing something in the surfaces which exhibit them. Whatever else we say about our experience of pictures, we should respect this fundamental and obvious fact. Thus the beauty of the marks is not hidden from us, not even when we see them in the special way they are meant to be seen. Indeed, it seems quite possible, at least within certain limits, to appreciate simultaneously the beauty of the marked surface and that of the item visible therein. (That this should be is, after all, no more mysterious than that we be aware of other properties of surface and depicted object at one and the same time.) A complete aesthetics for pictorial art would accommodate this central and important phenomenon. My interest, however, is rather more focused. I want to concentrate on the representation of beauty, to try to understand its importance for pictorial art.

Consider again the distinction between represented beauty, i.e. beauty the world is shown as containing, and beauty the world really contains. Above I argued that pictures let us savour the beauty represented in them. However, I might have argued the case for the beauty things really possess. We can savour the beauty something, the Taj Mahal say, really possesses *through* savouring the beauty represented in pictures of it, provided those pictures are accurate. What is the aesthetic significance of this fact? Answering this will help us see the further significance of savouring beauty which is *merely* represented.

Suppose the only beauty pictures let us savour was beauty things really possessed. If so, the distinctive value of pictures would lie in providing a special means of access to something itself aesthetically

18. See *Laocoon*, ch. 3 and Savile *Aesthetic Reconstructions*, ch. 1.

valuable, the beauty of various items in the world. They would enable us to enjoy that beauty, even if the items which exhibited it were distant, had ceased to exist, or were in some other way inaccessible to us. The feature of pictures which would be the source of their value would be a sort of transparency.[19] At least as far as the beauty of things went, they would be windows on the real world, letting us engage with that beauty through looking at them.

Although I have not explicitly defended my position as it applies to real beauty, I think that this application is correct, and thus that the last paragraph does capture some of the value of pictorial art. But I also think that pictures let us savour beauty which is *only* represented, beauty not found in the world outside the picture. We can contemplate the beauty of a depicted mausoleum, even if the picture shows the Taj Mahal's counterpart in black marble, planned but never built. Thus pictures do not simply provide a new route to existing beauty, they *create* new beauty. They allow the beauty they represent to engage our sensibilities, for all that there is no such beauty. This might be because—as with the black Taj—there is no actual thing the picture depicts; or because, although some such thing is indeed represented, it is shown as having a beauty it does not in fact enjoy—as in a flattering portrait. Either way, pictures provide access to beauty which the world does not contain, and the world onto which they provide a window transparent to our sensibilities is not merely the actual world, but that of the possible too.

It is worth noting that, on this view, while pictures are valuable for a distinctive reason, in one sense it is false that what we value in them is not found elsewhere. On the contrary, it is precisely so, in the beauty of things around us. This is obvious when the beauty represented is beauty the world really contains—the beauty the true-to-life portrait conveys is the very same quality which engages us when we see the sitter face-to-face. But it also holds when the savoured beauty is only represented. Here too what the picture lets us savour is just another instance of the property material objects enjoy, and which we savour in seeing them—what Lessing called 'material beauty'. What is special about pictures is that they extend

19. There have been several other senses in which it has been suggested, or denied, that pictures are transparent. For two such senses, see Savile *Aesthetic Reconstructions* chs. 1–3, and Walton 'Transparent Pictures', *Critical Inquiry* 11 (1984).

the range of material beauty accessible to us. They can let us appreciate the beauty of things too remote to be experienced at first hand, and they can let us appreciate material beauty which is not there to be experienced at all.

Since Lessing has come up again, this may be a good point to ask whether my cogitations provide a way to make concrete the thought he was reaching for. I am not exegetically competent here, but I can note that the translation of Lessing's key claim provides a decent slogan for my position. Lessing said that pictures imitate material beauty, while literary works do not. If we take 'imitate' in at least one natural way, as to copy or reproduce, that claim nicely encapsulates the thoughts of the last paragraph. Pictures imitate, in the sense of copy, the beauty of existing material objects. But they also copy material beauty in that they make more of that same general good available to us, by *creating* such beauty for us to savour.[20]

However, perhaps anxieties persist about the negative part of Lessing's claim, that literature is impotent in this regard. Earlier I conceded that literature could permit us to *judge* represented beauty, through leading us to visualise. Might it not thereby also let us *savour* that beauty? And if so, what is aesthetically distinctive about pictures?

To answer this question, we need to examine in more detail the possibilities pictures offer for aesthetic interaction with the represented scene. There are many features we might note here, but the following sample should suffice. The represented scene may be highly complex, and the beauty we savour may be dependent on that complexity. We are free to direct our attention within this, possibly complex, scene, concentrating our attention on various aspects of what is depicted at the expense of others. Even when the represented scene is not very complex, there is the permanent possibility of surprise, or of disappointment—of

20. It is perhaps hyperbole to speak of pictures *creating* beauty. I would certainly not allow that they create instances of the other properties they represent—cubicness, or redness, for instance. Whether beauty is in the same boat as these other represented properties depends on its ontological status, an issue on which I would like to stay neutral. If beauty's presence requires little more than that we exhibit the response I have called 'savouring', then pictures may indeed create beauty. If much more is required, probably they do not. Even if so, I hope to be forgiven the hyperbole, since pictures certainly offer us all that we seek in beauty—the opportunity to respond in the way we respond to it. If they do not create it, they do the next best thing.

noticing some elusive feature (perhaps organizational) of what is represented which may intensify our pleasure in it, or undermine that pleasure almost completely. In all these respects, savouring beauty in pictures mimics savouring it in the flesh. The aesthetic significance of the latter can thus attach to the former.

These features of our interaction with the represented scene are all more or less directly dependent on the fact that in the pictorial case the experience which allows us to savour beauty is sustained by the surface before us. The resulting experience is readily available without exertion on our part, stable, and sensitive to minute features of the surface.

Now visualising contrasts quite sharply in these respects. When we visualise we must ourselves sustain the experience which would make savouring possible. Even if a description can tell us precisely what to visualise (something about which I earlier expressed scepticism), we must expend effort to bring this about. The limitations of our attention and memory constrain how complex the visualised scene may be—for many of us a severe constraint, and one that can only be lifted by abandoning directed visualising for the free play of fancy. The upshot of all these differences is that it is in practice very difficult for visualising to support savouring with any of the features just noted.

Of course, what is in practice very difficult may still be quite possible in principle. But the possibility here is beginning to seem quite thin—requiring our psychological capacities to be less restrictive than they are, and literary descriptions to guide complex visualising better than they do. And this raises the question how relevant these possibilities are to what we value in the literary arts as they are practised. The answer, I think, is that they are not relevant at all. As the literary arts are, it is rare, if not completely unknown, for represented beauty to be savoured at all; and certainly is not the case that savouring ever occurs with any of the refinements noted above. In the pictorial arts, in contrast, such savouring is commonplace. Savouring which exhibits anything like the richness and range of savouring beauty seen face-to-face, the savouring which is central to the value of contemplating beauty at all, provides a distinctive reason for caring about the pictorial arts, not only as matters happen to be, but as they readily could.

I close with two further points of clarification. First, it is important that I speak of beauty, and not of its opposite, ugliness, or whatever property, if there is one, that falls between the two. For my claim is that pictures let us savour an aesthetically valuable feature of what they depict and, of the three properties just mentioned, only beauty is plausibly taken to be aesthetically valuable. Had I not concentrated on beauty, the value my discussion attributed to pictures would be more cognitive in nature. It would be the value of informing us of the aesthetic standing, as beautiful, ugly or whatever, of something with the (other) properties ascribed to the object represented. If pictures performed such a function, they would still be distinctive in doing so, and it might still be taken as providing them with distinctive *aesthetic* merit. For who is to say that the aesthetic and the cognitive do not overlap, especially if what we are learning about is the aesthetic aspect of things? However, that merit is not the one I am interested in, and had it been my discussion would have taken a rather different course. It would have concentrated on pictures' ability to let us *judge* represented beauty, and left savouring aside.

The second point is to note a limit on the normative consequences of my view. It is a consequence of my position that certain sorts of picture provide the purest examples of pictures exhibiting the value I have identified. The ideal landscapes of Claude are an obvious instance. However, it is no part of my claim that these pictures represent the highest form of pictorial art. I have not suggested that all valuable pictures should exhibit the feature in question. I have not denied that there are other things to value in pictures, or that those other things are to be valued as much or more than this. I have not even suggested that this is the *only* distinctively pictorial value. All I have tried to do is to explore, in a tentative way, one reason for caring about pictures that would not be a reason for caring about the literary arts.[21]

Department of Philosophy
University of Birmingham
Birmingham B15 2TT
r.d.hopkins@bham.ac.uk

21. Thanks are due to Paul Boghossian, Malcolm Budd, Barrie Falk, Penelope Mackie, Derek Matravers, David Owens, Marion Thain and Kendall Walton.

ON WITTGENSTEIN'S PHILOSOPHY OF MATHEMATICS

Hilary Putnam and James Conant

II—James Conant

Putnam says, in his contribution to this symposium, that his Wittgenstein is neither a philosophical realist, nor a an anti-realist, but only someone who is concerned to defend 'commonsense realism'.[1] What does *that* mean?

The following represents an attempt to get clearer about the approach to reading Wittgenstein that Putnam recommends. I begin by canvassing a fairly standard proposal for what is involved in offering a 'realist' interpretation of Wittgenstein[2] and a proposal for how to oppose such an interpretation; and I try to see why Putnam's Wittgenstein is not the one who figures in either of these proposals. I then try to underscore some of the differences between Putnam's approach to Wittgenstein and that of various other commentators by elaborating some of his suggestions concerning how to read (and how *not* to read) Lectures XXV and XXVI of Wittgenstein's 1939 *Lectures on the Foundations of Mathematics* and, in particular, Wittgenstein's enigmatic discussion in those lectures of G. H. Hardy's claim that mathematical propositions 'correspond to a reality'.

I

Alternative ways of reading Wittgenstein. Simon Blackburn offers a helpful overview of what he takes to be the three different clusters of interpretations of Wittgenstein's later work that dominate 'the

---

1. Putnam's contribution is published in *Proceedings of the Aristotelian Society*, Supplementary Volume LXX (July 1996), pp. 243–264. It, in turn, is a shortened version of a longer paper. All subsequent unqualified references to page numbers are to the version in *Proceedings of the Aristotelian Society*.

2. When I say 'a fairly standard proposal for what is involved in offering a "realist" interpretation of Wittgenstein', I mean standard mostly among those who reject such an interpretation and prefer to read Wittgenstein as some sort of anti-realist.

contemporary scene'.[3] The first cluster—as Blackburn sum-
marizes it—'makes Wittgenstein into a... "realist" of a fairly
specific kind'—one who affirms that 'we need not blush to talk
about truth, facts, knowledge, and certainty' in areas such as ethics
any more than in any other area in which 'realistic thought and
language is perfectly in place'; the second cluster takes
Wittgenstein to be committed to some sort of anti-realist (or quasi-
realist) position with respect to 'areas' such as ethics;[4] the third
cluster insists that Wittgenstein is rightly seen as neither a realist
nor an anti-realist but a quietist who eschews the resolution of
philosophical problems.

Blackburn seems to take these three alternatives, as he
characterizes them, to exhaust the standing alternatives for
interpreting Wittgenstein. Blackburn himself opts without
hesitation for the second, on the grounds that the first alternative is
exegetically and the third philosophically unsustainable. Of the
three, the second is the option which Putnam, in his contribution to
this symposium, is most clearly concerned to reject.[5] Where then
are we to locate Putnam's Wittgenstein on Blackburn's grid? Well,
Putnam starts off by saying that his 'aim in this essay is to show
that Wittgenstein's work as a whole defends commonsense realism'
(p. 243), and, indeed, this fits a recent trend in Putnam's work of
purporting to expound Wittgenstein while, all the while, proudly
flying the banner of (something Putnam calls) realism.[6] All this
suggests that his interpretation falls squarely into Blackburn's first
category. But later on, in his contribution to this symposium, we
find a number of remarks which will seem to Blackburn to tend in
a contrary direction. The following passage will suffice as a
preliminary example: 'The problem with commonsense realism,
many will say, is that it isn't a philosophical position at all.
Wittgensteinians will agree; Wittgenstein himself tells us that it is
not his *intention* to put forward "theses"' (p. 251). Now this would

3. Simon Blackburn, 'Review of Paul Johnston, *Wittgenstein and Moral Philosophy*'
(*Ethics*, April 1993); p. 588.

4. Commentators who fall within this cluster are permitted to differ over the nice question
whether Wittgenstein himself realized that he was so committed.

5. I will not attempt, in what follows, to rehearse or assess Putnam's reasons for rejecting
this option. My business lies elsewhere: in trying to get clearer about the option he doesn't
reject.

6. See, for example, chapters 12–15 of Putnam's *Words and Life* (Cambridge, Ma.: Harvard
University Press, 1994).

seem to smack more of Blackburn's third category: the quietist interpretation. If one accepts Blackburn's way of specifying the options for reading Wittgenstein, then the simultaneous presence in Putnam's essay of remarks of the former kind (which suggest that he opts for a 'realist' interpretation) and remarks of the latter kind (which suggest that he opts for a 'quietist' interpretation) will seem to provide grounds for concluding that Putnam does not really know who he wants his Wittgenstein to be.

I shall assume otherwise. If Putnam's reading of Wittgenstein can be so easily seen not to fall neatly into any of Blackburn's three standing alternatives for how to read Wittgenstein (and, indeed, if Wittgenstein's own remarks about what he is up to, exhibit a similar irresoluteness) then, before concluding that Putnam (or Wittgenstein himself) does not know what he wants, we should take a closer look at the philosophical assumptions built into Blackburn's way of carving up the logical space of possible ways of reading of Wittgenstein.

II

*A kind of 'realist' Wittgenstein is **not**.* Blackburn says that those who belong to the first category of interpreters 'make Wittgenstein into a "realist" of a fairly specific kind'—and he cites John McDowell, Sabina Lovibond and Susan Hurley as exemples of commentators who make Wittgenstein into a 'realist' of this kind. Is Putnam's Wittgenstein a further example of a 'realist' of this fairly specific kind? Judging from Blackburn's preliminary characterization of the kind (as resting on the affirmation that 'we need not blush to talk about truth, facts, knowledge, and certainty' in areas such as ethics and mathematics any more than in any other area), the answer would appear to be affirmative. But, as Blackburn goes on to refine his characterization of the kind, it becomes less and less clear that this is the right answer. The crucial refinement comes when we are further told that proponents of this interpretation hold that for Wittgenstein in ethics and mathematics 'truth, knowledge, and the rest are in place as firmly and *in the same way* as everywhere else' [my emphasis].

Let us begin by considering a Wittgenstein who at least at first can seem to be—and who Blackburn takes to be—a 'realist' of this fairly specific kind: Sabina Lovibond's Wittgenstein.[7] Lovibond writes:

> What Wittgenstein offers us... is a homogenous or 'seamless' conception of language. It is a conception free of invidious comparisons between different regions of discourse.... On this view, the only legitimate role for the idea of 'reality' is that in which it is coordinated with... the metaphysically neutral idea of 'talking about something'.... It follows that 'reference to an objective reality' cannot intelligibly be set up as a target which some propositions—or rather, some utterances couched in the indicative mood—may hit, while others fall short. If something has the grammatical form of a proposition, then it *is* a proposition: philosophical considerations cannot discredit the way in which we classify linguistic entities for other, non-philosophical, purposes....
>
> The only way, then, in which an indicative statement can fail to describe reality is by *not being true*—i.e. by virtue of reality not being as the statement declares it to be....
>
> Thus Wittgenstein's view of language confirms us—provisionally, at least—in the pre-reflective habit of treating as 'descriptive', or fact-stating, all sentences which qualify by grammatical standards as propositions. Instead of confining the descriptive function to those parts of language that deal with a natural-scientific subject-matter, it allows that function to pervade all regions of discourse irrespective of content....
>
> Wittgenstein's view of language implicitly denies any metaphysical role to the idea of 'reality'; it denies that we can draw any intelligible distinction between those parts of assertoric discourse which do, and those which do not, genuinely *describe* reality.[8]

Lovibond's Wittgenstein refuses to draw any metaphysically invidious distinctions between different regions of assertoric discourse; he takes language to be 'metaphysically homogenous'. He acknowledges that there are various dimensions along which we might distinguish regions of discourse; but he holds that all of

7. I say 'who at least *at first can seem* to be a "realist" of this fairly specific kind' because as one reads further on (than the passages quoted below) in Lovibond's book—into the portions of her book in which she attempts to account for the differences between ethical and other kinds of knowledge, and to do justice to what she takes to be the genuine insights underlying non-cognitivism about ethics (concerning which the non-cognitivist himself provides a metaphysical misconstrual)—it becomes increasing doubtful that her Wittgenstein qualifies as a 'realist' of Blackburn's 'fairly specific kind'. But, since my present business is to defend Putnam's Wittgenstein, I will confine my remarks about 'Lovibond's Wittgenstein' to the passages from her quoted below, pretending (along with Blackburn) that her Wittgenstein does so qualify and thus riding roughshod over many of the details of her elegant and nuanced reading of Wittgenstein.

8. Sabina Lovibond, *Realism and Imagination in Ethics* (Oxford: Blackwell, 1983), pp. 25–27, 36.

these regions stand in the same relation to reality. Each region of discourse describes or represents what is the case. Ethical discourse represents ethical features of reality, and so on. The differences between different regions of discourse lie not in *how* they bear on reality, but only in *what* they bear on. Ethical, mathematical and empirical discourse are each concerned with a different kind of feature or aspect of reality.

Blackburn's response to this would seem to be: '*This* is supposed to be a reading of Wittgenstein?' Here is what he says:

> This interpretation would be nice if there were evidence for it. Unfortunately it flies in the face of innumerable texts, and indeed of the whole spirit of the later Wittgenstein. Far from finding a fundamental identity in our different assertoric activities, Wittgenstein wants to force the difference between different 'language games' right down our throats. He is constantly suggesting that underneath a superficial similarity of linguistic form there is a deep difference of function. There is no area he considered in the later work where this approach is not found.[9]

Blackburn evidently has trouble taking what he calls a 'realist' interpretation seriously as a *reading* of Wittgenstein. What is the source of his incredulity? Here are two things Blackburn says about Wittgenstein: (1) he constantly wants to force the difference between different language games right down our throats, and (2) he is constantly suggesting that underneath a superficial similarity of linguistic form there is a deep difference of function. He notices remarks of Lovibond's which appear to deny (2),[10] and he thus takes her to be concerned to deny (1) as well. With respect to the generic denial of (1), he seems to me to be quite mistaken about Lovibond;[11] but with respect to the denial of (2), Blackburn does have his finger on a substantive difference between himself and Lovibond—a difference that is made all the sharper by the (unnecessarily) extreme terms in which Lovibond expresses her denial of (2).

9. Blackburn, *op. cit.,* p. 589.

10. Remarks such as 'the descriptive function pervades all regions of discourse irrespective of content'.

11. In so far as it is important to Blackburn to claim that a 'realist' reading of Wittgenstein fails to acknowledge that 'Wittgenstein wants to force the difference between different "language games" right down our throats', it is by no means clear that Lovibond's Wittgenstein can furnish an example of what Blackburn wants to call a 'realist'. For her Wittgenstein is as interested as Blackburn's is in the difference between different 'language games', but locates the source of the differences in a different place (namely, in what Lovibond calls 'differences in relationships of intellectual authority').

In her eagerness to deny (2), Lovibond allows herself to wander into formulations of the doctrine she attributes to Wittgenstein which are very difficult to sustain exegetically. The clash between what Wittgenstein himself says and what she says on his behalf is perhaps most evident in her attribution to Wittgenstein of the principle that 'if something has the grammatical form of a proposition, then it *is* a proposition'.[12] Wittgenstein, on Lovibond's reading of him, would seem to be positively hostile to the idea that there could so much as be a significant philosophical task which consists in the investigation of whether, in a given case, an indicative sentence which appears to be a proposition is only misleadingly of that appearance. More to our present purpose, he would seem to be equally hostile to the idea that there could be a significant philosophical task which consists in the investigation of whether, in a given case, a proposition which appears to be of a particular sort— say, for example, a description—is only misleadingly of that appearance.[13] Yet, if any credence is to be lent to Wittgenstein's own descriptions of what he is up to, the prosecution of these twin philosophical tasks would appear to form the central business of the better part of his corpus (both early and late). Hence Blackburn's incredulity. The first of these tasks is summarized in §464 of *Philosophical Investigations*: 'My aim is: to teach you to pass from a piece of disguised nonsense to something that is patent nonsense.' In so far as this is Wittgenstein's professed aim in philosophy, it is arguable that no principle is more basic to his philosophical practice than the negation of the one which Lovibond ascribes to him: not everything which appears to be a proposition is one.[14] Allusions to the second task can be found in Wittgenstein's warnings to his reader against mistaking a certain sort of proposition 'whose form makes it look like an empirical proposition' for an empirical proposition, or against construing the grammar of a certain sort of expression 'on the model of "object and designation"'.[15] Arguably the second most basic principle to Wittgenstein's philosophical practice might be put

12. Lovibond, *op. cit.*, p. 26.

13. This shortcoming of Lovibond's reading of Wittgenstein is discussed by Cora Diamond in her article 'Wittgenstein, Mathematics and Ethics' (in *The Cambridge Companion to Wittgenstein*, edited by Hans Sluga and David Stern, Cambridge University Press: Cambridge, 1997). Throughout the remainder of this essay, I am indebted to this article and to conversations with Cora Diamond on these topics.

14. See, for example, *Philosophical Investigations*, §520.

15. As in §251 and §293 respectively of *Philosophical Investigations*.

somewhat tendentiously as follows: not every proposition which appears to be a description is one.

In so far as Lovibond's formulations tend towards denying that Wittgenstein holds to either of these principles, it is difficult not to sympathize with Blackburn's sense that what we are being offered is no longer a reading of Wittgenstein. For Wittgenstein is constantly concerned to show us how we can be misled by the similarities of grammatical appearance between empirical propositions, on the one hand, and ethical or mathematical or psychological propositions, on the other; and how these superficial similarities hide from us the distinctive kind of relation each of these latter kinds of proposition bears to reality. His point is not that we cannot use the word 'description' to encompass all of these different cases.[16] But that we will mislead ourselves if we suppose that, among all these diverse sorts of proposition, there runs some common thread which is usefully characterized as *the* descriptive function.[17]

One hint as to why Lovibond might feel wedded to the claim that it is Wittgenstein's view that 'the descriptive function pervades all regions of discourse' emerges in her characterization of what she takes the alternative to her own reading of Wittgenstein to be. She does not see how to allow for the passages in Wittgenstein's work which run contrary to her reading without ascribing to Wittgenstein a conception of reality that she justly feels he would wish to set himself against: a conception of reality as a *target* ('a target which some propositions—or rather, some utterances couched in the indicative mood—may hit, while others fall short'). She appears to think that the alternative to (what she calls) 'a homogenous view of language' must be such a conception: a conception which assigns (what she calls) 'a metaphysical role to the idea of "reality"'—so that any reading of Wittgenstein which denies that he holds the principle she ascribes to him (that everything which appears to be a description is one) thereby ascribes to him an intention of seeking to rank sentences into those that are metaphysically first-class (and really do represent things

16. This is what is 'somewhat tendentious' about my formulation of the second most basic principle to Wittgenstein's philosophical practice: it makes it seem as if his concern were to legislate how to use the word 'description'.

17. See, for example, *Philosophical Investigations*, §24 ('think how many different kinds of thing are called "description"'), and §§290–291 ('the word "describe" tricks us here').

as they are) and those that are metaphysically second-class (and purport to—but do not really—represent things as they are).

Locating where Putnam's Wittgenstein stands in regard to the disagreement between Lovibond and Blackburn is a tricky matter. To the extent that Blackburn is merely concerned to affirm that Wittgenstein does indeed hold to his two 'basic principles' (enunciated in the preceding paragraph but two), Putnam will want to side with Blackburn. But there is something in Lovibond's 'realism' which Putnam wants, nevertheless, to try to hang on to— the idea that ethical and mathematical propositions are *bona fide* instances of assertoric discourse: ethical and mathematical thought represent forms of reflection that are as fully governed by norms of truth and validity as any other form of cognitive activity. But he is not friendly to the idea that, in order safeguard the cognitive credentials of ethics or mathematics, one must therefore suppose that ethical or mathematical thought bears on reality *in the same way* as ordinary empirical thought; so that, in order to safeguard talk of the truth of propositions such as 'it is wrong to break a promise' or '2+2=4', one must suppose that, like ordinary empirical propositions, such propositions, in each sort of case, 'describe' their own peculiar sort of state of affairs. There is an assumption at work here that Putnam wants to reject—one which underlies Blackburn's way of distinguishing 'realism' and 'anti-realism'—the assumption that there are just two ways to go: either (i) we accept a general philosophical account of the relation between language and reality according to which all indicative sentences are to be classified equally as 'descriptions of reality'; or (ii) we accept an alternative philosophical account of the relation between language and reality which rests on a metaphysically-grounded distinction between those sentences which do genuinely describe reality (and whose cognitive credentials are therefore to be taken at face value) and those which merely purport to describe reality (and whose claims to truth are therefore to be taken as chimerical).

III

*A kind of 'anti-realist' Wittgenstein is **not**.* Putnam's interpretation clearly does not qualify as 'realist' in Blackburn's ('fairly specific') sense, in so far as it explicitly repudiates a central tenet of that realism—that language is (as Lovibond puts it) 'metaphysically homogenous', that in ethics and mathematics (as Blackburn puts it) 'truth, knowledge, and the rest are in place in the same way as everywhere else'. This repudiation can be found in a passage such as the following:

> The problem in all of these cases... is that we wish to impose a *pattern* of what it is to be true, a pattern devised largely from the successes of the physical science, on all of our discourse.... In contrast, the Wittgensteinian strategy, I believe, is to argue that while there is such a thing as correctness in ethics... [and] in mathematics, the way to understand that is not by trying to model it on the ways in which we get things right in physics, but by trying to understand the life we lead with our concepts in each of these distinct areas. The problems in the philosophy of mathematics are not precisely the *same* as the problems in metaethics... because the way the concepts work is not the same in these different areas, but what drives the sense that there is a problem—a problem which calls for either a 'skeptical solution' or an absurd metaphysics—can be the very same preconceptions about what 'genuine' truth, or 'genuine' reference must look like. (pp. 262–4)

Putnam's Wittgenstein denies here precisely what Blackburn's 'realist' is most concerned to affirm: that the kind of relation propositions bear to reality conforms throughout all regions of assertoric discourse to a single pattern. Putnam insists rather that in ethics, in mathematics, and in physics 'the way the concepts work is not the same', and that the avoidance of philosophical confusion concerning the differences between such concepts can be won only at the cost of a painstaking philosophical labour of 'trying to understand the life we lead with our concepts in each of these distinct areas'. Putnam's Wittgenstein thus shares with the Wittgenstein who figures in Blackburn's second cluster of interpretations a commitment to the following two ideas: (1) that superficial similarities of linguistic form can mask profound differences in function; (2) that we must come to *understand* these differences if we are to avoid being misled, in our philosophizing, by them.

To see where the differences lie between Putnam's and Blackburn's preferred ways of refusing (what Blackburn calls) 'realism', consider how Blackburn characterizes the philosophical morals which he thinks are to be drawn from Wittgenstein's efforts 'to force the difference between different "language-games" right down our throats':

> [Wittgenstein] is constantly suggesting that underneath a superficial similarity of linguistic form there is a deep difference of function. There is no area he considered in the later work where this approach is not found. Philosophical statements are not what they appear; they are rules of grammar. Mathematical statements are often not what they appear; they do not have the use of statements but of rules. Apparent self-descriptions are not what they appear; avowals are forms of self-expression. Statements attributing consciousness to others, or describing acts as voluntary, have the use of expressions of attitude. Ethical and aesthetic and theological assertions are not what they appear; the form of life in which they are found is not that of describing how the world is but of reacting emotionally to it.

> Bully for Wittgenstein, say I. But now remember too that 'philosophy leaves everything as it is.' So can we continue to talk of truth, fact, knowledge, and the rest in these non-descriptive areas without blushing? It seems a good question, and I do not think Wittgenstein ever confronted it squarely. His answer is going to be that we can, but it is not at all plain how he gets to it, for the difference of activity he harps on is introduced precisely by *contrast* with describing and representing the way of the world, and those are the activities that most obviously must conform to norms of truth and fact. Wittgenstein seems to leave unfinished business.... The business would be understanding how ejaculations, expressions of emotion, rules, and the rest can properly don the garb of assertions in the first place.[18]

There are two tendencies at play in how Blackburn characterizes what emerges from Wittgenstein's grammatical investigations which Putnam is bound to regard as unfaithful to Wittgenstein.

The first is a tendency to characterize non-descriptive forms of linguistic activity so that (in refusing to assimilate them to the category of descriptions) one assimilates them instead to some non-discursive category—so that they no longer seem to qualify even as regions of assertoric discourse. Blackburn does not say—as Wittgenstein is forever saying—that it helps to mitigate certain puzzling features of a given language-game if one *compares* (an aspect of) what one is doing in thus using language with certain non-linguistic forms of behaviour. Blackburn suggests rather that what Wittgenstein is concerned to claim is that certain forms of

18. Blackburn, *op. cit.*, p. 589.

words that appear to be descriptions are (not only not descriptions, but) not even, in any obvious sense, assertions at all—what they *really* are is, *mere* ejaculations, or *mere* expressions of feeling, or *mere* forms of emotional reaction. If one thinks *this* is what Wittgenstein is saying, then one is bound to think that he left unfinished philosophical business (namely, the business of addressing the question: how can one 'continue to talk of truth, fact, knowledge, and the rest' in connection with mere ejaculations or sub-cognitive emotional reactions or other bits of intrinsically non-assertoric behaviour?). Such a characterization of these (non-descriptive) regions of discourse invites us to conceive of them as being, in the first instance, utterly without connection to those regions of our discourse that most obviously do conform to norms of truth and fact, and hence threatens to render them no longer *regions* of discourse at all. Once this threat is realized, any subsequent rescue attempt (which allows one to continue to speak along with the vulgar of truth, fact, knowledge, and the rest in connection with these 'regions') comes too late. It will amount to nothing more than an attempt to show how various forms of non-assertoric linguistic behaviour can (as Blackburn puts it) 'don the garb of assertions', while remaining in substance, underneath the misleading outward garb, a wholly distinct kind of performance—one that falls outside the game of truth and falsity altogether.

The second of the two tendencies (at play in how Blackburn characterizes what emerges from Wittgenstein's grammatical investigations) is a tendency to set-up a single overarching contrast: on the one hand, there is language which 'describes and represents the way of the world', and, on the other hand, there is all this other stuff—and then examples follow, such as *mere* ejaculations, *mere* forms of emotional reaction, etc. A general positive character-ization of 'all this other stuff' is thereby insinuated through the character of the examples. The bulk of this other stuff looks as if it could be summed up in some single heading such as 'all this *merely expressive* stuff'. It then looks as if there is a single outstanding philosophical question: how can talk of truth, knowledge and the rest gain a foothold with respect to this latter sort of (merely expressive) stuff. So we appear to have an obligation to look for *the* story which answers this question (and it can seem as if Wittgenstein has inexcusably evaded this obligation).

The differences Wittgenstein seeks to teach are not (as Blackburn tends to suggest) primarily ones that obtain between one central kind of statement (namely descriptive statements) and the rest of language, but, more often than not, ones that obtain *within* the very broad category of uses of language that are not primarily concerned with representing or describing the world. Where Blackburn seeks to erect a single broad (non-descriptive) category and pose a single question about all of the cases which fall under it ('how do *these* sorts of proposition all manage to don the garb of assertions?'), Wittgenstein is concerned to show us how different the various cases which fall under this category are from each other. If one looks at what Wittgenstein has to say about the examples which Blackburn himself adduces—avowals, mathematical theorems, ethical statements—it is evident that he thinks that each of these regions of discourse has its own distinctive grammar, and that precisely what confuses us is our tendency to run these cases together with each other (as well as with ordinary empirical statements). Each of these non-descriptive regions, according to Wittgenstein, is caught up in the business of speaking truth in a different way. The anti-realist's determination to find *the* story (about how all these regions of our discourse are to be brought within the scope of a single contrast with empirical description) is thus identified by Wittgenstein as being as great a source of mischief as the determination of (what Blackburn calls) the 'realist' to find a single overarching story about how each sort of proposition corresponds to its own region of reality.

IV

A preliminary example: avowals. To further see the difference between Blackburn's and Putnam's Wittgensteins, it will help to explore for a moment a preliminary example—one that Blackburn himself adduces, that of avowals.

Wittgenstein's interest in avowals rests exclusively on an interest in dispelling the philosophical puzzlement occasioned by certain features of avowals. *One* such feature is that they possess first-person authority. If we take this authority to be continuous with the sort of authority that ordinary empirical reports possess—yet somehow extraordinarily less corrigible —we are bound to become puzzled. Wittgenstein suggests that, if we wish to understand the nature of the authority of avowals, we do well to consider the sort of (internal) relation that obtains between a smile and the joy which the smile expresses, and then to consider the way in which linguistic avowals often play the same sort of expressive role in our lives that such pre-linguistic non-verbal forms of behaviour, such as smiles, play. The point of the comparison is to bring out the expressive dimension of avowals (because it is partly a neglect of that dimension, Wittgenstein thinks, that renders the phenomenon of first-person authority puzzling).

The point of such a comparison however is not thereby to strip avowals of their assertoric dimension. If one sees non-descriptive uses of language as being simply a form of non-assertoric language-use, one will obscure from view how such uses of language interweave with those regions of our discourse that most obviously do conform to norms of truth and fact. When I say 'I am happy', I am expressing my happiness through a linguistic mode of behaviour. But such an utterance cannot simply be equated with a cry of joy. For when I say 'I am happy' there is something which is my telling the truth with respect to this matter. If I say 'I am happy', I issue an inference-license, and you may now say of me 'He is happy'; and what you say of me, assuming I am telling the truth, will be true. The grammatical and logical relations that obtain between my statement and yours cannot obtain between a non-assertoric bit of behaviour and a statement—say, between my smile or my cry of joy and your saying of me 'He is happy'. A smile or a cry of joy is neither true nor false, whereas an avowal is. The philosophical difficulty here, on Wittgenstein's view, lies in obtaining a perspicuous overview of the interplay between the various functions of avowals (among which are its expressive and assertoric functions).

Blackburn is certainly right that Wittgenstein thinks that the linguistic form of avowals masks their expressive function. Blackburn's formula for reading Wittgenstein, however, tends in the direction of hearing him say that philosophical clarity is achieved by simply exchanging one understanding of *the* function of avowals for another. *The* function of a bit of language is not only not simply what it appears to be; according to Blackburn's Wittgenstein, it is in reality not at all what it appears to be. *The* function of a bit of language is rather to be identified with that function which is masked by its linguistic form. Putnam's formula for reading Wittgenstein rests on trying to bring out how much philosophical trouble we get into when we start talking about '*the* function of a bit of language'. Those language-games which puzzle us most when we are doing philosophy, according to Putnam's Wittgenstein, are precisely those that possess the most complex and multi-layered structure—a structure which enables them to serve various kinds of function at once. The philosophical trick then lies in seeing how, in a given case, within a set of apparently mutually exhaustive accounts of a particular region of discourse (ethics, mathematics, avowals), each alternative account contains, and each occludes, a piece of the whole truth.

Putnam says 'the Wittgensteinian strategy' is to try to show how there can be such a thing as *correctness* in ethics and in mathematics, but not by trying to impose a single *pattern* or *model* on all regions of discourse, but rather by trying to understand the life we lead with our concepts in each of these distinct areas. But an appreciation of what correctness comes to in each of these distinct areas turns on an appreciation of the distinctive way in which each of these regions of our discourse is interwoven with those portions of our discourse where talk of truth, knowledge and the rest seems least problematic. When Wittgenstein, in his *Remarks on the Foundations of Mathematics*, says that a certain species of realism is the hardest thing in philosophy,[19] this does not, according to Putnam, refer to the task of finding a way to shoehorn the diverse regions of our discourse into a single general 'realistic' account of the relation between language and reality (such that each region of language is accorded its own region of reality for it to be 'about'); rather it refers to the task of providing a fully *realistic depiction* of the ways in which the different regions of our discourse are inextricably entangled in one another. Thus when Wittgenstein speaks of realism in philosophy, he means the word not in the philosopher's sense (as an account of some domain of fact that is out there anyway and which provides a target for thought to hit or fall short of), but rather in something more like the novelist's sense (i.e. a faithfulness to the complexity of everyday reality in depicting our lives with one another and in the world).[20]

19. *Remarks on the Foundations of Mathematics* (Oxford: Blackwell, 1967), VI, §23.

20. For an elaboration of this suggestion concerning how to understand what Wittgenstein means when he says he aspires to realism in philosophy, see chapter I of Cora Diamond *The Realistic Spirit* (Cambridge Ma.: MIT Press, 1991).

V

Quietism? Given that Putnam's Wittgenstein falls into neither the first nor the second of the clusters of interpretations of Wittgenstein's later work that Blackburn allows for, the question arises as to how he fares with respect to the third. Here is how Blackburn characterizes the third:

> The third cluster of interpretations wants elements from the second and from the first. It properly remembers Wittgenstein's love of motley. But it leaves no unfinished business—after all, how can Wittgenstein, with his hostility to the idea that philosophy is trying to find explanations of anything, admit to a feature of our language games that needs philosophical explanation? The true Wittgensteinian reaction is just to find *more* motley.... [This] is true to much in Wittgenstein, yet its problem is obvious: it denies Wittgenstein any words to say what he wanted about the differences that the position starts by celebrating.[21]

The third cluster wants to combine an element from the second cluster with an element from the first: from the second it keeps the idea that Wittgenstein wants to show us how very different ethical or mathematical propositions are from empirical descriptions (that he wants to teach us differences), from the first it keeps the idea that he takes us as far as we should want or need to go in philosophy (that he leaves no unfinished business). The problem, according to Blackburn, is that these elements cannot be combined without further ado: a mere exhibition of differences cannot by itself solve the very problems which force themselves upon us as soon as we take these differences to heart (problems such as: how can mere ejaculations don the garb of assertions?). Blackburn congratulates Wittgenstein on having unearthed some interesting and important philosophical problems; but for this very reason he is perplexed by Wittgenstein's apparent refusal to engage in the sort of constructive philosophizing that (Blackburn takes it) these very problems cry out for.

This renders the following exegetical question urgent for Blackburn: if grammatical investigation consists in a mere exhibition of differences, and if Wittgenstein's grammatical investigations unearth puzzling philosophical questions, then why

21. Blackburn, *op. cit.*, pp. 589–90.

does Wittgenstein think that, after having completed his grammatical investigations, he leaves no unfinished business? There is one answer to this question which has of late become something of an interpretative commonplace: Wittgenstein, we are told, espouses *quietism*. This is evidently the answer which Blackburn has in mind here. Elsewhere he offers the following characterizations of quietism:

> [T]he attitude which I christen *quietism* or *dismissive neutralism*... urges that at some particular point the debate is not a real one, and that we are only offered, for instance, metaphors and images from which we can profit as we please.[22]

> [Q]uietism... [is] the doctrine associated with Wittgenstein that there is no standpoint from which to achieve the traditional philosophical goal of a theory about some concept or another (e.g. truth, experience).[23]

Is Putnam's Wittgenstein a quietist? If one rests with the character-izations of quietism provided in these passages, the question is difficult to answer. For there is an unclarity in expressions such as 'urging that the debate [about X] is not a real one' and '[asserting] that there is no standpoint from which to achieve the goal [of providing a theory about X]'—an unclarity which has done much to obstruct the possibility of an encounter with Wittgenstein's philosophy.

One way of understanding these expressions is to take quietism to be (to borrow Blackburn's apt phrase) a form of *dismissive neutralism*. There is a debate we might engage in, but, while remaining neutral towards the parties currently so engaged, we quietists roundly dismiss the entire activity of so engaging oneself. Quietism, thus understood, is a call for renunciation: there is something which would be partaking in the debate in question, but the quietist urges us instead not to partake; there is something which would be attaining to the philosophical 'standpoint' in question, but the quietist urges us instead not to try to attain it. 'Quietism' is an apt label for such a call for renunciation. The original quietists, followers of the Spanish mystic Michaelis de Molinos, were participants in the seventeenth-century Catholic

---

22. *Spreading the Word* (Oxford: Oxford University Press, 1984), p. 146.

23. Simon Blackburn, *The Oxford Dictionary of Philosophy* (Oxford: Oxford University Press, 1984), p. 315.

Counter Reformation. They sought to withdraw from the world of the senses, to abstain from outward activity, and to absorb themselves in continuous passive devotional contemplation and prayer, hoping by this means gradually to effect an annihilation of the will (and therewith to attain beatitude). For the original quietists, there was, of course, a clear standing alternative to the rigours of their ascetic spiritual discipline: namely, indulging in an ordinary life of activity and absorption in the world of the senses— an alternative which most people embraced, but which they chose to renounce.[24] A quietist reading of Wittgenstein similarly takes there to be a clear standing alternative to the master's ascetic credo: indulging in an activity of constructive philosophizing—an alternative which most philosophers embrace, but which the true Wittgensteinian chooses to renounce. This fits in nicely with the thought that Wittgenstein's teaching means to leave us with no unfinished business. If we are true disciples of Wittgensteinian quietism we will have no stomach for the business that the unconverted feel we leave unaddressed. To say that Wittgenstein espouses quietism, so understood, is to say that there is a form of activity that he thinks we might engage in, but he urges us instead not to engage in it, urging us instead just to *stop*—and to renounce the activity altogether.[25]

Given such an understanding of quietism, is Putnam's Wittgenstein a quietist? No. To see why not, consider an alternative way of resolving the unclarity in the expressions that Blackburn employs in his characterization of quietism (such as 'urging that the debate [about X] is not a real one' and '[asserting] that there is no standpoint from which to achieve the goal [of providing a theory about X]'). On this alternative understanding, the aim is not merely

24. The term 'quietism' first came into professional philosophy, as far as I know, through Schopenhauer who thought the followers of Molinos were on to something, and was thus happy to declare: '[I]f, in the judgement of contemporaries, the paradoxical and unexampled agreement of my philosophy with quietism... appears an obvious stumbling block, yet I, on the other hand, see in this very agreement a proof of its sole accuracy and truth.' (*The World As Will and As Representation*, Vol. II, New York, NY: Dover, 1958; p. 615).

25. Various reasons can be (and have been) given for why Wittgenstein might think we should heed such a call for renunciation (e. g. there are reasons to think we will never be able to succeed in the activity in question, the activity itself is a frivolous one, etc.). It is immaterial to my purposes to enter into this level of detail. As soon as one thinks one owes an answer to the question 'Why does Wittgenstein think we ought to try to leave off philosophizing?', one's reading of Wittgenstein qualifies as quietist in the sense here outlined.

to *urge* that we leave off debating a certain question, but to *show* that there is no question to debate—to show that a certain apparent debate 'is not a real one', that the forms of words we avail ourselves of when we seek to describe the standpoint in question only apparently describe a standpoint. Thus the aim is not simply to withdraw from the debate, but rather to attempt to bring the debate to a satisfactory resolution. Thus Putnam writes:

> Wittgenstein... did *not* wish to sweep any problem under the rug; what he was rather trying to do is see just what picture 'holds us captive'—to find the roots of our conviction that we *have* a genuine problem, and to enable us to see that when we try to state clearly what it is, it turns out to be a nonsense problem. (p. 252)

A very different way of understanding Wittgenstein, from any of the three for which Blackburn allows, is encoded in this passage.

Putnam's Wittgenstein diverges from (what I have been calling) quietism in the following seven respects: (1) his philosophical practice is not exhausted by the activity of merely describing the differences between language-games; partly because (2) genuinely grasping what such differences come to itself requires an extensive positive effort of *understanding* (one of 'trying to understand the life we lead with our concepts in each of these distinct areas'), and because (3) the achievement of such understanding is itself in service of an ulterior elucidatory aim—one of *enabling us* to see something about ourselves:[26] that sometimes we mean nothing when we think we mean something (if 'we try to state clearly what the problem is, it turns out to be a nonsense problem');[27] this activity of elucidation itself presupposes an equally extensive task of *diagnosis* ('trying to see just what picture "holds us captive"— to find the roots of our conviction that we *have* a genuine problem'); thus (5) when a problem is made to disappear it is not because we succeed in averting our gaze from the problem, leaving it unaddressed, but because *the problem itself* is made to disappear; hence (6) we are not called upon to renounce anything (but rather to see that *there is nothing to renounce* where we thought that there

---

26. Where it is important that this is something that each person, in each such case, must come to see for him- or herself.

27. None of Blackburn's three clusters allows one to see how Wittgenstein's own descriptions of his aim in philosophy (in passages such as *Philosophical Investigations*, §464) could be anything but misdescriptions.

was something);[28] and, finally, (7) these twin philosophical tasks of understanding and elucidation never come to an end—each of us, necessarily always under the pressure of taking thought, will necessarily always provide the philosopher (in each of us and in each other) with plenty of unfinished business.[29]

VI

Wittgenstein on Hardy. The text on which Putnam leans most heavily in his discussion is Lectures XXV and XXVI of Wittgenstein's 1939 Cambridge *Lectures on the Foundations of Mathematics.* It is clear why the 1939 lectures provide an attractive text for Putnam's purposes. In those lectures, Wittgenstein is concerned both to deny precisely what 'realists' (in Blackburn's sense of the word) affirm and to deny what anti-realists affirm. Or, to put the point positively, in those lectures Wittgenstein is concerned to affirm both (1) that the kind of relation that mathematical propositions bear to reality is of an entirely different sort than that of empirical propositions; and (2) that this does not mean that we should conclude that talk of the truth or falsity of mathematical propositions is a misleading *façon de parler.*

In Lecture XXV, Wittgenstein begins by considering a remark of G. H. Hardy's:

> Consider Professor Hardy's article ('Mathematical Proof') and his remark that 'to mathematical propositions there corresponds—in some sense, however sophisticated —a reality'.[30] (The fact that he

28. The following passages can be read as a disavowal of (what I have been calling) quietism:

[P]hilosophy does not lead me to any renunciation, since I do not abstain from saying something, but rather abandon a certain combination of words as senseless....

If I am correct, then philosophical problems must be completely solvable....

If I say: here we are at the limits of language, then it always seems as if resignation were necessary, whereas on the contrary complete satisfaction comes, since *no* question remains.

The problems are dissolved in the actual sense of the word—like a lump of sugar in water. (*Philosophical Occasions*, Indianapolis, IN: Hackett, 1993, pp. 161, 181, 183).

29. Wittgenstein never comes close to saying 'My aim in philosophy is to leave no unfinished business' or anything of the sort! In my introduction to Putnam's *Realism with a Human Face* (Cambridge, Ma.: Harvard University Press, 1990), I discuss some of the passages in his work which have occasioned such a misreading and why it is essential to (Putnam's understanding of) Wittgenstein's conception of philosophy that it necessarily leave unfinished business.

30. What Hardy actually says is: '[Mathematical theorems] are, in one sense or another, however elusive and sophisticated that sense may be, theorems concerning reality...' (Hardy, 'Mathematical Proof', *Mind* 38 (1929); p. 18). Hardy does not anywhere in this article speak of a '*correspondence*' to reality'!

said it does not matter; what is important is that it is a thing which lots of people would like to say.)

Taken literally, this seems to mean nothing at all—*what* reality? I don't know what this means. But it is obvious what Hardy compares mathematical propositions with: namely physics.[31]

Hardy thinks that mathematics is about mathematical features of reality in the same way that physics is about physical features of reality. The view that Wittgenstein here ascribes to Hardy nicely parallels the one that we earlier saw Lovibond ascribe to Wittgenstein: the truth or falsity of a particular sort of statement depends on whether the statement in question accurately describes or represents the relevant sorts of features of reality. Hardy says that the truth (or falsity) of mathematical statements depends on their *correspondence* (or lack of correspondence) to mathematical reality. Hardy's picture is the same as that of Blackburn's 'realist': mathematics and physics have different subject-matters, but in each of these regions of discourse language functions in a parallel way. Its function in each case is to describe the corresponding region of reality. Wittgenstein continues:

Suppose we said first, 'Mathematical propositions can be true or false.' The only clear thing about this would be that we affirm some mathematical propositions and deny others. If we then translate the words 'It is true...' by 'A reality corresponds to...'—then to say a reality corresponds to them would say only that we affirm some mathematical propositions and deny others. We also affirm and deny propositions about physical objects.—But this is plainly not Hardy's point. If this is all that is meant by saying that a reality corresponds to mathematical propositions, it would come to saying nothing at all, a mere truism: if we leave out the question of *how* corresponds, or in what sense it corresponds.[32]

According to Wittgenstein, when Hardy says that a reality corresponds to mathematical propositions, he wants to be saying more than just that we affirm some mathematical propositions and deny others. He wants to be saying how, or in what sense, a reality corresponds; and his answer to that question is: *in the same way* that empirical features of reality correspond to empirical propositions.

31. *Wittgenstein's Lectures on the Foundations of Mathematics: Cambridge, 1939*, ed. Cora Diamond (Chicago: University of Chicago Press, 1976) [henceforth referred to as *LFM*]; p. 239.

32. *LFM*, p. 239.

It is Wittgenstein's criticism of this idea that Putnam is centrally concerned to elucidate in his essay:

> Wittgenstein was scornful of the idea that talk of numbers or sets is analogous to talk of objects.[33] We should not think that set theory has discovered an unimaginably large 'universe' of intangible objects; this is all confusion....
>
> Wittgenstein claimed that it is nonsense to say that following rules involves a special relation to mental (or Platonic) objects. Can't one respond, 'then what does make these sorts of claims true'? Isn't that a *real* question? Are you praising Wittgenstein for ignoring it?
>
> But this supposed 'real question' rests on the following picture: truth is what results when a statement 'is made true by' (or 'corresponds to') *something*. But, while that picture fits *some* statements, for example, the statement that a sofa is blue may 'correspond' to a certain blue sofa on a particular occasion—it doesn't fit other familiar statements without strain. (pp. 247, 253)

Putnam's way of summarizing Wittgenstein's point here is to say that we have a certain picture, derived from the case of empirical description (and, in particular, from physics), of what it is for truth to result when a statement 'is made true by' (or 'corresponds to') *something*; and, although we do (and should feel free to continue to) speak of mathematical statements as being true or false, we go awry when we try to extend this picture of what it is for something 'to correspond to a reality' to mathematics.

A little later on, Putnam writes:

> [W]hat of the question, 'Are mathematical propositions about reality?' I remind you of Wittgenstein's remark that our paradigm of a reality is the thises and thats we can point to.[34] As we get farther and farther away from away from these, our 'hold' on the notion weakens. This is not to say that the only realities there are [are] observables, but it is to say that the less what we are talking about is analogous to the thises and thats we can point to, the less sense it has to ask about whether what we are talking about is or is not a 'reality'. (pp. 261–2)

This passage suggests that insofar as we are talking about 'the thises and thats we can point to' it makes perfect sense to speak of a reality to which our talk corresponds; but, as we move farther and farther away from this particular language game—from this particular

---

33. Putnam here footnotes Lecture XXVI of *LFM*.
34. Putnam here footnotes the beginning of Lecture XXV, *LFM*, p. 240.

'paradigm of a reality'—it makes less and less sense (even in those regions of our talk where we distinguish between truth and falsity) to speak of a reality to which our talk corresponds.

Though this touches on a central feature of what Wittgenstein is up to in the *Lectures on the Foundations of Mathematics*, it is not quite a faithful paraphrase of what Wittgenstein says in the passage in question. What he says is:

> We have here a thing which constantly happens. The words in our language have all sorts of uses; some very ordinary uses which come into one's mind immediately, and then again they have uses which are more and more remote.... A word has one or more nuclei of uses which come into everyone's mind first....
>
> So if you forget where the expression 'a reality corresponds to' is really at home—
>
> What is 'reality'? We think of 'reality' as something we can *point* to. It is *this*, *that*.
>
> Professor Hardy is comparing mathematical propositions to propositions of physics. This comparison is extremely misleading.[35]

Wittgenstein's point is not that there is a paradigmatic context in which the expression 'a reality corresponds to' is at home and if we deviate too far from that context we necessarily fail to make sense. Rather his point is that we need to distinguish different kinds of things we can (and do) mean by this expression. We can deviate very far from this (paradigmatic) context and still make sense. There are perfectly good things that we can mean by calling on this expression in the context of talking about mathematics. Since we (rightly) feel that there is something to be meant when we call upon this expression in the context of talking about mathematics, we are not going to be (nor should we be) satisfied by someone who comes along and tells us that we fail to make sense when we attempt to use this expression in this context.

Putnam is quite right, nevertheless, that Wittgenstein thinks that there is a danger that, in our philosophizing about mathematics, we will end up employing the expression 'a reality corresponds to' in a way that fails to make sense; and this is indeed what he thinks happens in Hardy's case. But his complaint about Hardy is not that he strayed too far from a certain paradigmatic use of the expression. (In a sense it is the opposite: that Hardy is unable to free himself,

35. *LFM*, pp. 239–40.

when employing the expression in an utterly different context, from imagining that he is somehow still employing it in a way that is closely akin to its paradigmatic use.) Wittgenstein's point, when cautioning us about the possibility of straying into nonsense when philosophizing, never takes the form of an injunction to the effect that 'you must use this expression in this way and no other or else you will be speaking nonsense.'[36] The source of our failure to mean something, on Wittgenstein's view, never lies with the form of words itself. (Indeed, Wittgenstein is a master at finding a context which reveals that there is something we might mean after all by some unusual—and at first not obviously intelligible—combination of words.) The trouble, according to him, comes when we unwittingly run together distinct sorts of uses to which such a form of words might be put.

Wittgenstein touches on this topic at the beginning of the above passage. ('A word has one or more nuclei of uses which come into everyone's mind first.') Whenever we fail carefully to distinguish between the possible uses to which an expression can be put, the tendency will be to have a certain 'nucleus of use' come into our minds, occluding and distorting our view of the expression's alternative possible uses.[37] What happens when we are thus 'bewitched' by a nuclear use of an expression is, according to Wittgenstein, that we end up trying to be in two language-games at once (and therefore not quite in either): in the (philosophically puzzling) language-game which we are trying to understand and, at the same time, in the (nuclear) one which the expression—viewed in isolation from its use—calls immediately to our mind. We view the former use through the lens of the latter, and become puzzled by the features of the latter sort of case which are missing from the former.

When, in doing philosophy of mathematics, we call upon the expression 'a reality corresponds to', then what we inevitably think of, Wittgenstein says, is the sort of 'reality' that we can *point* to (and about which we can say: 'It is *this*, *that*.').[38] When we then try to

36. To the extent that he has an injunction to offer at all at this level of generality, it would be better put thus: 'Say whatever you like, as long as you don't confuse yourself!'.

37. This can happen even when the core or nuclear use in question has an utterly unrelated grammar from that of the use of the expression to which we presently wish to attend; and even when the alternative use is of a firmly established and familiar nature.

38. This is the point of the remark ('What is "reality"? We think of "reality" as something we can *point* to. It is *this*, *that*') which Putnam misunderstands.

go on and understand what it means when one says 'mathematics corresponds to reality', we try to understand what is meant on the model of the sort of relation that 'There is a sofa in my living-room' bears to the state of affairs that it is about. The solution here, according to Wittgenstein, lies not in denying (à la the logical positivists) that there is something to be meant by such a way of talking, but by showing what *can* be meant by it. Wittgenstein devotes the next several lectures of *Lectures on the Foundations of Mathematics* to providing an overview (what he, in *Philosophical Investigations*, later calls a perspicuous representation) of the different things that one might mean by the expression 'statements of such-and-such type *correspond to* (or: are *responsible to*) a reality'. This requires distinguishing, among other things, the various sorts of things this expression can mean when it is applied to mathematical statements[39], and the various sorts of things it can mean when it is applied to other sorts of statements. The use to which Hardy attempts to put the expression is to be seen in the end as a confused attempt to amalgamate several of these available possibilities of use in such a way as to fail in the end to be saying anything at all.

VII

The importance of mixed statements. 'Science', Putnam observes, 'doesn't divide into a part which is empirical and a *different* part which is mathematics. It contains 'mixed statements', statements which are empirical but which speak of... functions and their derivatives as well as of physical entities' (p. 250).

Even if we concede that propositions of pure mathematics are not about reality in the same way that propositions of physics are about reality, what about the case of mixed statements? Are we to conclude that such statements are 'about' physical entities, but are *not* 'about' functions and their derivatives? In Lecture XXVI of the 1939 lectures, to which Putnam refers us in this connection,

39. There is one thing that such an expression might perfectly well be taken to mean that Wittgenstein mentions in these lectures only in order to put aside—the case of (what he calls) 'mathematical responsibility': 'Given certain principles and laws of deduction, you can say certain things and not others.' He takes this to be a kind of responsibility which mathematical propositions can only bear to one another, rather than to something over and above the mathematical framework itself. Thus he goes on to say: 'But it is a totally different thing to ask: "And now what is *all* this responsible to?"' (*LFM*, p. 240). By the time he writes *Philosophical Investigations*, he has gained a much deeper appreciation of how puzzlement about the sheer possibility of normative constraint as such can help fuel a platonist appeal to a 'super-reality'.

Wittgenstein resists this conclusion: '[M]athematical propositions do not treat of numbers. Whereas a proposition like "There are three windows in this room" *does* treat of the number 3.'[40] Wittgenstein insists, however, that we must be careful here to distinguish between the sense in which mixed statements 'treat of' numbers (or functions and their derivatives) and the sense in which they 'treat of' physical entities. His route to this point is a characteristically roundabout one.

Lecture XXVI begins, rather peculiarly, as follows:

> If one talks about a reality corresponding to mathematical propositions and examines what that might mean, one can distinguish two very different things.
>
> (1) If we talk of an experiential proposition, we might say a reality corresponds to it, if it is true and we can assert it.
>
> (2) We may say that a reality corresponds to a *word*, say the word 'rain'—but then we mean something quite different. This word is used in 'it rains', which may be true or false; and also in 'it doesn't rain'. And in this latter case if we say 'some phenomenon corresponds to it', this is queer. But you might still say something corresponds to it; only then you have to distinguish the sense of 'corresponds'.[41]

What does Wittgenstein mean when he says 'we may say that a reality corresponds to a *word*'? He is here inventing a new way of speaking—one which he hopes will provide a useful point of comparison when considering what it might mean to say of mathematical propositions that they correspond to—or are responsible to—a reality. Wittgenstein continues:

> We *can* explain the *use* of the words 'two', 'three', and so on. But if we were asked to explain what the reality is which corresponds to 'two', we should not know what to say. This? [Wittgenstein raised two fingers and pointed to them.] But isn't it also six, or four?
>
> We have certain words such that if we were asked, 'What is the reality which corresponds?', we should all point to the same thing—for example, 'sofa', 'green', etc. But 'perhaps', 'and', 'or', 'two', 'plus' are quite different.[42]

If you were asked what reality corresponds to words such as 'sofa' and 'green', then you might answer by simply pointing to a sofa

---

40. *LFM*, p. 250.
41. *LFM*, p. 247.
42. *LFM*, p. 248.

or to something green; but in the case of words such as 'perhaps', 'and', 'plus' or 'two', you would be at a loss as to what to point to. Wittgenstein suggests that we say of such words that the reality which corresponds to them is our having a use for them; and he suggests that this is analogous to something one might mean in talking of the reality which corresponds to a proposition of mathematics:

> So with these words 'and', 'or', etc., we can say that the reality which corresponds to them is that we have a use for them.
>
> What I want to say is this. If one talks of the reality corresponding to the propositions of mathematics or of logic, it is like speaking of a reality corresponding to these *words*—'two' or 'perhaps'—more than it is like talking of a reality corresponding to the *sentence* 'It rains'....
>
> To say 'A reality corresponds to "2 + 2 = 4"' is like saying 'A reality corresponds to "two"'. It is like saying a reality corresponds to a rule, which would come to saying: 'It is a useful rule, *most* useful—we couldn't do without it for a thousand reasons, not just *one*.'[43]

Wittgenstein, at the end of Lecture XXV, suggests that we can speak of 'a reality corresponding to a rule'. Yet, he says there of this correspondence that it won't be 'of the kind we first expect', but rather will lie in the rule being of such a sort that it is rendered important and justified by all sorts of facts—facts about the world and about us—so that we shall not want (and perhaps may not even know what it would mean) to do without it. We are thus presented with the following suggestion for what it is for there to be a reality corresponding to a rule: for there to be any number of facts (mostly of a very general—and therefore easily overlooked—nature) about us and about the world which make it very useful to have the rule as part of the overall package of thought and language which provides us with our means of description. Wittgenstein takes this way of thinking about how rules can be responsible to reality to provide a way of understanding what it might mean to say of a mathematical proposition that it corresponds to a reality. Building on this suggestion, in Lecture XXVI, he draws attention to some of the differences between activities in which we first lay the groundwork for our means of description and employments of language which then go on to deploy those means of description.

43. *LFM*, p. 249.

'You might say' that mathematical propositions are in this respect more akin to 'preparations for a use of language', and can be thought of in this respect as 'part of the apparatus of language' rather than 'part of the application of language'.[44] Wittgenstein goes on to say:

> It is the whole system of arithmetic which makes it possible for us to use '900' as we do in ordinary life. It prepares '900' for the work it has to do. In this sense, mathematical propositions do not treat of numbers. Whereas a proposition like 'There are three windows in this room' does treat of the number 3.[45]

In this sense of 'propositions treat of numbers', coming to understand the sense in which propositions can treat of numbers requires first understanding the role mathematics plays in mixed statements—even such elementary mixed statements as 'There are three windows in this room'.

There are diverse kinds of mixed statements—diverse ways in which mathematical rules and methods are integrated into empirical statements, and diverse ways in which mathematical and non-mathematical language-games interweave with one another— as many as the sorts of application mathematics has in our lives. It is this diversity of function to which Wittgenstein thinks we need to attend, not merely in order to wallow in the motley, but because it is the interplay of these functions which occasions our puzzlement. Despite the tremendous differences at the level of detail, Wittgenstein's treatment of mathematics can in this respect be seen in its general approach to parallel his treatment of avowals (outlined in section IV). In both cases, he seeks to show how non-descriptive and descriptive dimensions of language are intertwined in—and interdependent on—one another. In the case of mathematics, what this means is that he seeks to uncover the diverse kinds of ways in which mathematics becomes embedded in forms of description. Two kinds of example come in for special attention in this regard in Lectures on the Foundations of Mathematics: (1) ways in which the formulation of a kind of ideal case enables us to describe various actual cases as departures of one or another sort from the ideal; and (2) ways in which mathematics is integrated into the body of standards for carrying out methods of arriving at descriptive propositions (as, for example, in locating miscounts or mistakes in

44. LFM, p. 249.
45. LFM, p. 250.

measurement). The point of such examples is to help us 'break free', as Putnam puts it, 'of the picture that if a statement is true there must be a *something* which 'makes' it true' (p. 252)—the picture that there must be a separate region of reality to which each region of assertoric discourse corresponds. Each of these examples are meant to underscore how mathematical propositions can be brought to bear on 'a reality' (not by describing how things are in some extra-empirical region of reality, but rather) by enabling the myriad kinds of application which constitute integral aspects of the framework within which the activity of empirical description takes place.

VII

Conclusion. The point of providing the preceding brief overview of Lectures XXV and XXVI of *Lectures on the Foundations of Mathematics* is to provide textual evidence for the following exegetical claim: in his discussion of the question of whether mathematical propositions 'correspond to' a reality, Wittgenstein aims to conclude neither (1) that they simply do correspond in the same way that any other proposition does, nor (2) that they simply don't, nor (3) that it would be a good idea to abstain from answering the question. Each of Blackburn's three interpretative strategies fails to account for large stretches of the text. Yet each of them can also point to stretches of the text which, taken in isolation from Wittgenstein's larger aims, will appear to support their inter-pretation. All three strategies share a common assumption: that Wittgenstein takes us to understand 'the question' as posed. (Hence the three interpretative strategies appear to exhaust the logical space of possible responses: the question as posed can be answered in only one of three ways—affirmatively, negatively, or evasively.) Whereas what Wittgenstein does instead is to begin by showing us the diverse questions we might be asking, when calling upon the words which we take to express the question—showing us that on some understandings of what we might be asking the answer is affirmative, on others negative; and that there is no answer to 'the question' as posed, because there is no clear question but only a form of words hovering indeterminately between these diverse possibilities of use.[46]

---

46. I am indebted to David Finkelstein for conversations on these topics.

XI*—METAPHOR AND THE UNDERSTANDING OF ART

by Berys Gaut

The language of art criticism is alive with metaphor. Lines may be delicate or gentle, colours warm or cool, brutal or sedate; musical notes may be high or low, chords open or filled; sounds may be fat, one musical passage may comment on, battle with, or answer another; a chord sequence may sharply increase in tension or gently relax towards a firm resolution. Yet such metaphors are staid and muted, the retired gentlefolk of critical discourse, compared to the soaring vocabulary of an art critic in full rhetorical flight. Robert Hughes writes of Susan Rothenberg's canvases that 'They carry a patina of doubt on every square inch of their surface. But they do breathe; light and air—of a rather claustral kind, but atmosphere just the same—bathe the bodies and unify them as objects in the world while threatening always to dissolve them as emblems of personality. The surfaces look as if they came via Philip Guston from Monet, picking up some of Giacomo Balla's Futurist dissections of light particles along the way—a sober flicker in which images flash and are gone like the sides of fish in dark weedy water.'[1] This wonderful passage, so brilliantly evocative of Rothenberg's work, jostles with metaphors, similes, comparisons and images, its rich imaginative density disclosing a literary achievement of some distinction. Yet its figurative density is not a hollow grandstanding of its author's talents: its interacting tropes conspire to be precisely descriptive, to delineate the look of Rothenberg's work in a way that is sharp and exact, yet revelatory of features of her paintings that it seems could only be disclosed by *these* words in *this* way.

Figurative language is central to critical discourse. But what is its significance? That question raises manifold issues concerning

1. Robert Hughes, *Nothing if not Critical: Selected Essays on Art and Artists* (London: Collins Harvill, 1990), p. 328.

*Meeting of the Aristotelian Society, held in the Senior Common Room, Birkbeck College, London, on Monday, 28th April, 1997 at 8.15 p.m.

the evaluation, interpretation and description of art. I here address but one of these issues: what does the pervasive use of metaphors to describe artworks reveal about the nature of aesthetic understanding and experience?

I

Even to pose this question is to invite a deflationary reply. For, as Goodman has reminded us, 'Metaphor permeates nearly all discourse; thoroughly literal paragraphs without fresh or frozen metaphors are hard to find in even the least literary texts.'[2] The essay before you and this very sentence come laden with metaphors. Given its omnipresence, nothing distinctive about aesthetic understanding is shown by the presence of metaphor in critical language.

In a way this objection is well-taken: metaphor is pervasive in discourse. Yet even to concede this leaves in place the question of what metaphor is doing in aesthetic understanding, even if what it is doing there is just what it is doing elsewhere. And it is a deep-rooted mistake of aesthetics to assume that there *must* be some interesting features which are unique to art. So even on the objection considered, there would still be a question for aesthetics to address. But one also wants to mark a difference between the use of metaphors in critical discourse and their deployment in some other domains, including philosophical ones. Goodman also writes that 'a metaphor is an affair between a predicate with a past and an object that yields while protesting'.[3] This statement of his theory of metaphor can have its metaphorical clothing stripped away to reveal the literal theory beneath. But how could one do that to Hughes' description of Rothenberg's paintings? Or to Rosalind Krauss's description of a Rodin sculpture: 'the female figure, doubled over into a ball of flesh, projects the feeling of both weight and buoyancy'?[4] Here any attempt to say literally what has been expressed metaphorically results in a flat-footed pastiche lacking the insight of the original. Philosophical metaphors are eliminable, decent art critical metaphors are not. This is not a point about paraphrase. Any literal transcription of Goodman's *bon mot* will

2. Nelson Goodman, 'Metaphor as Moonlighting' in Mark Johnson (ed.), *Philosophical Perspectives on Metaphor* (University of Minnesota Press, 1981), p. 226.

3. Nelson Goodman, *Languages of Art: An Approach to a Theory of Symbols*, 2nd ed. (Indianapolis: Hackett, 1976), p. 69.

4. Rosalind E. Krauss, *Passages in Modern Sculpture* (MIT Press, 1977), p. 25.

lose those features which ground its humour, and diminish its capacity to generate new thoughts by its retelling of a metaphor's application as an amorous adventure. Rather, the point is that a literal rendering of Goodman's words can be given that preserves the part of its content that is relevant for the purpose of stating a philosophical theory. For we know which of the remark's features are relevant for this purpose. But in the case of the art critical metaphors, we cannot determine which literal rendering of the metaphor is sufficient to preserve the content relevant for the purposes of art-critical insight.

II

What then does the use of metaphorical description reveal about our understanding of art? What is going on when Hughes describes Rothenberg's surfaces as 'a sober flicker in which images flash and are gone like the sides of fish in dark weedy water'? Describing the phenomenology here is a delicate matter. We want to say that the metaphor and its dependent simile draw our attention to features of the painting we might otherwise have missed: a certain quality of movement, of unsteadiness, in its surface. Yet these are more metaphors, the surface neither really moving nor really being unsteady. But such metaphors allow us, we say, to see something that is really there, for instance that the surface contains marks which are sufficient to suggest a representation without being sufficient to establish precisely which representation it is. And with this description we move to the literal realm. But now we have lost reference to those aesthetic qualities of restlessness and motion which first made Hughes' description seem apt and conditioned our experience of the painting. It seems then that somehow imagining and experiencing are here intertwined, that Hughes has us imagine a quality of restlessness and motion of the surface, and to do so in a way that is inextricable from our experiencing something in it. We naturally talk here of a penetration of imagination into experience, a conditioning of experience by imagination, a kind of imaginative experience. Coming to understand the qualities of the surface seems to involve experiencing them in a way inseparable from imagination.

Such talk captures the phenomenology of our application of metaphors to art, and has the merit of drawing on notions of imagination and experience that many have supposed to play a crucial role in aesthetic understanding. But these observations also seem intolerably vague: what precisely is the relation of imagination and experience gestured towards? And even in its vaguely specified state the description may seem false, placing imagination in too prominent a position in our perceptual trans-actions with art. Nevertheless, I am going to argue that the idea of imagination conditioning experience does capture the role of metaphor in our appreciation of art, and it can be rendered into a precise account of the phenomena with which we are concerned. That account will lead to a development of a two-level theory that involves distinguishing different senses of 'seeing-as', both of which are essentially involved in aesthetic experience. But to approach this theory we need first to consider a fundamental objection to it.

III

According to the perceptualist the notion of imagination conditioning the experience of art is false. The aesthetic qualities of art works are simply and literally seen. With no sense of discomfort we talk of seeing the boldness and violence of a colour scheme, of hearing the delicacy and frailty of a musical passage or the tension in a chord change. The metaphoricality of these descriptions does not threaten the claim that we are seeing the aesthetic qualities described. If imagination enters here at all, it is only in the sense that one may need imagination to discover what is in front of one if it is not obvious: imagination does not condition the experience of the objects of one's perception. The discovery of patterns in the photograph of a cloud-chamber may require imagination, for there may be some previously unknown patterns present, but it does not show that one does not simply see those patterns. For the perceptualist a metaphor is merely a kind of device for focusing vision, a kind of visual aid, a way of pointing to properties in the work which the critic's audience can then see.

Both Frank Sibley and Monroe Beardsley are in this sense perceptualists. Both acknowledge the importance of metaphor in our descriptions of art, yet both insist that we simply see aesthetic qualities, even though seeing these qualities may require the active exercise of various skills. Sibley stresses the importance of metaphor in aesthetic descriptions, but still talks about seeing aesthetic qualities, where it is a condition of seeing them that one has taste, a special kind of sensitivity to such qualities.[5] And Beardsley holds that human regional qualities of works of art (roughly, expressive qualities such as sadness and serenity) are described using metaphors, but that we perceive these qualities. 'To understand a piece of music is simply to hear it, in the fullest sense of this word, that is, to organize its sounds into wholes, to grasp its sequences of notes as melodic and rhythmic patterns, to perceive its kinetic qualities and, finally, the subtle and pervasive human qualities that depend on all the rest.' [6]

IV

Suppose I remark of a Kandinsky painting that it is alive with movement. The remark is metaphorical: the painting is static and certainly not alive. The perceptualist objection holds that what I am doing is pointing out features literally possessed by the painting. So, for instance, I am drawing attention to the fact that the painting has violent colours, is comprised of jagged lines, has a taut construction and dynamically interacting parts. These descriptions preserve reference to the quality of aliveness of the painting. But they are themselves metaphorical: colours do not physically threaten one, lines do not literally have cutting edges, the painting is not literally in a state of controlled tension and nothing in the picture has dynamism in the way a motor does. So let us try again: the painting has zigzag lines in it, its composition is centred around two intersecting diagonals, its colours are mainly primary and laid down next to each other without any intervening areas of colours that lie between them on the spectrum of colours. The problem now is that we no longer refer to those distinctive aesthetic qualities which we were trying to characterise by our metaphorical description. So we can confront the perceptualist with a dilemma: either the descriptions of the artwork use metaphors, in which case we have not paraphrased away the metaphors, or the descriptions do not use metaphors, in which case they do not capture the distinctive aesthetic properties in which we are interested. And that means that we cannot say *what* the literal

5. Frank Sibley, 'Aesthetic Concepts' in Joseph Margolis (ed.), *Philosophy Looks at the Arts: Contemporary Readings in Aesthetics*, 3rd ed. (Temple University Press, 1987).

6. Monroe Beardsley, *Aesthetics: Problems in the Philosophy of Criticism*, 2nd ed. (Indianapolis: Hackett, 1981), p. 337. For his account of human qualities, see p. 328 f.

properties of the painting are to which the metaphor is supposed merely to point. And if we cannot literally say what they are, we cannot notice them, and hence metaphor cannot be a mere device for bringing them to our attention.

In reply, the perceptualist might hold that we *can* give a literal description of the properties picked out without using metaphor. For some aesthetic descriptions are non-metaphorical: beauty, elegance, gracefulness, daintiness, ugliness, garishness, and so forth. So he can wriggle out from the dilemma threatening him. But the problem with this response is the paucity of such terms available to us. Some aesthetic terms commonly used are themselves metaphorical, such as 'delicacy' or 'fragility'. And the ones that remain are insufficient to make all the discriminations necessary: the colours in the Kandinsky need not be garish or ugly. What they are is dynamic, and so we cannot state what these distinctive properties are without recourse to metaphor.

The best response for the perceptualist is simply to deny a premise that is needed to generate the dilemma. For his difficulty was supposed to stem from the fact that he claimed a metaphor is merely a device for indicating the presence of some aesthetic property, but that he was unable to say what this property is without using metaphors. Yet he may say that this is because some properties cannot be referred to by literal uses of predicates. Our thoughts about objects outrun our capacity to speak of them literally, and only on the assumption that this is not so is he caught in a dilemma. It is clear that our thoughts about aspects of the world can in general escape our capacity for linguistic expression. Many of our beliefs are carried by sensory images, not by linguistic entities. I have beliefs about the colours and shapes of my wallpaper that are embodied in visual images, not in language (indeed the struggle to put into words what I know would be incomprehensible were this not so). I have beliefs about the smell of seaweed, the sound of waves crashing on the beach, the taste of honey that are carried by sensory images, not by linguistic statements. This is possible because the propositional content expressing what is remembered or noticed is constituted by a structure of concepts that need not be linguistically expressible. It may be maintained, for instance, that the propositional content is given by an analysis in terms of possible worlds. Metaphor is, then, a linguistic device for pointing to what can be thought, but cannot be said literally: the phenomenal qualities of experience escape any attempt to capture them in literal discourse.[7]

<h1 style="text-align:center">V</h1>

This perceptualist reply teaches us something important. It reveals a genuine function of metaphor in aesthetics: we can think of and notice what we cannot put into literal language. Further, because of the importance of subtle *perceptual* discriminations in aesthetic understanding, it is unsurprising if metaphors should be required in art criticism more than in other areas to capture those qualities in which we are interested. This account also explains the linguistic ineliminability of metaphor, by denying that we must be able to find some other linguistic description for what it is that the metaphor gets us to see. The view of imaginative experience defended here should not deny that this is a genuine function of metaphor and explains some of its purpose in art critical deployment. The issue is whether this is the whole story of what happens when we successfully use a metaphor in art criticism.

It is not in fact the whole story, for were the perceptualist correct, our experience of art would be very different from the way it is. According to the perceptualist, we can think of the use of a metaphor as a kind of pointing at genuinely possessed aesthetic properties of works. A metaphor's function in art criticism is exhausted by its role in getting us to see aesthetic properties. It may perform this function, depending on the theory of metaphor held, either just by causing us to notice these properties, or by having a metaphorical meaning and so denoting them. But in either formulation, the metaphor simply has the role of drawing these aesthetic properties to our attention. If this is so, then the metaphor is in an important sense dispensable: there could be someone who had exactly the same experience of an artwork as we have, because she is aware of the same genuinely possessed aesthetic properties, but who had never thought of or been aware of the metaphor. The problem for the perceptualist however is that this is scarcely

7. For this general perceptualist strategy, see Nicholas Zangwill, 'Metaphor and Realism in Aesthetics', *The Journal of Aesthetics and Art Criticism*, 49 (1), Winter 1991, pp. 57–62. For a discussion of ineffability in relation to metaphor, see Richard Moran, 'Metaphor', section IV, in Bob Hale and Crispin Wright (eds.), *A Companion to the Philosophy of Language* (Oxford: Blackwell, forthcoming).

credible, because of the role of metaphor in classification. Classification is internal to experience: we experience things as being of one kind or of another, and our experience of something would be different were our classifications of it different. Now consider the statement 'the painting is alive with movement'. The metaphor classifies together a motley bunch of properties: properties of vibrancy, subdued violence, extreme contrasts of saturation and hue, having jagged edges, acentric composition, a sense of fluctuation in pictorial depth, and so on. Some of these descriptions are literal, some metaphorical. How does one decide how to extend this list? There is such diversity here that we have no sense of how to carry on—except by use of the master-metaphor of being alive with movement. And certainly there is no reason to classify together these diverse properties other than because of their connection to the metaphor. So the metaphor cannot be discarded: it guides our ability to group these properties with each other, grounds our sense that they belong together.

Further, we are aware not just that these properties belong together, but also that what makes this the case is that they are all connected to the metaphor. Suppose there *were* someone who classified aesthetic objects and properties together in a way that is extensionally equivalent to our classification of them under the predicate 'being alive with movement'. This person when asked about her classification and its relation to live and moving things denies that there is any such relation, perhaps because she can make no sense of the claim that there could be such a relation (paintings are not living, and do not move). This would be grounds for saying that she understood and experienced the work in a way radically different from ours, for it is internal to our classification that we are disposed to explain it in terms of its connection to living, moving things. The point is even more evident if one supposes, as many have argued, that the application of emotion terms to art is metaphorical. A person who classified together all and only artworks we call 'sad', but denied any connection between them and sadness, would have failed to grasp the aesthetic property we were indicating—would have failed to grasp the sadness of these things, and so would have missed what was of primary interest to us.[8] Hence there could not

8. The argument about sadness is in Roger Scruton, *Art and Imagination: A Study in the Philosophy of Mind*, 2nd ed. (London: Routledge, 1982), pp. 38–9.

be a person whose experience and understanding of a work was as ours is, but who did not have a grasp of the metaphor in terms of which we classify features of the work. Thus the perceptualist view of the role of metaphor in criticism is false.

However, the perceptualist may respond that all that has been shown above is that we need to use metaphors to grasp (think of) aesthetic properties, for otherwise we cannot classify those properties in the way we do; but we have not shown that use of the metaphor conditions our *experience* of the artwork. So while imagination as exercised in the application of metaphors may still be required to get us in a position to see those properties, it does not enter into the perceptual experience itself.

This response however is unfaithful to the phenomenology of aesthetic experience. When I say that the Kandinsky moves with life, this is not simply a thought that strikes me as useful in the search for the aesthetic properties of the work: it conditions the way I experience the painting. I may for instance see its dense entangled lines as growing upwards, striving after new paths, entwining each other in a competition for space. In so seeing the lines, I may see them as taut or as drooping, as thrusting or as decaying. The metaphorical description is elaborated into many more. Here the use of the metaphor of aliveness is not at a superficial level, which might be characterised as a mere thought about the painting; the metaphor generates a whole network of interrelated and dependent metaphors which cannot be stripped away without altering our experience of the painting. Indeed, unless we could experience the painting in terms of these metaphors, we would not be so successful in being able to generate and apply related metaphors: it is because I see the painting as alive with movement that I am driven to see it as taut, as vital, or as aggressive. And awareness of these properties gives my experience of the painting much of the unity it has: were I to try to experience the painting only in terms of its genuinely possessed and largely ineffable aesthetic properties, my experience would be of a set of rather dissimilar properties, which lacked a great deal of the density of interconnections that I in fact experience the painting as having. So the use of metaphors does indeed condition our experience of the painting.

VI

The perceptualist objection to the claim that imagination conditions aesthetic experience fails. But what are we to conclude from this failure? One view is that it shows that strictly speaking we do not perceive aesthetic properties at all. The metaphorical nature of aesthetic description entails that one cannot perceive aesthetic properties: metaphorical descriptions are false, so the properties ascribed are not genuinely possessed by objects, hence one cannot perceive them instantiated in those objects. Roger Scruton has developed such a view as a core part of what he terms an 'affective' theory of art.[9] But this response ignores the possibility of metaphorical meaning, of predicates gaining a new meaning in their metaphorical usage and of being true of objects in this use, a position that for instance Beardsley has defended.[10] Or if it does not ignore this possibility, it needs an argument against the existence of metaphorical meaning and the cognitive content of metaphors. Such an argument has been advanced by Donald Davidson, but it has been subjected to serious critique on several grounds.[11] Scruton's affective theory is also threatened, irrespective of whether one agrees with his account of metaphor, by the possibility mentioned earlier that metaphors can get us to notice genuine aesthetic properties which cannot be referred to by literal uses of language. If this is so, then metaphors may be devices for drawing attention to ineffable aesthetic properties genuinely possessed by objects.[12]

A more cautious response to the failure of perceptualism is to note that it is consistent with the argument developed above that we do perceive certain aesthetic properties, but that more than mere

9. Roger Scruton, 'Understanding Music' in his *The Aesthetic Understanding: Essays in the Philosophy of Art and Culture* (London: Methuen, 1983), esp. pp. 86–7.

10. See his 'The Metaphorical Twist' in Johnson, ibid.

11. See Davidson, 'What Metaphors Mean' in Johnson, ibid.; for critiques see Goodman, 'Metaphor as Moonlighting', ibid., and Richard Moran, 'Seeing and Believing: Metaphor, Image, and Force' in *Critical Inquiry* 16 (August 1989), pp. 87–113.

12. See Zangwill, ibid. Zangwill's own position combines a Davidsonian view of metaphor with realism about aesthetic properties. Given his Davidsonian convictions, he has to hold that strictly speaking all metaphorical statements—including metaphorical aesthetic statements—are false, since their only meaning is their literal meaning, and they thus yield falsehoods when applied to artworks. Yet we confidently hold that certain of these aesthetic ascriptions are true. An error theory of metaphorical aesthetic statements is a high price to pay, particularly when it can be avoided by discarding the flawed theory of metaphor on which it draws.

perception is involved in our experience of metaphorically described properties. But what is this mysterious surplus? And what account of metaphor must one give to allow for such a possibility?

The account of metaphor must allow that metaphors can get us to notice aesthetic properties which we may be unable to describe in literal terms, for we have seen the plausibility of the view that this is part of what a metaphor does. Secondly, the account of metaphor must allow that more than this is involved in the functioning of a metaphor, for otherwise we permit the possibility (which we have denied) of someone having the same experience of an artwork as ourselves even though, unlike us, he does not apply metaphorical descriptions to it. Further, a metaphor clearly involves an exercise of imagination: if I say that war is hell, then what I am doing amongst other things is imagining war as hell. Similarly, if I say that a Kandinsky is alive with movement, I am imagining the painting as being alive with movement. Such imaginings, we have seen, guide us in what properties we notice. So what we need is a theory of metaphor that both allows us to notice properties that may not be otherwise linguistically expressible, and also gives a role to imagination. There is such a theory, which has been developed on independent grounds by Richard Moran.[13] The theory holds that there are two dimensions to metaphor: the dimension of cognitive content (a propositional content that the metaphor communicates), constituted by our beliefs about what properties the objects compared literally possess, beliefs which may be ineffable; and the dimension of the framing-effect, by which we see one object in terms of the other. Thus in the metaphor 'man is a wolf' the first dimension is constituted by beliefs such as those about the viciousness of men and wolves, the second by seeing men in terms of wolves. The claim that metaphors have a cognitive content has the advantage of allowing metaphors to be true, and in the case of aesthetic metaphors this permits aesthetic properties to be genuinely possessed by artworks. But the role of the framing-effect also creates a place for imagination. Moran frequently talks of the framing-effect as seeing one thing in terms of another, but clearly the seeing here is not always or usually literal, for I may use the metaphor 'man is a wolf' without *seeing* anyone or anything at all. The notion aimed at is *thinking* of one thing in terms of another.

13. Richard Moran, 'Seeing and Believing: Metaphor, Image, and Force', and 'Metaphor'.

Now imagining that something is the case, whatever else it may
involve, involves entertaining a proposition, where to entertain a
proposition is simply to think of it, to have it in mind, without
asserting it; belief, in contrast, involves asserting the proposition
thought of.[14] Since the framing-effect involves thinking of man in
terms of a wolf, but not believing that man is a wolf, this thought is
unasserted, and falls into the domain of imagination. The framing-
effect also controls the formation of further beliefs, i.e. thinking of
a man in terms of a wolf guides us in looking for literal features of
men and of wolves. It is this notion of control or organisation that
is required to explain how our grasp of metaphor can guide our
formation of new beliefs about what aesthetic properties are
genuinely possessed by objects and can connect genuinely
possessed aesthetic properties to ones only metaphorically
described and not genuinely possessed. Thinking of a canvas as
alive with movement, we classify together otherwise divergent
aesthetic properties, and we also preserve the connection with
aliveness and movement that is essential to our classification and to
our experience of the work. Acknowledgement of the framing-
effect thus removes the difficulties which the perceptualist account
encountered.

VII

There is then a theory of metaphor which allows a role for both
imagination and belief when we apply metaphors to art. But to note
this still leaves untouched our main claim that imagination enters
into and conditions the *experience* of art. It is time to redeem the
pledge to characterise the relation more precisely.

Ever since Wittgenstein introduced the notion of seeing-as, it has
seemed plausible to many that this phenomenon should be central
to our understanding of aesthetic experience. But to deploy it
properly requires a distinction between two kinds of seeing-as.
Suppose I see a whale, and I know that a whale is a large mammal.
This knowledge may not condition my perception: it is not brought
to bear on the look of the whale. But one day the knowledge may
strike me with fresh force, I may *see* the whale *as* a large mammal:

14. Supporters of this view, or variations thereof, include Alvin Plantinga, *The Nature of
Necessity* (Oxford: Oxford University Press, 1974), pp. 161–2; Scruton, *Art and Imagination*,
pp. 97–8; and Nicholas Wolterstorff, *Works and Worlds of Art* (New York: Oxford University
Press, 1980), pp. 233–4.

the knowledge that it is so enters into my perception of it, I see its blow-hole as a single nostril, its flippers as vestigial legs, its body as a bloated variant of mine. Such a shift in perception can be startling, can radically change the way the whale looks to me, can render feelings of amusement, shock or wonder appropriate to the animal which were not part of my previous repertoire of feelings towards it. This kind of seeing-as involves application of the concept of being a large mammal to what I see as part of the process of seeing it. Whatever position we take on the question of whether all perception involves concept-application, it is clear that in this type of seeing-as concept-application does indeed occur.[15] For there is a systematic transformation in the way the whale looks to me that is specifiable only by using the concepts mentioned above. There is a sense in which seeing the whale in this way requires imagination, for it requires a degree of originality to apply my knowledge to what I see, to allow it to infuse and transform my perception. But it does not involve imagination in the sense that my thought of the whale as a large mammal is unasserted: I believe that it is such, and I believe that its flippers are vestigial limbs. So this kind of seeing-as involves beliefs, concepts are applied assertively to objects, and we can term it *doxastic seeing-as*.

On the other hand, I may see the whale as an ungainly, abandoned child, and this thought may also colour my perception: I may hear its calls as helpless, hopeless cries, I may see its movements as writhings of frustration and despair, I may see its bulk as a distension of rage and hunger. This kind of seeing-as also renders apt a range of feelings, such as feelings of sympathy and concern, that may not have been especially appropriate before. Again, I may merely think of the whale this way, or the thought may enter into my perception. But unlike doxastic seeing-as, the thought here is not asserted of the object, for I do not believe that the whale really is an abandoned child. Rather, the concept of a child here is entertained of the whale, without being asserted of it.[16] Because the thought is not here asserted, we can speak of *imaginative seeing-as*.

15. See Tim Crane, 'The Nonconceptual Content of Experience' in Tim Crane (ed.), *The Contents of Experience: Essays on Perception* (Cambridge University Press, 1992), for a critique of the concept-application model of seeing; and D. W. Hamlyn, 'Perception, Sensation and Non-conceptual Content', *The Philosophical Quarterly*, 44 (175), 1994, pp. 139–53, for a defence of the model.

16. For this way of construing the matter, see Scruton, *Art and Imagination*, chapter 8, esp. p. 120.

Exercises of these two kinds of seeing-as are common in constituting experiences, and they affect the way we feel about what we see, and can be exercises of originality. I may see clouds as huge condensations of water-vapour and be surprised that water should look so white, or I may see them as huge animals floating above the ground. I may see a tree as a large plant and feel wonder at so extraordinary a growth, or I may see it as a man with upturned arms and wonder why he is so animated. The two kinds of seeing-as are also important in our dealings with art. I can see a Kandinsky painting as an early modern work, as a part of the European artistic tradition, or simply as a Kandinsky. These are cases of doxastic seeing-as, for I believe that the painting really has these properties. In which of these categories I see the painting can be crucial to what other properties I ascribe to it, as Kendall Walton has demonstrated.[17] Seen as a part of the European tradition, it may look a riotous assault on form, seen as a Kandinsky it may look admirably restrained. I can also, however, see the painting as alive with spiritual power, as taut and tense, as dashingly exuberant. These are cases of imaginative seeing-as, for I do not believe that the painting is really alive, tense or exuberant.

These observations about seeing-as link naturally to the earlier remarks about metaphors, and to the role of imagination and belief in our responses to art. For the framing-effect of a metaphor is, we noted, an exercise of imagination. I may say of the Kandinsky that it is moving with life, and when I do so I use a metaphor. In doing so, I get my audience to think of one thing (the painting) in terms of another (an object that moves with life). And when my audience experiences the painting in the light of the metaphor, they *see* the painting *as* moving with life. So the application of the framing-effect of the metaphor to the experience of the painting constitutes an exercise of imaginative seeing-as. It does not involve believing that the painting really possesses the quality of aliveness. The quality is imagined of the painting, my experience of the painting involves entertaining the concept of the painting; but it is not believed of the painting, we do not doxastically see the painting as alive. In imagining this of the painting, we are led to look for properties actually possessed by the painting, properties that make this imaginative seeing-as apt. This making apt or appropriate is

17. See his 'Categories of Art' in Margolis, ibid.

how imaginative seeing-as controls the quest for relevant aesthetic properties. For some of these properties we have literal descriptions (the Kandinsky is beautiful, elegant, etc.), for most we do not: as we noted, our perception extends beyond the grip of literal language. But the aesthetic properties we are cued to look for by the application of imaginative seeing-as are properties really possessed by the painting, even if they are ones we cannot speak of literally. Thus we employ doxastic seeing-as to detect them: we apply concepts assertorically to the object (the concepts need not be linguistically expressible). And what we see determines the cognitive content of the metaphor of aliveness used of the painting. Yet that cognitive content is determined in its extension by seeing the painting as alive, so that we cannot discard our awareness of the framing-effect, nor therefore of the metaphor and our experience of imaginatively seeing the painting as alive. And we also cannot discard seeing the painting as alive, without having a radically different experience to someone who sees it purely as having genuinely possessed aesthetic properties.

What our investigation of the application of metaphors to works of art reveals then is that the kind of understanding of art involved in such applications is constituted by the having of an imaginative experience of the work, where imaginative experience is to be understood in a two-level manner. The first level is imaginative seeing-as, and it corresponds to the framing-effect of the metaphor. Here properties are entertained of the work without being held actually to apply to the work. The second level is doxastic seeing-as, and here the content of some of the beliefs involved is identical with the cognitive content of the metaphor. At this level the properties ascribed are actually possessed by the work. In the invention of the metaphor by the critic, genuinely possessed aesthetic properties make apt a certain metaphor, and then application of this metaphor in imaginative seeing-as structures the search for genuinely possessed aesthetic properties. At this stage the first level controls the search for properties at the second level: it is by seeing the work as alive with movement that I am enabled to see other of its aesthetic properties that may elude linguistic expression.

This two-level theory yields the more exact statement of imaginative experience promised earlier. It also generates a diagnosis of the received opinions in this area. We can explain the attractions of perceptualism and its failures: the perceptualist correctly holds that metaphors can be used to discover genuine aesthetic properties which we can perceive, but fails to realise that this is not all that goes on in the use of metaphor, for he fails to see the importance of imaginative seeing-as in constituting an aspect of our aesthetic experience of the work, and he also fails to see its role in guiding our search for genuinely possessed aesthetic properties. On the other hand, the affective theorist, who thinks the use of metaphor shows we do not perceive aesthetic properties, realises the importance of imaginative seeing-as in our experience of art, but fails to notice that this is compatible with holding that doxastic seeing-as (genuine perception) of aesthetic properties is involved as well, and that here our perceptual abilities may outstrip our linguistic expressive capacities. The two-level theory shows that an attractive theory of metaphor and a distinction between two kinds of seeing-as allows one to reconcile what is correct in Scruton's account and what is correct in Beardsley's and Sibley's account, and so to defuse and transcend the dispute between them.

VIII

This theory of aesthetic experience transfers readily to the other non-visual arts. In music, there are similarly two senses of hearing-as: we can hear a passage as Brahmsian, or as in sonata form, or as being in the key of D major; we can also hear it as responding to another passage, as being full of tension, or as having a fat sound. So the story we have told about imaginative experience and metaphor applies smoothly here. And the theory also applies to literature insofar as its sensory dimension (the sound and look of words) is important, something most salient in the case of poetry, where the sound of the words—their rhythm, assonance, alliterative patterns—matters a great deal, and the look of the words on the page—the line length, spacing, etc.—may matter too. Similar observations apply to novels, though such sensory features are likely to be less aesthetically important there.

The interpretation of literature, of course, concerns many other things beside its sensory dimension, notably the interpretation of the characters and events featuring in the work. About such matters our theory is silent. But our question was what the application of metaphors to *works of art* tells us; the question was not what their application to *objects* (characters or events) denoted or described by works of art has to tell us about our understanding of those things. We do not perceive these objects, nor is the two-level theory committed to holding that we do. Our concern has been with what the use of metaphors tells us about what are sometimes termed 'formal' properties of works of art, insofar as these properties are described by metaphors.

This response may disappoint: surely a theory of aesthetic understanding should have a large degree of generality? Yet there are good reasons for holding that any attempt to develop a comprehensive, general theory of understanding of all aspects of art cannot succeed. The problem is that understanding art consists of such a diverse set of activities, involving so many different kinds of questions about such a motley set of matters, that any attempt to generate a simple overarching theory about these diverse activities must fail. We need to develop a plurality of theories of understanding, covering the diverse properties which are the objects of interpretation.[18] Into this patchwork of different theories the two-level theory fits as a component part. And even within this more modest compass, I have not tried to lay down a complete account of the constraints on what counts as imaginatively experiencing the work correctly. We ought to perceive only those aesthetic properties which are present in the work, and our imaginative seeing-as must be appropriate to the work. Just what constraints count on appropriateness (other than it being apt to disclose aesthetic properties really possessed) has not here been addressed. Rather, I have been concerned with specifying the mode of understanding involved—one involving a penetration of imagination into experience—and with drawing out its distinctness from and superiority to the perceptualist and affective theories.

IX

I close with two observations about the implications of what has been established for the nature of aesthetic understanding. We can approach the first by noting a distinction between two ways to understand metaphors. In 'war is hell', the critic may show the metaphor to be appropriate by listing the literal features shared by

18. See Berys Gaut, 'Interpreting the Arts: The Patchwork Theory', *The Journal of Aesthetics and Art Criticism*, 51 (4), 1993, pp. 597–609.

war and hell: they are noisy, hot, dangerous, involve torture, and
so forth. This dimension of understanding is an *explication* of the
metaphor, a statement of what features are literally possessed by
the objects metaphorically compared. But the task of understanding a metaphor can proceed in a different manner, not stating
literal likenesses, but creating a new set of metaphors which
develop the original metaphor further. So the critic may respond to
the metaphor by noting that if war is hell, generals are demons,
guns are pitchforks, the poor bloody infantry are suffering sinners,
bomb explosions are infernal fires, and marching towards the
battlefront is a journey to the inner circles of hell. In this kind of
understanding the critic does not explicate the metaphor, for her
remarks are themselves new metaphors: rather, she *elaborates* the
metaphor, works it outwards, extends its field of application by
inventing new and related metaphors.[19]

When a critic offers us a metaphor as appropriate to a work of
art, our and her understanding of it can proceed in both of these
ways. If she remarks that the canvas is alive with movement, that
then raises questions of whether the movement is tense or relaxed,
joyous or crabbed; and when we choose one term of the pair over
the other, we elaborate the metaphor of lively movement. On the
other hand, we can look for literal likenesses between the canvas
and such movement, noting that both have an organised structure
with a whole and parts, can be elegant and original. These two ways
of understanding the aesthetic metaphor are ones that can be
embodied in our experience of the work: we imaginatively see the
painting as taut and crabbed, and doxastically see it as original and
elegant. It is an advantage of the two-level view that it fits smoothly
with the distinction between the two ways of understanding
metaphors in general.

There is a further significance to the critic's use of metaphors. A
good metaphor has a degree of originality in reconfiguring our
conceptual map; it offers new insight into its object; its power
depends very much on the exact words chosen and how they are
deployed; it is capable of giving delight to its audience by their
appreciation of its originality, appropriateness, and its capacity to

19. See Moran, 'Seeing and Believing: Metaphor, Image, and Force', pp. 107–11, for a
related discussion of elaboration, though the contrast he draws appears to be somewhat
different from that made above.

be elaborated; it is something the interpretation of which eludes precise rules, for this depends on its context; and most works of literary art incorporate a great many metaphors. In virtue of these features, then, a good metaphor looks remarkably like a small work of art. Indeed, Aristotle remarks that for the poet 'the greatest thing by far is to be a master of metaphor.... it is also a sign of genius, since a good metaphor implies an intuitive perception of the similarity in dissimilars'.[20]

If we take seriously the view that a good metaphor is an artistic achievement, then the good critic, amongst other things a master of appropriate metaphor, becomes something of an artist too. And this sits comfortably with the observation that some of the best critics have themselves been poets or novelists, and with the literary felicity of Hughes' description of Rothenberg's work. Criticism at its best is on this view a kind of second-order art, an art comprised of observations about other forms of art. Like first-order art, it has constraints on success, and requirements to get it right, to imagine well. And if this line of thought is correct, then we have the final and perhaps deepest answer to our question about what the use of metaphor by critics shows about the nature of aesthetic under-standing. The answer is not just that the employment of metaphors shows that our understanding of art involves imaginative experience; it is that our understanding of art at its best is an artistic achievement. So it turns out that in a more radical sense than normally intended, criticism is indeed an art. And it is pleasant to end a paper so concerned with metaphor with the observation that I mean that remark quite literally.[21]

Department of Moral Philosophy,
University of St. Andrews,
St. Andrews, Fife KY16 9AL,
Scotland.
e-mail: bng@st-andrews.ac.uk

20. Aristotle, *Poetics*, 1459a5–8 in Jonathan Barnes (ed.), *The Complete Works of Aristotle: the Revised Oxford Translation* (Princeton University Press, 1984).

21. I am grateful for their comments to audiences at Virginia Commonwealth University and at conferences of the British Society of Aesthetics and the American Society for Aesthetics, to whom earlier versions of this paper were delivered. I also thank John Brown, Oswald Hanfling, Robert Howell, Peter Lamarque, Jerrold Levinson, Nick Zangwill and Eddy Zemach for their helpful comments.

XII*—*GRUNDLAGEN* §64

by Bob Hale

In *Grundlagen* §64, Frege writes:

> The judgement 'line a is parallel to line b', or, using symbols,
>
> a//b,
>
> can be taken as an identity. If we do this, we obtain the concept of direction, and say: 'the direction of line a is identical with the direction of line b'. Thus we replace the symbol // by the more generic symbol =, through removing what is specific in the content of the former and dividing it between a and b. We carve up the content in a way different from the original way, and this yields us a new concept

How is the procedure which Frege here describes by means of the metaphor of carving up the content in a new way best understood? Is there a way of understanding that procedure on which it can defensibly be applied to yield the results which Frege aimed to achieve? While my primary concern here will be to explain and argue for an answer to the first question,[1] I believe that the answer I shall defend goes some part of the way towards justifying an affirmative answer to the second, and I shall try to say something to support this view. Why it will go only part of the way may be appreciated by reflecting briefly on the context in which my opening passage occurs.

In §§55–57, exploring the possibility of defining number words contextually, Frege tries a recursive explanation of statements of the form 'The number n belongs to the concept F'. This he quickly rejects as unsatisfactory—it cannot serve to introduce number words as proper names (singular terms), standing for objects, because

---

1. I should probably emphasise that this is not an exercise in Fregean exegesis. My primary interest is in locating, if possible, a philosophically viable understanding of our passage which accords with Frege's general aims. I shall not be making, or trying to defend, detailed claims about what he actually meant, or is most plausibly taken to have meant.

*Meeting of the Aristotelian Society, held in the Senior Common Room, Birkbeck College, London, on Monday, 12th May, 1997 at 8.15 p.m.

we can never—to take a crude example—decide by means of our definitions whether any concept has the number JULIUS CAESAR belonging to it, or whether that same familiar conqueror of Gaul is a number or not

It is, Frege complains, 'only an illusion that we have defined 0 and 1'—and, he might have added, only an illusion that he has defined the number belonging to the concept F. Instead, all that has been done is to fix the sense of a series of second-level predicates of the form 'the number n belongs to ...'—or as we might put it, a series of numerically definite quantifiers '$\exists_0 x...x...$', ..., '$\exists_n x...x...$', ... Nothing has been done to justify the use of numerals or other numerical expressions as singular terms, or quantifiers binding variables ranging over numbers. Frege does not immediately abandon the idea of introducing numerical singular terms contextually. The moral he draws is rather that the proposed definition focuses on the *wrong* kind of sentential context. What is needed, if 'number words are to be understood as standing for self-subsistent objects' is to explain the sense of identity-statements linking such words. §§62–67 then examine whether this may be done by taking propositions of the form: 'the number belonging to F = the number belonging to G' to be equivalent with corresponding propositions of the form: 'there is a 1–1 correlation of the Fs with the Gs'. Frege's discussion of this proposal is conducted at one remove, in terms of the simpler example of the analogous definition of directions by means of the *Direction Equivalence*:

D=   the direction of line a = the direction of line b iff lines a and b are parallel

He reviews (§§63–7) three doubts or objections. Of these, he thinks the first two are misplaced. Our opening passage forms part of his answer to the first, which complains that it is an error to define identity specially for the case of numbers. Frege's reply is that this is precisely what he is *not* doing: the idea is, rather, to 'use the concept of identity, taken as already known, as a means for arriving at that which is to be regarded as being identical'. By the end of §67, however, he has convinced himself that the third objection—a re-run of the Julius Caesar problem—is unanswerable, and so abandons the project of defining number contextually and switches to his famous explicit definition in terms of extensions. Clearly, then, an affirmative answer to my second question cannot be fully justified without providing a positive solution to the Caesar problem. I think that Frege's pessimism on that score was premature, but will not attempt to justify that opinion here.

I

Content, Thought and Truth-Value. A crucial question, clearly, is how 'content' is to be understood. This is especially problematic in view of Frege's subsequent rejection of the notion of 'judgeable content', or content of a declarative sentence, and replacement of it by the contrasted notions of *thought* and *truth-value* (cf. Frege 1892 p. 47). The bearing of this change on our opening passage is not quite straightforward, since what Frege there envisages being carved up anew is not (directly, anyway) the content of a *complete sentence*, but that of the content of *the symbol for parallelism*. But it will bear indirectly, if we suppose, plausibly, that the content of a subsentential expression is part of the content of any complete sentence containing it, so that any recarving of the content of the former is eo ipso a recarving of the latter. In any case, we are surely bound to ask: Is there a coherent doctrine which survives Frege's introduction of the sense/reference distinction? How, if what Frege formerly spoke of as 'content' splits into reference and sense, is our passage is to be understood: should we take content as lying on the reference side, or on the sense side?

There are more or less obvious difficulties involved in taking the first course. In Frege's view, sentences refer to truth-values. The immediate difficulty in interpreting our passage in terms of this idea is that it appears to make no sense at all to speak of carving up truth-values. Truth-values are indeed objects, at least on Frege's eventual view, but they seem not to be the kind of object which can be carved up, like pieces of cheese. It is no help that Frege is obviously speaking figuratively, since there seems to be no sensible way to take the metaphor in the crucial case—the True and the False could not, it seems, be thought of as structured objects without depriving them of their capacity to be the referents of *all* true and *all* false sentences respectively. The view that truth-values are simple objects might be thought anyway to be imposed by Frege's doctrine that truth and falsehood are indefinable.

It might be proposed that we could build enough structure into the True—say by identifying it with the totality of facts, or, perhaps, the actual world, and taking the False as the totality of non-actual states of affairs, or, perhaps, the union of merely possible worlds. But this is no remedy, since it would lead to the unsatisfactory result that each true sentence shares its content with every other, with the unwanted upshot that 'the direction of line a = the direction of line b' would now bear no closer relation to 'lines a and b are parallel' than it bears to, say, 'Tuesday precedes Wednesday'.

Taking the content of a sentence to be the *particular* (actual or possible) *state of affairs* it represents—though not sanctioned by anything in Frege's writings—may seem a more attractive course, if only because states of affairs (as usually conceived) possess the kind of structure needed to give talk of recarving a toehold. In particular, it might be claimed, the state of affairs consisting in line a's being parallel to line b and that consisting in the direction of line a's being identical with the direction of line b just are one and the same state of affairs, differently described or conceptualised in alternative, equally permissible, ways. This approach must face up to a familiar difficulty, however. If identification of sentential contents with states of affairs (actual or possible) is to be viable, there will be needed some satisfactory general account of how states of affairs are to be individuated, and of when different sentences represent the same state of affairs. But a well-known argument—the 'Slingshot'—has it that on not obviously unacceptable principles governing when different sentences should be regarded as depicting the same state of affairs, there will be just two (possible) such—one to which all the true sentences correspond, and the other corresponding to all the false ones. The principles are—in Donald Davidson's version[2] of the argument—that interchange of co-referential singular terms within a given sentence does not change what state of affairs it depicts, and that logically equivalent sentences correspond to the same state of affairs. Then, where P is any true sentence:

the x such that $(0 = x \ \& \ P)$ = the x such that $0 = x$

2. Davidson 1969.

is logically equivalent with, and so represents the same state of affairs as, P. But if Q is any other true sentence, 'the x such that 0 = x & Q' co-refers with 'the x such that 0 = x & P', so that:

the x such that (0 = x & Q) = the x such that 0 = x

depicts that same state of affairs. But this is in turn (reversing the opening move) logically equivalent with Q. Whence Q represents the same state of affairs as P. So any two (and so all) true sentences represent the same state of affairs. And likewise, so do all false sentences. Unless this argument can be blocked, taking the content of a sentence to be a (possible) state of affairs brings after all no advantage over the clearly unsatisfactory course of identifying a sentence's content with its truth-value.

The argument is not obviously irresistible, of course. In particular, reservations about its driving principles—centred on the point that they allow unrestricted introduction of 'new' references —might suggest a more selective conception of states of affairs according to which, roughly speaking, sentences depict the same state of affairs iff they involve reference to the same objects and attribute the same properties to them. Clearly this will need refinement if it is to be proof against a revamped Slingshot that makes mischief over which predicates pick out the same property. But I shall not pursue that delicate issue here, since it seems equally clear that no refinement of this conception of states of affairs is going to be helpful in the present context. Frege wants us to accept 'the direction of line a = the direction of line b' and 'line a is parallel with line b' as different carvings of the same content. But they will not be so, if contents are taken to be states of affairs in the sense suggested, since the former involves reference to objects absent from the latter. Frege's procedure requires that we may regard two sentences as representing the same content, even when they speak of different objects and attribute different properties (just as the first of this pair speaks of certain directions and declares them to be identical, while the latter speaks of certain lines and declares them to be parallel).

It does not follow that no suitable conception of states of affairs can be circumscribed. But we are, I think, in position to draw two intermediate conclusions. First, it cannot be criterial for the identity of states of affairs depicted by two sentences that they make reference to just the same objects and attribute the same properties to them. And second, whatever its precise detail, the appropriate criterion of identity will not be purely extensional, on pain of vulnerability to some adaptation of the Slingshot argument. These—and especially the second—suggest that we would do well to look more closely at the alternative of construing content as lying on the sense side of Frege's distinction.

II

Content as Sense. The option of construing content as belonging to the realm of sense is, perhaps, both more attractive and more plausible.[3] But—as Michael Dummett argues[4]—it too faces a difficulty, which becomes apparent when we reflect on Frege's purposes. His object is to describe a route by which someone lacking the concept of *direction* may come to possess it. Further, the concept so introduced is—though of course Frege himself does not put it this way—to be a *sortal* concept: roughly, a concept under which fall objects, which may be singled out by terms of the form 'the direction of line a'. These commit him to two claims about the left and right sides of $D^=$:

Priority: $D^=$**(right)** is to have explanatory priority over $D^=$**(left)**

Syntax: the surface syntax of $D^=$**(left)** is to be semantically active

Priority requires that someone should be able to receive $D^=$ as an explanation of direction-talk, on the basis of her prior understanding of its right component. *Syntax* requires that the surface syntax of $D^=$**(left)** is to be taken at face value as reflecting its semantic structure—so that it involves a genuine occurrence of the identity predicate, with the result that the expressions 'the direction of line a' and 'the direction of line b' are to be reckoned genuine singular terms—so that the truth of (any instance of)

3. Linsky (1992), after evincing some initial sympathy with the idea that content should be understood as something like an objective state of affairs, rejects it for reasons akin to those rehearsed here, in favour of an interpretation of content as sense. But it seems to me that he completely fails to come to grips with the difficulty with which this section is concerned.

4. Dummett 1991, pp. 167–76. Considerations of space obliged me, regretfully, to forego discussion of points of agreement and disagreement with those numerous passages in Dummett's earlier writings—especially those dealing with the distinction between 'analysis' and 'decomposition'—which bear on my central question. Most of the relevant passages are to be found in Dummett 1981, chs. 12–17.

D=(left) calls for the existence of objects—directions—to which they refer.

The difficulty, as Dummett presents it, is that we cannot *further* impose the requirement (expressed by what he calls the *Synonymy Thesis)* that the two components express the same sense, *and* uphold *both Priority* and *Syntax.* Taking 'line a is parallel to line b' as a mere definitional abbreviation of 'the direction of line a = the direction of line b' allows us to uphold *Syntax* and the *Synonymy Thesis*; but it reverses the direction of explanation Frege plainly intends, and so sacrifices *Priority.* Viewing surface syntax of **D=(left)** as without semantic import—so that 'the direction of line a' and 'the direction of line b' are mere sham proper names, and effect no genuine reference to objects—lets us uphold *Priority* and the *Synonymy Thesis,* but at the cost of *Syntax.* What it seems we cannot do is maintain all three requirements. This is because, if a statement involves reference to objects of a certain kind, that is a feature of its sense. Understanding the statement will then require grasp of a concept under which those objects fall. In particular, then, *Syntax* requires that one who grasps the sense of **D=(left)** possesses the concept of a *direction.* But then, by the *Synonymy Thesis,* **D=(right)** must likewise involve an implicit reference to directions, and no one who lacks the concept of a *direction* will be able to grasp *its* sense. But *Priority* demands that one should be able to *advance from* understanding **D=(right)** *to* a grasp of the concept of a *direction,* which requires that one need *not* already possess that concept in order to grasp its sense. The three requirements are thus incompatible.

The argument just given relies on the assumption that Frege's notion of sense is *strongly compositional.* It is uncontroversial that Fregean sense (likewise reference) is *weakly* compositional, i.e. that the sense of any complex expression *is a function of* the senses of its constituents (likewise for reference). What the argument relies on is the further claim (which is obviously false for reference) that the sense of a complex expression *is actually composed of* the senses of its constituents in such a way that one cannot grasp the sense of the whole without grasping those of its parts. The attribution of this view to Frege—though repeatedly and confidently made by Dummett, for one—is not unchallengeable.

Probably the closest Frege comes to endorsing it is *Grundgesetze* Vol 1, §32:

> The names, whether simple or themselves composite, of which the name of a truth-value consists, contribute to the expression of the thought, and this contribution of the individual [component] is its *sense*. If a name is part of the name of a truth-value, then the sense of the former name is part of the thought expressed by the latter name.

But even this passage probably cannot be taken as unequivocally enforcing strong compositionality as the argument requires it. I can and shall leave the exegetical question here open. It is more important, for my purposes, to observe (1) that the objection to construing content as sense only has force as against such a strongly compositional notion, and so leaves space for construing content in terms of an appropriately weaker notion of sense, which allows that two sentences may express the same sense even though a thinker able to understand one of them may yet lack concepts required if he is to be in position to understand the other; and (2) that a solution to our problem along the lines just suggested will require a criterion for identity of sentence-sense on a suitably weaker interpretation.

III

Interlude: Begriffsschrift §9 and Grundlagen §64. Before turning to that task, I want to say something about the way in which I expect appeal to a weaker notion of sense to help us to arrive at a good interpretation of our opening passage.

In *Begriffsschrift* §9, Frege discusses the possibility of analysing or decomposing one and the same sentence in different ways which preserve what he there terms its conceptual content. He observes that 'Cato killed Cato' may be decomposed into function and argument in different ways, according as we view the first, the second, or both occurrences of the name 'Cato' as replaceable— giving 'ξ killed Cato', 'Cato killed ξ' and 'ξ killed ξ', respectively, as the functions involved. In the same vein, he might have observed (although he didn't in fact do so, here anyway) that the same sentence can be seen as formed, like 'Brutus killed Caesar', from the 2-place predicate 'ξ killed ζ', by filling the two argument-places with the same name. Someone might grasp the conceptual content of the whole sentence, via her understanding of this predicate, and only afterward come to grasp the sense of the new predicate 'ξ killed ξ' when her attention is first drawn to the possibility of that decomposition. It is at least doubtful that alternative decompositions could preserve conceptual content, if that is equated with strongly compositional sense. But if we acknowledge a weaker notion of sense along the lines suggested, the thought may appear tempting—even inescapable—that the *Begriffsschrift* discussion holds the key to our problem. Indeed, Dummett claims[5] that it must have supplied the model for Frege's talk of content-carving.

There are, however, at least two reasons why our *Grundlagen* §64 cannot happily be seen as implementing a procedure anticipated in *Begriffsschrift* §9. *Begriffsschrift*-style alternative analyses depend upon the possibility of different syntactic parsings of a single sentence. The claim is that a single sentence retains its conceptual content under different such parsings. But in the case of $D^=$, the two sentences which are to have the same content are quite different. The suggested model could, therefore, get a grip only if it could be maintained that there are alternative syntactic analyses of $D^=$(**right**), such that we can think of $D^=$(**left**) as being directly stipulated as equivalent to one of them, and then—via the claim that $D^=$(**right**) retains the same sense under the two analyses—as indirectly equivalent to the other. But no such alternative analyses of 'line a is parallel to line b' are in sight.

A related difficulty is that whilst Frege's *Begriffsschrift*-procedure is well-adapted to the formation of new (complex) predicates, it is quite unclear how alternative syntactic analyses of the kind there envisaged could disclose new *singular terms*; but that is precisely what would be needed, for it to apply to the *Grundlagen* §64 cases.

Oddly, Dummett in effect recognises that the preconditions for applying the *Begriffsschrift*-procedure are not met in the present case, but complains that Frege has illicitly transferred the model to cases in which it cannot properly be applied.[6] A more plausible account of what has gone wrong is that the mistake lies not in Frege, but in the attempt to assimilate his procedure in *Grundlagen*

5. Dummett 1991 p. 173 ff.

6. Dummett 1991, p. 175. The disparity between the two procedures is forcefully emphasised in Dummett 1981, p. 333.

§64 to that described in *Begriffsschrift* §9. The difference between the two is so obvious and striking that it seems unlikely that it can have escaped Frege's notice. Additional evidence that he pretty certainly had something else in mind comes from his speaking, in §64, of dividing up the content of the *symbol* for parallelism—in sharp contrast with the *Begriffsschrift* examples, where different parsings of a complete sentence are in view.

On the alternative account I favour, the procedure Frege envisages is as follows:

(1) We introduce 'the direction of line a = the direction of line b' as a (content (= weak sense)-preserving) redescription of the state of affairs consisting in the two lines being parallel, whilst simultaneously stipulating that its logical form is precisely what its surface syntax suggests.

(2) Since that shared content is available to one who understands the statement about parallelism, it can be appreciated without possession of the concept of direction. (That concept does not, therefore, lie hidden within the shared content, awaiting disclosure by analysis).

(3) By accepting the equivalence we come to know the content—but not yet the (fully compositional) sense—of its left hand side. But if we further accept this as having the logical form Frege intends, and so discern in it a genuine occurrence of the familiar identity-predicate, we shall be led to recognise the expressions flanking it as singular terms which, provided they have reference at all, stand for objects of a kind whose identity-conditions are given by the equivalence. The new sortal concept of *direction* may then be introduced as applying to objects of that kind.

IV

Weak sense and truth-conditions. Since the notion of weak sense that I want to characterise corresponds to one way of understanding talk of truth-conditions, I shall (with a degree of legislation) appropriate that term for it.

A very weak notion of truth-condition—perhaps the weakest that is at all plausible—may be defined by stipulating that sentences share their truth-condition iff they coincide in truth-value at all possible worlds. This meets the minimal requirement, implicit in Frege's procedure as I am understanding it, that the truth of **D=(right)**, for example, should suffice for the existence of the objects (directions) mentioned in **D=(left)**. But it is too weak. For one thing, arbitrary pairs of necessary truths will share very weak truth-conditions, yet are not plausibly taken as reconceptualisations of same state of affairs. Another closely connected cause for dissatisfaction derives from the wider philosophical interest of **D=**, which lies in the possibility of invoking its counterpart for numbers:

N=   The number of Fs = the number of Gs iff the Fs correspond 1–1 with the Gs

in defence of a broadly Fregean version of logicism. Anyone whose sympathies lie in this direction will want to regard **D=** and **N=** as *analytic of* the concepts of *direction* and *number*. But this surely requires identity of truth-conditions of their left and right sides in a stronger sense than is captured by the requirement of coincidence in truth-value across all worlds.

With a view to identifying a suitably stronger relation of identity in truth-condition—one closer to, but still weaker than, identity in fully compositional sense—let us consider a pair of sentences which are, independently of present concerns, plausibly taken to instantiate it.

                 (a) There are husbands

and   (b) There are wives

These are plausibly taken to share the same truth-condition, in a quite strong sense, whilst differing in (strongly compositional) sense, or thought expressed.[7] Their shared truth-condition is, of course:

                 (c) $\exists x \exists y (x$ is male $\& \ y$ is female $\& \ x$ is married to $y)$

That they differ in strongly compositional sense follows from the fact that someone might wonder whether there are husbands iff there are wives, without wondering whether there are husbands iff there are husbands. Their difference in compositional sense arises because, whilst formed ultimately from the same basic predicates

7. I am ignoring complications introduced by the possibility of homosexual marriage.

('ξ is male', 'ζ is female', 'ξ is married to ζ'), they are formed from them in different ways. The first comes by existential closure of the complex predicate:

(d) $\exists y(\xi$ is male & y is female & ξ is married to y)

while the second comes by existential closure of the different complex predicate

(e) $\exists x(x$ is male & ζ is female & x is married to $\zeta)$

Someone might understand (c) (and (a)) without having recognised the possibility of extracting the complex predicate (e) from (c), and thus without possessing the concept of *wife*.

Clearly (a) and (b) satisfy the weak requirement for identity of truth-condition already discussed. Our interest is in what stronger requirements they fulfil. One quite strong requirement is that anyone who understands both sentences should be able to tell immediately (i.e. without inference) that they must have the same truth-value. This is in fact the requirement which Dummett takes Frege to have accepted as both necessary and sufficient for identity of thought expressed by two sentences.[8] Dummett argues, correctly in my view, that it gives only a necessary, not a sufficient, condition for thought identity. However, since the reason why it fails to be sufficient is, at bottom, that it leads to violations of compositionality, and since we are, in effect, exploring the possibility of framing a criterion which captures the residue of the condition for identity of Fregean sense, when the compositionality requirement is subtracted, it is natural to ask whether this require-ment might nevertheless stand as *both* necessary *and* sufficient for identity of truth-condition.

The answer, I think, is that it is certainly sufficient, but probably cannot be taken to be necessary, if we wish to regard such pairs as (a) and (b) as coinciding in truth-condition. This is because it is at least very questionable that someone who understands both of these sentences could tell, without any inference at all, that they must have the same truth-value. More generally, the requirement that no inference of any kind, however simple, should be involved in recognising that the two sentences must coincide in truth-value seems both unmotivated and unduly exacting, if what is in question

8. cf. Dummett 1991, p. 171.

is identity of truth-condition rather than identity of thought expressed. This suggests weakening to:

> Two sentences have the same truth-condition iff anyone who understands both of them can tell that they have the same truth-value

The obvious worry is that this is now *too* weak. Weakening so as to permit (deductive) reasoning will let in arbitrary pairs of necessary truths which are (separately) knowable a priori. Thus not only will:

$$\text{(f)} \quad Nx: x \neq x = Nx: x \text{ is even \& } x \text{ is prime \& } x > 2$$

and   (g) The concepts $x \neq x$ and *x is even & x is prime & x > 2* can be one-to-one correlated

qualify as having the same truth-condition—so will (f) and

(h) Tuesday precedes Wednesday

yet we should hardly wish to view (f) as effecting a recarving of the same content as (h).

It is not in fact clear that this result is anything to worry about. It *would* be so, if the claim were that two sentences being alike in content is *not only* necessary, *but also sufficient*, for one of them to be properly seen as effecting a recarving of the content of the other. As against this, it might be held that coincidence in truth-condition (as defined) suffices *as far as the requirement of sameness in content goes*, but that this does not preclude the imposition of further conditions on the sentences involved, if Frege's procedure is to be properly applied (e.g. that the right hand side of any suitable equivalence should be to the effect that an equivalence relation holds among entities of some (already recognised) sort). Nonetheless, it is of interest to enquire whether a more selective conception of identity in truth-condition is available, instantiation of which *would* suffice for proper recarving.

Not just any pair of a priori knowable necessary truths will meet the following strengthened condition:

> Two sentences have the same truth-condition iff anyone who understands both of them can tell, *without determining their truth-values individually*, that they have the same truth-value

But some will, and so will many pairs of contingent statements one of which is, as it were, merely a logical complication of the other. These cases are straightforwardly illustrated by the pairs:

(i) $P \vee \neg P$ and $Q \vee \neg Q$

(ii) P and $(P \& Q) \vee (P \& \neg Q)$

One might seek to exclude such cases by strengthening the criterion so as to require that understanding S and S´ is not only sufficient (modulo competence in deductive reasoning) to enable a thinker to recognise their material equivalence, but also necessary. But this has the drawback that it also excludes—presumably undesirably—such pairs as

(iii) $P \& Q$ and $Q \& P$

A better remedy is to further restrict the kind of reasoning allowed. Thus far, we have been allowing any purely deductive reasoning— that is, any reasoning all steps of which correspond to true (classical) entailments. Such entailments will depend upon the semantic contributions made by key items of logical vocabulary, but will not in general be sensitive to those of non-logical vocabulary. A more selective notion of entailment—introduced for other purposes by Crispin Wright—is that of *compact entailment*. As Wright explains it, 'an entailment is defined as compact just in case it is liable to disruption by uniform replacement of *any* non-logical constituent in its premises, (but not in its conclusion)'. [9] In other words:

$A_1,...,A_n$ *compactly entail* B iff (i) $A_1,...,A_n$ entail B, and

                      (ii) for *any* non-logical constituent E occurring in $A_1,...,A_n$, there is *some* substitution E´/E which applied uniformly through $A_1...,A_n$, yields $A_1´,...,A_n´$ which do *not* entail B

The effect of (ii) is to disallow entailments in which the premises contain parts which are 'passengers', in the intuitive sense that their specific content makes no essential contribution to the holding of the entailment. Thus the entailments of '$P \vee \neg P$' by '$Q \vee \neg Q$' and

9. cf. Wright 1989, p. 612.

of 'P' by '(P & Q) v (P & ¬Q)' fail of compactness, since no uniform substitution on 'Q' can disrupt either. The entailment of 'P&Q' by 'Q&P' will be compact, however, whenever 'P' and 'Q' are both atomic, as well as in many cases where they are not. Not all instances of the schema 'A & B ⊨ B & A' will be compact entailments, of course, since one of the conjuncts may be a logical truth. A snag with compact entailment as defined is that it is not reflexive, since no logical truth compactly entails itself. But this defect is easily handled by allowing any entailment as compact if it is a substitution-instance of an entailment that is compact by the definition above.[10]

Employing this notion, my more refined proposal is that:

> Two sentences have the same truth-condition iff anyone who understands both of them can tell, without determining their truth-values individually, and by reasoning involving only compact entailments, that they have the same truth-value

In terms of this notion of truth-condition (in either its more or its less exacting form), we may introduce a derivative notion of states of affairs: two sentences will represent the same state of affairs iff they have the same truth-condition. We may then speak—conveniently, but not ineliminably—of one sentence involving a reconceptualisation of the same state of affairs as another.

The conception of states of affairs corresponding to the more liberal notion of truth-condition sustains (a restricted version of) one of the two principles to which the Slingshot appeals: all logically equivalent contingent sentences—and some (but not all) logically true (and some (but not all) logically false) sentences— will represent the same state of affairs. It avoids vulnerability to (a correspondingly restricted) Slingshot, however, by rejecting the other principle: interchange of co-referential terms is not guaranteed to preserve reference to the same state of affairs.[11]

---

10. Thanks to Peter Milne for drawing attention to the point, and the remedy. Note that with this adjustment, all instances of the schema 'A & B ⊨ B & A' will be compact, since each will be a substitution-instance of an entailment of this form where the conjuncts are atomic, and which is therefore compact under the earlier definition.

11. Clearly the notion of state of affairs matching the more exacting version of the criterion will be invulnerable to the Slingshot for the same reason. Indeed, on the more exacting version, the other step involved in the collapsing argument will fail too, since the entailment of P by '(ιx)(0=x & P) = (ιx)(0=x)' is not compact.

The two halves of **D=**, **N=**, etc., will coincide in truth-condition in my sense. Indeed, they will satisfy the stronger requirement imposed by the Fregean criterion for thought-identity, since anyone who understands a statement of direction-identity via the stipulation of **D=** can tell, without inference, that it must have the same truth-value as the corresponding statement of parallelism. But the point, of course, was to elucidate the *general* notion of truth-condition that is in play—only if that is done can the intended effect of the stipulation be clear.

V

Inflation? Frege's primary objective in the passage with which we began is to explain how **D=** may serve to introduce the concept of *direction*. But if this account of how his metaphor of carving content is good, it speaks also to the charge that the proposed explanation is objectionable because ontologically inflationary. That charge enjoys at least initial plausibility, simply because **D=(left)** makes explicit reference to objects of two sorts—lines and their directions—while **D=(right)** makes reference only to lines. The lynch-pin in the Fregean response to it is that the question what kinds of objects there are is not properly separable from the question what true statements, incorporating singular terms, can be made. In particular, it suffices for the existence of directions that there are true statements to be made, featuring terms which, if they have reference at all, refer to directions. If **D=** affords an acceptable means of introducing direction-terms, there are statements (sc. statements of direction-identity) the truth of which suffices for the existence of directions. And since, according to that explanation, those statements share their truth-conditions with the correlated statements of line-parallelism, the existence of directions calls for the obtaining of no states of affairs beyond what are already required for lines to be parallel. The thought that the direction of line a = the direction of line b is indeed a *distinct thought* (deploying different concepts) from the thought that lines a and b are parallel. But the sentences which express them are to be understood as different, equally correct, descriptions of the same state of affairs. It is in this sense, and for this reason, that the proposed explanation is not ontologically inflationary.

It is not open to the objector to accept the explanation but protest that lines could be parallel without there being such 'additional' objects as directions, since to accept the explanation is precisely to accept that the truth of statements of line-parallelism is sufficient for that of statements of direction-identity. Nor can he refuse to accept the explanation on the ground that the stipulation of identity in truth-condition of the two halves of $D^=$ builds additional and suspect ontological commitment into otherwise innocent statements of line-parallelism. This objection presupposes concepts of *direction* and *parallelism* for which it is an open question whether parallel lines have the same direction (or even have directions at all). It is quite unclear what this concept of *direction* is, or how it might be explained; but even if a coherent such concept can be contrived, it will not be the concept Frege sought to introduce by means of $D^=$, so that the objection is at best irrelevant. If the objector repudiates any commitment to some such non-Fregean concept of *direction*, and insists only that since one could be competent in parallelism-talk whilst lacking the concept of *direction*, so that the existence of directions is not implicit in the concept of *parallelism*, the Fregean may reply that this is true, but again beside the point—the proposal was not that we can *extract* the concept of *direction* from that of *parallelism*, but that we can build the former concept out of the latter, together with the general concept of identity. If the objector replies that since directions are objects over and above lines, *any* way of constructing the concept of *direction* out of that of parallelism—or any which would have us see statements to the effect that lines are parallel as requiring the existence of directions—must be objectionably inflationary, then he is simply begging the question.

Even if it is conceded that Frege's procedure is not intrinsically inflationary—in the sense that every application of it must result in an expanded domain of objects—the charge of inflation may be developed along different lines, focusing upon those applications which are of greatest philosophical interest, where the abstraction is grounded in an equivalence relation defined not on objects (as with $D^=$) but on concepts (as with $N^=$). $N^=$ itself, it may be observed, is satisfiable only in domains comprising least a countably infinite collection of objects. More generally, it may be argued that, however things may stand with first-order abstractions, there are bound to be second- or higher-order abstractions, resulting from the application of Frege's procedure, which *are* inflationary, and objectionably so. For suppose the universe comprises just k objects, for some (possibly infinite) cardinal k. Then there will be 2^k distinct first-level Fregean concepts definable on this universe. And there will certainly be at least one (second-level) equivalence relation *Eq* on these concepts which partitions them into as many (i.e. 2^k) equivalence classes. Since the associated Fregean equivalence: $\sigma(F) = \sigma(G) \leftrightarrow Eq(F,G)$ associates each equivalence class of concepts with a distinct σ-object, the universe must comprise at least $2^k > k$ objects!

There is no disputing that $N^=$ calls for an at least countable infinity of objects—indeed, it would be useless for Frege's purposes if it did not. Since there may be only finitely many concrete objects, it follows that it may call for the existence of more objects than there are concrete objects. But that does not make it inflationary, unless it is assumed that the concrete objects are all the objects there are. The more general argument calls for a more general response. What is questionable in it is the assumption that the universe (of objects) may be treated as a determinate fixed totality, of assignable bounded cardinality. Without that assumption, the idea that higher-order abstractions must result in expansion of the universe—as opposed to disclosing previously unrecognised reaches of it—gets no purchase. It may be that there is no positive warrant in Frege's work to think of the universe of objects as, in Dummett's words, indefinitely extensible; but neither, so far as I know, is there anything essential to his thought which is inhospitable to such a conception.[12]

Dept of Philosophy
University of Glasgow
Glasgow G12 8QQ
email: rlh@arts.gla.ac.uk

12. Earlier versions of this paper were presented to a Glasgow research seminar, a British Society for Philosophy of Science Conference in Sheffield, a meeting of the Cambridge Moral Sciences Club and a conference on Frege in Stirling. I am grateful to all these audiences for helpful discussion. Particular thanks are due to Jim Edwards, Hugh Mellor, Alex Oliver, Philip Percival, Michael Potter, Ian Rumfitt, Peter Sullivan, Nick Zangwill and, as usual, to Crispin Wright.

REFERENCES

Davidson, Donald	1969 'True to the facts' *Journal of Philosophy* vol.66, pp. 748–64.
Dummett, Michael	1981 *The Interpretation of Frege's Philosophy* London, Duckworth.
	1991 *Frege: Philosophy of Mathematics* London, Duckworth.
Frege, Gottlob	1879 *Begriffsschrift* Halle, L.Nebert; part translated in Peter Geach and Max Black *Translations from the Philosophical Writings of Gottlob Frege* Oxford, Blackwell 1952.
	1884 *Die Grundlagen der Arithmetik*, Breslau, W.Koebner, reprinted with English translation by J.L.Austin as *The Foundations of Arithmetic* Oxford, Blackwell 1950.
	1892 'Über Begriff und Gegenstand' *Vierteljahrsschrift für wissenschaftliche Philosophie* vol.16, pp.192–205, and translated as 'On concept and object' in Geach and Black.
	1893 *Grundgesetze der Arithmetik* vol.1 Jena, H.Pohle, part translated into English by Montgomery Furth in *The Basic Laws of Arithmetic* Berkeley, University of California Press 1964.
Linsky, Bernard	1992 'A Note on the "Carving Up Content" Principle in Frege's Theory of Sense' *Notre Dame Journal of Formal Logic* vol. 33 no.1, pp. 126–135.
Wright, Crispin	1989 'The Verification Principle: Another Puncture—Another Patch' *Mind* vol.98, no. 392, pp. 611–22.

XIII*—REASON AND AGENCY

by Thomas Pink

I

Motivation-based theories of agency. What is common to all that we deliberately do? What characteristics are essential to human agency? One very common approach to this question, at least within English-language philosophy, is to appeal to the way in which agency is motivated and explained. What all our agency has in common is a distinctively practical motivation—a distinctive *purposiveness*. To be motivated to act deliberately or intentionally is at least to be motivated to do something for a purpose—for the sake of or as a means to an end.[1] Hence our agency is always explained by a pro attitude directed at an end—by some psychological state or other that motivates us to pursue that end—combined with the belief that our agency, in a respect in which it is deliberate, would or might further that end.

We find this view in Davidson. As he puts it, if someone performs an action of type A for a reason, that he does A must be explained by the fact that the agent has:

> …a pro attitude toward actions of type B… and a belief that in performing an action of type A he will be (or probably will be) performing an action of type B… There must be such rationalising beliefs and desires if an action is done for a reason…[2]

For Davidson, purposiveness is the essentially practical form of motivation. There are passive occurrences which are motivated too—for which we can have our reasons. Just as we can perform actions for reasons, we can come to hold desires for reasons. But

---

1. If we understand the means–end relation widely, so that it can be constitutive as well as causal, this can be true even where there is no *further* end to our doing of A. Even here, A is still being done for a purpose—for its own sake: the end attained is wholly constituted by the means.

2. 'Intending' pp. 86–7 in D. Davidson *Essays on Actions and Events* (Oxford: Oxford University Press, 1980).

---

*Meeting of the Aristotelian Society, held in the Senior Common Room, Birkbeck College, London, on Monday, 26th May, 1997 at 8.15 p.m.

even though motivated by reasons, our coming to hold a particular desire is not usually a matter of our own deliberate doing. And the Davidsonian explanation for why this is so is simple. Desire-formation is not usually purposive. Unlike our actions, our desires are not usually formed as a means to any end. Desires to do A may be explained by further desires or pro attitudes towards attaining ends E; but the beliefs that combine with those further pro attitudes to get us to want to do A are characteristically beliefs about how *doing A* would further those ends—not beliefs about how *desiring to do A* would further those ends.

To answer the question, *Is intending an action?*, Davidson therefore again appeals to how the formation of particular intentions, in our decision making, is motivated. And, in Davidson's view, intending is no action precisely because the formation of particular intentions, like desire formation but unlike the performance of the actions intended, is non-purposive:

> The coming to have an intention we might try connecting with desires and beliefs as we did other intentional actions… But the story does not have the substantial quality of the account of intentional action…[3]

And Davidson is surely right that, characteristically, particular decisions to act aren't taken purposively—aren't taken as means to ends.[4] If I take a decision to perform an action A, rather than some alternative B, my decision won't normally have been based on any pro attitude towards an end and belief that deciding to do A would further that end. The deliberation on which my decision and intention to do A is based will have been deliberation about whether to do A—and not deliberation about whether to decide or intend to do A. The beliefs that will have moved me to form an intention to do A rather than B will have been beliefs about what ends *doing A* would further—not beliefs about what ends *deciding or intending to do A* would further.

Davidson's characterisation of human agency in terms of a distinctively practical motivation—as essentially purposive—is

---

3. 'Intending' p. 90.

4. Davidson puts forward the view of intention motivation which follows on pp. 213–14 of his replies in *Essays on Davidson* eds B. Vermazen and M. Hintikka (Oxford: Oxford University Press, 1985).

not new. We find essentially the same account in Hobbes who claimed:

> ...a Voluntary Act is that, which proceedeth from the Will, and no other.[5]

For Hobbes, to talk of the will just was to talk of the beliefs and pro attitudes—or *appetites*, as he termed them—that provide the purposes for which we act. A Hobbesean will to do A just is a combination of pro attitudes towards ends with beliefs that doing A might further those ends—a combination of purposes for doing A that overrides any purposes we might have for doing anything else, and disposes us actually to do A.

Hobbes's motivation-based conception of human agency as essentially purposive—the very conception which we see perpetuated in Davidson—was opposed to an earlier, scholastic conception of human agency. Where Hobbes and his successors characterised our agency in terms of its mode of motivation and explanation, Aquinas, by contrast, characterised it in terms of its mode of rationality, or the way in which it is governed by reason. Aquinas characterised human agency, not as something essentially purposive, but as the exercise of a distinctively practical rationality. And with this conception of human agency came a quite un-Hobbesean conception of the human will, not as mere appetite, but as an *appetitus rationalis*—as an action-motivating capacity to apply practical reason.

II

Aquinas's practical reason-based theory of human agency. Aquinas did make use of a motivation-based theory of agency— but only to characterise the agency of non-rational animals. The agency of animals did indeed consist simply in pursuing ends, motivated by appetites for those ends and guided in so doing by states that at least mimicked, in the form of instinct, beliefs about how their agency would further those ends. But this was not Aquinas's account of adult human agency. For in his view, adult humans possessed a capacity for practical rationality—a capacity which animals as supposedly non-rational beings wholly lacked.

---

5. *Leviathan* (1651) chapter 6, p. 44. References are to the edition of R. Tuck (Cambridge: Cambridge University Press, 1991).

Unlike animals, adult humans had the capacity to reason and form judgments about which actions they would be justified in performing, and to act on the basis of those judgments.

So humans were not motivated simply by mere appetites as animals were. Since humans had a capacity for practical rationality, they possessed a *rational appetite* or *will*: an action-motivating capacity for decision-making and intention formation whereby they could respond, well or defectively, to reason in practical form —to available rational justifications for and against performing specific actions.[6]

Human agency could then be characterised by Aquinas precisely as the exercise of a capacity for practical rationality. Notice that such exercise, though of a capacity for rationality, might still be defective in various ways. It is, after all, the very fact that our capacity for practical rationality can be exercised defectively that allows some of our agency to count as genuinely irrational—as constituting a genuine misapplication of reason.[7]

So, in Aquinas's view, any exercise, whether competent or defective, by us of our capacity for practical rationality just was an action (or if not an action, an equally voluntary refraining from action). As Aquinas put it:

6. I endorse, as essential to a practical reason-based account of agency, Aquinas's conception of the human will as a rational or reason-applying appetite. But I omit from the main text, as inessential to a practical reason-based account, a further important aspect of Aquinas's conception of the will—his *intellectualism*.

Aquinas conceived the will—our capacity for decision making and intention formation—as tied to our deliberative capacity to reflect and form practical judgments about how we should act. As involving the will, human actions, in Aquinas's view, were based on a view of the good. The acts of *electio* by which we decide to perform actions A were given their content by corresponding judgments that it would be good to do A. The will was notionally a power distinct from the intellect: but its actual operations were conceived by Aquinas as integrated with and informed by a corresponding exercise of the practical intellect.

In my *The Psychology of Freedom* (Cambridge: Cambridge University Press, 1996) I defend a rival, *voluntarist* theory which firmly distinguishes intellect and will. On this theory, our capacity for decision making and intention is still a rational appetite—a capacity for applying reason. For the will has precisely the function of executing practical judgments about how we should act. But decisions and intentions are quite distinct from the prior practical judgments which it is their function to execute—so that we can sometimes, irrationally, decide to act contrary to our judgments about how we should act. The will's reason-applying role is purely executive, not deliberative.

7. For a typically forceful expression of Hobbes's failure to understand this point, see *Leviathan*, chapter 6 p. 44:

The Definition of the *Will*, given commonly by the Schooles, that it is a *Rationall Appetite*, is not good. For if it were, then there could be no Voluntary Act against Reason.

An act is voluntary when it is an operation of reason.[8]

This practical reason-based conception of human agency had one immediate consequence. It naturally supported belief in a further, action-generating agency located in the very decision making that guided our actions.

On a practical reason-based conception of agency, we are active whenever we count as conforming to, or violating, the requirements of a practical, agency-governing reason. Now it seems natural to suppose (what I shall anyway be arguing below) that it is in our decision making, in particular, that we conform to or violate such requirements—that it is in our decisions about which actions to perform, in particular, that we are practically rational or irrational. Accordingly, our decisions to act must, as exercises of rationality in practical form, be cases of agency too.

And so Aquinas held a dual order theory of agency. The voluntary includes not only actions such as deliberately getting up and the like, and deliberate refrainings from such, but also the prior willing or deciding to perform or refrain from these actions. Just as it is up to us or within our control which actions we eventually perform so, as equally an exercise of our capacity for agency, it is equally up to us or within our control which actions we first decide or will to perform:

> But we have control both over whether we act or refrain from acting, and whether we will or refrain from willing.[9]

Aquinas's account of agency led him, then, to accommodate an important feature of agency as we ordinarily conceive it. For we do indeed ordinarily believe in just such an agency of the will. The taking of a particular decision is something we naturally take to be our own deliberate doing. When faced with options A or B, it can be entirely up to me which I decide to do—just as much as, when the time for action comes, it can be up to me whether I actually do A or do B. Deciding to do A rather than B is as much an exercise of my deliberate agency as is actually doing A rather than B.

8. *Summa Theologiae* (1265–74) 1a 2ae q6 a1, p. 54. Page references are to volume 2 of the BAC edition, Madrid 1985. There is a translation by J. Oesterle of this part of the *Summa* dealing with agency entitled *Treatise on Happiness* (Notre Dame: University of Notre Dame Press, 1983).

9. *Summa Theologiae* 1a 2ae q6 a3 p. 56.

Daniel Dennett is in fact something of a sceptic about the reality of an agency of the will. But he has noticed our natural belief in such agency. As he puts it, sometimes our own decisions about what we shall do seem

> ...the preeminently voluntary moves in our lives, the instants at which we exercise our agency to the fullest.[10]

And there are at least two respects in which taking a particular decision does seem to be a 'preeminently voluntary' move. First, taking a particular decision to act seems a doing which is essentially deliberate. That I take a particular decision to act, does not seem to be something that I can ever do inadvertently or unintentionally.

But there is a second respect in which, in decision making, our agency seems to be 'exercised to its fullest'. For it is at the point of taking a particular decision to act that we actually determine what we shall do—that we determine and control our agency as a whole. The point of taking decisions about which actions to perform, after all, is precisely to settle how in the future we shall be acting. In decision making, we not only settle what decision we take now; we also settle what actions we shall be performing thereafter, and so our agency into the future. Decisions to act are—what the actions decided upon are not—deliberate doings that determine our own deliberate doings generally. In taking decisions to act, we exercise, and exercise deliberately, a capacity for active self-determination —a determination and control of our agency as a whole through time.

Our concept of agency is deployed at two levels. It applies initially to such uncontroversial actions as deliberate hand raising and the like. These actions constitute our *first order* agency. But then the motivation for this first order agency can arise from our own agency too—from prior decisions by which, through our own deliberate doing, we leave ourselves motivated to perform particular actions. So in addition to our first order agency, we have a prior capacity for *second order* agency—a capacity, by our own deliberate agency, to leave ourselves motivated to perform particular first order actions.

We've seen that, unlike Davidson, Aquinas thought that the taking of a particular decision is itself an action. But notice that no

10. Elbow Room (Oxford: Oxford University Press, 1984) p. 78.

more than Davidson did Aquinas suppose that decision making need be purposive. Aquinas distinguished two kinds of action: *elicited* actions and *commanded* actions.[11]

Suppose that I am deliberating about whether to stand up or stay sitting down, on the basis of considering what ends these actions might further, and conclude that I should get up. My deliberation has then left me, as Aquinas puts it, commanding myself to get up—getting up hence counting as an *actus imperatus* or commanded action which, as based on beliefs about what ends its performance might further, is accordingly purposive.

But there is also the prior action of deciding to get up—an action which I haven't been deliberating about, which has been explained instead simply by my deliberation about whether to get up, and so simply by my beliefs about what ends getting up would further, and which is, accordingly, non-purposive. This action Aquinas regards as an *actus elicitus:* an action which is elicited by my practical reason, rather than commanded by it. And so, for Aquinas, we have the possibility of deliberate will agency that is motivated in non-purposive form. What makes such decisions actions themselves, is the fact that they as much count as exercises of a distinctively practical rationality as do the actions decided upon which they explain.

Some sort of belief in a capacity for second order agency was widespread in the high middle ages. Controversy then was often about the detail—and in particular about whether to conceptualise this second order agency in intellectualist terms as a freedom of the practical intellect, or in voluntarist terms as a freedom of the will apart from the intellect.[12] But fierce disputes about the very reality of second order agency were a striking feature of early modern ethical and psychological theory.[13]

11. The distinction is made in *Summa Theologiae* 1a 2ae, in the introduction to question 6 'On the voluntary and involuntary' p. 53. Elicited actions are dealt with in questions 8 to 16 pp. 67–111, commanded actions in question 17, pp. 112–121.

12. See Bonnie Kent *Virtues of the Will: the transformation of ethics in the late thirteenth century* (Washington, D.C.: CUA Press, 1996).

13. A variety of considerations against second order agency are proposed in, for example, the second book of Calvin's *Institutes of the Christian Religion* (1559), by Hobbes in *The Questions concerning Liberty, Necessity and Chance* (1656), and in qualified form in the chapter on power in Locke's *Essay Concerning Human Understanding* (1690). Considerations for are to be found in, for example, the nineteenth of Suarez's *Metaphysical Disputations* (1597) and Bramhall's *A Defence of True Liberty from Ante-cedent and Extrinsecall Necessity* (1655).

This early modern debate involved a complex variety of issues. But it was importantly part of a wider debate between two models of human agency. On one scholastic model, human agency was to be characterised as an exercise of practical rationality: an exercise that could occur prior to our first order agency, in the operations of a rational appetite—a capacity to motivate ourselves on the basis of practical reason. On the other model, human agency was to be characterised in terms rather of a purposive motivation—a motivation that is characteristically to be found in our first order agency, but not in our second.

III

Reason in practical form. Central to a practical reason-based account of human agency are the following claims. The agency performed by humans, at least, admits of rational justifications for and against its performance—justifications that are provided by reason in its distinctively practical or agency-governing form, and to which humans have a capacity to respond. The human capacity for agency, then, is essentially a capacity to apply and be guided by such practical justifications.

So human agency comprises those exercises of our rationality governed by reason in practical form. What unites all cases of human agency, then, is the common and distinctively practical way in which rational justifications for and against their performance are determined.

So to characterise what all agency has in common, we need to understand what it is for reason to take practical or agency-governing form—what it is for a mode of justification to be practical. And there is one particularly natural theory on this question. Suppose you want to argue someone into performing an everyday action—such as going for a walk or reading a book. You will always do so by seeking to persuade them that performing the action would likely constitute, or cause, some desirable outcome. So perhaps what distinguishes reason in its distinctively practical form, is that it governs agency by reference to the desirability of the ends which that agency is itself likely to further. Agency, on this view, is *means–end justifiable*. Performing an action A counts as agency only because its rationality depends on that same doing— doing A—being likely to further desirable ends.

Why should it be exercises of rationality in means–end justifiable form which count as our agency? The answer to this question lies, I think, in a natural connexion between agency and the exercise of control. It's not that to perform agency is ipso facto to exercise control. For we can lack control of what we do—as when as agents we are subject to compulsion or manipulation. But the nature of anything which counts as our agency—as something we deliberately do—must at least be consistent with our actually exercising control over and through its occurrence. If some occurrence—say, the taking of a decision—does count as a genuine doing, then the nature of that occurrence, *including* the way that it is governed by reason, shouldn't rule out its ever constituting an exercise of control. Perhaps then a distinctively practical rationality is that kind of rationality that must govern any exercise of control.

But means–end justifiability just *is* reason as it governs the exercise of control. For what does the rational exercise of control involve, but producing outcomes likely to be desirable, or preventing outcomes likely to be undesirable? And means–end justifiable doings are made rational precisely by the fact that they would likely produce desirable outcomes and prevent undesirable ones.

On this view, we can explain the common intuition that desires are essentially passive states—that, as we have already noted, forming a particular desire isn't something that we deliberately do. But this time, we no longer appeal to the non-purposiveness of desires. Instead we refer to the nature of desire rationality. Plausibly, what makes desiring to do A rational is the likely desirability (desire-worthiness) of doing A—which in turn depends on there being desirable ends which doing A might further. In which case a desire isn't a means–end justifiable state, justified as it is by reference to the desirability of ends likely to be furthered by its object, not by reference to the desirability of ends furthered by the desire itself.

Correspondingly, deciding or forming an intention to do A is going to count as agency only if the rationality of forming an intention to do A is determined in a non-desirelike, actionlike way—only if the rationality of intending to do A depends on the likelihood of intending to do A furthering desirable ends, and not simply on the likelihood of the intention's object, doing A, furthering desirable ends. Deciding or intending to do A counts as agency only if the taking of a particular decision to act is means–end justifiable.

Now elsewhere[14] I have argued that a decision to act is indeed a means–end justifiable occurrence. And that is precisely because the will is an *appetitus rationalis*—a capacity which we exercise in the application of practical reason. For decision making has the function of facilitating the application of reason as it governs our first order agency—a function decisions fulfil by coordinating the performance of our actions through time. By deciding in advance about which actions we shall perform, we settle and so leave ourselves knowing in advance which actions we shall be performing in the future. And that means that we can coordinate our present actions with those future actions. Decision making thereby helps ensure that the actions which we perform at one time are justified given the actions which we perform at other times.

The important point, as I argue elsewhere, is that their action coordinatory function means that decisions to act are means–end justifiable. It's not just that, in view of this action-coordinatory function, deliberating and taking a decision *one way or the other* about how to act is means–end justifiable—justifiable in terms of the desirable action-coordinatory end furthered by decision making in general. That's certainly true. But what is also true is that the taking of particular decisions to act—decisions say to do A rather than B—is means–end justifiable too.

Remember that our ordinary belief in second order agency is precisely that deciding on this particular action rather than that is something we deliberately do, so that it is up to us *which* actions we decide to perform. And that's only going to be true if justifications for deciding to perform particular actions A are to be explained in terms of the ends likely to be furthered by those decisions themselves—and not simply, as with desires, by reference to the ends likely to be furthered by the doing A decided upon.

Now the ends furthered by now deciding to do A and the ends furthered by later doing A can sometimes differ—and in a way which matters to the effective coordination of our agency through time. No matter how desirable performing or even attempting to

14. See *The Psychology of Freedom*, chapter 8.

perform an action may be compared to alternatives, it may still not be rational to decide on that particular action. Decisions to act enable us to coordinate our agency through time by settling in advance how we shall be acting. But they only do that if they ensure a continuing motivation to act as decided—a motivation which persists up to the time for action. Now if the decision to perform a particular action is not likely enough to ensure a continuing motivation to act as decided—if for example there's a risk that we might abandon that particular decision through some subsequent change of mind—then no matter how desirable the action in question, it might still not be rational to decide to perform it. Action coordinatory justifications for taking a particular decision depend on that particular decision's efficacy as a reliable motivator of the action decided upon—a consideration that has to do with ends furthered by taking that particular decision, and not simply with ends furthered by the action decided upon. And so deciding to perform a particular action A is itself a means–end justifiable action.

But can decisions be means–end justifiable without being purposive as well? Indeed they can. There is certainly an important link between means–end justifiability and purposiveness. If some doing X is means–end justifiable—if doing X can be justified by the fact that it would further some desirable end—then I take it that it must be possible for an agent rationally to do X on that basis, motivated by the belief that to do X would be to further that end. That doing X is to be justified as a means to ends does imply, then, that a doing of X can also occur in purposive form, motivated by beliefs about what ends doing X would further. But occurrences that are means–end justifiable can also be motivated in non-purposive form as well. From the facts that doing X is means–end justifiable, and that an agent is motivated to do X, it importantly doesn't follow that the agent is ipso facto being motivated by beliefs about what ends doing X would further—that the agent is doing X purposively, as a means to an end.

Justifications for intending to do A, we've seen, depend on the ends which forming that particular intention to do A would be likely to further—and are not straightforwardly determined by the ends which doing A would be likely to further. What shows this, I've suggested, is that action coordinatory justifications for deciding to do A depend on that decision's being a good action coordinator—on that decision's actually being likely to leave one with a continuing motivation to do A. Where a decision to do A is less than likely to lead to the doing or even the attempting of A, then the ends likely to be furthered by now deciding to do A, and the ends likely to be furthered by later doing A or even attempting it, can be very different. The question of whether or not it would be good in the future to do or at least attempt doing A won't then settle the question of whether now to decide to do A.

But ordinarily decisions are good at producing a continuing motivation for the actions decided upon. In which case the ends likely to be furthered by our now deciding to do A rather than B, needn't differ materially from the ends likely to be furthered by our future doing or at least attempting A rather than B. And so the question of which decision to take needn't be considered separately from the question of which action it would be desirable to perform or attempt—a question which as practical deliberators we have to consider in any case. Hence typically our practical deliberation is simply about the actions between which we have to decide, and not also about which decision to take or which intention to form.

The default decision procedure, then, can be and is to ignore completely the question of what ends our decisions might further. The beliefs that move us to decide to do A in particular, then, are going to be beliefs simply about what ends doing or attempting A would further, not beliefs about what ends now deciding to do A would further. And so our first order actions are purposive; but our second order actions characteristically are not. To use Aquinas's terminology, our first order actions are commanded by our reason; but our second order actions can be merely elicited.

Notice that Aquinas thought that all that fell within our control— our voluntary agency in general—was means–end justifiable. For he held that, as much as the actions which they explained, our decisions or willings could rationally be deliberated about as means to ends, and so take the form of commanded acts—*actus imperati:*

> ...omne quod est in potestate nostra, subiacet imperio nostro—all that falls within our control, is subject to the command [of our reason].[15]

15. *Summa Theologiae* 1a 2ae q17 a5, p. 116.

And:

> …just as reason can judge that it would be good to will something, so reason can command someone to will. From which it is clear that an act of the will can be commanded.[16]

But that fact was quite consistent with the possibility that actions of the will take a non-purposive, merely elicited form. What was essential to human agency was its practical mode of justification, not its purposive motivation. To act is to exercise our rationality—and to exercise it as governed by reason in action-governing form.

IV

The development of motivation-based accounts of human agency. On the one hand, we have in Aquinas a theorist who naturally conceives of human agency in terms of its practical rationality—in terms of rationality in means–end justifiable form—and whose conviction that the human will is a locus of agency is correctly combined with and reinforced by a true belief that decisions to perform specific actions are, in particular, means–end justifiable.

On the other hand, we have in the later Hobbesian tradition, theorists who naturally conceive of human agency in terms of a purposive motivation, and who are sensitive to the equally clear fact that the taking of particular decisions is typically not a purposive activity. These thinkers are led to doubt whether there really is an agency or freedom of the human will at all. How, in early modern Europe, did this second tradition gain strength? There are at least three importantly different sources of support for the motivation-based view.

- *radical anti-Pelagianism and scepticism about human practical rationality.*

Belief in a human, second order agency of the will, I've argued, comes with belief in human practical rationality. But where Christianity has influenced theories of human nature, this belief in a human practical rationality has often been in tension with belief in the Fall and original sin. For in western Christianity in its anti-Pelagian forms, the Fall is seen as at least seriously damaging to

16. *Summa Theologiae* 1a 2ae q17 a5, p. 116.

our practical rationality.[17] Now this damage need not be seen as total. Though fallen, we may still be seen as retaining some capacity for practical rationality, the will still remaining a rational appetite. But anti-Pelagianism always provides the potential for an outright denial of our practical rationality—a denial that means giving up a practical reason-based conception of our agency.

We find such an outright denial in the early modern period in, for example, John Calvin. For Calvin, it wasn't simply that the will was a rational capacity that was damaged, so that our will no longer reliably followed our reason. The reason of fallen humanity had, for Calvin, no motivational power whatsoever. Our rational judgments about how we should act no longer had any effect whatsoever on what actions we were motivated to perform. The human will was no longer a rational appetite at all:

> Since reason, therefore, by which man distinguishes between good and evil, and by which he understands and judges, is a natural gift, it could not be completely wiped out; but it was partly weakened and partly corrupted, so that its misshapen ruins appear. John speaks in this sense: The light still shines in the darkness, but the darkness comprehends it not [John 1:5]. In these words both facts are clearly expressed. First, in man's perverted and degenerate nature some sparks still gleam. These show him to be a rational being, differing from the brute beasts, because he is endowed with understanding. Yet secondly, they show this light choked with dense ignorance, so that it cannot come forth effectively. Similarly, the will, because it is inseparable from man's nature, did not perish, but was so bound to wicked desires that it cannot strive after right.[18]

It followed that the agency of fallen humanity was no longer the exercise of a distinctively practical rationality. It had to be conceptualised in the same terms as animal agency—in terms of a purpose-providing motivation provided by simple appetite. And just as in fallen humanity there was no longer a rational appetite, so too there was no longer a freedom and agency of the will:

> And actually, if you consider the character of this natural desire of good in man, you will find that he has it in common with animals.

17. Pelagius was the British theologian who in the early 5th century maintained that Adam's fall had not removed our own capacity to avoid sin, perfection through our own efforts remaining a possibility for us—and whose views were discredited for subsequent orthodoxy by Augustine.

18. *Institutes of the Christian Religion* book 2, chapter 2, 'The knowledge of God the Redeemer', pp. 270–1—page reference to volume 1 of the translation by F.L. Battles, ed. J. T. McNeill (London:S.C.M. Press, 1961).

For they also desire their own well-being; and when some sort of good that can move their sense appears, they follow it. But man does not choose by reason and pursue with zeal what is truly good for himself according to the excellence of his immortal nature; nor does he use his reason in deliberation or bend his mind to it. Rather, like an animal he follows the inclination of his nature, without reason, without deliberation. Therefore whether or not man is impelled to seek after good by an impulse of nature has no bearing on freedom of the will. This instead is required: that he discern good by right reason; that knowing it he choose it; that having chosen it he follow it.[19]

Calvin however had still not entirely abandoned a practical reason-based conception of human agency. Such a conception was still intelligible to him. It delineated, after all, the past agency of unfallen humanity—precisely the rational capacity which the Fall had removed. It is in a thinker such as Hobbes that we find an even more marked departure from the practical reason-based conception.

- *The reconceptualisation of rational agency.*

Aquinas's account of human rationality and agency left human psychology radically discontinuous with the non-rational psychology of animals. First, our rational agency was characterised as involving kinds of psychological attitude—states of intellect and will—quite absent from the animal psychology. Secondly, this theory of our agency was expressed within the metaphysics of reason-dualism. Though the non-rational passions and sensory capacities which we shared with the animals were material, the distinctively rational faculties of intellect and will essential to our agency were immaterial.

Now Hobbes accepted that humans could reason practically as animals could not. But a materialist account of human nature was a central feature of Hobbes's metaphysical and political project. Concerned to develop an economical action-explanatory theory in materialist terms, Hobbes sought to characterise human psychology as continuous with, and so a more developed form of, a material animal psychology. It is not that, as agents, we had psychological attitudes of immaterial kinds which animals lacked.

19. *op. cit.* p. 286.

We possessed the same action-explanatory psychological attitudes
—but with more complex and various contents. Hence Hobbes
deployed what was previously a theory of animal agency alone to
provide his account of human agency as well. As we have seen, all
agency, human or animal, was a product of a Hobbesean will—was
purposive motion explained, in human and animal alike, by the
same deliberative interaction of desires for ends and beliefs about
how those ends are to be attained.

Distinctively human practical reasoning came not with special
immaterial psychological faculties, but with language. Language
served to record and express beliefs and appetites—psychological
states which were themselves language-independent. Reasoning,
in Hobbes's view, then consisted in drawing out the implications
of the general terms of a language:

> Out of all which we may define… what that is, which is meant by
> this word *Reason*, when wee reckon it amongst the Faculties of the
> mind. For REASON, in this sense, is nothing but *Reckoning* (that
> is, Adding and Subtracting) of the Consequences of generall names
> agreed upon…[20]

Hobbes saw language, and the reason which came with it, as an
invented tool that was permitted by our greater intelligence, and
which in turn enabled us to reach general conclusions from
particular cases. Beyond this, reasoning beings did not have
radically different psychologies from non-reasoning beings, any
more than those who enjoy the invention of, say, writing have
different psychologies from those who lack that tool.

Hence though Hobbes was certainly no sceptic about practical
reason—the laws of nature in *Leviathan* are requirements of reason
on our agency—he did not appeal to reason in his account of what
human agency was. To have characterised human agency in terms
of our distinctive capacity for rationality would have introduced
the very discontinuity between human and animal agency which,
with its dualist associations, Hobbes wanted to avoid. The chapter
of *Leviathan* on motivation, will and agency directly follows those
on language and reason. But it is expressly framed to deal with
animals generally, in terms that include human agency as simply
one case.

---

20. *Leviathan* chapter 5, p. 32.

● *Scepticism about practical reason itself*

A further source of support for a motivation-based account of human agency is, of course, scepticism about practical reason itself. There may seem little point in characterising our agency in terms of the way it is governed by reason if, in fact, as Hume expressly claimed, our agency is not governed by reason at all.[21] It is no surprise then that Hume's general conception of agency and the will was based firmly within the motivation-based tradition. Far from being a locus of rational appetition and second order agency, the will for Hume was simply a phenomenological marker for subsequent action:

> ...by the *will*, I mean nothing but *the internal impression we feel and are conscious of, when we knowingly give rise to any new motion of our body, or new perception of our mind.*[22]

Of course, scepticism about practical reason need not be quite so tightly linked with the motivation-based conception. For as such a sceptic one could still allow that a practical reason-based conception of agency is acceptable at least as an analysis of common sense psychology—that it gets our ordinary conception of our own agency perfectly right. Scepticism about practical reason could then feed through into a corresponding scepticism about whether our ordinary conception of our own agency actually applies.

But this has not been a common position. Those who espouse a motivation-based conception of agency as essentially purposive have generally put that theory forward as an account, not just of agency, but of agency as we ordinarily conceive it. Indeed, in *The Questions concerning Liberty, Necessity and Chance*, Hobbes himself belligerently attacked belief in an agency of the will precisely as being a scholastic invention without any basis in the common sense either of his own or of previous times.

Yet this last claim, at least, seems to be false. Belief in an agency of the will is enough part of common sense, after all, for Dennett to register it as such. And this belief in the agency of our decision

---

21. See *Treatise of Human Nature* (1739–40), book 2, part 3, section 3 'Of the influencing motives of the will'. Page references will be to the edition of L.A. Selby-Bigge/P.H. Nidditch (Oxford: Oxford University Press, 1978).
22. *Treatise* p. 399.

making, I have argued, can perfectly well be accounted for in terms of a practical reason-based conception of agency combined with a compelling account of decision rationality. Our decisions and the actions they explain, however dissimilar in their motivation, are governed by one and the same kind of practice-governing reason.

The practical reason-based conception of human agency has been neglected by modern philosophers of action. But it is a quite central feature of the intellectual history of their subject. More than that, it seems to provide our ordinary conception of our own agency too. Perhaps it will turn out that a practical reason-based conception cannot apply to reality because, say as Hume suspected, agency, whether human or otherwise, isn't really governed by reason after all. But that is a matter for discussion elsewhere.

What must be true, is that too many modern philosophers of action have been ready just to assume the motivation-based conception. That Davidson, in particular, should have assumed it, shows just how unreflective philosophical adherence to this conception has become. For he at least does not obviously share the intellectual preoccupations that helped popularise such a conception of human agency in the first place. Who would accuse Davidson of a radically anti-Pelagian theological anthropology, or of eschewing the normative in his account of human psychology— of being driven by a desire to secure a language-independent and reason-independent continuity between human and animal psychological attitudes and faculties—or by outright reason-scepticism?

Department of Philosophy
King's College London
Strand
London
WC2R 2LS

XIV*—DOES THE PROBLEM OF MENTAL CAUSATION GENERALIZE?

by Jaegwon Kim

According to the standard textbook account, Cartesian substance dualism foundered on the rocks of mental causation. Descartes was immediately confronted by his contemporaries, notably Pierre Gassendi and Princess Elizabeth of Bohemia, with this question: How can there be causal commerce between minds and bodies, substances whose natures are totally alien to one another? By what mechanism can a mental substance, lacking all physical properties and not even located within physical space, exert its causal powers on lumps of matter, moving them hither and thither? As we know, Descartes hemmed and hawed in his replies, and it seems fair to say that he was in the end unable to produce an intelligible response. Again, according to the textbook account, this failure was chiefly responsible for the demise of mental substance and substance dualism.

An interesting, and in many ways ironic, development in philosophy of mind during the past two decades is the return of mental causation as a contentious issue for anti-Cartesian physicalists. Whether mental causation can be made intelligible within a physicalist framework has become a serious question— serious enough to force some physicalists to consider, in obvious despair, the prospect of having to live with epiphenomenalism. In the first part of this paper, I want to give credence to this development by presenting an argument to show that a shared commitment of all serious versions of physicalism, namely, mind–body supervenience, apparently leads to an epiphenomenalist conclusion. I call this 'the supervenience argument'. I will then consider a popular attempt to dissipate the sting of this argument by urging that the argument shows too much because, when suitably generalized, it would show that there is no causation in geology and biology any more than in psychology. The recommended

*Meeting of the Aristotelian Society, held in the Senior Common Room, Birkbeck College, London, on Monday, 9th June, 1997 at 8.15 p.m.

conclusion of course is that since there surely is biological and geological causation, the supervenience argument must be incorrect. This objection opens an instructive avenue for thinking about some general issues concerning causation in the special sciences, and I believe this can shed light on some central problems that define the current mind–body debate.

I

The Supervenience Argument, or Descartes' Revenge. Mind–body supervenience is sometimes thought to be a precondition for the possibility of mind–body causation. Jerry Fodor writes: 'If mind/ body supervenience goes, the intelligibility of mental causation goes with it'.[1] To my knowledge, Fodor has never explained why he said this (and not just once), but one possible explanation lies in the physicalist's commitment to *the causal closure of the physical domain*. This is the principle that says: If you pick any physical event and trace its causal ancestry or posterity, that will never take you outside the physical domain. That is, no causal chain will cross the boundary between the physical and the nonphysical. Descartes' interactionist dualism is in clear violation of this principle. If you reject this principle, you are ipso facto rejecting the in-principle completability of a physical theory of all physical phenomena (never mind a physical theory of *all* phenomena). For you would be saying that any complete explanatory theory of the physical domain must invoke nonphysical causal agents. No serious physicalist will entertain such a prospect.

If mind–body supervenience fails, with the mental domain floating freely, unanchored in the physical domain, causation from the mental to the physical would obviously breach the physical causal closure. Mind–body supervenience grounds every mental phenomenon in the physical domain by providing for it a set of physical conditions that necessitates it. Further, no mental phenomenon can occur, and no mental property can be instantiated, unless an appropriate physical base condition is present. Every mental event, be it a sensation like pain or itch, or an intentional

1. *Psychosemantics* (Cambridge: MIT Press, 1987), p. 42. I, too, used to say something like this, e.g., in 'Epiphenomenal and Supervenient Causation', *Midwest Studies in Philosophy* 9 (1984): 257–270. See also Ausonio Marras, 'Nonreductive Physicalism and Mental Causation', *Canadian Journal of Philosophy* 24 (1994): 465–493.

state like belief or desire, must be physically grounded: it occurs because an appropriate physical base is present, and it would not occur if such a basis was absent.[2] These claims can be put in terms of 'realization', a familiar idiom associated with the functionalist approach to mentality. Instead of saying that mental phenomena supervene on physical phenomena, one might say that they are 'realized' (or 'implemented') by physical/biological processes. But on a standard conception of realization, realization entails supervenience: systems in identical physical conditions will of necessity realize identical mental properties. So if the argument works with mind–body supervenience as a premise, it should work for those who prefer the realization formulation of the mind–body relation.

In any case, mind–body supervenience brings mental phenomena within the ambit of the physical: in a tolerably clear sense, the mental depends on, and is determined by, the physical, and in that sense the mental does not constitute an ontologically independent domain that injects alien causal influences into the physical domain. It is another question whether mind–body supervenience brings the mental *close enough* to the physical to evade the constraint of the physical causal closure.[3] But we will set this question aside here and pursue another line of reasoning.

We are now ready to begin the supervenience argument:

(i) Mind–body supervenience holds.

But what exactly does mind–body supervenience assert? For our purposes, the following will suffice:

> *Mind–body supervenience*: For every mental property M if anything has M at t, there is a physical subvenient (or base) property P such that the thing has P at t, and necessarily anything that has P at t has M at t (such a P is called a 'base' or 'subvenient' property of M).

Note that a base property is 'necessarily' sufficient for the supervenient property, where the necessity is taken to be at least

2. Contentful mental states are widely believed not to supervene on *internal* physical properties of the subject, but physicalists will not deny their supervenience on the subject's extrinsic/relational physical properties. For the present paper, we ignore the issues that arise from content externalism.

3. See my 'Postscripts on Mental Causation' in *Supervenience and Mind* (Cambridge: Cambridge University Press, 1993). See also Tim Crane, 'The Mental Causation Debate', *Proceedings of the Aristotelian Society Supplementary Volume* 69 (1995): 211–236.

nomological necessity—so that if mind–body supervenience holds, it holds in all worlds that share the fundamental laws of our world. Further, a mental property can supervene on *multiple physical bases*; thus, mind–body supervenience accommodates the familiar observation that mental properties are 'multiply realizable' in diverse physical substrates.

We first explore how mental-to-mental causation fares under supervenience:

(ii)   Suppose that an instance of mental property M causes another mental property M^* to be instantiated.

We may take 'instances' or 'instantiations' of properties as events, states, or phenomena. For brevity, we will often speak of one property causing another; this is to be understood to mean that an *instance* of the first causes an *instance* of the second.[4] Returning to the argument: it follows from (i), the supervenience premise, that:

(iii) M^* has a physical supervenience base, P^*.

We now face this critical question: *Where does this instance of M^* come from? How does M^* get instantiated on this occasion?* Two answers seem available:

(iv) M^* is instantiated: (a) because, as assumed, M caused M^* to be instantiated; (b) because P^*, the supervenience base of M^*, is present on this occasion.

There is an obvious tension between these two answers: mind–body supervenience tells us that M^* occurs because its supervenience base, P^*, is present, and that given that P^* is there on this occasion, M^* must occur *no matter what other events had preceded this instance of M^**—in particular, regardless of whether or not there was a prior instance of M. This apparently puts the causal claim of M in jeopardy: P^* alone seems fully responsible for, and capable of explaining, this occurrence of M^*.[5] The presence of P^* by itself absolutely guarantees the occurrence of M^*, and unless P^*, or another physical base, is there on this occasion, M^* can't be there

4. Strictly speaking, we should add: one property instance causes another *in virtue of the fact that the first is of an F-instance and the second is a G-instance* (where F and G are the properties involved).

5. This argument is based on what I have called 'the principle of causal/explanatory exclusion'; see, e.g., my 'Mechanism, Purpose, and Explanatory Exclusion', reprinted in *Supervenience and Mind*.

either. Given this, the only way anything can have a role in the causation of M^* has to be through its relationship to P^*, and a plausible and natural way of saving the claim of M to be a cause of M^* seems available, namely this:

(v) M caused M^* *by causing* P^*. That is how M caused M^* to be instantiated on this occasion.

There may be a general principle involved here: *To cause a supervenient property to be instantiated, you must cause its base property (or one of its base properties) to be instantiated.* To relieve a headache, we take aspirin: we causally intervene in the brain processes on which the headache supervenes. That's the only way we can do anything about headaches. To make your painting more expressive or more dramatic, you must physically alter the painting—that is, change the physical supervenience base of the aesthetic property you want to improve. There is no direct way of making your painting more beautiful or less beautiful; you must work on it physically if you want to change it aesthetically—there is no other way.

But (v) implies:

(vi) M causes P^* to be instantiated.

This is mental-to-physical causation. Whence this somewhat surprising result: *Under mind–body supervenience, mind-to-mind causation presupposes mind-to-body causation—that is, unless the mind can causally affect the body, it cannot causally affect itself.* So the question that we must now face is whether we can make sense of mental-to-physical causation.

Going back to (vi), we see that the supervenience thesis yields:

(vii) M itself has a physical supervenience base, P.

We must now compare M and P in regard to their causal status with respect to P^*. When we reflect on this, I believe we begin to appreciate reasons for taking P as preempting the claim of M as a cause of P^*. If you take causation as grounded in nomological sufficiency, P qualifies; for since P is sufficient for M and M is sufficient for P^*, P is sufficient for P^*. If you choose to understand causation in terms of counterfactuals, again P seems to qualify: If P hadn't occurred, M would not have occurred (we may assume, without prejudice, that no alternative ('fail-safe') physical base of M was available on this particular occasion), and given that if M

had not occurred $P*$ would not have occurred, we may reasonably conclude that if P had not occurred, $P*$ would not have occurred either on this occasion.[6] Moreover, it is not feasible to think of this situation as involving a causal chain from P to $P*$, with M as an intermediate link. For the relation from P to M is not happily thought of as a causal relation; in general, the relation between base properties and supervenient properties cannot be construed as causal. For one thing, the instantiations of the related properties are wholly synchronous, whereas causes are standardly thought to precede their effects; second, it is difficult, perhaps even incoherent, to imagine a causal chain, with intermediate links, between the subvenient and the supervenient properties. What intermediary stages could link the beauty of a painting with its physical properties? What intermediate events could causally connect a mental event with its subvenient physical base? Would such intermediaries be themselves mental or physical, or perhaps neither?

It seems, then, that the most natural way of viewing the situation is this:

(viii) P causes $P*$, with M supervening on P and $M*$ supervening on $P*$.

This explains the observed regularities between M-instances and $M*$-instances, and M-instances and $P*$-instances.[7] These regularities are not accidental; they are law-based, and may be capable of supporting counterfactuals. However, if we understand the difference between genuine, productive causal processes on the one hand and the noncausal regularities that are observed because they are parasitic on them, we are in a position to understand the picture emerging here. In the case of supposed M-to-$M*$ causation, the situation is rather like a series of shadows cast by a moving car: there is no causal connection between the shadow of the car at one instant and its shadow an instant later—rather, each is an effect of the moving car. The moving car represents a genuine causal process, but the series of shadows it casts, no matter how regular and lawlike, does not constitute a causal process. We, therefore, seem forced to conclude:

6. I am not assuming transitivity for counterfactuals in general.

7. Note, however, that these regularities are likely to be restricted in generality. The reason is that M's alternative supervenience bases cannot be counted on to cause $P*$ and hence $M*$.

(ix) The M-to-M^* and M-to-P^* causal relations are only apparent, arising out of a genuine causal process from P to P^*

This, then, is the supervenience argument against mental causation. Its force, I believe, cannot be ignored by serious physicalists. In what follows, I'll discuss one way one might to wish to undermine it, what I call 'the generalization objection'.

II

The Generalization Objection. The return of mental causation as a philosophical problem has elicited the following sort of deflationary response from a wide group of philosophers: The supposed 'problem' is easily generalizable to all the special sciences, like chemistry, biology, and geology, and this shows that the problem is a bogus problem, something not worth worrying about. Tyler Burge writes:

> The existence of a closed system reflects a pattern of causal relations and of causal explanation that needs no supplementation from the outside.... It does not follow from this that such a system excludes or overrides causal relations or causal explanation in terms of properties from outside the system. Indeed, if it did follow, as has often been pointed out, there would be no room for causal efficacy in the special sciences, even in natural sciences like chemistry and physiology.... But few are tempted by the idea that physical events cannot be caused in virtue of physiological properties of physical events.[8]

Burge's claim is that if the causal closure of the physical domain excluded mental-to-physical causation (that is, the causal efficacy of mental properties in relation to physical properties), the same considerations would show that no special-science properties—for example, chemical, biological, and physiological properties—could be causally efficacious in the physical domain. To put it another way: just as the causal closure of the fundamental physical domain does not exclude the causal efficacy of properties in the physical special sciences, like chemistry and biology, it does not exclude the causal efficacy of mental properties.

In a similar vein, Lynne Baker writes:

8. Burge, 'Mind–Body Causation and Explanatory Practice', in *Mental Causation*, ed. John Heil and Alfred Mele (Oxford: Clarendon Press, 1993), p. 102.

Moreover, I want to show that the metaphysical assumptions with which we began inevitably lead to scepticism not only about the efficacy of contentful thought, but about macro-causation generally. But if we lack warrant for claiming that macro-properties are generally causally relevant, and if we take explanations to mention causes, then most, if not all, of the putative explanations that are routinely offered and accepted in science and everyday life are not explanatory at all.[9]

This strategy is fairly common: Defuse worries about mental causation by pointing out that mental properties are in the same boat as all other special-science properties. Robert Van Gulick puts the point this way:

... reserving causal status for strictly physical properties... would make not only intentional properties epiphenomenal, it would also make the properties of chemistry, biology, neurophysiology and every theory outside microphysics epiphenomenal... If the only sense in which intentional properties are epiphenomenal is a sense in which chemical and geological properties are also epiphenomenal, need we have any real concern about their status: they seem to be in the best of company and no one seems worried about the causal status of chemical properties.[10]

Perhaps no one is worried about the causal efficacy of chemical properties or biological properties, but then not many people are really 'worried' about mental causation either. What some of us are worried about is finding an intelligible *account* of mental causation. This is a different worry and, I believe, a philosophically legitimate one. In any case, are we sure that we have a clear understanding of the causal efficacy of geological or biological properties in relation to fundamental physical properties? Perhaps, the correct moral to be drawn is not that mental causation is not a problem for us, but rather that geological and biological causation, too, is a problem. If anyone were to retort, 'Who *needs* an account of the efficacy of geological or physiological properties?', I don't believe that that is the kind of philosophical attitude we should commend. Further, how can we be sure that an account that works, say, for chemical properties will also work for mental properties?

9. Baker, 'Metaphysics and Mental Causation', in *Mental Causation*, ed. Heil and Mele, p. 77.

10. 'Three Bad Arguments for Intentional Property Epiphenomenalism', *Erkenntnis* 36 (1992), p. 325.

What forms the background of the issues being raised here is the standard hierarchical model of the world. Things of this world, and their properties, are pictured in a vertically arranged micro-to-macro hierarchy of levels, from the elementary particles of microphysics to atoms and molecules, and their aggregates, and then upward to cells and organisms, and so on—a picture that has led to the familiar 'levels' talk, as in 'levels of description', 'levels of analysis', 'levels of explanation', and the like.

Much of our thinking about mentality and psychology has been shaped by this picture: psychology is a special science located at one of these levels, toward the upper end, in this multi-layered system, and mentality is a distinctive set of properties that make their first appearance at this level. It is natural for those who share this picture to see nothing special about mental causation: if there is a difficulty in the mental-neural case, we should expect the same difficulty to attend every level in relation to its lower levels. Since there is, or at least appears to be, no special problem at other levels, why should we think there is a problem at the mental level? The implied answer of course is no. Whence 'the generalization objection'.

As you will recall, the supervenience argument against mental causation does not require an elaborate characterization of the dependence or supervenience relation, or any special characteristic of the mental except for its supervenience. Reasoning that leads to the generalization objection is based on the belief that the mental-neural relationship is, *in all relevant respects*, the same relationship that characterizes, say, the chemical-microphysical, or biological-physiochemical, case. The supervenience argument shows that where there is supervenience there is a potential problem about the causal efficacy of the supervenient properties. This means that if, as would widely be acknowledged, chemical, biological, and other special-science properties supervene on basic physical properties, their causal status would also be threatened by the supervenient argument.

III

Properties: 'Levels' and 'Orders'. One aspect of the supervenient argument that you may find troubling is this: its general strategy seems to be one of showing that causal relations at any given level are only apparent, being reflections of 'real' causal processes at a lower level. This makes the argument iterable for each lower level, giving credence to Van Gulick's suggestion that worries about mental causation have the consequence that all causal powers seep downward and get deposited at the microphysical level, leaving microphysics as the only theory capable of generating causal explanations. Moreover, what if there is no bottom level (as Ned Block challenges us to consider[11])? If there is no absolute lowest level, causal powers would drain away into a bottomless pit and there wouldn't be any causation *anywhere*!

Fortunately, Van Gulick's and Block's worries are unfounded. What their thinking neglects is the fact that the supervenient-subvenient relation does not track the macro-micro relation. Return to our statement of mind–body supervenience: it is evident that both the supervenient mental properties and their subvenient base properties are properties *of the same entities*. A human is in pain and is in an appropriate neural state (say, his c-fibres are firing). Or consider ethical supervenience: it is the same Socrates who exemplifies both the moral property of goodness and the nonmoral properties of being truthful and courageous.

Functionalists take mental properties as 'second-order' functional properties with physical/neural properties as their 'realizers'. Let D be a set of ('first-order') properties: a *second-order property* over D is the property of having some property in D satisfying a certain specification C. Where C involves causal relations (that is, C specifies a 'causal role'), we may call the second-order property a *functional property*. Properties in D satisfying C are the *realizers* of the second-order property in question. Consider dormitivity (Block's example): the dormitivity of a sleeping pill is the second-order functional property of having some property or other that causes people to fall asleep. In Seconal pills, dormitivity is realized by the chemical secobarbital; in Valium pills the realizer is diazepam. Notice that a second-order property and its realizers are had by the same entities: it is the Seconal pill that has both dormitivity and the property of containing secobarbital. Consider pain as functionally conceived: to be in pain is to be in some state (i.e., instantiate some property) that is caused by tissue damage and that causes winces and groans. C-fibre excitation, they say, is a realizer of pain in humans. If so, it is one and the same human who

11. In personal communication.

is both in pain and in a c-fibre-excitation state. It is evident that *a supervenient property and its base properties, and a second-order property and its realizers, are at the same level on the micro-macro hierarchy; they are properties instantiated by the very same objects and systems.* That is a direct consequence of what 'supervenience' and 'second-order property' mean. The series of properties generated by the supervenient/subvenient relation, or the second-order/first-order relation, does not track the levels in the micro-macro hierarchy; it stays entirely within a single level.

We may usefully distinguish, then, between 'higher-level' and 'higher-order' when speaking of properties in an ordering, reserving the 'order' idiom for property series generated by existential quantification over the given set of properties (that is, first-order, second-order,... properties) and using the 'level' idiom for tracking the micro-macro hierarchy. This in itself is a mere terminological matter, but there is an important point to keep in mind. As we saw, the first-order, second-order,... progression does not track the micro-macro ordering: these properties apply to entities at the same micro-macro level. In contrast, spin, charm, and such are properties of basic particles, and have no application to atoms, molecules, and other objects at higher levels of the micro-macro hierarchy. Transparency, ductility, and inflammability are properties of aggregates of molecules, and have no meaning for atoms or basic particles. Consciousness and intentionality are properties of individual biological organisms, or their neural systems, and have no application to entities that are micro in relation to them. These groups of properties, then, do track the micro-macro relation.

Consider the property of having a mass of ten kilograms. It is a property of certain aggregates of molecules, like my desk and filing cabinets, and clearly no proper part of my desk has this property. However, the property is *micro-based* in the following sense: for my desk to have this property is for it to have two parts, a top and a base, such that the first has a mass of six kilograms and the second a mass of four kilograms.

I believe we can make use of David Armstrong's notion of 'structural property'[12] to explain the idea of 'micro-based property':

12. For details see Armstrong, *A Theory of Universals*, Vol. II (Cambridge: Cambridge University Press, 1978), chapter 18.

P is a *micro-based property* just in case *P* is the property of having proper parts, $a_1, a_2, \ldots, a_n$, such that $P_1(a_1), P_2(a_2), \ldots, P_n(a_n)$, and $R(a_1, \ldots, a_n)$.

Being a water molecule, therefore, is a micro-based property in this sense: it is the property of having two hydrogen atoms and one oxygen atom in a such-and-such bonding relation. Being a cube, too, is a micro-based property in our sense. A micro-based property, therefore, is constituted by micro-constituents—by the micro-parts of an object and the properties and relations characterizing these parts. But such a property is a macroproperty, not a microproperty.

These considerations suffice to show that the generalization objection does not have the full generality its advocates see in it. In particular, the worries generated by the supervenience argument are *intralevel* worries and do not generalize across micro-macro levels; hence, they do not have the dire consequences warned against by Block, Van Gulick, and others, namely that, according to the argument, all causal powers bleed downward toward the micro, either ending up at the most basic level of microphysics or vanishing altogether if there is no bottom level.

That this cannot be so should be obvious from the most mundane examples. This desk has a mass of 10 kilograms, and having this mass represents a well-defined set of causal powers. But no micro-constituent of this desk, none of its proper parts, has this property or the causal powers it represents. H_2O molecules have causal powers that no oxygen or hydrogen atoms have. A neural assembly consisting of many thousands of neurons will have causal powers that are distinct from the causal powers of its constituent neurons, or subassemblies, and human beings have causal powers that none of their individual organs have. *Macroproperties have their own causal powers that go beyond the causal powers of their micro-constituents*. This means that at higher levels in the micro-macro hierarchy we must expect to find properties with new causal powers.[13] Nothing in the supervenience argument conflicts with this fact.

This answers some, but not all, of the points raised by the generalization objection. The part that has been answered is the worry that the only causally active agents in this world might turn

13. This does not mean that these new causal powers are 'emergent' in the sense of classic emergentism.

out to be basic particles and their microphysical properties, and that the familiar objects of our daily experience, like tables and chairs, and their properties might be deprived of causal powers. But the heart of the generalization objection has not so far been addressed, and it is this: If supervenience puts psychological properties in trouble as causally effective properties, why doesn't it put all other supervenient properties, like chemical and biological properties, in the same trouble?

IV

Just How Far Does the Supervenience Argument Generalize? We will approach our problem in a somewhat roundabout way. Let us begin by considering the idea of a 'physical property'. I am not here seeking a definition or a general criterion. The question is rather this: Assuming that the properties and magnitudes that figure in basic physics are physical properties, what other properties are to be counted as members of the physical domain? When we speak of the physical, or physical properties, in discussing the mind-body problem, we standardly include chemical, biological, and neural properties among physical properties. Without invoking a general definition of 'physical', can we give some principled ground for this practice? And when we speak of the causal closure of the physical domain, just what should be included in the physical domain, and why? We assume that the entities and properties of basic physics are in this domain, but what else goes in there and why?

Some philosophers, especially those tempted by the generalization objection, often sound as though they are in the grip of an excessively, and unjustifiably, narrow conception of the physical domain. Perhaps, the standard micro-macro hierarchical model abets the idea that ultimately the physical domain only comprises the lowest microphysical level—only microphysical particles and their properties. But this is wrong. The physical domain must also include aggregates of basic particles, aggregates of these aggregates, and so on, without end; atoms, molecules, cells, tables, organisms, mountains, planets, and all the rest belong, without question, in the physical domain. What then of properties? What properties, in addition to the properties and relations of basic particles, are to be allowed into the physical domain? Obviously, mass of one kilogram should be in; although no basic particle has this property, aggregates of basic particles can have this property, and the property is clearly a physical one.

But what makes mass of one kilogram a physical property? Perhaps this is a silly question, but there is an instructive answer: Because it is a micro-based property whose constituents are physical properties and relations, for we can think of this property as the property of being made up of proper parts, a_i, each with a mass of m_i, where the m_is sum to 1 kilogram. It seems appropriate, then, to consider the physical domain to be closed under formation of micro-based properties: If P is a micro-based property of having parts $a_1,\ldots,a_n$, such that $P_1(a_1),\ldots,P_n(a_n)$, and $R(a_1,\ldots,a_n)$, then P is a physical property provided that $P_1,\ldots,P_2$ and R are physical properties and relations, and each a_i is a basic particle or an aggregate of basic particles.

On this understanding, then, being a water molecule is a physical property, and being composed of water molecules (that is, being water) is also a physical property. It is important that these micro-based properties are counted as physical, for otherwise the physical domain won't be causally closed. Having a mass of 1 kilogram has causal powers that no smaller masses have, and water molecules, or the property of being water, have causal powers not had by individual hydrogen and oxygen atoms.

Are there other properties to be allowed in? Consider second-order properties. Again, it seems entirely proper to count as physical any second-order property defined over physical properties. Thus, if D is a set of physical properties, any property defined over D by existential quantification, in the manner of 'the property of having some property P in D such that $H(P)$', where 'H' specifies a condition on members of D, is also a physical property. Something further must be said about the vocabulary in which the condition H is specified, but it seems safe to assume that causal and nomological concepts can be included.

These, then, are three closure conditions: first, any entity aggregated out of physical entities is physical; second, any property that is micro-based on entities and properties in the physical domain is also physical; third, any property defined as a second-order property over physical properties is physical. Are there other closure conditions? I am not sure. Conjunctive properties can be taken as a special case of micro-based properties (if we can waive the condition that the constituents of such properties must be nonoverlapping proper constituents): having P & Q is being composed of parts a_1 and a_2, where $a_1 = a_2$, such that a_1 is P and a_2 is Q.[14] But disjunctions and complementations are not in yet; these operations give rise to some well-known complications that need not be discussed here.

What we have seems sufficient to let in chemical properties. Dispositional properties get in either as second-order properties or micro-based properties. Transparency is the property of passing light rays without altering them, and thus counts as a second-order functional property. If transparency is identified with micro-structure, it qualifies as a micro-based property. The same can be said of such properties as water-solubility, thermal conductivity, inflammability, and the like. How about biological properties? Without going into details, I believe they behave like chemical properties: they qualify as physical in virtue of one or the other of two closure rules on physical properties. Being a cell may be a micro-based property; being a heart may be a second-order functional property (i.e. being a heart is plausibly viewed as being an organ/device with powers to pump blood[15]).

Functional properties, as second-order properties, do not bring new causal powers into the world: they do not have causal powers that go beyond the causal powers of their first-order realizers. If M has two realizers, P_1 and P_2, each M-instance is either a P_1-instance or P_2-instance, and those M-instances that are P_1-instances have the causal powers of P_1, and, similarly, the M-instances that are P_2-instances have the causal powers of P_2. There is, therefore, no special problems about the causal efficacy of functional properties. If mental properties are functional properties, there are no special problems about their causal efficacy either; they will simply inherit the causal powers of their realizers. Thus, mental properties turn out to be heterogeneous as causal properties (to the extent that their realizers are causally heterogeneous), but they are causally efficacious nonetheless. It is those mental properties that resist

14. I believe Armstrong has made this suggestion.

15. Some would want to say that for something to be a heart, it must have the 'function' of pumping blood. This will introduce some new complications.

functionalization whose causal potency is still in question. So long as we think there are nonfunctionalizable mental properties—on most accounts, qualia are the prime candidates—the problem of mental causation will continue to trouble us.

What of the causal powers of micro-based physical properties? These properties are constructed out of more basic, lower-level physical properties and relations. And if we assume that properties are primarily individuated in terms of causal powers, we must also consider their causal powers to be determined by the details of the microstructure involved. But this only means that the causal powers of the micro-based property P are *fixed*, or *determined*, by the causal powers of the properties and relations, $P_1,\ldots, P_n$, and R, that figure in P's construction, but they need not be, and are not likely to be, *identical* with the causal powers of these constituent properties and relations. There is a world of difference between *determination* and *identity*. That is how micro-based properties can bring new causal powers into the world.

We can see that the case of micro-based properties is not parallel to the case of supervenient psychological properties. In the latter case, the physical base properties, presumably certain neuro-biological properties, are at the same level as the psychological properties. This is part of what generates the problem about mental causation: the causal role of a mental property had by me is threatened with preemption by another property, a neural property, also had by me. My causal powers seem fully explicable in terms of the causal powers of my neural/biological/physical properties without adverting to my mental properties.

Difficulties of this sort do not arise for micro-based properties in relation to their constituent properties, because the former do not supervene on the latter taken individually or as a group. It is an interesting question whether or not the causal powers of a given micro-based property can be *predicted* or *explained*, on the basis of its micro-constituents and the way they are configured (for determination as such implies neither predictability nor explainability). Answers will vary depending on the particular properties involved and available scientific theories. This issue is directly tied to the doctrine of property emergence. There is much more to be said about micro-based properties, their causal powers, and the status of scientific theories about them.[16]

The upshot, then, is that we can, and do, grant novel causal powers to micro-based properties at higher levels—novel in the sense that these causal powers are not had by any lower-level properties that constitute them. And the supervenience argument does not apply to them, and their causal roles are not threatened by it. The difficulty with mental properties stems from the fact that they (or at least a subset of them) seem neither functionalizable nor construable as micro-based physical properties.

What all this means is that the supervenience argument would generalize only to those nonmental properties, if any, that, though supervenient on other properties, resist functionalization in terms of their base properties. If we think of functionalization as reduction,[17] as I would recommend, the problem of mental causation generalizes only to supervenient properties that are not reducible to their base properties. If you are a nonreductive physicalist, you take mental properties (at least a distinguished subset of them) as irreducible though supervenient, and that is why you land yourself in deep trouble with mental causation. In contrast, it is not obvious that there are such properties in other special sciences—that is, supervenient but nonfunctionalizable properties. As we saw, some special-science properties are micro-based properties, but we should keep in mind that the supervenience argument does not apply, and is not intended to apply, to these properties. We may conclude, then, that the claim that the supervenience argument renders all special-science properties epiphenomenal is far from proven, and that it is probably false.

Department of Philosophy
Brown University
Providence
Rhode Island 02912
USA

16. Some more details are to be found in my 'Explanation, Prediction, and Reduction in Emergentism', forthcoming in *Intellectica*. In particular, we need to deal with the question whether some micro-based properties supervene on other, more basic, micro-based properties, and the attendant question of their respective causal powers.

17. See my 'The Mind–Body Problem: Taking Stock After Forty Years', forthcoming in *Philosophical Perspectives*, 1997.

XV*—MEANING AND MORALITY[1]

by Susan Wolf

I

Bernard Williams' critique of impartial morality. Through a series of books and articles, Bernard Williams has launched an attack against the universalist, impartialist moralities that have dominated nineteenth and twentieth century thought. The attack is often referred to as the objection that morality is too demanding. Thus, in 'A Critique of Utilitarianism', Williams asks us to consider a man who 'is identified with his actions as flowing from projects and attitudes which in some cases he takes seriously at the deepest level, as what his life is about'. 'It is absurd to demand of such a man, when the sums come in from the utility network', he continues, '...that he should just step aside from his own project and decision and acknowledge the decision which utilitarian calculation requires'.[2] He makes the same point in 'Persons, Character and Morality', where he goes on to note that

> the Kantian, who can do rather better than (the utilitarian), still cannot do well enough. For impartial morality, if the conflict really does arise, must be required to win; and that cannot necessarily be a reasonable demand on the agent. There can come a point at which it is quite unreasonable for a man to give up, in the name of the impartial good ordering of the world of moral agents, something

1. I gratefully acknowledge the Guggenheim Foundation and the Australian National University for providing me with the opportunity to think and write about the issues in this essay. Thanks are also due to many audiences and colleagues in Australia and the U.S., and especially to Hilary Kornblith, Arthur Kuflik, Robert Nozick, Philip Pettit, Amelie Rorty, Michael Smith, and Milton Wachsberg, whose comments on an earlier draft of this essay have been immensely helpful to the development of my thought on these matters. I regret that many of their challenges and insights are not adquately addressed and reflected here, but I hope that further work will more fully incorporate what I have learned from them.

2. J. J. C. Smart and Bernard Williams, *Utilitarianism For & Against* (Cambridge: Cambridge University Press, 1983) p. 156.

*Meeting of the Aristotelian Society, held in the Senior Common Room, Birkbeck College, London, on Monday, 23rd June, 1997 at 8.15 p.m.

which is a condition of his having any interest in being around in that world at all.[3]

We may sum up by saying that according to Williams it is absurd, or at any rate, unreasonable for morality to insist that a person do X or refrain from Y even at the cost of robbing himself of what gives meaning to his life. Since, however, as Williams sees it, morality is committed to doing just that, morality, if it is to be thought of as an institution to which we are to be universally, unconditionally and proudly committed, is in serious trouble.

Since Williams' work has generated enormous interest and provoked much discussion, one cannot complain that it has not been taken seriously. But I think something important in it has generally been missed. Specifically, the responses have not attended to the specific nature of the sacrifice Williams contemplates being demanded of the agent, namely, a sacrifice of that which gives the agent his reason for living, or, more generally, his reason for caring about anything in the world at all. The responses to Williams' critique, in other words, have been generally insensitive to the difference between happiness and meaning. Attending to this difference, I think, makes Williams' arguments more compelling and the challenge he poses for traditional conceptions of morality harder to meet. In some sense, this makes his work more threatening to those of us—most of us, I presume— who want morality and people's commitment to it to be reasonable and secure. At the same time, however, attending to the difference between happiness and meaning opens up new lines of inquiry and discussion, or at any rate revives dormant ones, that have the potential to strengthen moral commitment and to add to the reasons people currently recognize themselves to have for living morally and for engaging in morally commendable projects.

II

Responses to Williams. There are at least two reasons why, at least at first glance, Williams' claims seem threatening to defenders of morality. One is the worry that if we grant Williams' charge that it is absurd for morality to demand a person to sacrifice something

3. Bernard Williams, 'Persons, character and morality', in *Moral Luck* (Cambridge: Cambridge University Press, 1981) p. 14.

of fundamental importance to himself, then morality will lose all its leverage, and even much of its content: anything would have to be permitted if it meant enough to the agent. On one fairly natural reading, Williams seems to be advocating the position that if Gauguin feels he has to abandon his family to follow his vocation, morality should step aside and let him.[4] And if that view is sound, what is morality to say about Caligula or Idi Amin or the child-molester who claims that his life would lose all meaning if he could not molest children?

Another worry is that if Williams' claim is granted, not just the practical but the theoretical heart of morality will be lost. For *a* fundamental fact, if not the fundamental fact of morality is the fact of human equality—that is, roughly, the fact that one human being is no more deserving of happiness, freedom, opportunity, than another. One person has no more right to a good life—including in that a meaningful life—than another. This being so, the idea that someone should be allowed to ignore or even worsen the situations of others whose opportunities for minimally decent lives are all but nonexistent, in order to get whatever it takes to fill her life with meaning seems to amount to an outright denial of the reasonableness of the moral point of view.

For both these reasons, if not for others, defenders of morality have resisted Williams' claims. We may classify their responses into three sorts.

First, there are those consequentialists, like Shelly Kagan and R. M. Hare, who deny the force of Williams' claims completely. They may point out that the sort of case with which Williams is concerned, in which maximizing utility requires an agent to make an ultimate sacrifice, is fairly rare. But when such cases do occur, they see no reason to back down from the view that morality requires them to make the sacrifice. It is sad when an agent has to give up so much, but, why, they respond, is it absurd? Nowhere is it written that morality would be easy.

Others, like Samuel Scheffler, though resisting Williams' conclusions, nonetheless make concessions aimed at minimizing his concerns. Thus, they acknowledge a need, as it were, to shrink back the demands of a full-fledged consequentialism to secure agents' room to express their personal points of view. Rather than

4. This refers to Williams' discussion of Gauguin in Williams, *ibid.*, Chapter 2.

require the literal maximization of utility, then, they build in agent-centred prerogatives or a more flexible and weaker requirement to make the world a better place, thus giving theoretical acknowledgement to the legitimacy of a person's special attachment to his own first-order projects and preferences.

Third are the philosophers who take Williams' critique to support rights-based or Kantian moral theories over consequentialist ones. Unlike consequentialist theories, these theories do not ask the agent to *weigh* her own projects against the projects of others. Rather they ask the agent to *limit* or *constrain* pursuit of her projects in accordance with a principle that acknowledges and respects something like the equal right of others to pursue theirs. Such theories may be said to build respect for the personal point of view into moral thought in a more central and fundamental way than consequentialism, and so seem more fully to recognize the privileged character of agents' relations to their own projects that forms the basis of Williams' critique. Though these theories are still too demanding to suit Williams, they may be thought to be a less appropriate and less vulnerable target for his attack.

Each of these responses deserves serious attention. Each has given rise to fruitful trains of thought that have thrown light on basic issues in moral theory. However, as I mentioned before, none of these responses pay particular attention to the fact that Williams' critique focuses on the way morality relates to what gives meaning to people's lives. Had Williams' complaint been that morality asks people to sacrifice too much in the way not of meaning but of self-interest or happiness or preference-satisfaction, the responses to his complaint would be essentially unchanged.

I will not speculate here on why this feature of Williams' position has been missed. It is perhaps natural enough in the context of the relevant texts to think that one can without much slippage paraphrase 'it gives his life meaning' with 'it means a lot to him'. But it is a mistake. For there are a number of salient facts about the sorts of things that can be said to give someone's life meaning that have no analogue when it comes to what makes someone happy or contributes to her well-being or satisfies her preferences.

III

Salient facts about what gives meaning to life. One such fact, which Williams emphasizes, is that what gives one's life meaning gives one a reason to live, or, more generally, a reason to take an interest in the world. A person for whom life has no meaning will, by contrast, have no such reason. This is not to say that people necessarily need a reason to live and to take an interest in the world. But some people do, and if such people have nothing that gives meaning to their lives, they will not find a reason. For such a person, it may be a matter of indifference whether she lives or dies. She may take no interest in herself. She may see no reason to get out of bed in the morning.

It would be fair to say that such a person not only finds life meaningless—she is extremely unhappy. And it may be true that most people who are happy have projects or interests or involvements that give their lives meaning. But happiness is no guarantee of meaning. More importantly, unhappiness is no guarantee of a lack of meaning, no guarantee of a lack of a reason to live or a reason to take an interest in the world. As Camus pointed out, if a thing is worth living for, it may also be worth dying for, and *a fortiori* it may be worth living with much pain and sorrow for. Having a reason to live, then, and a reason to care about the world in which one lives, is linked fundamentally not with happiness but with meaning.

A second fact about meaning, on which Williams at least implicitly relies, is that what, if anything, gives meaning to one's life is not, at least not wholly, a matter of choice or will, and it is certainly not a matter of anyone else's choice or will. One cannot simply decide to get meaning in life, or to get it specifically from this activity or that, and one cannot effectively be ordered or commanded to take meaning from some project to which one has been assigned.[5] Paradigmatic examples of what gives meaning to people's lives are vocations, to which one feels oneself called, and close relationships with people to whom one feels oneself drawn. This is not to say that will and determination do not have important

5. There may be a different, external, sense of 'the meaning of one's life' in which one's meaning consists in the playing out of a role to which one has been assigned. That one's life has meaning in this sense, however, may not be fulfilling or satisfying to oneself in the least. It may thus not give one a reason (an internal, motivating reason) to live.

roles to play. Still, it seems right that we speak of *finding* meaning in our lives, and not of choosing it.

The third, and last, fact about meaning that I want to introduce is foreign to the spirit of Williams' concerns and may well be unacceptable to him. But it is no less true for that. It has to do with the sort of thing that can give meaning to life.

As a psychological fact, there is no doubt that certain sorts of projects, relationships, involvements characteristically answer to the call of meaning; others, even though they may be popular and generally perceived as pleasant or satisfying do not comfortably fit that role. I have already mentioned, as fitting into the first category, vocations, as one might take oneself to have toward the priesthood, or to a career in teaching, or a life dedicated to music—and certain sorts of loving relationships. That there should be a sense of destiny connected to these activities, however, is far from essential to their serving the cause of meaning. For many of us, what gives meaning to our lives are things we more or less stumbled onto—philosophy, perhaps, or attachment to a particular community or political cause. Some activities and interests, however, are not well-suited to be meaning-providers. Much as I love ice cream, I cannot say that the opportunity to eat it regularly and often, even, we might imagine, without negative side-effects, gives me any reason to live whatsoever. Nor would the ongoing availability of crossword puzzles or mystery novels.

The hypothesis I wish to put forward here, with little defence but I hope lots of plausibility, is that the activities, interests, and commitments that give meaning to people's lives are those that people are disposed to see as objectively worthwhile. Meaningfulness in life, in other words, arises out of people's responding to things that are and that they see to be *worth* responding to. One's life is meaningful in proportion to the degree to which one can see oneself as bound up with things, people, activities or projects of worth in a deep and positive way.[6]

Insofar as meaningfulness in life is a subjective matter—insofar, that is, as the meaningfulness of a person's life depends on her seeing it, or being disposed to see it as meaningful—it is important to stress her *perception* of activities or the objects of the activities

6. This account of meaningfulness and its relation to happiness are discussed in my 'Happiness and Meaning: Two Aspects of the Good Life', in *Social Philosophy and Policy* 14 (1) Winter, 1997.

with which she is involved as having objective worth. But there is also an objective aspect to the question of whether a person's life is meaningful. In order for a person not just to think that she has a meaningful life, but to actually have one, the activities with which she is engaged must not just seem to her worthwhile—they must really be so. Acknowledgment of this point is necessary to explain how a person whose life till now seemed meaningful to her can come to change her mind about it and *be right*. For example, a woman who has dedicated her life to the care and comfort of a man whom she now finds has been using her, or a corporate executive who, having made her way to the top at the cost of her weekends, her personal relationships, and her health, might now see the goals she has achieved as shallow and worthless. It is also necessary in order to explain the kind of approval and respect we have both for people who live meaningful as opposed to meaningless lives, and for people who care about the meaningfulness of their lives as opposed to those who are indifferent to it.

Building this point more explicitly into my proposal about what gives meaning to lives and integrating this with the previous point about meaning not being wholly a matter of choice or will yields an account of meaning we may put in terms of a slogan—namely, that *meaning arises in a person's life when subjective attraction meets objective attractiveness*. In other words, a person finds meaning in her life insofar as she finds herself gripped or engaged by something she sees to have positive value and has the opportunity to interact with it in a positive and fruitful way.

We might bring this into more imaginative grasp if we think of the world as a value-filled place, a place, that is, with countless things, or even countless realms, of value. No one person—perhaps even no one culture or society—can honour, appreciate, or engage with them all. But, if a person is lucky, she will find herself engaged with some of them. That is, she will be struck, inspired, drawn by some value or some object of value in a way that moves her to respond—by honouring, preserving, creating, studying, loving—so as to attach or identify herself with that value, in a way that allows her to see her life at least partly in terms of her relationship to it.[7] This picture is crude and simplistic, and perhaps because of

7. This is perhaps something like David Wiggins' image of an individual's having a particular lantern-like focus on the value-rich world in his 'Truth, Invention, and The Meaning of Life', *Proceedings of the British Academy* LXII (1976).

this, dangerous. We shouldn't make too much of this picture, especially without qualifications and elaborations. But the principal thought the image is meant to convey is that meaningfulness in life, that which gives us both a reason to live and a reason to care about the world in which we live, requires a kind of evaluative attachment—a relationship in which we subjectively value things or goals or activities that are objectively worth valuing—that roots us motivationally to the world and to other reasons.

Reflections both on what gives meaning to life and on the motivational role the sense of meaningfulness plays for us are intrinsically interesting in their own right. But what, to return to the starting point of this paper, do they have to do with ethics or moral theory?

IV

Williams' critique reconsidered. Attention to the difference between what gives meaning to someone's life and what merely 'means a lot' to him in the sense of being a major determinant of his happiness or state of satisfaction will at least in one respect make Williams' attack on traditional morality seem less deeply threatening or subversive. Since meaning, unlike happiness and satisfaction, can only come from involvement with projects of value, it follows that even if we accept Williams' claim that morality cannot reasonably be expected to trump in cases where it conflicts with meaning-providing activities, this would not imply that, so to speak, anything goes. Were a child-molester to claim that his life would lose all meaning if he could not molest children, it would be in order to reply that if that were really true then his life would be meaningless anyway. Child-molesting, since it is lacking in value, is not the sort of thing that can give meaning to one's life. For that matter, it seems to me appropriate, at least as a first response to Williams' version of Gauguin, to ask why the ability to express himself as a painter requires Gauguin to leave France for Tahiti, abandoning his wife and children in the process. Though one cannot decide, much less let someone else decide to take meaning from whatever one's lot in life gives one, neither can one decide that as background to the pursuit of one's especially identified projects, nothing short of unbridled freedom or a high level of comfort will do. The thought that one's life will lose all meaning if one cannot abandon one's family and move to Tahiti ought at least to arouse suspicion—either of inauthenticity or self-indulgence or both.[8]

For related reasons, attention to the fact that Williams' worry is about the relation of morality not to happiness but to meaning qualifies and softens the worry that Williams' views are antithetical to the theoretical heart of morality. For the figure against whom Williams finds the demands of morality to be unreasonable or absurd is not that of the traditional enemy of morality, the incorrigible egoist. It is rather someone whose opportunity to pursue some objectively valuable project with which she identifies is threatened by the requirements of impartial morality. Such a person need not think that her happiness or freedom is any more important that the next person's—indeed, she need not think or care about her own happiness or freedom at all.

If the focus on meaning and its distinction from happiness and satisfaction make Williams' attack seem less subversive to morality, however, it also, makes it more difficult to deflect or defeat. When we focus on someone whose life is so devoid of meaning that she sees no reason to live, it does seem absurd to say to her that she should go out there and maximize utility, or, to remove the technical and abstract aspect of the appeal, that she should go save the rainforests or the whales, that she should pass out condoms or dole out soup. The point is not just that it would be foolish of us to expect these exhortations to be effective. It is that the thought that they ought rationally to be effective seems wholly detached from and out of touch with human psychology.

To the suggestion that she should get up and make the world a better place, the deeply depressed person might well reply, 'Why should I? Why am *I* responsible for the well-being of the world or the whales? Why can't you give the job to someone else and leave me in peace?' So far as I can tell, the moralist has nothing to say in answer.

The consequentialist, who seems especially targeted by this scenario, cannot just accept this point, taking comfort in the

8. A similar response might be made (again at least as a first response) to the second case Williams discusses in *Moral Luck, op.cit.*—viz., the case of Anna Karenina. After all, she has her son whom she professes sincerely and deeply to love. This is not to say that in either Gauguin's or Anna's case, further details will not lead us to accept the description Williams offers.

thought that it represents a very special case. The situation of the extremely depressed person reveals something about the situations of ordinary people, who have no difficulty finding reasons for living or for taking an interest in the world, as well. Reflecting on the extremely depressed makes us recognize that the questions 'Why is it my responsibility to improve the world, or to keep it from deteriorating?', 'Why should I try to make the world a better place?' can be legitimate questions, and not, as moralists tend to imagine, mere inauthentic protests of a selfish, greedy nature. Indeed, these questions may be unanswerable in the case of those who have no interest in themselves or the world. Once one has admitted this, however, one cannot but admit that a person who does care about herself or about some part of the world can also legitimately ask whether and why she should care about the world at large.

It seems to me that in most cases we have an answer to this. For example, 'You care about your own happiness (or your child's happiness), don't you? But your happiness (or your child's happiness) is objectively no more important or good than another person's happiness.' But this does not imply, as the consequentialist must think it does, that we have reason to care about the world at large above all else. It does not imply that we have reason to hold this interest above all others, as that before which all other interests must bend, including those interests without which one's interest in life and so in the world at large would vanish.

Consequentialism holds that a person morally ought to do whatever brings about the most good. That is to say that a person should have, as her dominant project, under which all other projects must be normatively subsumed, the project of making the world (the universe) as good as possible. But why should a person have this as a project? In the case of a person for whom life has no meaning, a person who takes no interest in the world (including herself) at all, there seems to be no satisfactory answer to this question. For her, there may be no reason to try to make the world better. But even for those of us who do take an interest in the world, and who do have a reason to want it be better rather than worse, it is not clear that this ought to dominate much less swallow up the less global interests that made our lives seem worth living.

These sorts of considerations seem to me to favour a Kantian approach to ethics over a consequentialist one. For if the recognition, say, of human equality (of the fact, that is, that our own welfare and the welfare of those others about whom we particularly care are no more objectively valuable or worthy of promotion than the welfare of any other human beings) does not rationally entail that we should care about all human beings equally or that we should practically commit ourselves to whatever maximizes the well-being of all human beings considered equally, it does seem to have some implications for how it is rational and reasonable to behave. The recognition of the moral arbitrariness of most of what distinguishes one person from another may augment the recognition of a common humanity, or deepen one's appreciation of it in such a way as to generate a direct, albeit unequal, concern for humans generally. Independently of that, the recognition of human equality should lead one to pursue one's own goals and interests in a way that acknowledges the legitimacy of others' efforts to pursue their goals and interests. Although the recognition of human equality does not support the total subsumption of one's personal projects and values into an impersonally weighted collection of goods to the world, then, it does seem to me to support a commitment to living in a way that coheres with an acknowledgment of something like universal human worth or dignity. It does, in other words, seem to support an at least vaguely Kantian morality, an acceptance of at least some positive duties to relieve suffering and to come to the aid of those less fortunate than oneself and of negative duties, or side-constraints, that restrict both what one may take as one's goals and how one may go about pursuing them.

It is, I think, less of an embarrassment to Kantian-style morality than it is to consequentialism that it has nothing to say to the extremely depressed—although Kant himself famously believed that pure reason did have something to say even to them.[9] It is not clear, for example, that a supporter of a Kantian morality (albeit not Kant's own morality) even wants to have something to say to a person who is extremely depressed. At least, if she is not hurting anyone else and if no one—that is, no one in particular, like a parent or a child or a friend—depends on her for his survival and well-

---

9. See, e.g., his discussions of the duty not to commit suicide.

being, it is not clear that the extremely depressed person ought morally to be doing something she is not doing. The Kantian, if she cannot cheer the person up—that is, bring her back into an interested and engaged relation to the world—may well just leave her in peace, or, more likely and more sadly, in her own private state of turmoil.

Still, I think Williams is right that familiar forms of Kantian morality, while doing better than consequentialism, do not do well enough in recognition of the fact that our commitment to morality is rationally, and not just practically, conditioned—conditioned, as I have been concerned to stress, not on an agent's retaining a measure of happiness or an opportunity to pursue it, but on her retaining a connection to something that makes her life meaningful to her, that gives her a reason to live and a reason to care about what happens in the world. As Williams notes, according to familiar conceptions of Kantian morality, if it does come down to an out-and-out conflict between the demands of morality and anything else, morality must be required to win. And that, says Williams, can be a quite unreasonable requirement on the agent.

Some have understood Williams' complaint as one aimed at getting the moralist to revise the content of morality—that is, some have thought that Williams wants morality to ask less of the agent than either Kantians or consequentialists think it does, so as unilaterally to permit an agent to do what is of fundamental importance to himself. That, however, would be a quite unreasonable requirement on morality. If a man must throw his 1000-page manuscript overboard—his life's work, we may imagine—in order to keep the lifeboat afloat—then he must, awful as it must be for him. If a woman must turn her son in to the police to prevent an innocent man from being wrongfully convicted, morality requires that she do so, regardless of the consequences of what will be left of her own life, not to mention her son's, afterwards.

One may, however, accept Williams' point that it is unreasonable to expect morality necessarily to win in the case of a conflict with a person's last grasp on meaning without thinking this calls for a revision in the content of morality. One may instead revise one's view of the rational force of morality. That is, one may acknowledge that in cases of conflict of this sort, morality may not be rationally overriding.

If we ask ourselves why people have reason to be moral in ordinary circumstances, leaving out of account the very prominent consideration that it is apt to be in their long-term self-interest, we will appeal to their sympathy and concern for humans or sentient beings in general, to their desire to make the world a better place, to their sense of fairness in light of the recognition of human equality, to an interest in justifying themselves to others, or to living in a way that affirms their membership in a community of mutually dependent and roughly equal persons. Williams' challenge, however, asks for a reason for people to be moral not only in ordinary circumstances but in circumstances in which being moral would leave them so shattered as to be perhaps without any further reason to live at all. Why should they care about justifying themselves to others more than they care about justifying themselves specifically to their children (with whom, perhaps, they see themselves in a relationship of unconditional commitment) or to their God (the obvious case is Abraham and Isaac) or to their self-imposed but publicly intelligible ideals of themselves?

Often it will be appropriate to respond to concrete challenges of this form by questioning the terms in which they are conceived. Perhaps there is an option left out of account that would allow one to be more faithful to both morality and the competing value than the ones first thought of (for example, the woman may somehow be able to bring out evidence to prove the innocence of the accused without leading the police to her son). Perhaps one should see the alternatives already conceived in a different light (for example, it may not be better for the son in the long run for the woman to shield him from the police now). If these strategies fail, the reasons why they fail may bring out reasons for weakening one's commitment to the value with which morality is in conflict. That is, one may find substantive reasons for finding morality, and one's fidelity to it, more important or more worthy than that which is in tension with it. A God who would require a father to sacrifice his son as a mere test of the father's loyalty may not merit one's allegiance. A son who would expect and want his mother to violate basic principles of justice to protect him from just prosecution by the law may not be worthy of the mother's love. More generally, a project that can only be carried out at the expense of deceiving or exploiting or injuring others may not be worth it.

Kant himself would speak in less qualified terms. According to Kant, no project whose pursuit conflicts with morality can be worth it. A person always has more reason to be moral than she has to do anything in conflict with morality. This is so for Kant because morality gets it source from pure reason itself and because our possession of the faculty of reason constitutes the deepest and most valuable part of us. A conflict between morality and some other value is for Kant a conflict between one's allegiance to rationality and one's allegiance to something else. To act immorally would be to break faith with one's rational nature—and that can never be worth it, for one's rational nature is more valuable and more essential to our identity than any other part of us.

Contemporary Kantians vary in the degree to which they follow Kant in connecting morality with rationality, and, especially, with a pure unempirical rationality. Some depart from the coldness of Kant's emphasis on reason, understanding morality to be an expression of a more fundamentally social aspect of our nature. Anyone, however, who thinks that in cases of conflict, morality is always overriding—that is, anyone who thinks that in cases of conflict it is always reasonable to expect morality to win—must believe there to be some aspect of ourselves, in virtue of which we are moral agents, that constitutes, for each and every one of us, our deepest and most valuable part.

This, I take it, Williams denies. To accept it would be to accept the view that what gives meaning to our lives, at the most fundamental level, is the same for all of us, and that it is, moreover, something that is dictated not by subjective attraction but by some independent fact. If one believes that people's lives can have or lack meaning, that people can have or lack reasons to live, that what gives meaning to one life may not give meaning to another, and that meaning is not wholly a matter of choice or of will, then it seems one must be committed to a contrary view. If one thinks that a person's having a reason to live can depend at the deepest level on her ability to express herself as an artist or to be in a suitably positive relationship with her children or to engage appropriately with some realm of value with which she feels a special affinity, then there can be no expectation about what reasonably should win in a conflict between some such ground-project and morality. A person faced with such a conflict might acknowledge that she will not be able to justify herself to others if she violates principle X. But what is it to her that she cannot justify herself to others, if the alternative is to do something that shatters her life, forces her to betray a value with which she identifies so closely that in its absence she finds no reason to live? It may be, of course, that whatever she does in such a case will shatter her life. One hopes that a serious violation of morality will also be viewed as a betrayal of something with which people closely identify themselves. But this would not make the moral choice more reasonable for her than the other choice. It would at best make it as reasonable.

V

Conclusions. If we agree with Williams that a person whose life is meaningless might lack any reason to live or to take an interest in the world, and agree also that morality itself, or the opportunity to engage in it, may not be sufficient to give meaning to life, then it seems to me that we are committed to agreeing also that morality is not unconditionally overriding. We cannot rationally expect a person to abandon all that gives her life meaning in order to, as it were, preserve the moral order—for were she to abandon what gives her a reason to live and to care about the world, she would give up as well her reason to care about the moral order. Moreover, the connections between having meaning in one's life and having reasons to care about morality would seem to have implications for what we should expect in less dire circumstances as well. The fact that meaningful activity tends to root people motivationally to their lives and to the world should make us want to give fairly wide berth to people's opportunities to find meaning and to 'indulge' in the activities or relationships from which their lives' meaning flows.

It is the subjective aspect of meaningfulness—the fact that perceiving one's life to be bound up with worthwhile activities provides one with a reason to live and to take an interest in the world—that grounds Williams' claims about the (limited) rational force of morality. To understand the import of these claims and their proper effect on our moral judgments, however, the objective aspect of meaningfulness (which Williams does not acknowledge) must be recognized as well. A concession to the legitimacy of an

individual's attachment to the activities that give her life meaning
is not a concession to egoism or selfishness, at least not as these
terms are ordinarily understood. Giving a wide berth to people's
opportunity to pursue and maintain what gives meaning to their
lives is not a matter of indulging people's potentially
disproportionate interest in securing their own happiness or in
satisfying their whims. To acknowledge and respect people's
attachment to what gives meaning to their lives is, rather, to
acknowledge people's interest in, or even need to see their lives as
bound up with something *worthwhile*, and though the sort of worth
in question may not be identical with moral worth (it is hard to
understand and evaluate, for example, the moral worth of various
intellectual and aesthetic enterprises that nonetheless seem prime
candidates for activities that have the sort of worth that can give a
life meaning), neither is it in any way conceptually opposed to it.
To the contrary, many of the most common sources of meaning in
people's lives are highly commendable from a moral point of view,
fostering, as they do, community, well-being, and virtue.

Williams' attack on impartial morality is, as I construe it, an
attack on the idea that what is often called 'the impersonal point of
view' gives us absolute and unconditional reasons. According to
Williams, our susceptibility to reasons generated by the impersonal
point of view is conditional on our having interests and reasons
that are not impersonal. In light of this, Williams argues, there can
be no guarantee that the impersonal reasons will always have the
rational authority to trump reasons given by the interests on which
the existence of impersonal reasons depend.

Since Williams' attack has been on the authority of the
impersonal point of view, interpreters have naturally taken him to
be speaking from, and defending the legitimacy of, the personal
point of view. If we take seriously the distinction between meaning
and happiness, however, and understand meaning as I have urged
above, then it is highly misleading to think in these terms. For the
reasons that are generated from the activities and interests that give
meaning to our lives do not stem from the view that pursuing these
activities will be best for us or from the view that they will
maximally satisfy our preferences any more than they come from
a belief that pursuing them will be best for the world. We would
not engage in these activities if we did not think them good

independently of us. Yet we engage in them not out of duty but out of a more personal attachment or love.

Recognizing the legitimacy of these reasons and their potential to compete with the claims of a more impartial morality presents difficulties for the enterprise of building a systematic theory or providing a unified structure in which all our legitimate reasons for action will fit. It is hard to know how to weigh these reasons against reasons that are generated from an impersonal point of view. Because of this, one might see these remarks as morally subversive, as posing a threat or at least a challenge to traditional conceptions of morality's authority. In practice, however, recognizing the legitimacy of people's interests in pursuing projects that give meaning to their lives is not likely to undermine or weaken our commitment to morality. To the contrary, its typical effect is more apt to be a strengthening of our commitments to and respect for specific projects, interests, and values that morality would wholeheartedly approve of and commend. Still, to recognize the legitimacy of these interests, weighted neither according to their role in contributing to personal happiness nor according to their role in contributing to the totality of happiness or preference-satisfaction in the world, is to recognize a form of nonmoral reason, a form of reason arising from the love or appreciation or respect for—more generally from the subjective attraction to—what we believe to be at least somewhat objectively good or worthwhile.

Department of Philosophy
Johns Hopkins University
347 Gilman Hall
3400 N. Charles Street
Baltimore
MD 21218-2690
USA

DISCUSSION

HABERMAS'S MORAL COGNITIVISM

by Gary Kitchen

Jurgen Habermas's recent paper[1] represents a timely contribution to the debate concerning the topic of truth in ethics.[2] Habermas certainly believes that truth in ethics is possible, but naturally seeks to avoid the pitfalls of a realist construal of moral judgements as referring to 'objective values'—improbable constituents of the universe disparaged by sceptics such as Mackie on the grounds of their ontological 'queerness'.[3] I will not dwell on the many virtues of Habermas's splendid body of work, but try to sketch out some difficulties his moral philosophy may encounter.

Habermas drops the requirement that moral judgements *are* truth claims and proceeds on the weaker assumption that they are *analogous* to truth-claims,[4] referring to the normative order that ought to govern society rather than the objective order of nature. The analogy is spelled out in an earlier paper:

> The noncognitivist position relies primarily on two arguments: first, the fact that disputes about basic moral principles ordinarily do not issue in agreement, and second, the failure...of all attempts to explain what it might mean for normative propositions to be true....The first argument loses its force if we can name a principle

1. Jurgen Habermas, 'On the cognitive content of morality', *Proceedings of the Aristotelian Society*, Volume XCVI, 1996, pp. 335–358. An elaborate statement of his position in moral philosophy, in which he presents a detailed attempt to combat scepticism about moral knowledge, is given in 'Discourse ethics—notes on a program of philosophical justification', *Moral Consciousness and Communicative Action*, MIT Press, 1990, pp. 43–115. Also useful are 'Remarks on discourse ethics' and the interview 'Morality, society and ethics', both in *Justification and Application*, Polity Press, 1993, pp. 19–111, pp. 147–176.

2. For a collection of recent papers on the same topic, see Brad Hooker, ed., *Truth in Ethics*, Blackwell, 1996. Habermas's perspective differs greatly from that of the contributors to this volume—which might help to explain why his work is not mentioned there—in that his moral philosophy is advanced together with a social theory which tries to conceptualise modernity as a whole. Though his own moral philosophy is Kantian, Habermas has a great deal in common with thinkers such as Alasdair MacIntyre and Charles Taylor who, inspired by Aristotle, link the problems of modernity with that of truth in ethics (MacIntyre, *After Virtue*, 2nd ed., Duckworth, 1985; Taylor, *The Ethics of Authenticity*, Harvard University Press, 1992, and *Sources of the Self*, Cambridge University Press, 1989, particularly Part I). To put it at its most simplistic, all three thinkers are responding to what Max Weber called the 'disenchantment' of modernity. I cannot go into these matters here.

3. J.L.Mackie, *Ethics: Inventing Right and Wrong*, Penguin, 1977, Chapter 1.

4. 'On the cognitive content of morality', p. 351.

that makes agreement in moral argumentation possible in principle. The second argument fails if we give up the premise that normative sentences, to the extent to which they are connected with validity claims at all, can be valid or invalid only in the sense of propositional truth.[5]

Habermas argues that a bridging principle analogous to the principle of induction is required in moral discourse. The basic bridging principle, 'U', which makes consensus possible, is this:

> a norm is valid when the foreseeable consequences and side effects of its general observance for the interests and value-orientations of *each individual* could be freely accepted *jointly* by *all* concerned.[6]

As an idealized expression of a fundamental democratic intuition, this 'principle of universalization' seems admirable. But Habermas contends that the norms that eventuate from it might be thought to constitute something analogous to moral truth. Hence consideration of 'U' in this context must focus on its status as a crucial ingredient in his moral cognitivism.

There are on the face of it several grounds why Habermas's cognitivism might fail. I will state these grounds in a rather stark way before going on to elaborate them a little. (I) As a matter of fact, 'U' might not lead to agreement on any norms; (II) 'U' might not lead to agreement on any norms in principle; (III) any convergence brought about by 'U' would be unstable and ephemeral; (IV) 'U' might not be justified. I will look at these points in order.

I

Habermas tells us that the goal of his moral philosophy is to try to reconceptualize Kant's ethics in such a way that the monological testing of norms according to the categorical imperative is replaced by some real process of cooperative effort at consensus. What guarantee is there that any norms will eventuate from such a procedure? A stringent interpretation of 'U' might lead us to believe that Habermas is suggesting that everyone's opinion on a hypothetical norm needs to be canvassed and joint agreement sought. One might object that a) the arrangements for such a procedure would be unworkable since it looks as if it would be necessary to canvass everyone's opinion and b) the scale of agreement required is unrealistic since one person's dissent would serve to invalidate the norm in question. It may be that if these consequences follow from a

5. 'Discourse ethics', p. 56.

6. 'On the cognitive content of morality', p. 354. A slightly different version is given in 'Discourse ethics', p. 65.

stringent interpretation of 'U' this may not be quite what Habermas has in mind. But there seems little doubt that c) in practice, the procedure may reveal conflict rather than consensus and it is possible that we will discover as a matter of fact that no norms can be thought acceptable to everyone. Is consensus at all feasible, except on the most insignificant scale? Habermas might respond that disagreement on the validity of a norm may indeed occur, and then the question will be temporarily left open 'on the assumption that only one side can be right'.[7] But if 'U' does not render agreement plausible, there is no reason to suppose that it can defeat non-cognitivism; rather than generating conviction, the procedure might reveal the extent of disagreement and undermine belief in the rational resolution of moral issues. If these plausible objections are correct then no agreement on valid moral norms—no 'moral knowledge', analogous to truth claims—might be expected to eventuate from the procedure.

II

It is unlikely in principle that there will be any agreement on norms via the procedure. This is because there are conflicting and incommensurable notions of justice in currency and it is hence unlikely that any such norm(s) can be thought to be acceptable to all. A very powerful statement of the basic incommensurability of fundamental conceptions of justice is given by Alasdair MacIntyre. MacIntyre discusses the theories of Rawls and Nozick and points out that Rawls' position gives priority to equality in respect of needs whereas Nozick's gives priority to entitlements. Both theories neglect an aspect of justice which MacIntyre himself considers to be important, that which centres on the notion of desert. How can a conflict between such competing principles be rationally resolved? These incompatible conceptions of justice exist side by side in the modern world, and it follows (so MacIntyre believes) that 'our society cannot hope to achieve moral consensus'—a fact which he deplores.[8] Habermas certainly accepts the existence of differing principles of justice:

> There are material principles of justice, such as 'To each according to his needs' or 'To each according to his merits' or 'Equal shares for all'. Principles of equal rights, such as the precepts of equal respect for all, of equal treatment, or of equity in the application of the law, address a different kind of problem. What is at issue here is not the distribution of goods or opportunities but the protection of freedom and inviolability. Now all of these principles of justice

7. 'Morality, society, and ethics', p. 158.

8. Alasdair MacIntyre, 'Justice after virtue: changing conceptions', *After Virtue*, 2nd ed., Duckworth, 1985, p. 252.

can be justified from the perspective of universalizability and can claim prima facie validity. But only in their application to particular concrete cases will it transpire *which* of the competing principles is the most appropriate in the *given* context.[9]

It seems to me that the move to see conflicting principles as involving problems of appropriate application rather than justification may be too hasty. It obscures the fact of moral conflict, which it is the purpose of 'U' to address. The following points are relevant: a) the principles of justice cited above have not been reached through a procedure like that prescribed by 'U', and hence it is unclear why they can claim even prima facie validity; b) many of the principles cited—e.g. those concerning distributive justice—are inconsistent with one another, which suggests some cognitive shortcoming if we accept that moral principles are analogous to truth claims; c) Habermas's definition of 'U' does not include any reference to prima facie validity, or explain how it relates to actual validity. If we acknowledge that actual validity may be strictly unattainable we will require some account of prima facie validity. Inevitably, it seems to me, inconsistency amongst norms that pass some prima facie test is likely to undermine belief in their cognitive status and call into question the ideal of consensus that underlies 'U'.

The upshot of (I) and (II) is that 'U' makes valid moral norms appear possible, but gives us no reason to think they can be actual. The abstract possibility of such norms is not sufficient to demonstrate moral cognitivism, just as the principle of induction alone—conceived in isolation from anything that anybody might take to be scientific knowledge—would not justify the belief that scientific knowledge might be actual.[10]

III

It is plausible to think that agreement on scientific knowledge might be guided by how things are independently of us. There is the presumption that an increase in explanatory power will accompany theory-change, with perhaps a gradual convergence on a better explanation of the phenomena in question. Bernard Williams has argued that there is 'no coherent hope' of such convergence in ethics.[11] It seems initially a great merit of Habermas's approach that he is able to give some clear intuitive sense to the idea of moral convergence: he thinks that the procedure designated by 'U' will reveal generalizable interests and that convergence

9. 'Morality, society and ethics', p. 152.

10. I put to one side the difficulties involved in the inductivist conception of science.

11. Compare Williams' discussion of science, ethics and convergence in *Ethics and The Limits of Philosophy*, Fontana, 1985, Chapter 8.

will be guided by clearer approximation to these. But it is important to see that, in Habermas's scheme, agreement on norms seems to be the key criterion of what might constitute generalizable interest; we do not come to agree on norms *because* they represent generalizable interests but rather come to see interests as generalizable because we can agree on norms that advance them. But agreement reached through any real procedure is likely to be inherently unstable if it is reached at all. The concept of truth suggests at the very least a kind of stability, and if moral principles cannot attain this then it is inappropriate to label this position cognitivist.

IV

'U' itself may not be justified. To advance his justification of 'U', Habermas draws on the device of what he has earlier called a 'performative contradiction'.[12] His strategy, following that of Karl-Otto Apel, is to try to show that the moral sceptic commits himself or herself to certain universal and necessary principles in the very process of argumentation and that these principles are incompatible with scepticism about moral knowledge. Specifically, he seeks to show that every possible argument relies on presuppositions from which 'U' can be derived:

> Every person who accepts the universal and necessary communicative presuppositions of argumentative speech and who knows what it means to justify a norm of action implicitly presupposes as valid the principle of universalization....[13]

If this is the case, then clearly the denial of 'U' will be self-contradictory.

Yet it is difficult to avoid the suspicion that there is something unsatisfactory about this idea. One reason for the suspicion, perhaps, is that this way of showing that moral judgements have cognitive status seems simply too good to be true. If moral cognitivism appears to follow from the rational presuppositions of argument, it is tempting to think that there may be something wrong with our conception of these presuppositions—presuppositions which entail that which is surely a crucial part of what needs to be established (i.e. whether there is or can be moral knowledge). It seems counter-intuitive to suppose that rational argument *about* the possibility of moral knowledge might be precluded if we only come to understand the necessary conditions of any such argumentation occurring. Moreover, by refusing to leave the non-cognitivist any defensible territory, Habermas seems to fail to acknowledge that there is a real debate here.

12. 'On the cognitive content of morality', p. 356. The phrase occurs in his essay on 'Discourse ethics'.
13. 'Discourse ethics', p. 86.

The idea of a performative contradiction is surely at the heart of Habermas's justification of morality, and we hence need to pay attention to it. According to Habermas, participants in rational argumentation cannot avoid the presupposition that

> the structure of their communication rules out all external or internal coercion other than the force of the better argument and thereby also neutralizes all motives other than that of the cooperative search for truth.[14]

He adduces some plausible considerations in support of this idea. It would be nonsensical to claim that we could legitimately convince someone of a particular proposition by utilising lies, for example, if the implicit goal of the endeavour was the search for truth. Argumentative discourse has to rely on the presupposition that speakers assert only what they really believe to be true. The claim being made by Habermas is not that empirical discourses do in fact always abide by these rules, but that they ought to be followed if 'error-free argumentation is to take place in real life'.[15] He acknowledges that 'real human beings [are] driven by other motives in addition to the one permitted motive of the search for truth'.[16]

From what has been said, it would not follow from the presuppositions of rational argument that some moral norms might claim validity. As Habermas acknowledges, the claim that moral judgements are true or false in just the same way as descriptive statements is problematic, and he avoids it by introducing 'U'. So 'U' certainly does not yet follow from the presupposition of a cooperative search for truth. But of course Habermas also believes that contested norms of action can be rationally justified via the procedure designated by 'U'. He suggests that performative contradictions can be demonstrated in the following statement:

> Having excluded persons A, B, C,...from the discussion by silencing them or foisting our interpretation on them, we were able to convince ourselves that [norm] N is justified'.[17]

There is undoubtedly something powerfully disconcerting about this statement. It seems unfair that persons affected by a norm's being put into effect should have no say in its formulation. The feeling is that only a norm which everyone has had an opportunity to comment on can claim to be legitimate. Habermas argues that the statement contradicts presuppositions of argumentation which prescribe that all competent subjects should be allowed to take part in a discourse and should not be prevented from

14. 'Discourse ethics', p. 88–9.
15. 'Discourse ethics', p. 91.
16. 'Discourse ethics', p. 92.
17. 'Discourse ethics', p. 91.

exercising their rights in the matter by any kind of coercion. He believes that these rules amount to an implicit acknowledgement of 'U':

> It follows from the aforementioned rules of discourse that a contested norm cannot meet with the consent of the participants in a practical discourse unless (U) holds...[18]

But the feeling of discomfort could be alleviated, I think, by simply including A, B, C...in the discussion, and this would by no means carry the intuition that one had to adopt 'U'. The discomfort may perhaps be due to the fact that this scenario contradicts our intuitions concerning democratic legitimacy (rather than moral validity); but legitimacy of this kind does not require consensus on contested norms and would be legislatively unworkable if it did. That is, we would not think that a decision lacked democratic legitimacy simply because some voted against it.

Habermas's emphasis on the derivation of 'U' somewhat diverts attention from a further highly problematic aspect of his moral philosophy, which is his belief that there is some fact of the matter about 'what it means to justify a norm of action'. At this point, we need to introduce a further principle. Habermas presents his work in moral philosophy as an attempt to replace Kant's categorical imperative with a discourse principle, 'D':

> only those norms can claim validity that could meet with the agreement of all concerned in their capacity as participants in a practical discourse.[19]

It now seems clear that the derivation of 'U' relies on 'D' as a premise:

> the discourse ethical idea of justification suggests that the basic principle 'U' can be derived from the implicit content of universal presuppositions of argumentation in conjunction with the conception of normative justification in general, as it is expressed in 'D'.[20]

Even if we grant that Habermas is correct in his delineation of the content of these presuppositions, it looks as if the plausibility of 'U' can be no greater than that of 'D'. Whatever the precise relationship, Habermas does not advance any formal justification of 'D' in this essay.

A better understanding of 'D' would require some account of Habermas's highly elaborate theory of communicative reason, whose detailed discussion would be outside the scope of my own brief and

---

18. 'Discourse ethics', p. 93.
19. 'On the cognitive content of morality', p. 347.
20. 'On the cognitive content of morality', p. 355.

tentative attempt to canvass some difficulties for his moral cognitivism. It seems plausible on the face of it to think that 'D', like 'U', will be subject to the same problems I have listed in points (I) to (III) above. One further line of attack on his cognitivism might turn on criticism of his account of what it means to justify a norm of action. Does 'D' really capture this? Is the connection Habermas makes between justification and consensual agreement at all plausible? For Habermas, communicative reason aims at understanding. But in his definition of what understanding involves—aided by the German language—Habermas already seems to freight it with what looks very much like an ethical purpose:

> The goal of coming to an understanding [*Verständigung*] is to bring about an agreement [*Einverstandnis*] that terminates in the intersubjective mutuality of reciprocal understanding, shared knowledge, mutual trust, and accord with one another.[21]

The claim that understanding requires agreement seems somewhat question-begging—in ethics, for example, people may understand one another's position perfectly well whilst strenuously disagreeing with one another. It may be that 'D' expresses this understanding of 'understanding' and offers a reforming rather than merely reportive definition of practical validity, which amounts to a recommendation to adopt the principle it prescribes and will undoubtedly require independent justification.[22, 23]

Department of Philosophy
University of Essex
Wivenhoe Park
Colchester

21. Jurgen Habermas, 'What is universal pragmatics?', in *Communication and the Evolution of Society*, Beacon Press, 1979, p. 3.

22. Cp. William Frankena's discussion of 'definist' accounts of morality in Chapter 6 of his *Ethics*, Prentice Hall, 1963, p. 84.

23. I would like to thank Andrew Chitty for his very helpful comments on an earlier draft.

SELF-RESPECT AND THE STEPFORD WIVES

by Catriona McKinnon

I

Self-respect, like dignity and integrity, plays a key role in the way we shape our lives yet it remains an underanalysed concept. Questions like, 'Could I live with myself if I did x?' or fears like the fear of failure address at some level the effect that x or failure may have on our self-respect. We all have levels to which we think we will not sink, and although these lower limits are not always determined by considerations concerning our self-respect, such considerations will often play a crucial role in defining what we will strive not to be or try to become. Self-respect is something that we are loath to give up even in the harshest of circumstances and quick to pursue even at the cost of great toil.

Self-respect has at least two components. The first component is connected with a person's conception of herself as having moral value, regardless of her reasons for viewing herself in this way. Sticks and stones cannot possess this general component of self-respect but Kantians, Utilitarians, Christians and Buddhists can all equally well achieve it. This aspect of self-respect is essentially a state of mind. But self-respect must be connected with more than what one believes; it must also be dependent upon what one does. Thus, the second component of self-respect is connected with a person's success at achieving or striving to achieve goals which she finds valuable. The measure of this success will depend upon the person's particular talents and abilities, such that success for the individual in activity x may not coincide with social conceptions of successful x-ing. For example, a tone deaf person might respect herself in virtue of being able to hold a tune, but she would not ipso facto be a great singer.

This outline of self-respect occurs at what could be called the meta-level. It gives a general and abstract description of the structural features of self-respect but remains silent on the question of how potential self-respecters should conceive of themselves as morally valuable, for example, or what kind of activity counts as striving to achieve a valued goal. Each self-respecter will evince these aspects of self-respect in a way that depends on their central values. In addressing my puzzle about self-respect—for reasons which will become clear—I will take it as a virtue of any proposed answer that it remains at this meta-level without making reference to any very specific values which need not be shared by all self-respecters.

The puzzle I want to focus on can be illustrated by considering the following cases. First, take Eric Cantona, the Manchester United striker. Let us assume that Eric conceives of himself as morally valuable, performs well according to his personal standards for all those activities he values, and has no hidden failures or secret despair. Given this it is clear that, love or loathe him, Eric has self-respect.

Second, consider the Stepford Wives. Ignoring the fact that the Stepford Wives in the film were automata, let us stipulate that these are women who perform well at all the activities forming the core of their conception of the good; they are maestros at washing up, masters of cake baking and geniuses at keeping their husbands fed, clothed and sexually satisfied. As one of the Stepford husbands in the film says of his Wife, 'She cooks as good as she looks'. Let us also assume that they conceive of themselves as morally valuable.

Given this it should follow that Eric and the Stepford Wives respect themselves to more or less the same degree. They all conceive of themselves as morally valuable and are all extremely successful in pursuing their personal goals; Eric is one of the best Premier League players, and no-one touches the Stepford Wives when it comes to housekeeping. But do we really want to make this unqualified claim? I would be reluctant to, for although the Stepford Wives may have some self-respect my intuitions are that they do not have as much as Eric. The puzzle I will examine is why we are reluctant to treat the Stepford Wives as exemplary self-respecters when, prima facie, they have many of the attributes and achievements which we normally take to be indicative of self-respect. There must be something about the Stepford Wives that Eric lacks which explains this unease. In trying to pinpoint the difference between them I hope to shed some general light on the complex concept of self-respect.

II

At first sight there are three ways to explain the difference between Eric and the Stepford Wives. First, one could focus on what they do. Second, one could concentrate on the extent to which they exercise certain capacities. And third, one could address the nature of their preferences. Although none of these approaches is acceptable, I will briefly address each of them so as to give a sense of how thorny the problem of the Stepford Wives is.

The most obvious way to explain the difference between Eric and the Stepford Wives is simply to claim that footballing is intrinsically and objectively more worthy of respect than housekeeping, and thus Eric respects himself more than the Stepford Wives because what he does gives him more objective reason to respect himself than what they do. This is an undesirable approach to the problem; self-respect does not necessarily depend upon the value that others place on your personal achievements, and thus the fact that we ourselves may think that housekeeping is inferior to footballing does not explain why we think that a group of housekeepers respect themselves less than a footballer. I believe it better to devote your life to music than to God, but I would not automatically conclude that all successful pianists respect themselves more than a community of chaste Carmelites.

The second approach is to claim that autonomy is a necessary condition for self-respect and Eric has, while the Stepford Wives lack, a high level of autonomy. So the difference between them is the degree to which they exercise their capacity for autonomy.

The main problem with this approach is that positing autonomy as a necessary condition for self-respect, regardless of whether the person in question values autonomy or not, is excessively chauvinistic in so far as it represents only one conception of self-respect that is dependent upon one specific set of values, that is, the values associated with autonomy.[1] One of the pre-analytical hallmarks of self-respect is that all sorts of people with diverse characters, capacities and values can equally well respect themselves. Positing autonomy as necessary for self-respect makes it the prerogative of those who value autonomy, but any plausible analysis of self-respect must reflect the diversity it encompasses. If self-respect is understood as dependent upon the exercise of capacities which are not held constant in value across many different perspectives then the analysis will be of one conception of self-respect only, rather than of the meta-characteristics which shed real light on this concept.

The third approach is to claim that a person cannot have self-respect unless the preferences she acts upon in pursuing valued goals are authentic.[2] Thus, authentic preference formation is a necessary condition for self-respect. One prominent account of authentic preferences defines them as objectively contributing to the development of a person as a flourishing human being according to an Aristotelian conception, but one could equally well adopt other conceptions of human flourishing to elucidate authenticity. One could argue, then, that Eric's preferences for

---

1. For example, independence, self-control and courage. Those conceptions of autonomy which are not associated with specific values like these lie outside the scope of the criticism.

2. Cf. Jean Hampton, 'Selflessness And The Loss Of Self' in *Altruism* eds. Paul, Miller and Paul (Cambridge: Cambridge University Press, 1993).

football contribute to his flourishing as an individual whereas the Stepford Wives' preferences for catering for their husbands to the exclusion of all else do not and thus Eric has, and the Stepford Wives lack, self-respect.

The authenticity based approach shares the basic flaw of the other two approaches; it requires that one describe a necessary condition for self-respect in terms of one very specific—in this case Aristotelian—set of values. Any analysis of self-respect which proceeds like this cannot reflect the way in which self-respect transcends value differences.

It might seem here that the attempt to address the puzzle of the Stepford Wives at the meta-level without invoking specific values is futile. In what follows I hope to give a satisfactory answer to the puzzle which shows that this is not the case. This answer will further illustrate how self-respect depends more on how one behaves rather than what one values, and illuminate the general structure of the life of a self-respecting person.

III

So exactly what is wrong with the Stepford Wives? What is it that they have or do which would explain our reluctance to point them out to children as self-respecting role models?

A clue to explaining this reluctance can be found by examining why the Stepford Wives so assiduously perform their household tasks. Their desire to please their husbands is generated—at least initially—by a fear of the censure or criticisms which they will receive if they fail to keep house well. When the primary motivation for an action is fear of this sort, the fear that one will be in some way punished if one fails to meet standards set for one by others then, I submit, that action cannot serve as a basis for self-respect.

This does not imply that the self-respecting person will not fear failure or attempt to avoid criticism per se. As already noted, one of the things we fear most is the loss of self-respect, the failure to succeed by our own lights. But fearing self-criticism is distinct from fearing the criticisms of others, even though these two worries are often intimately connected. People sometimes internalise the criticisms of others and develop a self-attitude which blinds them to their personal successes. One difference between Eric and the Stepford Wives can be found in the explanations we give of their respective fears of failure. Eric's self-criticisms are dependent upon his failure according to what he counts as success, whereas the Stepford Wives' self-criticisms are dependent on a desire to please their spouses, originally inculcated in them by a fear of incurring the censure of their husbands in virtue of what they count as success for their Wives.

We are now more easily able to pinpoint what is worrying about the Stepford Wives and their self-respect. The reason why they fear their husbands' censure is their perception of them as their moral superiors, as worth more than they are, and they desire to promote their husbands' interests in virtue of this belief. A person who acts in this way is subservient, and it is the probable subservience of the Stepford Wives that distinguishes their case from that of Eric and explains our unease over their claims to self-respect. In general we could claim that when a person promotes the interests of another primarily because they believe themselves to be morally inferior to that other then they are subservient, and subservience is incompatible with self-respect, however one gains it.[3] [4]

The claim that subservient activity cannot ground self-respect is harmonious with three general, meta-features of self-respect implied by the outline given earlier. First, a person's self-respect is intimately connected with how they behave over and above what they believe, and subservience also manifests itself in behaviour. Subservient behaviour, then, cannot ground self-respect. Second, self-respect is not an all-or-nothing affair, but rather a matter of degree. One can conceive of oneself as more or less morally valuable and be more or less successful at striving to achieve personal goals. Subservience is similarly a matter of degree; more or less of one's actions can be more or less subservient. Third, self-respect is rarely totally absent; a person who conceives of themselves as utterly valueless and has never striven to achieve any personal goals is hard to picture. One explanation of why this is difficult is now available: that it is extremely hard to be totally subservient; to succeed in this all of a person's other-directed actions would have to be premised on a conviction of their moral inferiority. These three claims about self-respect are all intuitively appealing, and it is a virtue of the account of the relationship between subservience and self-respect sketched above that it reflects them.

This strategy avoids the problems associated with the three approaches outlined earlier by importing only a minimum of values into the explanation. In pinpointing the source of our worries about the Stepford Wives in their probable subservience I have avoided addressing the question of the worthiness of housekeeping per se or the Wives' failure

3. For a similar account of this relationship see Chapter 1 of *Autonomy And Self-Respect* (Cambridge: Cambridge University Press, 1991) by T. E. Hill Jnr. Hill's account differs from mine in that he defines servility in terms of a failure to appreciate the importance of, or perhaps even to acknowledge the existence of, one's rights.

4. It is compatible with the Stepford Wives' subservience that they are also motivated to promote their husbands' interests out of love or affection. Nonetheless, they remain subservient if their primary motivation is their perception of themselves as morally inferior to their husbands.

to live up to various ideals of the good life. To avoid subservience one must view the other who benefits from one's actions as no more valuable than oneself, and this belief is compatible with any number of perspectives. Eric avoids the self-disrespect of the Stepford Wives partly by avoiding subservient behaviour, but if his footballing successes were primarily motivated by a desire to please his dominant wife then this would not be the case. Alternatively, if the Stepford Wives excel at housekeeping but are indifferent to their husbands' commands then—at least in keeping house—they avoid subservience. Subservience has been defined in such a way that many different kinds of lives based around diverse sets of values can evince a subservient structure. This account of the structure of subservience mirrors the account of the structure of self-respect in so far as subservience is not exclusively linked to any one type of life or person. In this way my answer to the puzzle of the Stepford Wives ensures that self-respect retains its character as an attitude not dependent upon the specifics of what a person holds valuable, but rather dependent upon the way in which a person structures their life so as conform to these values.[5]

Department of Philosophy,
University College London,
London WC1E 6BT.

5. I would like to thank Véronique Munoz-Dardé, Neil Storer and Jo Wolff for many helpful discussions on earlier versions of this paper.

LIST OF MEMBERS

Please notify the Executive Secretary, University of London, Senate House, Malet Street, London WC1E 7HU, of any errors and omissions.

ABDELHAY, Mr Sofyan A., Hail Region Electricity, P.O. Box 68, Hail, Saudi Arabia [1997]

ABERDEIN, Mr Andrew, 1 Crescent Avenue, Formby, Liverpool L37 2ES [1994]

ABIMBOLA, Mr K.O., Dept of Philosophy, LSE, Houghton Street, London WC2A 2AE [1990]

ACKARY, Mr Mark, 37 Muswell Hill Place, London N10 3RP [1992]

ACTON, Mrs B., 5 Abbotsford Park, Edinburgh 10 [?]

ADAMS, Fred, Dept of Philosophy, Central Michigan University, Mt. Pleasant, MI 48859, USA [1996]

ADDIS, Mr Mark R., Dept of Philosophy, University of Leeds, Leeds LS2 9JT [1992]

ALEXANDER, Professor P., 10 West End Grove, Farnham, Surrey GU9 7EG [1945]

ALEXANDRU, Mr Stefan, Wesendonckstr. 5, D-53115 Bonn, Germany [1995]

ALI, Ms Samal, 268 Rhodeswell Road, London E14 7UE [1995]

ALI, Mr Shahrar, Senior Member, Commonwealth Hall, Cartwright Gardens, London WC1H 9EB [1993]

ALLEN, Mr C., 33 Bartle Avenue, East Ham, London E6 3AJ [1984]

ALLEN, Professor H. J., Dept of Philosophy, Adelphi University, Garden City, NY 11530, USA [1966]

ALLPORT, Dr P. P., Dept of Physics, University of Liverpool, Oxford Street, Liverpool L69 3BX [1995]

ALMOND, Professor B.M., Dept of Philosophy, The University, Hull HU6 7RX [1961]

ALTHAM, Dr J. E. J., Gonville & Caius College, Cambridge CB2 1TA [1972]

ALTRICHTER, Professor F., Dept of Philosophy, University of North Carolina, Wilmington, NC 28406, USA [1986]

ALVAREZ, Ms Maria, 29 Pembridge Square, London W2 4DS [1988]

AMINI, Mr Majid, 15 Glen Albyn Road, London SW19 6HB [1984]

ANSCOMBE, Professor G. E. M., 3 Richmond Road, Cambridge CB4 3PP [1956]

ANTONIOL, Ms Lucie, High Beleg, Duninoby, St Andrews KY16 8LZ [1995]

ANTONIOL, Mrs Lucie, 6 Castle Court, Stirling FK8 1EL [1995]

APATA, Gabriel, 125 Ebdon Way, Kidbrooke, London SE3 9PJ [1996]

APPIAH, Professor A., 106 Pembroke Street, Boston, MA 02118, USA [1983]

ARCHARD, Dr David, Dept of Moral Philosophy, St. Andrews University, St Andrews, Fife KY16 9AL [1995]

ARENAS, Sherry Austin, 805 Leavenworth Street #103, San Francisco, CA 94109, USA [1994]

ARIKHA, Ms Noga A., Windmill Hill House, Windmill Hill, London NW3 6SJ [1993]

ARMOUR, Professor Leslie, 473 Besserer Street, Ottawa, Ontario, Canada K1N 6C2 [1994]

ARMSTRONG, Mr John, 4130 E. Hayne St., Tucson, AZ 85711, USA [1994]

ARNEY, Mr D. J., 4 Seaview Terrace, Cottesloe, WA 6011, Australia [1994]

ARNOLD, Dr Denis, 1120 Cliff Avenue #402, Tacoma, WA 98402 USA [1995]

ARREGUI, Dr Jorge V., Linaje 4, 8° A, Málaja, Spain [1988]

ASHBY, Dr Ron, 14 Knoll Court, Farquhar Road, London SE19 [1985]

ASHCROFT, Dr R. E., Dept of Philosophy, University of Liverpool, 7 Abercromby Square, Liverpool L69 3BX [1991]

ASQUITH, Mr Nathan, 1 Quality Street, High Shincliff, Durham DH1 2PP [1995]

ATHANASOPOULOS, Dr Constantinos, 6 Hiolkou Street, Kamatero, Athens 13451, Greece [1992]

ATKINS, Mr Robert, 119 Glenville Grove, London SE8 4BJ [1996]

ATKINSON, Mr Anthony, Dept of Experimental Psychology, South Parks Road, Oxford OX1 3UD [1995]

ATKINSON, Professor R. F., 211A Exwick Road, Exeter EX4 2AU [1957]

AUGER, Mr M., Flat 1, 27 Denmark Avenue, Wimbledon, London SW19 4HQ [1984]

AUSTEN, Andrea, 102–12 Passy Crescent, North York, Ontario, M3J 3L2, Canada [1994]

BACKHOUSE, Mr J., Royal Russell School, Coombe Lane, Croydon, Surrey CR9 5BX [1995]

BACON, Ms A. E. M., 28 Queen's Gate Mews, London SW7 5QL [1992]

BACRAC, Mr N., 26 Kenver Avenue, London N12 0PG [1986]

BAGGOT, Jennifer, 75 Morehampton Square, Donnybrook, Dublin 4, Ireland [1995]

BAGHRAMIAN, Dr Maria, Dept of Philosophy, University College Dublin, Dublin 4, Republic of Ireland [1992]

BAIGENT, T. J. H., 182 Wiltshire Close, Rosemoor Street, London SW3 2NZ [1994]

BAKAOUKAS, Mr Michael, 90 South Clerk Street, Edinburgh EH8 9PT [1995]

BAKER, Miss Amy Marie, 11 Old St. Paul's, Russell Street, Cambridge CB2 1HA [1993]

BAKER, John, Dept of Politics, University College Dublin, Dublin 4, Ireland [1996]

BAMBREY, Mr R. J., Glangwili, Ystrad Aeron, Lampeter, Dyfed SA48 7PG [1995]

BAMBROUGH, Mr J. R., St John's College, Cambridge CB2 1TP [1960]

BARNES, Professor Jonathan, Départment de Philosophie, Université de Genève, 1211 Genève 4, Switzerland [1969]

BARNETT, Mr Peter A., 33 Longmore Road, Shirley, Solihull, W. Mids. B90 3DZ [1996]

BARRY, Professor Brian, 14 Russell Chambers, Bury Place, London WC1A 2JU [1996]

BAR–ON, Dr Dorit, Dept of Philosophy, University of North Carolina at Chapel Hill, Chapel Hill, NC 27599-3125, USA [1995]

BATCHELOR, Dr Gawaine, 51 Ondine Road, London SE15 4ED [1994]

BATES, Mr D. F., 8 Danes Close, Kirkham, Preston, Lancs. PR4 2YS [1995]

BATTY, Mr Jim, 22 Benhill Wood Road, Sutton, Sussex 1SM 4HQ [1995]

BAXTER, Rev. Dr Anthony, St Mary of the Angels, Moorhouse Road, London W2 5DJ [1975]

BEADLE, Dr Elaine, Dept of Philosophy, University of Reading, Whiteknights, Reading GR6 2AA [1991]

BEALE, Mr Jonathan, 9 Candover Close, Harmondsworth, Middlesex UB7 0BD [1995]

BEANEY, Dr Michael, Dept of Philosophy, University of Leeds, Leeds LS2 9JT [1985]

BEAVER, Mrs Bonnie, 55 Yale Court, Honeybourne Road, London NW6 1JQ [1991]

BEDFORD, Mr E., 23 Farmer Street, London W8 7SN [1956]

BEEBEE, Dr H., Dept of Philosophy, University College, Gower Street, London WC1E 6BT [1993]

BEHAR, Mrs Georgette, 54 Hanover Gate Mansions, Park Road, London NW1 4SN [1982]

BEHRENDT, Ms K.A., 49 Summertown House, 369 Banbury Road, Oxford OX2 7RA [1996]

BELSEY, Andrew, Philosophy UWCC, PO Box 94, Cardiff CF1 3XB [1975]

BENDALL, Ms Karen, 68 Oakley Square, London NW1 1NJ [1994]

BENN, Dr P. M. W., Dept of Philosophy, University of Leeds, Leeds LS2 9JT [1987]

BENNETT, Mr P. J., 82 Fort Road, Newhaven, E. Sussex BN9 9EJ [1987]

BENTLEY, Dr Russell K., Dept of Politics, Keele University, Keele, Staffs. ST5 5BG [1993]

BERENSON, Dr Frances, 13 Landsdowne, 9/10 Carlton Drive, London SW15 2BY [1970]

BERGES, Ms S., 26 Loraine Road, Holloway, London N7 6EZ [1991]

BERMÚDEZ, Dr José Luis, Faculty of Philosophy, University of Cambridge, Sidgwick Avenue, Cambridge CB3 9DA [1995]

BERRY, D., 260 Southlands Road, Bromley, Kent BR1 2EQ [1982]

BERRY, Dr G. J., Longwood House, The Broadway, Woodhall Spa, Lincs. LN10 6SH [1992]

BERTASI, Ms Debora, Dept of Philosophy, Birkbeck College, Malet Street, London WC1E 7HX [1994]

BIGGAR, Dr Peter, Hillhead, Craighton, North Kessock, Inverness IV1 1YG [1986]

BIGGIERO, Miss Fiona, Max Rayne House, 109 Camden Road, London NW1 [1993]

BIGGS, Dr Michael A.R., Faculty of Art & Design, University of Hertfordshire, Manor Road, Hatfield, Herts AL10 9TL [1990]

BINDERUP, Lars, Dept of Logic & Metaphysics, University of St Andrews, St Andrews, Fife KY16 9AL [1996]

BIRD, Dr A. J., Dept of Philosophy, Edinburgh University, David Hume Tower, George Square, Edinburgh EH8 9JX [1993]

BIRD, Professor G. H., Dept of Philosophy, The University, Manchester M13 9PL [1955]

BJARUP, Professor Jes, Juridiska Institutionen, Stockholms Universitet, S 106 91 Stockholm, Sweden [[1996]

BLACK, Dr Oliver, 21 Andrews House, Barbican, London EC2Y 8AX [1992]

BLACK, Robert, Dept of Philosophy, University of Nottingham, University Park, Nottingham NG7 2RD [1971]

BLACKWOOD, Mr Andrew, Flat 4, 64 Cambridge Gardens, London W10 6HR [1992]

BLOCK, Professor N., Dept of Philosophy, New York University, Main Building, 100 Washington Square East, New York, NY 10003-6688, USA [1987]

BLUM, Professor Alex, Dept of Philosophy, Bar-Ilan University, Ramat-Gan 52900, Israel [1985]

BOARD, Mr E. J., 5 Escuan Lodge, 17 Aberdeen Park, London N5 2AQ [1980]

BODEN, Professor M., School of Cognitive & Computing Sciences, University of Sussex, Falmer, Brighton BN1 9QM [1961]

BOGDANOVIC, Dr Marko, 51 Ridgmount Gardens, Bloomsbury, London WC1E 7AU [1994]

BONINO, Guido, Via G-Zambelli 7, 10137 Torino, Italy [1993]

BONZON, Dr Roman, Dept of Philosophy, Augustana College, Rock Island, Illinois 61201, USA [1990]

BORG, Ms Emma, 4 Paddenswick Road, London W6 0UB [1996]

BORST, Mr C. V., Dept of Philosophy, University of Keele, Newcastle-under-Lyme, Keele, Staffs ST5 5BG [1974]

BORSTNER, Dr Bojan, Kotlje 125, 62390 Ravne na Koroskem, Slovenia [1992]

BOSOWSKI, Mr John, 13A Park Crescent, Brighton BN2 3HA [1995]

BOWLES, Mr Michael T. P., 14 Plymouth Place, Leamington Spa, Warwickshire CV31 1HN [1995]

BOYCE, Mr Raymond, 28 Abinger Drive, Redhill, Surrey RH1 6SY [1990]

BOYD, Miss Veronica, 8 Kilmorey Gardens, Twickenham TW1 1PY [1994]

BRADSHAW, Mr Norman, 6/34 Johnston Street, Annandale, NSW 2038, Australia [1989]

BRADY, Mr Michael S., Dept of Philosophy, University of California, Santa Barbara, California 93106-3090, USA [1994]

BRAINE, David, Dept of Philosophy, King's College, Old Aberdeen, Aberdeen AB9 2UB [1989]

BRANDON, E. P., Office of Academic Affairs, University of the West Indies, Cave Hill, Barbados [1970]

BRANQUINHO, Dr Joao Miguel B. V., R. Cesario Verde 6–C/V Esq., 1100 Lisboa, Portugal [1989]

BREACH, Mrs J. J., 9 Devonshire Close, London W1N 1LE [1989]

BRELADE, Mrs Susan, 13 Eastgate Street, Winchester, Hampshire SO23 8EB [1983]

BREWER, Dr Bill, St Catherine's College, Oxford OX1 3UJ [1987]

BRIERTON, Mr Darren, 6/4 Sienna Gardens, Edinburgh EH9 1PG [1988]

BRITTEN, Mr Bob, 36 Carlton Mansions, Holmleigh Road, London N16 5PX [1995]

BROACKES, Professor J. D., Dept of Philosophy, Brown University, Providence, RI 02912-1918, USA [1985]

BROADIE, Dr A., Dept of Moral Philosophy, University of Glasgow, Glasgow G12 8QQ [1967]

BRODY, Dr Alan, 39 Fifth Avenue, New York, NY 10003, USA [1992]

BROOKS, Professor D. H. M., Dept of Philosophy, University of Capetown, Private Bag, Rondebosch 7700, South Africa [1985]

BROOME, Dr John, Dept of Philosophy, The University, St Andrews, Fife [1977]

BROWN, Mr Alan, St Cross College, Oxford OX1 3LZ [1994]

BROWN, Curtis, Dept of Philosophy, Trinity University, 715 Stadium Drive, San Antonio, TX 78212, USA [1993]

BROWN, Professor D. G., Dept of Philosophy, University of British Columbia, 1866 Main Hall, E-370, Vancouver, Canada V6T 1Z1 [1991]

BROWN, James, Dept of Philosophy & Politics, University of Ulster at Coleraine, Cromore Road, N. Ireland BT52 1SA [1982]

BROWN, Dr Jessica, Dept of Philosophy, University of Bristol, 9 Woodland Road, Bristol BS8 1TB [1993]

BROWN, Mr Michael, Exeter College, Oxford OX1 3DP [1995]

BROWN, Robert, Dept of Social Philosophy, Australian National University, Canberra 2600, Australia [1954]

BROWN, Professor S. C., 45 Westoning Road, Harlington, Dunstable, Beds LU5 6PB [1962]

BRÜMMER, Professor V., Laurillardlaan 3, 3723 DL Bilthoven, The Netherlands [1979]

BRUMSEN, Mr Michiel, High Beley, Dunino by St. Andrews, Fife KY16 8LU [1994]

BRUNNING, Mr P. D., 27 Tintern Road, London N22 5LU [1974]

BRYANT, C., Dept of Moral Philosophy, The University, St Andrews, Fife KY16B 9AL [1974]

BUDD, Professor Malcolm, Dept of Philosophy, University College, London WC1E 6BT [1985]

BULLARD, Mr Edward, 23 Rochester Terrace, London NW1 9JN [1996]

BURNYEAT, Professor M. F., Robinson College, Cambridge, CB3 9AN [1964]

BURWOOD, Dr S.A., Dept of Philosophy, University of Hull, Hull HU6 7RX [1992]

BUTTERFIELD, Dr J., Jesus College, Cambridge CB5 8BL [1983]

BUXTON, Mr Ian, 2 Homer Close, Barnehurst, Bexleyheath, Kent [1993]

BYNUM, Mr Jonathan, 14 W. Cold Spring LN #705, Baltimore, MD 21210, USA [1993]

BYRNE, Dr A., Dept of Linguistics & Philosophy, 20D–213, MIT, Cambridge, MA 02139, USA [1987]

BYRNE, P. A., Dept of Philosophy of Religion, King's College, London WC2R 2LS [1975]

CALLCUT, Mr Daniel John, Dept of Philosophy, Johns Hopkins University, 3400 North Charles Street, Baltimore, MD 21218, USA [1993]

CALLNON, Mrs L. M., 63 Dulverton Road, Ruislip, Middlesex HA4 9AF [1991]

CALVERLEY, Mr J. E., Garden Flat, 58 Blenheim Crescent, London W11 1NY [1989]

CAMERON, J. R., Dept of Philosophy, King's College, University of Aberdeen, Aberdeen AB9 2UB [1977]

CANDLISH, Mr Stewart, Dept of Philosophy, University of Western Australia, Nedlands 6009, W. Australia [1974]

CARD, Mr Robert, 248 Nine Mile Ride, Wokingham, Berkshire RG40 3PA [1996]

CARPENTER, Mr D., 47 Waverley Road, Southsea, Hants. PO5 2PJ [1987]

CARR, Mr Jeffrey V., Flat 6, 10/6 Blacket Avenue, Edinburgh EH9 1RS [1992]

CARRUTHERS, Professor P. M., Dept of Philosophy, Sheffield University, Sheffield S10 2TN [1980]

CARSTON, Ms R. A., Dept of Phonetics & Linguistics, University College, London WC1E 6BT [1982]

CARTER, Mr Tim, Rt. 1 Box 170, Mansfield, TN 38236, USA [1994]

CARTWRIGHT, Professor Helen, 6 Whittier Place, Apt. 3-N, Boston, MA 02114, USA [1985]

CARUANA, Mr Louis, St Edmund's College, Cambridge CB3 0BN [1994]

CARVALHO, Sr Manoel Joaquim de, Jr., M. J. de Carvalho & Cia. Ltda., Caixa Postal 97, Bahia, Brazil [1988]

CARVER, T., Dept of Politics, University of Bristol, 12 Priory Road, Bristol BS8 1TU [1975]

CASALEIRO, Abel, 153–175 Whitechapel Road, London E1 1DP [1994]

CASSAM, Dr Quassim, Wadham College, Oxford OX1 3PN [1995]

CASSELL, Ms Jacqueline A., 5 Priory Street, Lewes, East Sussex BN7 1HH [1990]

CATSOULIS, C., Mozartstraat 4, B-2018 Antwerp, Belgium [1994]

CAUSSE, Ms Christine, 42 Gloucester Place, London W1H 3HJ [1992]

CHALTON, Miss Nicola, The Well House, Austins' Place, Old Town, Hemel Hempstead, HP2 5HN [1995]

CHAMPLIN, Dr T. S., Dept of Philosophy, University of Hull, Cottingham Road, Hull HU6 7RX [1992]

CHANNON, Mr D. J., 91 Ingram Road, Thornton Heath, Croydon CR7 8EH [1995]

CHAPPELL, Dr T. D. J., Dept of Philosophy, University of Manchester, Manchester M13 9PL [1990]

CHAPPELL, Professor V. C., RR No. 7, 17 Harkness Road, Pelham, MA 01002, USA [1959]

CHARLTON, Professor W., Dept of Philosophy, University of Edinburgh, David Hume Tower, George Square, Edinburgh EH8 9JK [1966]

CHART, Mr David, Dept of History & Philosophy of Science, Free School Lane, Cambridge CB2 3RH [1994]

CHÁVEZ-ARVIZO, Professor Enrique, Union College, Humanities Centre, Philosophy Department, Schenectady, NY 12308-2371, USA [1994]

CHERBONNIER, Professor E. L., 843 Prospect Avenue, Hartford, CT 06105, USA [1963]

CHERRY, C. M., Eliot College, The University, Canterbury, Kent [1974]

CHEUNG, Dr Kam Ching Leo, Dept of Religion & Philosophy, Hong Kong Baptist University, Kowloon Tong, Hong Kong [1993]

CHILD, Dr T. W., University College, Oxford OX1 4BH [1990]

CHITTY, Mr Andrew, 16 Oldlands Avenue, Balcombe, West Sussex RH17 6LY [1991]

CHOI, Mr W., Flat 2, Tannery Square, Green Road, Meanwood, Leeds LS6 4LT [1994]

CHOPRA, Y.N., 37 Clovelly Court, Blenheim Gardens, London NW2 [1982]

CHRISLEY, Dr Ronald L., School of Cognitive & Computing Sciences, University of Sussex, Falmer, Brighton BN1 9QH [1994]

CHRISTOFIDOU, Dr Andrea, Worcester College, Oxford OX1 2HB [1996]

CHUNG, Dr Man C., Wolverhampton University, School of Health Sciences, 62–68 Lichfield Street, Wolverhampton WV1 1DJ [1995]

CLARK, M., Dept of Philosophy, The University, Nottingham NG7 2RD [1963]

CLARK, Dr Peter, Dept of Logic & Metaphysics, University of St Andrews, St Andrews, Fife, Scotland KY16 9AL [1987]

CLARK, Professor S. R. L., 1 Arnside Road, Oxton, Birkenhead, Merseyside L43 2JU [1975]

CLARKE, Mr Jonathan, 16 kings Hall Road, Beckenham, Kent BR3 1LU [1994]

CLEMENTZ, Docteur F., 38 Rue d'Angivillers, 78000 Versailles, France [1985]

CLIFTON, Mr Barry, Lilac Cottage, Western Road, Jarvis Brook, Crowborough, East Sussex TN6 3EW [1993]

COATES, Dr P., 23 Woodland Rise, London N10 3UP [1976]

COCKBURN, Dr D. A., Dept of Philosophy, St David's University College, Lampeter, Dyfed SA48 7ED [?]

CODY, Professor Arthur, 2573 Pine Flat Road, Santa Cruz, CA 95060, USA [1970]

COFFEY, D. J., 86 Hare Lane, Claygate, Esher, Surrey KT10 0QU [1990]

COHEN, Professor G.A., All Souls College, Oxford OX1 4AL [1963]

COHEN, Professor L. J., The Queen's College, Oxford OX1 4AW [1948]

COHEN, M. D., Dept of Philosophy, University College, Singleton Park, Swansea SA2 8PP [1968]

COLES, Mr Norman, 19 Old Humphrey Avenue, Hastings, E. Sussex TN34 3BT [1977]

COLLINS, Mr J. E., 47 Grange Park, London W5 3PR [1992]

CONWAY, David, Middlesex Polytechnic, Queensway, Enfield, Middlesex EN3 4JF [1977]

COOPE, Christopher, Dept of Philosophy, University of Leeds, Leeds LS2 9JT [1996]

COOPER, Professor David E., Dept of Philosophy, University of Durham, 50 Old Elvet, Durham DH1 3HN [1986]

COOPER, Professor N. L., 2 Minton Place, Dundee, Scotland DD2 1BR [1959]

COPELAND, Dr J., Dept of Philosophy, University of Canterbury, Christchurch, New Zealand [1983]

COPELAND, Dr J., Dept of Philosophy, University of Canterbury, Christchurch, New Zealand [1983]

CORAZZA, Dr Eros, Dept of Philosophy, University of Nottingham, University Park, Nottingham NG7 2RD [1996]

CORNWELL, Mr James M., 56 Mill Street, Osney, Oxford OX2 0AL [1993]

CORRIGAN, Kevin, Dean, St. Thomas More College, University of Saskatchewan, 1437 College Drive, Saskatoon, Saskatchewan, Canada S7N 0W6 [1996]

CORROLL, Mr A., 30 Biddestone Road, Islington, London N7 9RA [1996]

CORSO, Teresa M., 124 Maryland Road, London N22 4AP [1996]

COTTINGHAM, Professor J. G., Dept of Philosophy, University of Reading, Reading RG6 2AA [1995]

COUTTS, Dr G. A., 57A Studley Grange Road, Hanwell, London W7 2LU [1987]

COYLE, Mr Sean, 0/2 11 Kelvindale Gardens, Kelvindale, Glasgow G20 8DW [1995]

CRANE, Dr Tim, Dept of Philosophy, University College, London WC1E 6BT [1983]

CRAWFORD, Mr M.S., Exeter College, Oxford OX1 3DP [1995]

CRISP, Dr R. S., St Anne's College, Oxford OX2 6HS [1983]

CRITCHLEY, Dr Simon, Dept of Philosophy, University of Essex, Colchester CO4 3SQ [1996]

CROMBIE, Mr I. M., Wadham College, Oxford OX1 3PN [1948]

CUA, Professor A. S., 7525 Cayuga Avenue, Bethesda, MD 20817, USA [1985]

CUI, Wei, Currier House Box 508, Harvard University, Cambridge, MA 02138, USA [1993]

CUMMINGS, Louise, 59 Ethel Street, Lisburn Road, Belfast BT9 7FT [1996]

CUNLIFFE, C. R., Abbot's Barn, Abbey Farm, St Bees, Cumbria CA27 0DY [1963]

CURTIS, Mr Brian A., 137 Hanover Road, London NW10 3DN [1990]

CUSACK, Pearse, Mount St Joseph Abbey, Roscrea, Co. Tipperary, Ireland [1996]

DALGARNO, Melvin, 16 College Bounds, Aberdeen [1975]

DAMMANN, R. M. J., School of European Studies, University of Sussex, Falmer, Brighton BN1 9QM [1977]

DANCY, Professor J. P., Dept of Philosophy, University of Keele, Keele, Staffs ST5 5PG [1975]

DANQUAH, Dr Joseph B., 65 Castle Road, Chatham, Kent ME4 5HX [1993]

DANQUAH, Dr Joseph B., 65 Castle Road, Chatham, Kent ME4 5HX [1993]

DATTA, Dr Rama, 510 Bloomfield Drive, Fayetteville, NC 28311, USA [1991]

DAVIES, D. J., 9 Brodorion Drive, Cwmrhydyceurw, Swansea SA6 6LP [1976]

DAVIES, Dr M. K., Corpus Christi College, Oxford OX1 4JF [1982]

DAWSON, Mr Angus J., 3 Watford Mount, New Mills, High Peak, SK22 4EP [1994]

DAWSON, Mr Paul, 6a Graham Road, Wealdstone, Middlesex HA3 5RF [1995]

DE JONGE, Ms Eccy, Flat 25, 46–7 Coram Street, London WC1N 1HE [1994]

DENARD, Mr W. V., 5 Eaton Brae, Shankill, Dublin 18, Ireland [1996]

DENNIS, Mr Daniel, 21 John Keall House, Henry Jackson Road, London SW15 1DJ [1993]

DENNY, Miss Susan, 49 Woburn Avenue, Theydon Bois, Epping, Essex CM16 7JR [1987]

DENYER, N. C. Esq., Trinity College, Cambridge CB2 1TQ [1988]

DEUGD, Prof. Dr C. de, Sint Jansgeleen 3, 6176 RA Spaubeek, The Netherlands [1969]

DIAMANDOPOULOS, Professor Peter, Adelphi University, Garden City, Long Island, NY 11530, USA [1991]

DIAMOND, Professor Cora, Dept of Philosophy, 521 Cabell Hall, University of Virginia, Charlottesville, VA 22903, USA [1962]

DIFFEY, Dr T. J., 9 Wilmington Close, Hassocks, West Sussex BN6 8QB [1979]
DIGGLE, Mr Phil, 46 Linden Road, Gosforth, Newcastle upon Tyne NE3 4HB [1995]
DILMAN, Dr Illham, Dept of Philosophy, University College of South Wales, Swansea [1955]
DIMOCK, Mr Steven, 7175 Highland, Powell, Butte, OR 97753, USA [1994]
DIMOV, Mr Venelin G., Ul. Konstantin Iretchek 7, Russe-7000, Bulgaria [1993]
DIVERS, Dr John, Dept of Philosophy, University of Leeds, Leeds LS2 9JT [1994]
DIVERS, Dr John, Dept of Philosophy, University of Leeds, Leeds LS2 9JT [1994]
DOHERTY, Mr Andrew, 49 Boneybefore, Carrickfergus, Co. Antrim, Northern Ireland BT38 7EQ [1996]
DOMINIONI, Stefano, 1999 Commonwealth Avenue, Apt. 9, Brighton, MA 02135, USA [1996]
DONEY, Professor Willis, Dept of Philosophy, Thornton Hall, Dartmouth College, Hanover, New Hampshire 03755, USA [1952]
DONNAN, Mr M. J., 39 Calshot Way, Enfield, Middlesex EN2 7BQ [1991]
DONOHUE, Miss Jennifer Grace Agnes, 18 Woodseer Street, London E1 5HD [1993]
DOOLEY, Dolores, Dept of Philosophy, Lucan Place, University College, Cork, Ireland [1996]
DØØR, Mr Jørgen, Dyrehøjvej 17, DK-5672 Brobyværk, Broby, Denmark [1981]
DOUTHART, Ms Jane, 4 Gresham Street, Edge Lane, Liverpool L7 9LU [1995]
DOVEY, Mr Matthew J., c/o Libraries Automation Service, 65 St Giles, Oxford OX1 3LU [1992]
DOW, Mr Jamie, 84 Hamilton Street, Stalybridge, Cheshire SK15 1LN [1994]
DOWER, Dr Nigel, Dept of Philosophy, King's College, University of Aberdeen, Old Aberdeen, Scotland AB9 2UB [1968]
DOWNIE, Professor R. S., Dept of Moral Philosophy, The University, Glasgow G12 8QQ [1961]
DRASAR, B. S., London School of Hygiene & Tropical Medicine [1969]
DREWERY, Ms Alice, c/o Centre for Cognitive Science, 2 Buccleuch Place, Edinburgh EH8 9LW [1994]
DRONSFIELD, Mr J., 49 Littlebury Road, Clapham, London SW4 6DW [1987]
DUCKWORTH, Mr N., 204 Chapter Road, London NW2 5NB [1995]
DUFF, Professor R. A., Dept of Philosophy, University of Stirling, Stirling FK9 4LA, Scotland [1994]
DUMMETT, Professor M., 54 Park Town, Oxford OX2 6SJ [1951]
DUNCAN, Professor E. H., Dept of Philosophy, Baylor University, B. U. Box 7273, Waco, Texas 76798-7273, USA [1967]
DUNDON, Mr Paul Anthony, 60 Thames Street, Oxford OX1 1SU [1993]
DUNLOP, Mr James, Flat 3, 78 Hemingford Road, Barnsbury, London N1 1DB [1987]
DUPRÉ, Professor John, Dept of Philosophy, Birkbeck College, Malet Street, London WC1E 7HX [1996]
DURKIN, Mr C. R., Magdalen College, Oxford OX1 4AU [1994]
DUTHIE, D. J., 35 Holmesdale Road, London N6 [1964]
DWYER, Mr John L., Q. C., Owen Dixon Chambers East, 205 William Street, Melbourne 3000, Australia [1970]
DYBIKOWSKY, J. C., Dept of Philosophy, University of British Columbia, Vancouver 8, BC V6N 3B9 Canada [1970]
DYKE, Ms Heather L. M., First Floor Flat, 45 Mattison Road, London N4 1BG [1993]

ECKERSLEY, Ms Maureen, Drivers Barn, Butchers Hill, Ickleton, Saffron Walden CB10 1SR [1989]

ECKHARDT, Mr Westley, Ravella 15 Principal 2a, 08021 Barcelona, Spain [1995]

EDDY, Crick, Dendermondestraat 48, 1785 Merchtem, Belgium [1996]

EDGINGTON, Mrs D. M. D., Dept of Philosophy, Birkbeck College, Malet Street, London WC1E 7HX [1969]

EDWARDS, Dr James S., Dept of Philosophy, University of Glasgow, Glasgow G12 8QQ [1991]

EDWARDS, Michael, 3 Westway, Raynes Park, London SW20 9LX [1974]

EGAN, Frances, Dept of Philosophy, Rutgers University, Davison Hall/Douglas Campus, New Brunswick, NI 08903, USA [1996]

EGEL, Dr Lawrence, 200 North Hammes Avenue, Joliet, Illinois 60435-6677, USA [1992]

ELAN, Mr M. A., 26 King Edward Street, St. Davids, Devon, Exeter EX4 4NY [1984]

ELLEDGE, Mr Timothy, 3112 Dow Drive, Knoxville, TN 37920, USA [1994]

ELLERBECK, Mr Volker, Jaarbrücker Str. 7, 10405 Berlin, Germany [1986]

ELLIS, Fiona, 10 Winchester Place, London N6 5HJ [1995]

ELLIS, Professor Anthony J., Dept of Philosophy, Virginia Commonwealth University, Richmond, VA 23284-2025, USA [1989]

ELWELL, Dr David, 57 Western Road, Oxford OX1 4LF [1984]

EMMETT, Professor D., 11 Millington Road, Cambridge CB3 9HW [1934]

ENG CHEE, Mr Rupert Seah, Block 210 Pasir Ris Street 21, #12–322, Singapore 510210 [1997]

ENGEL, Professor Pascal, 4 Pas Montbrun, Paris 75014, France [1985]

ENGLISH, Mr R. W. H., 20 Commondale, Putney, London SW15 1HS [1992]

ETUKUDO, Mr Abraham, 72 Sarsfeld Road, London SW12 8HP [1996]

EVANS, Mr Ellis, 102 Woodhead Road, Holmbridge, Huddersfield HD7 1NL [1956]

EVANS, Professor J. D., Dept of Philosophy, The Queen's University, Belfast BT7 1NN [1974]

EVANS, Professor J. L., The Dingle, Danybryn Avenue, Radyr, Nr. Cardiff [1946]

EVELING, H. S., College East, Fettes College, Carrington Road, Edinburgh EH4 1QX [1958]

EVERARD, Mr C. D., Dept of Philosophy, King's College, Strand, WC2R 2LS [1991]

EVERITT, Mr N., School of Social Studies, University of East Anglia, University Plain, Norwich NOR 88C [1968]

EVERSON, Mr S., St Hugh's College, Oxford OX2 6LE [1987]

EYNON, Mr T. P., 107 D Mountview Road, Hornsey, London N4 4JH [1995]

FACEY, Dr K. K., 105 Kings Head Hill, London E4 7JG [1991]

FALK, Dr B., Dept of Philosophy, University of Birmingham, P. O. Box 363, Birmingham B15 2TT [1974]

FANE, Mr C. E., 6 Aberdeen Road, Redland, Bristol BS6 6HT [1995]

FARGE, E. J., 50 Grove Avenue, Twickenham, Middlesex TW1 4HY [1971]

FARIS, Professor J.A., 15 Coney Island, Ardglass, Co. Down BT30 7UQ [1996]

FARKAS, Katalin, Dept of Philosophy, Eötvös Loránd University, Budapest, Piarista Köz 1, 1052 Hungary [1995]

FARRELL, Mr B. A., Corpus Christi College, Oxford OX1 4JF [1947]

FARRELL, Dr Tom, 24 Glandore Road, Griffith Ave, Dublin 9, Ireland [1996]

FARRINGTON, Mr Roger, 77 Marsham Court, Marsham Street, London SW1P 4LA [1991]

FARRUGIA, Mr Marco, 5/2, St Peter's Court, Resort Street, St Paul's Bay, Malta [1996]

FAWCUS, Mr Keir, 45 Jessell House, Judd Street, London WC1 [1993]
FEIT, Mr Neil P., 234 Elm Street, Northampton, MA 01060, USA [1994]
FERGUSON, Mr Stephen, 45a South Street, St. Andrews, Fife [1994]
FERNANDEZ-DIEZ-PICAZO, Mr E. Gustavo, 132 Leslie Road, Leytonstone, London E11 4HG [1993]
FERRAND, Mr David, Foxlark, Smithan Hill, East Harptree, Nr. Bristol BS18 6BZ [1993]
FERREIRA, José R. Martins, Rua Joaquim Antunes 977 Ap. 122, Pinheiros/SP, Sao Paulo CEP 05415-012, Brazil [1992]
FIELD, Mrs Jennifer, 5 Laurel Rise, Exmouth, Devon EX8 4RT [1991]
FIELDS, Mr Lloyd, Dept of Philosophy, University of Dundee, Dundee DD1 4HN [1974]
FILIPPOU, Mr Michalis, 211 Willesden Lane, London NW6 [1994]
FILOZOFSKA ISTRAZIVANJA, Odsjek za Filozofiju, Filozofski Fakultet, Ul. Djure Salaja 3, Zagreb, Croatia [1983]
FINIGAN, Mr Charles P., The Presbytery, Plowden, Lydbury North, Shropshire SY7 8AG [1991]
FISHER, Mr D. R., 36 Wellesley Crescent, Twickenham, Middlesex TW2 5RT [1975]
FLOWERS, Mr Jason Ian, Flat 1C3, New Block, Camden Road, Camden Town, London NW1 [1996]
FØLLESDAL, Professor Dagfinn, Staverhagan 7, 1300 Sandvika, Norway [1994]
FOOT, Mrs P, 15 Walton Street, Oxford [1948]
FORBES, Professor G., Dept of Philosophy, Tulane University, New Orleans, LA 70118-5698, USA [1984]
FORREST, Mr R. J., 2 Montolieu Gardens, Putney, London SW15 6PB [1990]
FORRESTER, Ms Lily A., Dept of Philosophy, Dundee University, Dundee DD1 4HN [1991]
FOSTER, Dr J. A., Brasenose College, Oxford OX1 4AJ [1980]
FOSTER, Dr Samantha, Garden Flat, 32 Talbot Road, London W2 5LT [1996]
FOULKES, Dr P., 24 Granville Park, London SE13 7EA [1954]
FOX, Thomas Esq., 61 West 108th St., Apt. 5A, New York, NY 10025-3244, USA [1993]
FOX, Mr Chris, 15 Foxhill Road, Reading RG1 5QS [1996]
FRANZEN, Mr John C., 905 Harlocke St., Apt. 2, Iowa City, IA 52246, USA [1994]
FRAZIER, Dr Robert L., Magdalen College, Oxford OX1 4AU [1991]
FREAKLEY, Mark, Faculty of Education, Griffith University, Nathan, Queensland 4111, Australia [1996]
FREMANTLE, Mr Samuel, 14A Montpelier Vale, Blackheath, London SE3 0TA [1996]
FRICKER, Dr E., Magdalen College, Oxford OX1 4AU [1981]
FRICKER, Miranda, Dept of Philosophy, Birkbeck College, Malet Street, London WC1E 7HX [1995]
FRIEND, Ms Michèle, The Old Vicarage, Pytchley, Nr. Kettering, Northants. NN14 1EP [1993]
FRIMANNSSON, Dr G. H., Faculty of Education, University of Akureyri, P. O. Box 224, IS-602 Akureyri, Iceland [1990]
FUHRMANN, Dr André, Universität Konstanz, Zentrum Philosophie, 78434 Konstanz, Germany [1983]
GAHIR, Mr Balvinder, 79 Roman Road, Ilford, Essex IG1 2NZ [1995]
GALBRAITH, J. W., Woodlands, Shore Road, Kilcreggan, G84 0HQ [1966]
GALLIE, Roger, Dept of Philosophy, University of Nottingham, University Park, Nottingham NG7 2RD [1968]

GALLIE, Professor W. B., Cilhendre, Upper Saint Mary Street, Newport, Dyfed, Wales [1937]

GARCIA, Mr S. Meckled, 38 St. George's Avenue, Tufnell Park, London N7 0HD [1994]

GARCIA Y ALONSO, Mr Antonio, 52 Pitcroft Avenue, Reading RG6 1NN [1993]

GARDINER, P. L., Magdalen College, Oxford OX1 4AU [1950]

GARDINER, Mr Stephen M., 1475 1/2 Slaterville Road, Ithaca, New York 14850, USA [1992]

GARDNER, Dr S., Dept. of Philosophy, Birkbeck College, Malet Street, London WC1E 7HX [1984]

GASELTINE, Mrs K. M., 12 Latham Road, Cambridge CB2 2EQ [1992]

GASKIN, Dr Hilary, Publishing Division, Cambridge University Press, The Edinburgh Building, Shaftesbury Road, Cambridge CB2 2RU [1995]

GASKIN, Dr Richard, School of English & American Studies, Arts Building, University of Sussex, Falmer, Brighton BN1 9QN [1992]

GAUT, Dr Berys N., Dept of Moral Philosophy, University of St. Andrews, St. Andrews, Fife KY16 9AL, Scotland [1992]

GAYLARD, Mr Michael, 43 Hillfield Park, Muswell Hill, London N10 [1994]

GAYNESFORD, Mr Max de, Dept of Philosophy, University of Reading, Whiteknights, Reading RG6 2AA [1993]

GAZDIK, Igor, Elinsborgsbacken 23, S-163 64 Spanga, Sweden [1991]

GEISENDORFER, Mr James, 1001 Shawano Avenue, Green Bay, Wisconsin 54303, USA [1977]

GHOSHAL, Mr P, 5 Daresbury Road, Charlton, Manchester M21 9NA [1994]

GIANNAROU, Ms Angeliki, 7 Siskin Close, Longridge Park, Colchester CO4 3FR [1993]

GIAQUINTO, Dr M. D., Dept of Philosophy, University College, London WC1E 6BT [1982]

GIBBARD, Mr Peter, Dept of Philosophy, University of Michigan, Ann Arbor, Michigan 48109, USA [1994]

GIBBER, Mrs Jessie, 22 Ringwood Avenue, London N2 9NS [1987]

GIBSON, Professor Q., Dept of Philosophy, Arts Faculty, Australian National University, Canberra 0200, Australia [1948]

GILBERT, Professor Margaret, Philosophy Dept U54, University of Connecticut, Storrs, Ct 06269, USA [1995]

GILL, Mr Tim, 34 Kyverdale Road, London N16 7AH [1994]

GILLAN, Mr Adrian, Flat on Top, 64 Meadow Road, London SW8 1PP [1994]

GILLETT, Mr G., Magdalen College, Oxford [1991]

GILMOUR, A. J., 68 Scholar's Road, Balham, London SW12 0PG [1975]

GLADWIN, Mr Gary, 7 Johnson House, Cranleigh Street, London NW1 1PH [1991]

GLASS, Mr Graham, 121A Whipps Cross Road, Leytonstone, London E11 1NW [1996]

GLOCK, Dr Hans-Johann, Dept of Philosophy, University of Reading, Whiteknights, Reading RG6 2AA [1994]

GOCHET, Professor P., 78 Boulevard Louis Schmidt, P.B. 35, 1040 Brussels, Belgium [1959]

GOFF, Mr John, 55 Cowgate Road, Greenford, Middlesex UB6 8HH [1996]

GOLD, Mr J. I., 131 Roding Road, Loughton, Essex IG10 3BS [1992]

GOLDSBURY, Professor P. A., Dept of English, Faculty of Integrated Arts & Science, Hiroshima University, Kagamiyama 1-7-1, Higashi-Hiroshima City 724, Japan [1969]

GOLINSKY, Mrs M. F., 72 Lexham Gardens, London W8 5JB [1992]

GONLEY, Mr James, 64 Heron Drive, Luton, Bedfordshire LU2 7LZ [1970]

GONZALEZ ARNAL, Stella, Dept of Philosophy, Keele University, Keele Hall, Keele [1996]

GONZÁLEZ, Professor Wenceslao J., Facultad de Humanidades, Calle Vázquez Cabrera, s/n Esteiro, 15403–Ferrol (La Coruña), Spain [1988]

GOODWIN, Professor Barbara, School of Economic & Social Studies, University of East Anglia, Norwich NR4 7TJ [1989]

GORMAN, Mr Alan, 88 High Street, Totnes, Devon TQ9 5SN [1994]

GOTTLIEB, Mr A., 20 Holly Hill, London NW3 6SE [1995]

GOUDAPPEL, Miss Miriam, Wolfson College, Oxford OX2 6UD [1994]

GOUGH, Mr Martin, Dept of Philosophy, University of Leeds, Leeds LS2 9JT [1994]

GOWLAND, Mr M. J., 52 Lincoln Road, East Finchley, London N2 9DL [1992]

GRAHAM, Gordon, Dept of Moral Philosophy, St Andrew's University, Fife, Scotland KY16 9AL [1959]

GRAHAM, Mr Peter, Dept of Philosophy, Stanford University, Stanford, CA 94305, USA [1994]

GRANDY, Count L. de, 73 Richmond Road, Freemantle, Southampton [1973]

GRAU, Mr Christopher Mark, Dept of Philosophy, Johns Hopkins University, 347 Gilman Hall, 3400 N. Charles St., Baltimore, MD 21218-2690, USA [1996]

GRAYLING, Dr A., Dept of Philosophy, Birkbeck College, London WC1E 7HX [1985]

GREENBAUM, Dr Louis, 43 Ringmore Rise, London SE23 3DE [1994]

GREENBERG, Mr Mark D., Jesus College, Oxford OX1 3DW [1992]

GREENE, Mr E. P. C., 45 Pembroke Street, Oxford OX1 1BP [1964]

GREENSTREET, Mr Stuart, Flat 2, 3 Wykeham Road, Hastings, East Sussex, TN34 1UA [1986]

GREENWOOD, T., Dept of Logic, University of Glasgow, Glasgow W2 [1969]

GREGORY, Mr D., Room F85, Ifor Evans Hall, 109 Camden Road, London NW1 9HA [1993]

GRIFFIN, Ms Jennifer A., 23 K, Westbourne Terrace, London W2 3UN [1993]

GRIFFIN, Nicholas, RR#1 Troy, Ontario LOR 2BO, Canada [1992]

GRIFFITHS, Dr David, Castle Bernard, Bandon, County Cork, Eire [1988]

GULLAN-WHUR, Dr Margaret, Orange House, Heacham, King's Lynn, Norfolk PE31 7EG [1992]

GUNTON, Professor C. E., Dept of Theology & Religious Studies, King's College London, Strand, London WC2R 2LS [1969]

GUTIERREZ-GIRALDO, Dr David, Jesus 66, 2-1, E-08870 Sitges (Barcelona), Spain [1996]

GUTOWSKI, Dr Peter, Dept of Philosophy, Catholic University of Lublin, Ul. Raclawickie 14, 20-950 Lublin, Poland [1996]

GUTTENPLAN, Dr S. D., Dept of Philosophy, Birkbeck College, Malet Street, London WC1E 7HX [1978]

HAACK, Professor Susan, Dept of Philosophy, College of Arts & Sciences, Miami University, P. O. Box 248054, Coral Gables, Florida 33124-4670, USA [?]

HAAS, Professor W., 40 Park Range, Manchester, M14 5HQ [1946]

HAGBERG, Dr Garry, Dept of Philosophy, Bard College, Annandale-on-Hudson, New York 12504, USA [1989]

HAIGHT, M. R., Dept of Philosophy, The University, Glasgow G12 8QQ [1982]

HAKSAR, Dr V., Dept of Philosophy, University of Edinburgh, David Hume Tower, George Square, Edinburgh EH8 9JX [1965]

HALDANE, Professor J. J., Dept of Moral Philosophy, University of St Andrews, Fife, Scotland KY16 9AL [1979]

HALL, Mr Martin, Flat B, 280 Rotton Park Road, Edgbaston, Birmingham B16 0JH [1995]

HALL, Roland, Dept of Philosophy, University of York, Heslington, Yorks [1957]

HALL, Sean, 33 Cradley Road, New Eltham, London SE9 2HD [1990]

HALL, Suzanne, 12 Thornbury Square, Hornsey Lane, Highgate, London N6 5YN [1991]

HALLER, Professor R., Kumarweg 5, A-8044 Graz, Austria [1959]

HAMILTON, Dr Andrew, Dept of Philosophy, University of Durham, Durham DH1 3HP [1987]

HAMILTON, Mr C. F., Römerstraße 70, 53111 Bonn, Germany [1987]

HAMLYN, Professor D.W., 38 Smithy Knoll Road, Calver, Derbyshire S30 1XW [1951]

HAMM, Mrs Celeste, 38 The Uplands, Harpenden, Herts. AL5 2NZ [1992]

HANDBY, Mr Jason, 22a Clifton Road, Brighton, E. Sussex BN1 3HN [1996]

HANDEL, Mr James, 67 St Quintin Avenue, London W10 6NZ [1995]

HANFLING, Professor O., Oakridge, Red Copse Lane, Boars Hill, Oxford OX1 5ER [1970]

HANNA, Mr Philip, 18 Lismurn Park, Ahoghill, Ballymena, Co. Antrim BT42 1JN [1994]

HANNAY, A., Institute of Philosophy, PO Box 1024, Blindern, 0315 Oslo 3, Norway [1959]

HARCOURT, Dr E., Lady Margaret Hall, Oxford OX2 6QA [1990]

HARE, Professor R. M., Bywater, The Street, Ewelme, Nr. Wallingford, Oxon. OX10 6HQ [1947]

HARLAND, Mr S. J., Gregory Harland Ltd, 14 High Street, Windsor SL4 1LD [1996]

HARMAN, Mr C., 13 Eastgate Street, Winchester, Hampshire SO23 8EB [1986]

HARPHAM, Mr Simon, 104 Willows Road, Balsall Heath, Birmingham B12 9QD [1995]

HARRISON, Andrew, Dept of Philosophy, University of Bristol, 9 Woodland Road, Bristol BS8 1TB [?]

HARRISON, Professor B., School of English & US Studies, Arts Building, University of Sussex, Brighton BN1 9QN [?]

HARRISON, Professor Jonathan, 10 Halifax Road, Cambridge CB4 2PX [1947]

HARRISON, M. T. Esq., 23 Bank Chambers, 25 Jermyn Street, London SW1Y 6HR [1984]

HARRISON, Dr R., King's College, Cambridge CB2 1ST [1971]

HARRISON, Dr Simon, St John's College, Cambridge CB2 1TP [1996]

HARROP, Mr Steve, 41 Kingswear Road, London NW5 1EU [1995]

HART, Dr W. A., Dept of Philosophy & Politics, The University of Ulster, Coleraine, Co. Londonderry, Northern Ireland, BT52 1SA [1978]

HART, Dr W. D., Dept of Philosophy (M/C 267), The University of Illinois at Chicago, Chicago, Illinois 60680-4348, USA [1975]

HASPER, Mr P. S., H. Colleniusstraat 6-A, 9718 KT Groningen, The Netherlands [1996]

HATZIMOYSIS, Mr Anthony E., Dept of Philosophy, University of Leeds, Leeds LS2 9JT [1994]

HATZISTAVROU, Mr Anthony, 116 Mayfield Road, Edinburgh EH9 3AH [1996]

HAWKINGS, F. M. A., 2B Cole Street, London SE1 [1983]

HAY, Professor W. H., 39 Bagley Court, Madison, Wisconsin 53705, USA [1946]

HAYLER, Mr R. W., Dept of Philosophy, University of Leeds, Leeds LS2 9JT [1995]

HAYNES-CURTIS, Dr Carole, Flat One, 52 Pennsylvania Road, Exeter, Devon EX4 6DB [1984]

HEAD OF DEPARTMENT, Dept of Philosophy, University of Dhaka, Dhaka-2, Bangladesh [1990]

HEAD OF DEPARTMENT, Dept of Philosophy, University of the West Indies, St Augustine, Trinidad [1990]

HEAL, Dr B. J., St John's College, Cambridge CB2 1TP [1977]

HEATH, Professor P. L., Dept of Philosophy, University of Virginia, Charlottesville, USA [1946]

HEBBLETHWAITE, The Rev. B. L., Queen's College, Cambridge CB3 9ET [1976]

HEEGER, Professor Dr R., Paulus Potterlaan 7, NL-3723 Ex. Bilthoven, The Netherlands [1979]

HEIL, Professor J., Dept of Philosophy, Davidson College, Davidson, NC 28036, USA [1987]

HELLMUND, Gunnar, Forbindelsesvejen 116, DK-9400 Nørresundby, Denmark [1996]

HEMP, Mr David, Jesus College, Cambridge CB5 8BL [1994]

HENDEL, Ms Giovanna E., Flat 28, 11 Endsleigh Gardens, London WC1H 0EH [1995]

HENDERSON, Mr Simon A., 73 Shortlands Road, Kingston-upon-Thames, Surrey KT2 6HF [1990]

HENDERSON, Professor T. Y., Dept of Philosophy, University of Saskatchewan, 9 Campus Drive, Saskatoon, Saskatchewan, Canada S7N 5A5 [1977]

HENDIN, Mr Richard J., 58 Thorparch Road, London SW8 4RU [1993]

HENLEY, Mr D. S., 21A Vincent Gardens, Neasden, London NW2 7RJ [1988]

HEPBURN, Dr E. R., Queensland Bioethics Centre, P.O. Box 3343, South Brisbane, Queensland 4101, Australia [1996]

HEPBURN, Professor R. W., Dept of Philosophy, University of Edinburgh, David Hume Tower, George Square, Edinburgh EH8 9JX [1955]

HERNER, Mr Richard, Pinhills Farm, Bowood Estate, Calne, Wiltshire SN11 0LY [1993]

HERRING, Mr N. J., 94 Steeds Road, London N10 1JD [1991]

HERRING, Mr Patrick, Flat 7, Victoria House, 121 Long Acre, Covent Garden, London WC2E 9PA [1991]

HERSHON, Mr E., 48 Rodney Street, Liverpool L1 9AA [1992]

HERTZBERG, Professor Lars, Vårdbergsgatan 8 B 31, FIN-20700 Åbo, Finland [1983]

HICKS, Professor David, 1 St Colme Drive, Dalgety Bay, Fife, KY11 5LQ [1965]

HIGGINSON, Mr Tim, 110 Waterloo Gardens, Milner Square, London N1 1TY [1994]

HIGGS, G. J. C., 11 Palmers Road, East Sheen, London SW14 7NB [1974]

HILGENBERG, Mr Timothy, 1 Bryanston House, Dorset Street, London W1H 3FQ [1995]

HILL, Dr C., The Vicarage, Church Road, Broughton, Clwyd CH4 0QB [1966]

HILL, Professor Susanne E., Dept of Philosophy, 132 Coughlin Hall, Marguette University, Milwaukee, WI 53233, USA [1991]

HILPINEN, Professor Risto, Dept of Philosophy, University of Miami, P. O. Box 248054, Coral Gables, Florida 33124-4670, USA [1994]

HILTON, John R., Hope Cottage, Nash Hill, Lacock, Wiltshire SN15 2QL [1949]

HINDLEY, Ms Anna, 86a Maygrove Road, London NW6 2ED [1995]

HINTIKKA, Professor Jaakko, Dept of Philosophy, Boston University, 745 Commonwealth Avenue, Boston, MA 02215, USA [1959]

HIRSCHMANN, E. E., 23 The Potteries, Barnet Lane, Barnet, Herts. EN5 2DH [1964]

HISABE, Mr Kazuhiko, 58A Sydenham Road, Croydon CR0 2EF [1993]

HOARE, Mr Richard John, 18 Woodseer Street, London E1 5HD [1993]

HOBSON, Mrs Dawn E., Flat 1, 1 Empress Avenue, Ilford, Essex IG1 3DE [1996]

HODGES, Ms Claire-Louise, 10 Salford Road, Marsden, Oxford OX3 [1994]

HODGSON, Mr M. J. C., 78 Rowley Street, Walsall, West Midlands WS1 2AY [1987]

HODSON, Mr T., 1 Hall Cottages, Alderton Road, Shottisham, Nr. Woodbridge, Suffolk IP12 3EP [1986]

HOERL, Mr Christoph, 55 Tavistock Court, Tavistock Square, London WC1H 9HG [1994]

HOFFMAN, Professor Robert, 98 Christian Avenue, Stony Brook, New York 11790-1202, USA [1960]

HOLBORROW, Professor L. C., Vice-Chancellor, Victoria University of Wellington, Private Bag, Wellington, New Zealand [1964]

HOLLAND, Professor R. F., 9 Ashleigh Road, Leeds LS16 5AX [1950]

HOLLINGS, Mr L. A., 13 Rowan Close, Fishponds, Bristol BS16 3LT [1968]

HOLLIS, Professor Martin, Dept of Philosophy, School of Economic & Social Studies, University of East Anglia, Norwich NR4 7TJ [1967]

HONDERICH, Professor T., Dept of Philosophy, University College, London WC1E 6BT [1962]

HOOKER, Dr B., Dept of Philosophy, University of Reading, Whiteknights, Reading RG6 2AA [1983]

HOOKWAY, Professor C. J., Dept of Philosophy, University of Sheffield, Sheffield S10 2TN [1979]

HOPKINS, Dr J., Dept of Philosophy, King's College, London WC2R 2LS [?]

HOPKINS, Dr R. D., Dept of Philosophy, University of Birmingham, Edgbaston, Birmingham B15 2TT [1992]

HORNER, Mrs Sylvia H., 76 Marble House, Elgin Avenue, London W9 3PT [1995]

HORNSBY, Professor Jennifer, Dept of Philosophy, Birkbeck College, Malet Street, London WC1E 7HX [1995]

HORTON, Keith, 63 Talbot Road, London N6 [1996]

HOSSACK, Dr K., 8 Fairlie Gardens, London SE23 3TE [1988]

HOWIE, Dr G. O., Dept of Philosophy, University of Liverpool, 7 Abercromby Square, P. O. Box 147 , Liverpool L69 3BX [1994]

HOY, Ronald C., Dept of Philosophy, California University of Pennsylvania, P.O. Box 409, California, PA 15419, USA [1996]

HUGHES, Dr Christopher, 37 Edge Hill Court, Edge Hill, Wimbledon, London SW19 4LL [1984]

HUGHES, Mr D. M., 51 Military Road, Heddon, Newcastle-upon-Tyne, NE15 0HA [1984]

HUGHES, Professor R. I. G. , Dept of Philosophy, University of South Carolina, Columbia, SC 29208, USA [1994]

HULL, Mr Stephen, 18 Shanrod Road, Katesbridge, Banbridge, County Down BT32 5PG [1995]

HUMPHREYS, Mr Alfred E., 22 Wantz Haven, Princes Road, Maldon, Essex CM9 7HA [1994]

HUNTER, Professor G. B., Dept of Philosophy, University College of North Wales, Bangor, Gwynedd LL57 2DG [1952]

HURST, F. J., 27 Nilverton Avenue, Sunderland, Tyne and Wear [1975]

HURSTHOUSE, Dr R., 91 Eynsham Road, Oxford [1978]

IGGULDEN, Mr David, 5 Malvern Way, London W13 8EB [1992]

IKPE, Dr I., Dept of Philosophy, National University of Lesotho, P.O. Roma 180, Lesotho [1987]

INGARDIA, Dr Richard, St John's University, 300 Howard Avenue, Staten Island, New York 10301USA [1993]

INGRAM, Dr P. G., 16 Castlekaria Manor, Castlehill Road, Belfast BT4 3QL [1981]

IRELAND, Dr M. P., Arts Building C, University of Sussex, Brighton BN1 9QN [1963]
ISAAC, Dr M. T., Surrey House, 80 Lewisham Way, London SE14 6NY [1990]
ISAACSON, Dr Daniel, Sub-Faculty of Philosophy, 10 Merton Street, Oxford OX1 4JJ [1985]
ISHIGURO, Professor Hidé, Dept of Philosophy, Faculty of Letters, Keio University, Mita 2-15-45, Minato-Ku, Tokyo 108, Japan [1960]
IVORY, Mr Mark, Flat 3, 27 Old Steine, Brighton BN1 1EL [1991]
JACK, Mrs J. M. R., King's College, Cambridge CB2 1ST [1967]
JACKMAN, Mr Henry, Dept of Philosophy, University of Toledo, Toledo, OH 43606-3390, USA [1992]
JACKSON, Edna, P. O. Box 2044, Flagstaff, Arizona, AZ 86004, USA [1994]
JACKSON, Jennifer, Dept of Philosophy, University of Leeds, Leeds LS2 9JT [1996]
JACOBSEN, Ms C., Dept of Philosophy, Birkbeck College, Malet Street, London WC1E 7HX [1990]
JAGER, Dr M., Frederick Hendricklaan 5A 2HG, 2582 BP Den Haag, 's-Gravenhage, The Netherlands [1980]
JAMES, Ms Gill, 1 Ridge View, Marshcroft Lane, Tring, Herts HP23 5PU [1993]
JAMES, Dr Susan, Faculty of Philosophy, Cambridge University, Sidgwick Avenue, Cambridge CB3 9DA [1985]
JANAWAY, Dr C., Dept of Philosophy, Birkbeck College, London WC1E 7HX [1986]
JANTZEN, Dr Grace M., Dept of Philosophy of Religion, King's College, Strand, London WC2R 2LS [1980]
JARAB, Dr Josef, Dept of Philosophy, UP Olomouc, Krizkovskeho 10, 77147 Olomouc, Czechoslovakia [1991]
JASZCZOLT, Dr K. M., Dept of Linguistics, Modern & Medieval Languages, Cambridge University, Sidgwick Avenue, Cambridge CB3 9DA [1996]
JAYASURIYA, Dr Hemal, 5 Chilvins Court, 172 Nether Street, West Finchley, London N3 1PQ [1991]
JENNINGS, Mr C., 74 Morton Road, London N1 3BE [1992]
JENKINS, Gary, BDDCA Harare, FCO, King Charles Street, London SW1A 2AH [1985]
JOHANNESSEN, Mr H., Idrettsvn 7, 5037 Solheimsviken, Norway [1970]
JOHN, Christopher J., 48 Aldridge Way, Nepean, Ontario, Canada K2G 4H8 [1991]
JOHNSON, Mr Jeffrey T., 335 Laurel Dr. Apt. 26A, Arcata, CA 95521, USA [1995]
JOHNSTON, Mr Martin, 34 Plover Street, Deepoale, Preston, Lancashire PR1 6TU [1996]
JOHNSTON, Mr Neil, 133 The Georgian Village, Castleknock, Dublin 15, Ireland [1996]
JONES, Dr O. R., Cilan, Cae Melyn, Aberystwyth, Dyfed SY23 2HA [1958]
JONES, R. T., Bissom Bungalow, Penryn, Cornwall [1964]
JONES, Ward E., Wadham College, Oxford OX1 3PN [1994]
JOURNAL OF PHILOSOPHY, 720 Philosophy Hall, Columbia University, New York NY 10027, USA [1979]
JUDSON, Dr R. L., Christ Church, Oxford OX1 1DP [1981]
KACHERE, Mr Romance, 9 Mitchell, Grahame Park Estate, London NW9 5UB [1993]
KAIL, Mr P. J. E., Clare College, Cambridge CB2 1TL [1995]
KANJI, Mr Aly, 1 Egerton Place, London SW3 2EF [1995]
KARAVAKOU-MOURNOURAS, Mrs Vicky, 29 The Shrubbery, Grosvenor Road, Wanstead, London E11 2EL [1992]

KASSMAN, A. A., 31 West Heath Drive, London NW11 7QC [1954]
KAUNE, Professor F. J., Am Stadtpark 30, 38667 Bad Harzburg, Germany [1985]
KEEFE, Ms R. J., Robinson College, Cambridge CB3 9AN [1992]
KEIL, Mr Stephen, Breslauer Str. 34, 40231 Düsseldorf, West Germany [1993]
KEKES, Professor John, 2041 Cook Road, Ballston Lake, NY 12019, USA [1980]
KELLY, Mr John, 18 Harraden Road, Blackheath, London SE3 8BZ [1985]
KEMP, Mr D. R. J., 45 Green Hill Close, Copped Hall, Camberley, Surrey GU15 1PG [1963]
KENNETT, Miss Maxine, Fuchsia Cottage, Sydenham, Oxford OX9 4LJ [1996]
KENNY, Ms Zehanne, 34 Darling Estate, Navan Road, Dublin 7, Ireland [1996]
KHATAMI, Mr Mahmoud, 19 Kepier Court, Durham DH1 1HX [1995]
KHILKOFF-BOULDING, Mrs M., Sandhills Maplesden, Stonegate via Wadhurst, East Sussex TN5 7EL [1994]
KHIN ZAW, Miss S., 4 Devereux Road, London SW11 6JS [1971]
KIERAN, Dr Matthew L., Dept of Philosophy, University of Leeds, Leeds LS2 9JT [1992]
KILPATRICK, Ms Thérèse, 31 Maury Road, London N16 7BP [1993]
KIM, Professor Jaegwon, Dept of Philosophy, Box 1918, Brown University, Providence, RI 02912, USA [1990]
KING, Dr Peter J., 31 Hendred Street, Oxford OX4 2EE [1993]
KIRK, Professor Robert, Dept of Philosophy, The University, Nottingham NG7 2RD [1967]
KIVY, Professor Peter, 37 West 12th Street, New York NY 10011, USA [1978]
KJELLERUP, Mr Kevin T., 1418 N. Adams St., Tallahassee, FL 32303-5525, USA [1994]
KLAUDAT, Mr André N., Flat 29, Summertown House, 369 Banbury Road, Oxford OX2 7RB [1992]
KNEALE, Mrs M., 4 Bridge End, Grassington, Nr Skipton, N. Yorks, BD23 5NH [1937]
KNIGHT, Ms Karen, Magdalen College, Oxford OX1 4AU [1991]
KNOPF, Mr Steven, 209A Willesden Lane, London NW6 7YR [1992]
KNOWLES, Mr Dudley, Dept of Moral Philosophy, University of Glasgow, Glasgow G12 8QQ [1976]
KNOWLES, Mr Jonathan, Dept of Philosophy, Birkbeck College, London WC1E 7HX [1991]
KOLBEL, Mr Max, Dept of Philosophy, King's College London, Strand, London WC2R 2LS [1992]
KONDAL, Mrs Elizabeth, 25 Shelgate Road, London SW11 1BD [1987]
KÖRNER, Professor S., 10 Belgrave Road, Bristol BS8 2AB [1946]
KOSZUTA, Mr Jan. A., 60 Bewdley Street, London N1 1HD [1990]
KRÁCHAN, Ms S., Flat C, 60c Culverley Road, London SE6 2LA [1994]
KRETSCHMER, Dr Martin, 8 Chevening Road, London SE10 0LB [1996]
KRIEGER, Mr Jerry, 1700 Civic Centre Dr. #616, Santa Clara, CA 95050, USA [1994]
KUPPERMAN, Professor Joel J., U-54 University of Connecticut, Storrs, CT 06269-2054, USA [1985]
KURUVILLA, Mr Anil, 141 Church Lane, London SW17 9PW [1989]
LACEWING, Mr Michael, 180 Herschel Crescent, Oxford OX4 3TY [1992]
LACEY, Dr A. R., Dept of Philosophy, King's College, Strand, WC2R 2LS [1954]
LADIMEJI, Mr D., Flat 5, 10A Airlie Gardens, Campden Hill Road, London W8 7AL [1987]
LADYMAN, Mr James, Dept of Philosophy, University of Leeds, Leeds LS2 9JT [1995]
LAKELIN, Mr P. J. M., 7 Cranmer Road, Cambridge CB3 [1993]

LAKHANI, Mr Jay, 6 Lea Gardens, Wembley, Middx HA9 7SE [1996]
LALL, Mr Nehru, 254 Grange Road, Guildford, Surrey [1991]
LAMBERT, A. C., 2 Shaw Court, Ninehams Road, Caterham, Surrey CR2 5LL [1976]
LAMPE, Mr Raymond, 7108 66th Street, Apt. L3, Glendale, NY 11385, USA [1994]
LANGTRY, Dr Bruce, Dept of Philosophy, The University of Melbourne, Parkville, Victoria 3052, Australia [1994]
LARGE, Mr D. N., 35 Easedale Avenue, Newcastle upon Tyne NE3 5TA [1985]
LARKIN, Mr William S., 216 W. Victoria #105, Santa Barbara, CA 93101, USA [1995]
LARRETA, Sr Juan, S. A. D. A. F., Bulnes 642, 1176 Buenos Aires, Argentina [1988]
LARVOR, Dr B., Dept of Philosophy, 7 Abercromby Square, The University of Liverpool, P.O. Box 147, Liverpool L69 3BX [1995]
LAURIER, Daniel, Dépt de Philosophie, Université de Montreal, C. P. 6128, Succursale A, Montreal, Québec H3C 3J7, Canada [1992]
LAVAL, Mr D., 81 New Concordia Wharf, Mill Street, London SE1 2BB [1987]
LAVERS, Mr Paul, 7 Marine Square, Kemptown, Brighton BN2 1DL [1993]
Le FEUVRE, Mrs P., 4 Probert Close, Aldermans Meadow, Leominster, Hereford HR6 8LH [1982]
Le POIDEVIN, Dr Robin, Dept of Philosophy, University of Leeds, Leeds LS2 9JT [1987]
LEAL, Dr Fernando, Paseo De Los Robles 4169–4, 45110 Guadalajara, Jal., Mexico [1996]
LECHNIAK, Mr Marek, Dept of Logic & Theory of Knowledge, Catholic University of Lublin, Lublin, Poland [1996]
LEE, Mr Barry J., 289 Wightman Road, Hornsey, London N8 0NB [1989]
LEE, Mrs Penny, 83, The Vineyard, Richmond, Surrey TW10 6AT [1995]
LEE, Robyn L., 1807 North Elm #408, Denton, Texas 76201-3023, USA [1994]
LEITE, Mr Adam J., 31 Philips St., Arlington, MA 02174, USA [1996]
LEMOS, Ms Irene Nikoias, Venice Yard House, Flat 1, 40 Smith Square, London SW1P 3HL [1994]
LEMOS, Professor Ramon, Dept of Philosophy, University of Miami, Coral Gables, Miami, FL 33124, USA [1956]
LEONTSINIS, Ms Eleni, Room 600, Lillian Penson Hall, Talbot Square, London W2 1TT [1994]
LEONTSINIS, Mr Nikos, Room 600, Lillian Penson Hall, Talbot Square, London W2 1TT [1994]
LETHBRIDGE, Mr J. B., Englische Seminar, Universität Tübingen, 50 Wilhelm-strasse, 72074 Tübingen, Germany [1995]
LEVINE, James, Dept of Philosophy, Trinity College, Dublin 2, Ireland [1996]
LEVINE, Professor M. P., Dept of Philosophy, The University of Western Australia, Nedlands, Western Australia 6907, Australia [1996]
LEWIS, Dr H. A., Dept of Philosophy, University of Leeds, Leeds LS2 9JT [1964]
LEWIS, Mr P. B., Dept. of Philosophy, University of Edinburgh, David Hume Tower, George Square, Edinburgh EH8 9JX [1973]
LILLEHAMMER, Mr Hallvard, Peterhouse, Cambridge CB2 1RD [1992]
LIN, L. M., 50-03, 203 Street, Bayside, NY 11364, USA [1994]
LIN, Dr Yunqing, Somerville College, Oxford OX2 6HD [1996]
LINDE, Mr L. K., 24 Baron Street, London N1 9ES [1993]
LINDSAY, Christopher J., 13 Golf View, Bearsden, Glasgow G61 4HH [1991]
LIPTON, Dr Peter, Dept of History & Philosophy of Science, Free School Lane, Cambridge CB2 3RH [1989]

LITTLEJOHN COOK, Mr Peter, 2nd Floor Flat, 2 Rosary Gardens, London SW7 4NS [1996]

LLOYD, Mr R., 32 Derwent Road, Harpenden, Herts. AL5 3NU [1987]

LLOYD-THOMAS, Mr D.A., 5 Sutcliffe Close, London NW11 6NT [1969]

LODGE, Paul, Dept of Philosophy, Davison Hall, Douglass Campus, Rutgers University, New Brunswick, NJ 08903-0270, USA [1989]

LOKARE, Dr V.G., 21 Ashleigh Gardens, Sutton, Surrey SM1 3EL [1959]

LONG, Professor A, Dept of Classics, University of California, Berkeley, CA 94700, USA [1969]

LONG, Peter, Dept of Philosophy, The University, Leeds 2 [1956]

LOWE, Dr E. J., Dept of Philosophy, University of Durham, 50 Old Elvet, Durham DH1 3HN [1980]

LOWE, Mrs S. L., Dept of Philosophy, University of Durham, 50 Old Elvet, Durham DH1 3HN [1985]

LUCAS, Mr J., Merton College, Oxford OX1 4JD [1955]

LUCAS, Professor R. E., Junior, 421 Spring Street, Fleetwood, PA 19522, USA [1980]

LUCHOWSKA, Anna, ul. Opawska 39, 48–340 Glucholazy, Poland [1996]

LUDWIG, Mr Eric, 6517 32nd Ave. N.W., Seattle, WA 98117, USA [1995]

LUMSDEN, Mr Michael, 20 Warblington Road, Emsworth, Hampshire PO10 7HQ [1992]

LUND, Mr James, Evergreen Hill, Spaniards Road, London NW3 7SJ [1982]

LYON, A. J., Dept of Social Science & Humanities, City University, Northampton Square, London EC1V 0HB [1970]

LYONS, Professor David, The Sage School of Philosophy, Goldwin Smith Hall, Cornell University, Ithaca, NY 14850, USA [1970]

LYONS, Professor W. E., Dept of Philosophy, Trinity College, Dublin 2, Ireland [1973]

MacBRIDE, Mr Fraser, Dept of Philosophy, University College London, Gower Street, London WC1E 6BT [1995]

MacCORMICK, Professor D. N., Dept of Public Law, University of Edinburgh, Old College, Edinburgh EH8 [1973]

MACDONALD, Mr Graham, 19 Blackburn Gardens, Didsbury, Manchester M20 9YH [1981]

MacDONALD, Mr N. Iain, Dept of Philosophy, The University of New Brunswick, Fredericton, N. B., Canada [1995]

MacDONALD, Professor R. C., Dept of Philosophy, The University of New Brunswick, Fredericton, N. B., Canada [1995]

MACKIE, Dr David W., Corpus Christi College, Oxford OX1 4JF [1993]

MACKIE, Dr P. J., Dept of Philosophy, University of Birmingham, Edgbaston, Birmingham B15 2TT [1983]

MACKINTOSH, Mr James, 6 Castle Villas, Stroud, Glos. GL5 2HP [1991]

MACPHERSON, Fiona, 17 Lyon Crescent, Bridge of Allan, Stirlinghire, Scotland FK9 4DN [1996]

MADDISON, Mrs Veronica, 6 Troutbeck Close, Twyford, Berks RG10 9DA [1995]

MADELL, Dr G. C., Dept of Philosophy, Edinburgh University, David Hume Tower, George Square, Edinburgh EH8 9JX [1979]

MAGEE, Professor Bryan, 12 Falkland House, Marloes Road, London W8 5LF [1972]

MAGILL, Dr Kevin, 33 Court Road, Wolverhampton WV6 0JN [1992]

MAGNELL, Professor T. A., Dept of Philosophy, Drew University, Madison, NJ 07940-4031, USA [?]

MAHLER, Mr O., 44 Manchester Street, London W1M 5PE [1984]

MAIBOM, Ms Heidi L., 18d Northwood Road, London N6 5TN [1994]

MALIKAIL, Professor J. S., 367 Templeton Street, Sandyhill, Ottawa, Ontario, Canada K1N 6X8 [1977]

MALONEY, Mr Ian, Eichholzweg 4, CH–6312 Steinhausen, Switzerland [1992]

MANDIC, Mr M., 9 Hillcrest Court, 301/303 Brownhill Road, Catford, London SE6 1AH [1989]

MANKOWITZ, Miss Olivia, 26 Longridge Road, London SW5 9SJ [1995]

MANN, Mr Robert G., 39 The Ridgeway, Radlett, Herts WD7 8PT [1995]

MARIANO, Dr José, Dean, CRC-College of Arts & Sciences, Pearl Drive, Ortigas Complex, Pasig 1600, Metro-Manila, Philippines [1990]

MARION, Dr Mathieu, Dept of Philosophy, University of Ottawa, P.O. Box 450, Station A, Ottawa, Ontario, Canada K1N 6N5 [1996]

MARKHAM, K. A., 41 Millbrook Road, Dinas Powys, South Glamorgan CF64 4BZ [1967]

MARSH, Mr M. G., 1 Hyde Road, Richmond, Surrey TW10 6DU [1987]

MARSH, Mr L., c/o 40 Sorrel Bank, Linton Glade, Croydon CR0 9LW [1990]

MARSH, Mr Michael S., 26 1/2 Methley Street, Kennington, London SE11 4AJ [1996]

MARSHALL, Dr G. D., Dept of Philosophy, University of Melbourne, Parkville 3052, Australia [1967]

MARSHALL, Ms S. C., 1 Seale Street, Chester Green, Derby DE1 3RT [1984]

MARSHALL, Miss S. E., Dept of Philosophy, University of Stirling, Stirling, Scotland [1969]

MARTIN, Dr Michael, Dept of Philosophy, University College, Gower Street, London WC1E 6BT [1991]

MARTIN, Mr Christopher, Dept of Philosophy, University of Glasgow, Glasgow G12 8QQ [1994]

MARTINIAN, Mr Alpha, University of London Hall of Residence, Hughes Parry Hall, Cartwright Gardens, London WC1H 9EF [1991]

MASH, Mr A. R., 88 Tudor Road, Upton Park, London E6 1DR [1994]

MASON, Ms Wendy, 42 Lansdowne Drive, London E8 3EG [1995]

MATRAVERS, Dr D. C., 2c Sedgwick Court, Sedgwick Street, Cambridge CB1 3AJ [1988]

MATRAVERS, Dr M. D., Dept of Politics, The University of York, Heslington, York YO1 5DD [1992]

MATTEO, Anthony, Dept of Philosophy, Elizabethtown College, One Alpha Drive, Elizabethtown, PA 17022, USA [1996]

MATTHEW, Mr Simon, 5 Woodbine Avenue, Leicester LE2 1AJ [1992]

MATTHEWS, Miss G. M., St Anne's College, Oxford OX2 6HS [1954]

MAUND, Mrs C., Spring Farm, Fittleworth, Sussex [1933]

MAXWELL, Professor M. J., Dept of Philosophy, Victoria University of Wellington, P. O. Box 600, Wellington, New Zealand 30882 [1995]

MAY, Mr Simon, 129 Riverview Gardens, London SW13 9RA [1994]

MAYO, Professor B., 4 Maynard Road, St Andrews, Fife KY16 8RX [1952]

MAYS, Dr W., Institute of Advance Studies, Manchester Metropolitan Univeristy, All Saints, Manchester M15 6BH [1947]

McADAM, Ms Lynne, 12A Montpelier Vale, Blackheath, London SE3 0TA [1995]

McCABE, Dr M.M., Dept of Philosophy, King's College London, Strand, London WC2R 2LS [1996]

McCLOUGHAN, Mr Meade, 149 Chevening Road, London NW6 6DZ [1995]

McCREE, Mrs M., 7 Poplar Close, Hitchin, Herts. SG4 9LZ [1987]

McCULLAGH, Mr Mark, Dept of Philosophy, University of Pittsburgh, 1001 CL, Pittsburgh, PA 15260, USA [1993]

McCULLOCH, Professor Gregory, Dept of Philosophy, University of Birmingham, Birmingham B15 2TT [1985]

McDONNELL, Mr S. S., 70 Temple Road, Temple Cowley, Oxford OX4 2EZ [1988]

McFARLAND, Mr Duncan, Dept of Philosophy, University of Birmingham, Edgbaston, Birmingham B15 2TT [1995]

McFEE, Professor Graham, 19 Vicarage Road, Eastbourne, E. Sussex BN20 8AS [1973]

McGOLDRICK, Miss P., 9 Station Approach, Sudbury, Middlesex HA0 2LA [1977]

McKENZIE, Ms Michele, 4 Erskine Road, Primrose Hill, London NW3 3AJ [1995]

McKINNON, Ms Catriona, 66 Aylesbury Road, London SE17 2EH [1992]

McKIRAHAN, Professor R. D., Dept of Philosophy, Pomona College, Claremont, CA 91711-6355, USA [1988]

McKNIGHT, C. J., Dept of Philosophy, Queen's University, Belfast BJ7 [1966]

McLAUGHLIN, Dr R. M., Philosophy Dept, Macquarie University, N.S.W. 2109, Australia [1967]

McMANUS, Dr Denis, Dept of Philosophy, University of Southampton, Highfield, Southampton SO17 1BJ [1995]

McNAUGHTON, D. N., Dept of Philosophy, University of Keele, Keele, Staffs. ST5 5BG [1973]

McQUEEN, D. A., Dept of Philosophy, The University, Nottingham [1967]

MEHMET, Mr Naci, 2 Upton Leaze, 63 London Road, Forest Hill, London SE23 3UD [1992]

MEIKLE, Dr S., Dept of Philosophy, University of Glasgow, Glasgow G12 8QQ [1996]

MELLOR, Professor D. H., Faculty of Philosophy, University of Cambridge, Sidgwick Avenue, Cambridge CB3 9DA [1966]

MENDUS, Professor S. L., Dept of Politics, University of York, Heslington, York YO1 5DD [1984]

MENZIES, Dr Peter, School of History, Philosophy & Politics, Macquarie University, North Ryde, Sydney NSW 2109, Australia [1992]

MERTENS, Ms Kerstin, 58 Strathearn Road, Edinburgh EH9 2AD [1993]

MIDGLEY, G. C., 1A Collingwood Terrace, Jesmond, Newcastle-upon-Tyne, NE2 2JP [1949]

MIGOTTI, Professor Mark, Dept of Philosophy, Hamilton College, 198 College Hill Road, Clinton, NY 13323, USA [1987]

MILLAR, Professor A., Dept of Philosophy, University of Stirling, Stirling FK9 4AL [1976]

MILLER, Dr Alexander, Dept of Philosophy, University of Birmingham, Birmingham B15 2TT [1988]

MILLICAN, Dr P., Dept of Philosophy, University of Leeds, Leeds LS2 9JT [1986]

MILLIOS, Mr Tom, 3 Hickin Street, London E14 3LW [1994]

MILLS, Mr Adam, 32 Arlington Avenue, Islington, London N1 7AY [1992]

MIND, Editorial Administrator, Dept of Philosophy, King's College, Strand, London WC2R 2LS [1991]

MIR, Miss Naseam, 49 Dixon Avenue, Queens Park, Glasgow G42 8EG [1996]

MIR, Mr Tariq, 49 Dixon Avenue, Queens Park, Glasgow G42 8EG [1994]

MITCHELL, Professor Basil, Oriel College, Oxford OX1 4EW [1949]

MITCHELL, Dr David, 4/29 Trinity Church Square, London SE1 4HY [1992]

MITCHELL, Mr James Stuart, South View, Potters Heath Road, Welwyn, Hertfordshire AL6 9SY [1995]

MIZOGUCHI, Mr Kenji, 2-3-20-603 Morigo-cho, Nada, Kobe 657, Japan [1990]

MOISEYEV, Alexei, Dept of Philosophy, University College London, Gower Street, London WC1E 6BT [1996]

MOMTCHILOFF, Mr Peter, Editor, Philosophy, Oxford University Press, Walton Street, Oxford OX2 6DP [1994]

MONCASTER, J. A [1962]

MONTEFIORE, Alan, Balliol College, Oxford OX1 3BJ [1952]

MOONAN, Dr Lawrence, 43 Ashhurst Way, Oxford [1992]

MOONEY, Mr Paul, Flat 3, 37/41 Gower Street, London WC1E 6HH [1995]

MOORE, Dr A. W., St Hugh's College, Oxford OX2 6LE [1985]

MORAN, Professor Dermot, Dept of Philosophy, University College Dublin, Belfield, Dublin 4, Republic of Ireland [1992]

MORDAUNT, Ms P. M., 16 Blenheim Road, Reading RG1 5NQ [1993]

MORICE, G., 46 Queen Street, Edinburgh EH2 3NH [1960]

MORLEY, Mr J. Thomas, P. O. Box 5155 PSU, Pembroke, NC 28372, USA [1994]

MORPHY, Mrs Frances, Arts and Reference, Oxford University Press, Walton Street, Oxford OX2 6DP [1991]

MORRIS, Dr M. R., Meadow Cottage, Ripe, Lewes, E. Sussex BN8 6AX [1985]

MORRISON, Ms Kirstie, University College, Oxford OX1 4HB [1991]

MORTIMORE, Mr J., 5 Sandfield Road, Thornton Heath, Surrey CR7 8AW [1996]

MORTON, Professor Adam, Dept of Philosophy, 9 Woodland Road, Bristol BS8 1TB [1991]

MOSELEY, Dr Darran A., 8 The Paddocks, Walton on the Wolds, Melton Mowbray, Leicestershire LE14 4AT [1996]

MOSER, Birgit, 128 Habsburgerstr., 79104 Freiburg, Germany [1991]

MOTHERSILL, Professor Mary, Dept of Philosophy, Barnard College, 3009 Broadway, New York NY 10027, USA [1989]

MOUNCE, H. O., Dept of Philosophy, University College of Swansea, Singleton Park, Swansea, Wales [1964]

MUDGE, Mr Ben, 39 Constantine Road, London NW3 2LN [1993]

MULLARKEY, Dr John, 56 Linskill Terrace, North Shields, Tyne and Wear NE30 2EP [1996]

MULLER, Mr Vincent C., Kegelhofstr. 44, D-20251 Hamburg, Germany [1991]

MULLINS, Anne, 7 Lower Common South, Putney, London SW15 1BP [1994]

MULLOCK, Philip, 7524 Graymore Road, Pittsburgh, PA 15221-3116, USA [1962]

MUMFORD, Dr Stephen, Dept of Philosophy, University of Nottingham, Nottingham NG7 2RD [1990]

MURCHO, Desidério O., Rua Bento de Jesus Caraça 16, Vale de Milhaços, 2855 Corroios, Portugal [1994]

MURPHY, Mr D. P., Graduate Dept of Philosophy, Davison Hall, Douglas Campus, New Brunswick, NJ 08903, USA [1993]

MURPHY, Mr M. J., 2 Spingate Close, Hornchurch, Essex RM12 6SW [1989]

MURRAY, Mr David, Dept of Philosophy, Birkbeck College, London WC1E 7HX [1959]

MYNOTT, Dr R. J., Managing Director, Publishing Division, Cambridge University Press, Edinburgh Building, Shaftesbury Road, Cambridge CB2 2RU [1989]

NAILS, Professor Debra, Dept of Philosophy, Mary Washington College, Fredericksburg VA 22401, USA [1985]

NAISH, Mr M., 11 Drayton Close, Irby, Wirral L61 2XS [1969]

NANI, Marco, Largo Pannonia 23, I-00183 Roma, Italy [1992]

NATHAN, Dr N. M. L., 133 Shrewsbury Road, Birkenhead, Merseyside L43 8SR [1965]

NELSON, Dr Mark, Dept of Philosophy, University of Leeds, Leeds LS6 3QF [1995]

NEUMUELLER, Mr Ralf, Schlesierweg 27, 66538 Neunkirchen, Germany [1989]

NEWFIELD, J. G. H., 96 Abbots Park, St Albans, Herts. AL1 1TP [1956]

NEWMAN, Professor A. J., Dept of Philosophy & Religion, University of Nebraska at Omaha, Omaha, Nebraska 68182-0265, USA [1981]

NEWMAN, Mr Jeremy P., 11 The Green, Clophill, Bedford MK45 4AD [1995]

NEWTON, Mr David, Flat 1, 5 Oakdale Road, London SW16 2HW [1993]

NEWTON-SMITH, Dr W., Balliol College, Oxford OX1 3BJ [1978]

NICLAUSS, Herr Norbert, Lehrstuhl für Philosophie, Universität Bayreuth, D-95440 Bayreuth, Germany [1990]

NOKES, S. M., Oak Tree Farm, Clay Hills Road, Kelsale, Saxmundham, Suffolk IP17 2PW [1991]

NOONAN, Mr H. W., 9 Margaret Grove, Harborne, Birmingham B13 9JJ [1984]

NOORDHOF, Dr P. J. P., Dept of Philosophy, University of Nottingham, University Park, Nottingham NG7 2RD [1988]

NORRIS, Mr Kevan, 54 Plimsoll Road, London N4 2EL [1989]

NUDDS, Mr Matthew, 65A Chesterton Road, Cambridge CB4 3AN [1994]

O'BRIEN, Mr Dan, 28 Forest Road, Moseley, Birmingham B13 9DH [1996]

O'BRIEN, Ms L. F., Dept of Philosophy, University College London, Gower Street, London WC1E 6BT [1993]

O'CASEY, Mr Martin, 42 Chalfont Road, Oxford OX2 6TH [1987]

O'CONNOR, Dr Brian, Dept of Philosophy, University College Dublin, Belfield, Dublin 4, Ireland [1996]

O'CONNOR, Professor D. J., Dept of Philosophy, The University, Exeter, Devon [1943]

O'CONNOR, Dr Tony, Dept of Philosophy, University College, Cork, Ireland [1996]

O'HAGAN, Timothy, School of Economic & Social Studies, University of East Anglia, Norwich NR4 7TJ [1996]

O'HEAR, Professor A., Interdisciplinary Human Studies, University of Bradford, Bradford, W. Yorkshire BD4 1DP [1975]

O'NEILL, Mr Basil, Dept of Philosophy, University of Dundee, Dundee DD1 4HN [1994]

O'NEILL, Maire, Dept of Philosophy, University College Dublin, Dublin 4, Republic of Ireland [1995]

O'NEILL, Dr O. S., Newham College, Cambridge CB3 9DE [1985]

O'SHAUGHNESSY, Brian, 22 Heath Hurst Road, Hampstead, London NW3 2RX [1990]

OAKESHOTT, Miss Anna, 45 Cranberry Lane, London E16 4PD [1993]

ODERBERG, Dr D. S., Dept of Philosophy, University of Reading, Reading RG6 2AA [1988]

ODLUM, Dr H. R., Burgh Cottage, Woodbridge, Suffolk IP13 6PT [1966]

OKA, Professor M., Fujidanchi 3–4 2 Chome, Ohmachi-Nishi, Asaminami-Ku, Hiroshima 731-01, Japan [1974]

OKASHA, Samir, 46A Western Road, Oxford OX1 4LG [1996]

OLIVER, Dr Alex, Queen's College, Cambridge CB3 9ET [1991]

OLIVIERI, Dr G., Dept of Philosophy, University of Leeds, Leeds LS6 2AU [1994]

OMELYANTCHIK, Dr Valentin, 252001 Kiev-1, Trochsviatitelska 4, Institute of Philosophy, Ukraine [1994]

ONOF, Dr C. J., 131 Geary Road, London NW10 1HS [1990]

OPPENHEIMER, Lady Helen, L'Aiguillon, Grouville, Jersey, Channel Islands [1962]

OPPLER, Mrs Corinna, Flat 154, 3 Whitehall Street, London SW1A 2EL [1990]

ORCHARD, Ms Vivienne, Ground Floor Flat, 54A Nightingale Lane, London SW12 8NY [1991]

ORENSTEIN, Professor Alex, Ph. D. Program in Philosophy/Box 520, Graduate Center, 33 West 42 Street, New York, NY 10036-8099, USA [1995]

ORTEGA, Miss Angela, 30 Mendora Road, London SW6 7NB [1993]

OSBORNE, Dr Catherine, Dept of Philosophy, University College, Singleton Park, Swansea SA2 8PP [1990]

OVER, Dr D. E., Sunderland Polytechnic, Forster Building, Chester Road, Sunderland SR1 3SD [1970]

OWENS, Dr David, Dept of Philosophy, University of Sheffield, Sheffield S10 2TN [1996]

OZSIVADJIAN, Nasip, 25 Cumberland Avenue, Guildford, Surrey GU2 6RQ [1993]

PADDON, Miss D. S., 4 Lewes Road, Ditchling, Sussex BN6 8TT [1994]

PAGET, Mr Terence, 163 St. Giles Road, Tile Cross, Birmingham B33 0PD [1989]

PAGONIS, Dr Constantine, 63A Thoday Street, Cambridge CB1 3AT [1991]

PALMER, Dr A. W., 1 Chichester Terrace, Brighton BN2 1FG [1962]

PALUMBO, Mr J., 117 Borden Street, Toronto, Ontario, Canada M5S 2N2 [1994]

PANK, Mrs P., 15 Torriano Cottages, London NW5 2TA [1987]

PAPINEAU, Professor David, Dept of Philosophy, King's College, Strand, London WC2R 2LS [1988]

PARKER, Mr Michael J., c/o Dept of Philosophy, University of Leeds, Leeds LS2 9JT [1994]

PARKER, Dr M. J., 5 Pages Lane, Muswell Hill, London N10 1PU [1991]

PARRY, Mr Gareth, Flat 10, 34 Spiers Wharf, Glasgow G4 9TB [1987]

PARRY, S. J., Dept of Philosophy, University of Leeds, Leeds LS2 9JT [1975]

PARTRIDGE, Mr M., Dept of Philosophy, King's College, University of Aberdeen, Old Aberdeen AB9 2UB [1987]

PASK, Mrs Elizabeth, 36 Conifer Cast, Wash Common, Newbury, Berks RG14 6RT [1995]

PASKINS, B., King's College, Strand, London WC2R 2LS [1971]

PASQUALE, Mr Pete, 2516 North Fremontia Drive, San Bernardino, CA 92404, USA [1995]

PATTERSON, Mr James W., 3 Dower Road, Four Oaks, Sutton Coldfied, West Midlands B75 6UA [1992]

PATTERSON, Dr S., Dept of Philosophy, Birkbeck College, Malet Street, London WC1E 7HX [1995]

PAULINO-ALVAREZ, Mr A., 35 Queen's Gate, London SW7 5JA [1987]

PAYA, Dr A., 16 Guinness Court, Cadogan Street, London SW3 2PE [1987]

PEACOCKE, Professor Christopher, Magdalen College, Oxford OX1 4AU [1984]

PEARS, Professor D., Christ Church, Oxford OX1 1DP [1948]

PEEBLES, Mr David J., 44 Dufton Road, Quinton, Birmingham B32 2PY [1993]

PENDLEBURY, Professor Michael, Dept of Philosophy, CB#3125 Caldwell Hall, The University of North Carolina, Chapel Hill, NC 27599-3125, USA [1986]

PENNINGTON, Mr C., 182 Enfield Chase, Guisborough, Cleveland TS14 7LG [1994]

PENSTON, Mr C. M., 67 Zion Road, Thornton Heath, Surrey CR7 8RJ [1993]

PEÑA, Professor Lorenzo, Instituto de Filosofía del CSIC, Pinar 25, E-28006 Madrid, Spain [1981]

PERRY, Professor John, Dept of Philosophy, Stanford University, Stanford, CA 94305, USA [1991]

PETTIT, Professor Philip, R. S. S. S., Australian National University, Canberra, ACT 0200, Australia [1979]

PHEMISTER, Dr Pauline, Dept of Philosophy, University of Liverpool, 7 Abercromby Square, Liverpool L69 3BX [1985]

PHILLIPS, Professor D. Z., Dept of Philosophy, University College of Swansea, Singleton Park, Swansea SA2 8PP [1962]

PHILOSOPHICAL REVIEW, 218 Goldwin Smith Hall, Cornell University, Ithaca, New York NY 14853, USA [1979]

PIGDEN, Dr Charles R., Dept of Philosophy, University of Otago, Box 56 Dunedin, New Zealand [?]

PIKE, J. E., c/o Dept of Philosophy, Glasgow University, Glasgow G12 8QQ [1994]

PINCHAM, Mr Don, 98 Carshalton Park Road, Carshalton, Surrey SM5 3SG [1990]

PIOTR, Dr Gutowski, Dept of Philosophy, Catholic University of Lublin, Ul. Raclawickie 14, 20–950 Lublin, Poland [1995]

PLITHAS, Mr Evangelos, 52 Aetideon Street, Athens 15561, Greece [1996]

PLOWDEN, S., 69 Albert Street, London NW1 [1961]

PODGER, Mr J. P. E., Flat 1, 103 Manor Avenue, Brockley, London SE4 1TD [1988]

POLLARD, Bill, Hatfield College, Durham DH1 3RQ [1996]

POLLARD, Mr Jason, New Block, Flat FDG5, 109 Camden Road, London NW1 9HA [1996]

POMPA, Professor L., Dept of Philosophy, PO Box 363, University of Birmingham, Birmingham B15 2TT [1962]

PONTIN, Mr Andrew, Flat 3, 30 Nottingham Place, London W1M 3FD [1994]

POTTER, Professor E. F., Mills College, 5000 MacArthur Blvd, Oakland, CA 94613, USA [1977]

POTTS, T. C., Dept of Philosophy, University of Leeds, Leeds 2 [1967]

PRESTON, Dr John M., Dept of Philosophy, University of Reading, White Knights, Reading RG6 2AA [1990]

PRICE, Mr A. W., Dept of Philosophy, University of York, Heslington, York YD1 5DD [1976]

PRINCE, Dr L. P., 149 Gillott Road, Edgbaston, Birmingham B16 0ET [1982]

PROSSER, Mr Alan, 7 Mellish Court, Ewell Road, Surbiton, Surrey KT6 6EU [1991]

PSILLOS, Dr Stathis, Centre for the Philosophy of Natural & Social Sciences, LSE, Houghton Street, London WC2A 2AE [1991]

PUNFORD, Mr M. A. U. H., Apartment Five, One to Two, High Street, via Fish Street, Shrewsbury, Shropshire SY1 1SP [1993]

PUTMAN, Professor Daniel, Dept of Philosophy, University of Wisconsin, Fox Valley, 1478 Midway Road, Menasha, WI 54952, USA [1985]

PYBUS, Dr Elizabeth M., 4 Northbank Cottages, Cameron, St Andrews, Fife KY16 8PE [1973]

QUAYLE, Mr Martin, 28 Craigmore Tower, Guildford Road, Woking, Surrey GU22 7RB [1995]

QUERALTÓ, Professor Dr., Ramón, Sales y Ferré 16, 41004 Sevilla, Spain [1983]

QUILTER, Mr John G., Dept of Philosophy & Theology, Australian Catholic University, P.O. Box 968, North Sydney, NSW 2060, Australia [1992]

QUINN, Mr Martin, Dept of Civil Engineering, Imperial College, London SW7 2BU [1993]

QUINTON, Lord, The Mill House, Turville, Henley-on-Thames, Oxon RG9 6QL [1950]

RADCLIFFE, Mr W. J., 32 Queens Road, Teddington, Middlesex TW11 0LR [1991]

RAFF, Professor Charles, Dept of Philosophy, Swarthmore College, 214 Rutgers Avenue, Swarthmore, PA 19081-1925, USA [1985]

RAHIMI, Mrs S., Flat D, 73 Carleton Road, London N7 [1992]

RAMACHANDRAN, Mr Murali, School of Cognitive & Computing Sciences, University of Sussex, Falmer, Brighton BN1 9QH [1986]

RANKIN, K. W., 4285 Cedar Hill Road, Victoria BC, Canada V8N 3C7 [1957]

RASEKH, Mr M., 7 Ruby Street, Manchester M15 6RS [1996]

RAWLINGS, Gayle, Clare Hall, Cambridge CB3 9AL [1995]

READ, Mr S. J., Burnt Cottage, Burnt Lane, Orford, Suffolk IP12 2NJ [1987]

READ, Dr S. L., Dept of Logic & Metaphysics, University of St Andrews, Fife KY16 9AL [1977]

READER, Dr C. S., 30 Harvey Goodwin Avenue, Cambridge CB4 3EU [1994]

REES, D. A., Jesus College, Oxford OX1 3DW [1947]

REES, Mr W. J., Hendre Jim, Lower Moor, St Davids, Haverfordwest, Dyfed SA62 6RP [1957]

REIBETANZ, Ms Sophia, Holywell Manor, Manor Road, Oxford OX1 3HU [1994]

RENNARD, Ray, Dept of Philosophy, Johns Hopkins University, Baltimore, MD 21218, USA [1996]

REQUATE, Dr Angela, Wittgensteinarkivet ved, Universitetet i Bergen, Harald Hårfagresgt. 31, N–5007 Bergen, Norway [1994]

RESTALL, Greg, Automated Reasoning Project, Australian National University, Canberra ACT 0200, Australia [1996]

RETALLICK, Mr Gary, Dept of Philosophy, King's College, Strand, London WC2R 2LS [1990]

REVILL-TAYLOR, Mr G. A. D., Flat 4C, 14 Benhill Road, Sutton, Surrey SM1 3RL [1995]

REVISTA DE FILOSOFÍA LATINOAMERICANA, Casilla de Correo 5379, 1000 Buenos Aires, Argentina [1994]

REX-TAYLOR, Mr David, 28 Pates Manor Drive, Bedfont, Feltham, Middlesex TW14 8JJ [1972]

RICE, Mr D. H., Christ Church, Oxford OX1 1DP [1987]

RICH, Professor Paul, Universidad de las Americas, Apartado Postal 100, Cholula 72820, Puebla, Mexico [1989]

RIDHA, Mr Shawky W., 55 Chestnut Grove, New Malden, Surrey KT3 3JJ [1992]

RIEGER, Mr Adam, 18 Berkeley Place, London SW19 4NN [1991]

RIFAT, Mr Serdar, 422 Larkshall Road, London E4 9JF [1995]

RIPLEY, Mr Matthew, 6 Trelake Road, St. Austell, Cornwall PL25 5NH [1991]

ROBBINS, Mrs M. J., Flat 1, 35 Elm Park Gardens, London SW10 9QF [1995]

ROBERTS, Professor T. A., Dept of Philosophy, The University College of Wales Aberystwyth, Hugh Owen Building, Aberystwyth, Dyfed SY23 3DY [1963]

ROBERTSON, Mr Colin, 20 Mary McArthur House, Hornsey Lane Estate, London N19 3BS [1992]

ROBERTSON, Dr Neil G., University of King's College, Halifax, Nova Scotia, Canada B3H 2A1 [1987]

ROBINSON, H. M., Dept of Philosophy, University of Liverpool, PO Box 147, Liverpool L69 3BX [1982]

RODIN, David, Magdalen College, Oxford OX1 4AU [1996]

RODRIGUEZ-VALLS, Dr Francisco, C/Castilla 139, 1°C, 41010–Sevilla, Spain [1989]

ROESSLER, Mr Johannes, Magdalen College, Oxford OX1 4AV [1994]

ROMNEY, Miss G., 32 Hanover Square, Leeds LS3 1AW [?]

ROONEY, Mr P., 46 Hale Gate Road, Halebank, Widnes WA8 8LZ [1990]

ROSE, Dr C. J., Garden Flat, 60 The Ridgway, London SW19 4RA [1976]

ROSS, Mr G., Flat 2, 7 Mornington Avenue, London W14 8UJ [1966]

ROSSITER, Anne, 31 Endymion Road, London N4 1EQ [1995]

ROWLAND, C., Peterhouse, Cambridge University, Cambridge [1996]

ROWLANDS, Dr Peter, 1 Sheerwater Close, Bruche, Warrington, Cheshire WA1 3JE [1995]

ROXBEE-COX, Mr J. W., 1 Rectory Barn, Halton, Lancaster LA2 6LT [1959]

RUBEN, Professor David, Dept of Philosophy, London School of Economics, Houghton Street, London WC2A 2AE [1971]

RUBINSTEIN, Mr Arthur, P.O. Box 10, Flagler Beach, FL 32136-0010, USA [1995]

RUIZ, Ingrid, 16 Broomhall Road, Sanderstead, Surrey [1991]

RUNDLE, Bede, Trinity College, Oxford OX1 3BH [1967]

RUST, Dr A.J., Balberstrasse 10, CH-8038 Zurich, Switzerland [1988]

RYAN, Mr Richard, 25 Millbank, West Derby, Liverpool L13 0BN [1994]

RYNHOLD, Mr Daniel, 3 Fir Tree Court, Allun Lane, Elstree, Herts WD6 3NF [1994]

SAAB, Dr Salma, Retama 82-B, Tlalpan, Mexico 14080 D.F., Mexico [1996]

SAAGUA, Professor J. de Deus Santos, Rua Martim Vaz 42, 2# Esq., 1100–Lisboa, Portugal [1992]

SABATES, Marcelo, Dept of Philosophy, Brown University, Providence, RI 02912, USA [1995]

SABIN, Mr Miles, 10 Pembroke Gardens, Hove, East Sussex BN3 5DY [1990]

SACKS, Dr M. D., Dept of Philosophy, University of Essex, Wivenhoe Park, Colchester CO4 3SQ [1983]

SADDINGTON, Mr John, 4 Peel Close, Holmefield Lane, Heslington, York YO1 5EN [1996]

SAINSBURY, Professor R. M., Dept of Philosophy, King's College, Strand, London WC2R 2LS [1969]

SAITO, Professor S., 1462 2-Chome Nakazato, Kiyose-shi, Tokyo, Japan [1979]

SALEHNEJAD, Mr A., Flat D, 73 Carleton Road, London N7 [1991]

SALES, Mr Francisco, Av. Resurgimiento #50, 24100 Campeche, Camp., Mèxico [1994]

SALLES, Professor Maurice, 1 Allée Du Bucquet, 14111 Louvigny, France [1989]

SALLES, Mr Ricardo, Chabacano 35-27, Delegacion Contreras, Mexico D.F. 10810, Mexico [1992]

SALMON, Professor Nathan, Dept of Philosophy, University of California, Santa Barbara, CA 93106, USA [1988]

SASONOW, Mr M., Highlands, 28 Pound Lane, Sonning, Berks. RG4 0XE [1988]

SAVAGE, Mr Peter, 7 Girton Close, Fareham, Hants. PO14 4QZ [1996]

SAVILE, Dr A. B., Dept of Philosophy, King's College, Strand, London, WC2R 2LS [1968]

SAW, Miss Than, Flat 22, 1/6 Dufours Place, Broadwick Street, London W1V 3FD [1994]

SAWADA, Ms Kaya, 1-6-13 Chiyogaoka Asao-ku, Kawasaki-shi, Kanagawa-ken, Japan 215 [1995]

SAWYER, Miss Sarah, Dept of Philosophy, King's College, Strand, London WC2R 2L [1992]

SCALTSAS, Mrs Patricia Ward, c/o Philosophy, DHT, George Square, Edinburgh EH8 9JX [1989]

SCALTSAS, Dr Theodore, Dept of Philosophy, University of Edinburgh, David Hume Tower, George Square, Edinburgh EH8 9JX [1982]

SCHEIN, Professor Barry, Dept of Linguistics, GFS 301, MC-1693, University of Southern California, Los Angeles, California 90089-1693, USA [1991]

SCHILBRACK, Mr Kevin, 17301 Southwest 94th Avenue, Miami, FL 33157-4426, USA [1994]

SCHMID, Dr Peter A., Badenerstr. 79, CH-8004 Zürich, Switzerland [1994]

SCHNEIDER, Mr Steven, Dept of Philosophy, Birkbeck College, Malet Street, London WC1E 7HX [1996]

SCHNIERTSHAUER, Rev. Richard, Riedbergstraße 3, D-79100 Freiburg, Germany [1992]

SCHOENMAN, Mr R., 38D Hilldrop Road, Tufnell Park, London N7 0JE [1994]

SCIENTIFIC INFORMATION, INSTITUTE FOR, (Book Acquisitions), 3501 Market Street, Philadelphia, PA 19104, USA [1986]

SCOTT, Dean, 5710 Rhodes Road, Apt. A, Kent, Ohio 44240, USA [1995]

SCOTT, Professor D. S., School of Computer Science, Carnegie Mellon University, 5000 Forbes Avenue, Pittsburgh, PA 15213-3891, USA [1972]

SCOTT, Ms Jenni, Oxford University Press, Walton Street, Oxford OX2 6DP [1995]

SCOTT-MACNAB, J., The Cottage, 50 Digswell Rise, Welwyn Garden City, Herts AL8 7PW [1995]

SEHGAL, Mr Rajeev Kumar, 24 Chasefield Road, London SW17 8LN [1996]

SEN, Miss Manidipa, Dept of Logic & Metaphysics, University of St Andrews, St Andrews, Fife KY16 9AL [1993]

SEN, Madhucchanda, Room LGB–5, Langton Close, Wren Street, London WC1X 0HD [1996]

SETIYA, Mr Kieran, The Graduate College, Princeton, NJ 08544, USA [1994]

SEWELL, Ms A., 9B Nelson Road, London N8 9RX [1996]

SEYMOUR, Mr Mark, Dept of Logic & Metaphysics, University of St Andrews, St Andrews, Fife KY16 9AL [1995]

SHAER, Mr Paolo, 19 Wellesley House, Church Way, London NW1 1LL [1992]

SHALKOWSKI, Dr Scott A., Dept of Philosophy, University of Leeds, Leeds LS2 9JT [1996]

SHAND, Dr John, 69 Cromwell Road, Stretford, Manchester M32 8QJ [1995]

SHARPE, Dr R. A., St David's College, Lampeter, Dyfed SA31 2HA [1971]

SHARPLES, Professor R.W., Dept. of Greek & Latin, University College, London WC1E 6BT [1977]

SHEELER, Dr R., 36 Avenue des Tilleuls, 1203 Genève, Switzerland [1979]

SHEERIN, Sheelagh, 8 Ashdale, Ballymena, Co. Antrim BT43 7AL [1993]

SHORTER, J. M., 3 Spring Lane, Horspath, Oxford [1970]

SILKIN, R. L. F [1979]

SILVERSTEIN, Professor Harry S., Dept of Philosophy, Washington State University, Pullman, WA 99164-5130, USA [1992]

SIMESTER, Dr Andrew, Law Faculty, University of Birmingham, Edgbaston, Birmingham B15 2TT [1991]

SIMMONS, Dr Keith, Dept of Philosophy, University of North Carolina at Chapel Hill, Chapel Hill, NC 27599-3125, USA [1995]

SINGER, Professor Marcus, 5021 Regents Street, Madison, Wisconsin 53705, USA [1952]

SINGLETON, Dr J., 39 Manorville Road, Hemel Hempstead, Herts. HP3 0AP [1979]

SINGLETON, Mr T. J., Dept of Philosophy, 605 Dale Hale Tower, 455 West Lindsey Drive, University of Oklahoma, Norman, OK 73072, USA [1992]

SIRICHAN, Mr Teerapot, 18 Hyndewood, Bampton Road, Forest Hill, London SE23 2BH [1996]

SKORUPSKI, Professor J. M., Dept of Moral Philosophy, University of St Andrews, St Andrews, Fife KY16 9AL [1975]

SMART, Professor J. J. C., 74 Mackenzie Street, Hackett, A. C. T. 2602, Australia [1948]

SMART, Professor R. N [1956]

SMEYERS, Prof. Dr. Paul, Faculteit der Psychologie en Pedagogische Weten-schappen, Katholieke Universiteit Leuven, Tiensestraat 102, 3000 Leuven, Belgium [1992]

SMILEY, Professor Timothy, Clare College, Cambridge CB2 1TL [1981]

SMITH, Dr Barry C., Dept of Philosophy, Birkbeck College, Malet Street, London WC1E 7HX [1984]

SMITH, Mr Basil, No. 5 Sherringham House, 68 Lisson Street, London NW1 5NY [1995]

SMITH, Dr Marc, Dept of Philosophy, St Thomas University, Fredericton, N.B. E3B 5G3, Canada [1996]

SMITH, Dr P., Dept of Philosophy, University of Sheffield, Sheffield S10 2TN [1971]

SMITH, Professor Robin, Dept of Philosophy, Texas A & M University, College Station, TX 77843-4237, USA [1990]

SMITH, Mr S. A., 9 Fontenoy Road, London SW12 9LZ [1987]

SMITHURST, Mr M., Dept of Philosophy, The University, Southampton SO9 5NH [1979]

SNELLING, Mr David, 15 Irene Road, London SW6 4AC [1992]

SNOWDON, Dr P. F., Exeter College, Oxford OX1 3DP [1978]

SODHI, Mr K. S., 45 Fairview Road, Norbury, London SW16 5PX [1995]

SOFAER, Ms Neema, E3 Great Court, Trinity College, Cambridge CB2 1TQ [1995]

SOLUM, Lawrence B., Dean, Loyola Law School, 919 S. Albany Street, P. O. Box 15019, Los Angeles, CA 90015-0019, USA [1989]

SOMERVILLE, Mr J. W. F., Dept of Philosophy, The University, Hull HU6 7RX [1964]

SORABJI, Professor R., Dept of Philosophy, King's College, London WC2R 2LS [1967]

SORELL, Professor Tom, Dept of Philosophy, University of Essex, Wivenhoe Park, Colchester CO4 3SQ [1984]

SOROOSH, Professor A., Academy for Philosophy, 6 Nezami Alley, France Avenue, Tehran, Iran [1996]

SOSA, Ms Beatrice, University Courts K-4, Martin, TN 38237, USA [1994]

SOTERIOU, Mr Matthew J., 26A Ridgmount Gardens, London WC1E 7AS [1994]

SOTERIOU, Mr Matthew J., 26A Ridgmount Gardens, London WC1E 7AS [1994]

SPARSHOTT, F. E., Victoria College, Toronto 5, Ontario, Canada [1951]

SPENCER-SMITH, Dr R. M., Middlesex University, Queensway, Enfield EN3 4SF [1992]

SPERBER, Dan, 2 Square de Port-Royal, 75013 Paris, France [1991]

SPICKER, Professor Stuart F., 145 Overlook Drive, Las Placitas, New Mexico 87043, USA [1970]

SPIERS, Ms Louise, 2 Burns Road, Alperton, Wembley, Middx HA0 1JR [1996]

SQUIRES, J. E., 5 Drumcarrow Road, St Andrews, Fife KY16 8SE [1972]

STALLEY, Mr Richard F., Dept of Philosophy, Unviersity of Glasgow, Glasgow G12 8QQ [1995]

STAMMBERGER, Mr Ralf M. W., Schulstraße 3, D-56414 Steinefrenz, Germany [1993]

STANDISH, Dr Paul, School of Educational Studies, University of Dundee, Dundee DD1 4HN, Scotland [1994]

STAVRINIDES, Mr Zenon, 17 Scott Hall Square, Leeds LS7 3JN [1982]

STAVROPOULOS, Dr Nicos E., 21 Democritou Street, 106 73 Athens, Greece [1990]

STCHEDROFF, M., Dept of Philosophy, The Queen's University, Belfast, Northern Ireland [1966]

STEIN, Christian, Graduiertenkursus Kognitionswissenschaft, Universität Hamburg, 22524 Hamburg, Germany [1995]

STEINER, H. I., Dept of Government, University of Manchester, Manchester M13 9PL [1974]

STELL, Mrs Jean, Frognal, 25 Berks Hill, Chorleywood, Herts. WD3 5AG [1994]

STERN, Axel, The Old Vicarage, 16 Egerton Road, Monton, Manchester M30 9LR [1964]

STERN, Professor David, 720 North Dodge Street, Iowa City, IA 52245, USA [1983]

STERN, Professor L., 2 Charlton Street, Apt. 4C, New York NY 10014, USA [1964]

STEVENS, Mrs J. M., Flat F, 3 Warwick Square, London SW1V 2AA [1980]

STEWARD, Dr Helen, Balliol College, Oxford OX1 3BJ [1991]

STOBBART, Mr J. B., 23 West Park Road, South Shields, Tyne & Wear NE33 4LB [1995]

STOCK, G. G. L., Dept of Logic, King's College, Old Aberdeen, Aberdeen [1965]

STOCK, Mr Guy, 9 Union Place, Montrose DD10 8QB, Scotland [1994]

STONE, Mr A., School of Science, Technology & Design, King Alfred's College of Higher Education, Sparkford Road, Winchester, Hampshire SO22 4NR [1986]

STONE, M. R. W., Flat 2, 23 Bolton Gardens, London SW5 0AQ [1994]

STONE, Dr M. W. F., Dept of Theology & Religious Studies, King's College, London WC2 2LS [1992]

STONEHAM, T. W. Esq., Sub-faculty of Philosophy, 10 Merton Street, Oxford OX1 4JJ [1990]

STORL, Dr Heidi, Dept of Philosophy, Augustana College, Rock Island, IL 61201, USA [1992]

STORRING, Mr Rod, 42 Felstead Road, London E11 2PJ [1988]

STOUT, Dr Rowland, 20 Dove House Close, Wolverrote, Oxford OX2 8PG [1996]

STOWELL, Ms Louie, 51 Elmfield Avenue, Teddington TW11 8BX [1995]

STRATTON, Mr S. J., 58 Whiteley Close, Dane End, Nr. Ware, Herts. SG12 0NB [1988]

STRAWSON, Dr G. J., Jesus College, Oxford OX1 3DW [1980]

STRAWSON, Professor Sir Peter, Magdalen College, Oxford OX1 4AU [1974]

STREET, Mr Edward, Gonville and Caius College, Cambridge CB2 1TA [1995]

STRUGNELL, Mr N. D., 253A Banbury Road, Oxford OX2 7HN [1993]

STUART, Mr J. J., 5 Meynell Grove, Sherwood Rise, Nottingham NG7 7NA [1992]

STUART, Dr Susan A. J., 4 Kirklee Quadrant, Glasgow G12 0TR [1988]

STUBBS, Mrs E., 70 Hodford Road, London NW11 8NG [1993]

STUBBS, J. P., 3 Burnside, Wigton, Cumbria CA7 9RE [1985]

STURGEON, Dr Scott, Dept of Philosophy, Birkbeck College, Malet Street, London WC1E 7HX [1991]

STUTT, Dr Arthur, KMI, The Open University, Milton Keynes MK7 6AA [1990]

STUTTARD, Mr Dafydd, Brasenose College, Oxford OX1 4AJ [1994]

STYTLE, Mr James R., Post Office Box 1231, Crawfordsville, Indiana 47933, USA [1995]

SUÁREZ, Mr Mauricio, Dept of Logic & Metaphysics, University of St Andrews, St Andrews, Fife KY16 9AL [1995]

SULLIVAN, Dr P. M., Dept of Philosophy, University of Stirling, Stirling FK9 4LA [1985]

SUNDT-OHLSEN, Mr Eilert, 94 Boileau Road, London W5 3AJ [1995]

SUSTER, Dr Danilo, Dept of Philosophy, University of Ljubljana, Askerceva 12, 61000 Ljubljana, Slovenia [1991]

SUZMAN, Professor L. J., Sadlers Grayswood Road, Haslemere, Surrey GU27 2SP [1984]

SWAIN, Miss Karen, 5 Franklyn Drive, Staveley, Near Chesterfield, Derbyshire S43 3YA [1993]

SWALE, Ms Eve J. L., 3 Greta House, 60 Hardy Road, London SE3 7PA [1995]

SWINBURNE, Professor R. G., Oriel College, Oxford OX1 4EW [1961]

SYDOW, Mr Momme v., Markt 37, D-53111 Bonn, Germany [1996]

SZAHAJ, Dr Andrzej, Institute of Philosophy, Nicolaus Copernicus University, 87–100 Torun, Podmurna 74, Poland [1990]

SZUBKA, Dr Tadeusz, Logic & Theory of Knowledge Department, Catholic University of Lublin, 20–950 Lublin, Poland [1995]

TANNER, Dr M. K., Corpus Christi College, Cambridge CB2 [1963]

TANNEY, Dr J., Dept of Philosophy, Darwin College, University of Kent at Canterbury, Canterbury, Kent CT2 7NY [1994]

TAPPENDEN, Paul, 1 Fairfield Gardens, London N8 9DD [1989]

TAPPOLET, Ms Christine, 28 Quai de Corsier, CH 1246 Corsier, Switzerland [1989]

TARNOWSKI, Dr Josef, Uniwersytet Gdanski, Instytut Filozofii i Socjologii, Ul. Wita Stwosza 55, 80-952 Gdansk, Poland [1990]

TARTAGLIA, James, 40 Oakcroft Road, London SE13 7ED [1996]

TAYLOR, Mr Craig D., 97 Kingsmead Road, Tulse Hill, London SW2 3HZ [1992]

TAYLOR, C. C. W., Corpus Christi College, Oxford OX1 4JF [1968]

TAYLOR, Mr John, Holywell Manor, Manor Road, Oxford OX1 3UH [1996]

TAYLOR, Dr Michael R., Dept of Philosophy, 226 Hanner Hall, Oklahoma State University, Stillwater, Oklahoma 74078-0220, USA [1993]

TAYLOR, Mr Nick, Holywell Manor, Manor Road, Oxford [1992]

TEBBIT, Dr Mark, 39 Archbishops Place, London SW2 2AH [1992]

TEICHMAN, Jenny, New Hall, Cambridge CB3 0DF [1996]

TEICHMANN, Dr R., 6 Tyndale Road, Oxford OX4 1JL [1983]

TELFER, Miss E., Dept of Philosophy, University of Glasgow, Glasgow G12 8QQ [1968]

TENNANT, Professor Neil W., Dept of Philosophy, Faculty of Arts, Australian National University, GPO Box 4, Canberra ACT 2601, Australia [?]

THE QUEEN'S UNIVERSITY BELFAST, Student Philosophy Society, Belfast BT7 1NN [1990]

THERO, Mr Daniel P., 33 Aspen Road, Latham, NY 12110-5227, USA [1995]

THOMAS, Dr G. L., 23 Bromwich Avenue, Highgate, London N6 6QH [1987]

THOMAS, Mr J. L. H., 4 North Lodge Cottages, Ladykirk, Berwick upon Tweed, TD15 1SU [1987]

THORNTON, Dr Tim, Dept of Philosophy, University of Warwick, Coventry CV4 7AL [1995]

THURLING, Dr R. T. D., 23 Kings Road, Kingston upon Thames, Surrey KT2 5JA [1984]

TIEGER, Mr Richard C., 452 West 261 Street, Riverdale, NY 10471, USA [1994]

TODD, Mr Ian, 146c Clarence Road, London E5 8DY [1991]

TOMIN, Dr Julius, 330 Banbury Road, Oxford OX2 7ED [1979]

TOMS, Mr Eric, 12 Burdiehouse Road, Edinburgh EH17 8AF [1972]

TORRANCE, Dr S. B., 13 Quernmore Road, London N4 4QT [1969]

TOWEY, Dr J.A., 5 Aldensley Road, London W6 0DH [1996]

TOWNSEND, Dabney, Dept of Philosophy, University of Texas at Arlington, Box 19527/305 Carlisle Hall, Arlington, Texas, TX 76019, USA [1996]

TRAMPOTA, Andreas MA, 221 Goldhurst Terrace, London NW6 3EP [1993]

TRAVIS, Professor C. S., Dept of Philosophy, University of Stirling, Stirling FK9 4LA [1987]

TREVIJANO, Carmen G., Teorema, Apartado 61. 159, 28080 Madrid, Spain [1984]

TRIGG, R. H., School of Philosophy, University of Warwick, Coventry, Warwickshire [1965]

TROTT, Elizabeth, 297 Bessborough Drive, Toronto, Ontario M4G 3K9, Canada [1994]

TRUNCELLITO, Mr David A., 3528 East 2nd Street, Apartment 76, Tucson, AZ 85716, USA [1994]

TSOCHAS, Ms Catherine, 9 Ockham Court, 22 Bardwell Road, Oxford OX2 6SR [1994]

TUCKER, Paul M. W., 24 Bow Brook, Gathorne Street, London E2 0PW [1981]

TUCKER, Sarah, 80 South Hill Park, London NW3 2SN [1995]

TURNER, Fr. Nickolas, St Mary's Vicarage, R. A. F. Ascension, B. F. P. O. 677 [1992]

TURNER, Mrs Sharon W., 417 James Street, Laurinburg, NC 28352, USA [1994]

TUSKE, Mr Joerg, Clare Hall, Cambridge CB3 9AL [1993]

UKPABI, Mr C. F., 6 Harlech Road, Southgate, London N14 7BX [1988]

UNIVERSITY COLLEGE DUBLIN, Dept of Philosophy, Dublin 4, Eire [1991]

UPTON, Mr Hugh, Centre for Philosophy & Health Care, University College, Singleton Park, Swansea SAZ 8PP [1979]

URMSON, J. O., 5 Appleton Road, Cumnor, Oxford OX2 9QH [1939]

UTTER, Professor Glenn, Dept of Political Science, Box 10030, Lamar University, Beaumont, TX 77710, USA [1983]

VALENTINE, Miss Victoria, 34 Tinwell Road, Stamford, Lincs. PE9 2SD [1993]

VAN BRAKEL, Professor J., Hoger Instituut voor Wijsbegeerte, Kardinaal Mercierplein 2, 3000 Leuven, Belgium [1988]

VAN DEN BROM, Professor L. J., Slauerhofflaan 80, 9752 HD, Haren (GN), The Netherlands [1979]

VAN DER LAAN, Paul MA, Prinsengracht 349H, 1016 HK Amsterdam, The Netherlands [1992]

VANZAN, Mr L., 10 Royal Mint Place, Tower Hill, London E1 8LS [1995]

VASYLCHENKO, Mr Andriy, 252001 Kiev-1, Trochsviatitelska 4, Institute of Philosophy, Ukraine [1994]

VERSALLION, Mr Mark, 143 Marlborough Hill, Harrow, Middlesex HA1 1UG [1995]

VIENNE, Professor Jean-Michel, 17 rue du Sénat, 44300 Nantes, France [1993]

VINCE, Mr Barrie, 20 Eccles Road, London SW11 ILY [1992]

VIRVIDAKIS, Dr Stelios, 4 Kroussovou Str, Illissia, 115 28 Athens, Greece [1987]

VISINTAINER, Mr John, 10080 Hawley Drive, N. Royalton, OH 44133, USA [1995]

VISION, Professor Gerald, 2113 Chestnut Avenue, Ardmore, PA 19003-3003, USA [1976]

VON TEVENAR, Gudrun, Dept of Philosophy, Birkbeck College, London WC1E 7HX [1993]

WALKER, Mr Andrew V., 25 Chambers Lane, Willesden Green, London NW10 2RJ [1983]

WALKER, Mr George, 16 Newton Mansions, Queens Club Gardens, London W14 9RR [1992]

WALKER, Dr Mark Thomas, Dept of Philosophy, University of Birmingham, Edgbaston, Birmingham B15 2TT [1996]

WALKER, Dr R. C. S., Magdalen College, Oxford OX1 4AU [1992]

WALL, Mr I. D., 2 The Meadway, Chelsford Park, Orpington, Kent BP1 6HW [1989]

WALLACE-COOK, Mr A. D. M., 29 Arle Road, Cheltenham, Gloucestershire GL52 8JT [1996]

WALLIS, Mr Hugh, 30 Park Mount, Kirkstall, Leeds LS5 3HE [1992]

WALSH, Mr David, 45 Hartham Road, London N7 9JJ [1991]

WALSH, Mr David, 29 Sydenham Rise, London SE23 3XL [1996]

WALSH, Mr Denis M., Dept of Philosophy, King's College, Strand WC2R 2LS [1991]

WALSH, Mr M. J., Flat 5, 68 Hopton Road, Streatham, London SW16 2EN [1992]

WALTER, Dr David John, 90 Green Dragon Lane, Winchmore Hill, London N21 2LH [1995]

WALTON, Ms C., Mullenders, Swan Lane, Nr Burford, Oxon OX8 4SH [1972]

WARBURTON, Dr Nigel, Dept of Philosophy, University of Nottingham, University Park, Nottingham NG7 2RD [1992]

WARD, Dr James M., Schafer House, 168 Drumond Street, London NW1 3HZ [1995]

WARNER, Martin, Dept of Philosophy, University of Warwick, Coventry CV4 7AL [1969]

WARREN, Mr G. J., 10 Desenfans Road, London SE21 7DN [1996]

WARSOP, Dr Andrew, 42 Sutherland Avenue, London W9 2HQ [1993]

WATERS, Mrs Rita, 147 Fellows Road, Swiss Cottage, London NW3 3JJ [1996]

WATKINS, Mr Graham, 40 Derby Street, Mansfield, Notts. NG18 2SE [1994]

WATKINSON, Mr Damian A., 15 Aysgarth Road, Birley Carr, Sheffield S6 1HU [1996]

WATLING, Dr J., 5 Meadow Close, Petersham, Surrey TW10 7AJ [1954]

WATTS, Mr Ian David, Flat 31, 28 St John's Road, Buxton, Derbys. SK17 6XQ [1993]

WEAVER, Mr Eric, 541 Hall of Languages, Dept of Philosophy, Syracuse University, Syracuse, NY 13210, USA [1996]

WEBB, Mr Stephen, 14 South 10th Avenue, Apt T, Highland Park, NJ 08904, USA [1993]

WEBER, Christine, 116 2nd St. South, Independence, OR 97351, USA [1996]

WEBSTER, Mr Henry, 168 Garron Lane, South Ockendon, Essex RM1 5LA [1996]

WEDGWOOD, Mr Ralph N., 12 Castle Street T/L, Edinburgh EH2 3AT [1994]

WEILAND, Mr Jan Peter, Flat A2, 6 Airlie Gardens, London W8 7AJ [1993]

WEINTRAUB, Dr Ruth, Dept of Philosophy, University College London, Gower Street, London WC1E 6BT [1996]

WEIR, Dr Alan, Dept of Philosophy, The Queen's University of Belfast, Belfast BT7 1NN [1995]

WEISS, Dr B., Dept of Philosophy, Birkbeck College, Malet Street, London WC1E 7HX [1994]

WELBOURNE, Mr M., Dept of Philosophy, University of Bristol, 9 Woodland Road, Bristol BS8 1TB [1977]

WELTY, Mr Kris R., Dept of Philosophy, Wayne State University, 51W. Warren, Detroit, MI 48202, USA [1995]

WENDELKEN, Dr D. R., Dept of Politics, University of Durham, 48 Old Elvet, Durham DH1 3LZ [1989]

WERSCHKUL, Ms Hilda T., 3530 S. W. Gale Avenue, Portland, Oregon 97201, USA [1994]

WESTPHAL, Dr J. A. G., Dept of English & Philosophy, Idaho State University, Pocatello, Idaho 83209, USA [1977]

WESTWOOD-DUNKLEY, Mr Clive, 71 Cornwall Gardens, London SW7 4BA [1995]

WHELAN, Joseph P., 1642 Westmount Blvd. N. W., Calgary, Alberta, Canada T2N 3G6 [1991]

WHEWELL, D. A., Dept of Philosophy, University of Durham, 50 Old Elvet, Durham DH1 3HN [1973]

WHITAKER, Ms B., Darwin College, Silver Street, Cambridge CB3 9EU [1994]

WHITE, Mrs Gabrielle, 23 Kelso Road, Leeds LS2 9PR [1972]

WHITE, J. P., Dept of Philosophy, Institute of Education, Malet Street, London WC1 [1966]

WHITE, Professor Morton, Institute For Advance Study, Princeton, New Jersey 08540, USA [1951]

WHITE, Mr Raymond W., 831 Persimmon Place, Columbus, Ohio 43213, USA [1993]

WHITE, R. M., Dept of Philosophy, University of Leeds, Leeds LS2 9JT [1975]

WHITE, Professor V. A., University of Wisconsin Center, Manitowoc County, 705 Viebahn Street, Manitowoc, WI 54220, USA [1985]

WHITELEY, Professor C. H., Edgbaston Beaumont, 32 St James Road, Birmingham B15 2NX [1936]

WIGGINS, Professor David, Dept of Philosophy, Birkbeck College, Malet Street, London WC1E 7HX [1962]

WIGHTMAN, George Esq., Church Farm House, Evenlode, Moreton-in-Marsh, Gloucestershire GL56 0NY [1960]

WILDE, Mr T., 1 Railway Cottages, Skillings Lane, Brough, N. Humberside HU15 1EU [1992]

WILKS, Professor Y., Computing Research Laboratory, New Mexico State University, Las Cruces, NM 88003, USA [?]

WILLARD, Professor D., School of Philosophy, University of S. California, Los Angeles, CA 90089-0451, USA [1985]

WILLIAMS, Professor Bernard, Corpus Christi College, Oxford OX1 4JF [1953]

WILLIAMS, Professor C. J. F., 1 Fossefield Road, Midsomer Norton, Bath BA3 4AS [1961]

WILLIAMS, Dr James, Dept of Philosophy, University of Dundee, Dundee DD1 4HN [1996]

WILLIAMS, S., 301 St Margaret's Road, Twickenham, Middlesex [1976]

WILLIAMSON, Professor Timothy, Dept of Philosophy, University of Edinburgh, David Hume Tower, George Square, Edinburgh EH8 9JX [1985]

WILLS, Mr Eric R., The Leaze, Little Leaze Lane, Catcott, Somerset TA7 9HL [1994]

WILSMORE, Dr S. J., Flat 27 Queen Court, Queen Square, London WC1N 3BB [1963]

WILSON, Mr B. G., Innisfree, St Thomas Street, Deddington, Oxon OX15 0SY [1974]

WILSON, R. D., Flat 3, St James Lodge, 60 The Crescent, Davenport, Stockport SK3 8SP [1974]

WINCER, Mr Kieron, 30 Arthur Road, Horsham, West Sussex RH13 5BQ [1993]

WINCH, Professor P. G., 310 West Hill Street, Apt. 3 W, Champaign, Illinois 61820, USA [1958]

WISBEY, Dr C. H., 5 Waring Drive, Orpington, Kent BR6 6DN [1995]

WOLENSKI, Professor Jan, Dept of Logic, Jagiellonian University, ul. Grodzka 52, 31-044 Krakow, Poland [1996]

WOLFF, Jonathan, Dept of Philosophy, University College, London WC1E 6BT [1987]

WOLLHEIM, Professor R. A., Dept of Philosophy, University of California, Berkeley, California 94720, USA [1950]

WOOD, Mrs Anne, Flat 13, Davey's Court, 33 Bedfordbury, London WC2N 4BW [1993]

WOOD, Mr John W., 35 Brompton Square, London SW3 2AE [1975]

WOOD, Dr Jonathan, 61 Highbridge Road, Aylesbury, Bucks HP21 7RX [1993]

WOOD, Mr Robert N., 13 Wilton Drive, Flat 0-1, Glasgow G20 6RW [1992]

WOODFIELD, Dr Andrew, Dept of Philosophy, 9 Woodland Road, Bristol BS8 1TB [1991]

WOODMAN, Mr I. M., 16 Chalkpit Hill, Chatham, Kent ME4 5TA [1984]

WOODS, Justin R., 22 Belham Park Road, London SW12 [1996]

WORRALL, D. I., Westward House, Chapel Lane, Pirbright, Surrey GU24 0JY [1976]

WORTH, Mr Andrew J., 69 Clova Road, Forest Gate, London E7 9AG [1991]

WRIGHT, A. C. H., Larters Farm, Spong Lane, Cratfield, Halesworth, Suffolk IP19 0DP [1970]

WRIGHT, Professor C. J. G., Dept of Logic and Metaphysics, University of St Andrews, St Andrews, Fife KY16 9AL [1975]

WRIGHT, Mr Jason, #26 Fischer Graduate Residence Hall, Apt. IC, University of Notre Dame, Notre Dame, Indiana 46556-5676, USA [1994]

WRIGHT, Professor Michael B., 165 Wood Street, Bristol, Rhode Island 02809, USA [1993]

WRIGHT, P. N., The Open University, Publishing Division, Walton Hall, Milton Keynes MK7 6AA [1975]

WRIGLEY, Mr Anthony, Dept of Philosophy, University of Leeds, Leeds LS2 9JT [1996]

WRINGE, Mr William G., Dept of Philosophy, University of Leeds, Leeds LS2 9JT [1996]

YAMAZAKI, Makoto, 408 Estate Maenocho, 2-1-20 Maenocho, Itabashi-ku, Tokyo 174, Japan [1991]

YEEN, Mr Wing Choy, St Michael's College, P. O. Box 662, Broadway NSW 2007, Australia [1995]

YOUNG, D. A., Dept of Philosophy, University of Sussex, Falmer, Brighton [1979]

YOUNG, Dr James O., Dept of Philosophy, University of Victoria, P. O. Box 3045, Victoria, B. C., Canada V8W 3P4 [1992]

YOUNG, Dr Roger, Dept of Philosophy, University of Dundee, Dundee DD1 4HN [1994]

ZAJAC, M., Lotnikow 85-12, 44-100 Gliwice, Poland [1983]

ZALABARDO, Dr José L., Dept of Philosophy, University of Birmingham, Edgbaston, Birmingham B15 2TT [1988]

ZECH, Mr Loren A. Jr., 12033 Livingston St., Wheaton, MD 20902, USA [1993]

ZEGLEN, Professor Urszula, Dept of Logic & Theory of Knowledge, Catholic University of Lublin, Lublin, Poland [1996]

ZIEDINS, Professor R., 25 Masters Avenue, Hamilton, New Zealand 2001 [1984]

ZUPKO, Dr Jack, Dept of Philosophy, Emory University, Atlanta, GA 30322, USA [1984]